Theater after Film

∴

Theater after Film

∵

Martin Harries

THE UNIVERSITY OF CHICAGO PRESS
CHICAGO AND LONDON

The University of Chicago Press, Chicago 60637
The University of Chicago Press, Ltd., London
© 2025 by The University of Chicago
All rights reserved. No part of this book may be used or reproduced in any
manner whatsoever without written permission, except in the case of brief
quotations in critical articles and reviews. For more information, contact the
University of Chicago Press, 1427 E. 60th St., Chicago, IL 60637.
Published 2025
Printed in the United States of America

34 33 32 31 30 29 28 27 26 25   1 2 3 4 5

ISBN-13: 978-0-226-83870-0 (cloth)
ISBN-13: 978-0-226-83871-7 (paper)
ISBN-13: 978-0-226-83872-4 (e-book)
DOI: https://doi.org/10.7208/chicago/9780226838724.001.0001

The University of Chicago Press gratefully acknowledges the generous
support of the Humanities Center at the University of California, Irvine,
toward the publication of this book.

Library of Congress Cataloging-in-Publication Data

Names: Harries, Martin, author.
Title: Theater after film / Martin Harries.
Description: Chicago : The University of Chicago Press, 2025. | Includes
  bibliographical references and index.
Identifiers: LCCN 2024041052 | ISBN 9780226838700 (cloth) | ISBN
  9780226838717 (paperback) | ISBN 9780226838724 (ebook)
Subjects: LCSH: Mass media and theater. | Motion pictures and theater. |
  Experimental theater—History—20th century. | Theater and society—
  History—20th century. | LCGFT: Theater criticism.
Classification: LCC PN1995.25 H26 2025 | DDC 791.43/657—dc23/eng/20240910
LC record available at https://lccn.loc.gov/2024041052

♾ This paper meets the requirements of ANSI/NISO Z39.48-1992
(Permanence of Paper).

For Jennie

∵

And in memory of my mother, Elizabeth Wanning Harries
Gather up the fragments that remain, that nothing be lost.

Now we are going out to the movies, as ever.

Tennessee Williams

Contents

ONE

Preface · 1

TWO

Incommunication · 3

THREE

Theater/Media · 4

FOUR

Demolition of a Theater (1901) · 6

FIVE

Residual Becomes Emergent · 8

SIX

Medium/Media/Remediation in Reverse · 14

SEVEN

Theater/Film · 20

EIGHT

Apparatus · 26

NINE

Williams, Beckett, Kennedy · 28

TEN

Walter Benjamin's Work of Art Essay · 31

ELEVEN

Benjamin's Medium · 41

TWELVE

Modernism: Shaw, Lorca, Brecht · 52

THIRTEEN

Participation in Postwar Theater · 61

FOURTEEN

Artaud's Voice against Radio · 85

FIFTEEN

Publics · 94

SIXTEEN

Handke's *Offending the Audience* · 97

TENNESSEE WILLIAMS

SEVENTEEN

Williams's Material · 111

EIGHTEEN

Learning Sexual Violence with Tennessee Williams, or *Streetcar* in Pictures · 114

NINETEEN

Lead Belly's Guitar and Williams's Counterpublics · 130

SAMUEL BECKETT

TWENTY

Beckett, Cinema, Politics · 151

TWENTY-ONE

Film and Its Audiences · 153

TWENTY-TWO

Catastrophe: Fixing the Audience · 179

TWENTY-THREE

Endgame, Postwar Mass Culture, and Forms of Address · 190

TWENTY-FOUR

Beckett, the Proscenium, Media · 201

TWENTY-FIVE

Product Placement · 214

ADRIENNE KENNEDY

TWENTY-SIX

Theater after Hollywood · 225

TWENTY-SEVEN

A Movie Star in 1976 · 233

TWENTY-EIGHT

The Author as Produced: Hollywood/Jim Crow · 247

TWENTY-NINE

Diary of Lights · 254

THIRTY

Afterword/After Theater · 258

Acknowledgments 261
Bibliography 265
Index 285

[ONE]

Preface

Genealogies with punctual points of origin are always myths, and I will indulge in a myth. This book began on the evening of September 24, 1983, in New York City, at the Harold Clurman Theater on 42nd Street. That evening, in the fall of my first year in college, I went with my parents, who were in the city for a night or two, to see three short plays by Samuel Beckett: *Ohio Impromptu, Catastrophe*, and *What Where*. I don't remember theater events, decades later, as well as some of my friends do, and I can't claim any astonishing recall of that evening. Later in this book I will look closely at details of some of Beckett's plays; here I wish I could convey the exceptional charge of that evening as a whole. The tableaux of *Ohio Impromptu* and *Catastrophe*—the two figures with their long dead white hair turning the pages of a book, the sculptural manipulated victim on his plinth—have stayed with me, as did the voice of the director in *Catastrophe* emerging from behind us in the small theater, and the eerie presence of the actor David Warrilow. Above all the night stays with me as an occasion of inassimilable strangeness. The memory of that evening perseveres as an intimation of how different theater could be, and of the difference theater can make.

∵

Theoretical claims have apparently changed so much: why has the apparatus of the scholarly book changed so little? Scholars often admit to limitations of position and of knowledge, and then return to a mode of writing structured around seeming omniscience, completeness, and authority that in other ways they resist. I think of the structure of this book as a way to respect both the experience of reading and the material I am writing about. I have put it together as a series of sections that are usually shorter and less deliberately sutured to each other than those of most scholarly books. One reason for this structure is my impatience with certain protocols of academic writing, in particular those gestures with which writers signal to readers what they will do rather than going about doing it: for example, "in chapter 1, I will . . ." As a reader, I often skip such pages, and so I don't want to write them. I have allowed for breaks and gaps between sections, and these gaps are real. The gaps are also, I think, only more obvious than those to which every book is subject: the concrete limitations of any intellectual project—limitations of time, and of space, and of my grasp—mean that there must be things that are relevant and yet unacknowledged. The gaps here are a way of acknowledging what I could not write about or do not know.

Yes, those gaps acknowledge absences, but they also, I hope, produce connections both somewhat anticipated and entirely unexpected, connections I could not make or guess. The idea of the book as an apparatus and the allure of a structure that allows for discontinuities between its pieces owes much to a montage aesthetic. Bertolt Brecht is at once one of the topics of this book and an influence on its form, as are the theorists with whom he was in dialogue. Why not let books such as *One-Way Street* or *Minima Moralia* continue to open up possibilities for different modes of writing and organization?[1] The following sections, some as short as a paragraph and some many pages long, are not as various in content or as paratactic in their relationships as are the pieces of those much more wide-ranging works. I have wondered, indeed, whether there is a disconnection between the relative continuousness of my argument and the relatively fragmentary form of the structure I have chosen. That structure, however, is also tied to the argument. I argue that the force of film remade theater in the decades after 1945. The forms of this remaking, however, varied, even or especially inside the works of individual playwrights. To have devised a single section on Tennessee Williams or Samuel Beckett or Adrienne Kennedy, for instance, might suggest that their work constitutes a single, consistent response to the complex ways film determined his drama. Discontinuous sections better reflect my sense of these plays as a set of related but discrete experiments with the problem of film and mass culture. I hope that, while the argument across the book will point to continuities, allowing for these breaks between sections will underline the singularity of the plays I consider and stress that an argument made about one play does not necessarily transfer to another. I also hope that some readers will supply, in their own thinking, teaching, and writing, pieces of what is missing here.

---

1. I have tried to keep in mind Walter Benjamin's "Teaching Aid," subtitled "Principles of the Weighty Tome, or How to Write Fat Books," in *One-Way Street*, 44–45.

[TWO]

Incommunication

Theater is a poor medium. In a time of so-called lossless formats, theater loses more than it saves. It does not communicate content as media are supposed to do. In the present, it may be that these deficiencies have become strengths, that theater's poverty as a medium of communication has made it a rich site for thinking again about what we want from a medium, from media, from communication, from art. A format programmed for loss might make us wonder about what we expect to be able to save.

[THREE]

Theater/Media

The previous section, in the present tense and about the present situation of theater, introduces but is also in crucial ways out of tune with, and even contradicts premises central to, the book that follows. This book makes no claims about theater as such and offers no generalizations about a set of practices, collectively dubbed "theater," with a long and contradictory history. Such claims give in to the glamour of an understanding of theory that sees its aim as the formulation of statements that are permanently true. I do believe my opening sentences accurately describe theater now. I also think that the relationship between theater and media has not been constant, has changed in the past, and will not remain as it is. There is no relationship between theater and media. There have been theaters, and there have been media, and no single ratio describes how theater and the media surrounding it have affected each other.

Contemporary theater is notable for its incorporation of media technologies into the mise en scène. This proliferation of media on stage has inspired an important and growing body of criticism and scholarship of theater's intermedial condition.[1] This book contributes to this scholarship in two ways. First, it challenges critical emphasis on the *presence* of media technologies on stage—of screens, video projections, live feeds, recorded pop songs—as the measure of the impact of the media surround. The impact of mass culture may be—may have been—at its most forceful when screens or other manifestations of cinematic or televisual technologies are or were absent. Second, I argue that the critical consensus that theater began to respond to media around 1970 is at once more or less correct, if one has one's eye on the proliferation of media onto the stage, and in need of rethinking.

---

1. For important instances among many, see Freda Chapple and Chiel Kattenbelt, eds., *Intermediality in Theatre and Performance*, Eckart Voigts-Virchow, *Mediated Drama/Dramatized Media*, Sarah Bay-Cheng, "Theatre Squared," and Sarah Bay-Cheng, Jennifer Parker-Starbuck, and David Z. Saltz, *Performance and Media*.

The argument of this book is that the vital and still reverberating period of theatrical experimentation in Europe and America in the decades after World War II marks an era in the history of the interplay between theater and film.

Cinema's debts to theater, and the familiar narrative of cinema's emancipation from those of its techniques that originated in or seemed to imitate theater, have been the subject of several important studies.[2] As its title suggests, this book makes a different argument, one that reverses this familiar trajectory from the stage to the screen. After 1945, apprehensions of the hegemony of cinema were widespread. Theater had nothing like cinema's ubiquity or subject-forming force, and in that relative poverty lay its strength in imagining different dramas and forms of spectatorship. The theater that came after film did not unmake cinema's hegemony. It did, however, provide a zone of contestation, a place where, by making that domination of the cultural field visible through negation or hyperbolic expansion, its power might be destabilized. A crucial material in postwar theatrical experiment was the mass cultural force that theater could channel and represent, and yet never possess. Theater's poverty as a medium made palpable the poverty of media.

2. For an influential early study, see A. Nicholas Vardac, *Stage to Screen*. In *Theatre to Cinema*, Ben Brewster and Lea Jacobs challenge Vardac's thesis and the more general argument that cinema finds itself as it sheds the trappings of theatricality: for Vardac, the destiny of a frustrated drive toward stage realism finds its technological solution in cinema. Brewster and Jacobs's richly historical disruption of quasi-evolutionary theories of cinema, and of the development of media forms more generally, has been influential in my conception of this book, the title of which acknowledges both of these predecessors.

[FOUR]

Demolition of a Theater (1901)

In April 1901, F. S. Armitage, a cameraman for the American Mutoscope & Biograph Co., used time-lapse techniques over the course of about thirty days to film the demolition of the Star Theatre from the northeast corner of Broadway and 13th Street in Manhattan.[1] The offices of the film company were across Broadway in the Roosevelt Building, and Armitage saw that the newer medium could capture the deliberate demolition of the venerable theater across the street. The Star Theatre had seen better days as the middle of three incarnations of Wallack's Theatre, one of the most important theatrical institutions in nineteenth-century New York City. In 1902, the American Mutoscope & Biograph Co. took out its copyright on the film by delivering a set of paper prints to the Library of Congress, which cataloged the prints as "Star Theatre." The film survives because these paper prints survived: the irony that many examples of a once new medium survived because of their preservation as printed stills is glaring. Under two minutes long, the short film is now more often known and discussed under variants of the more elaborate title, "Demolishing and Building Up the Star Theatre," a title that indicates how the film was shown to its first audiences. The film company took advantage of its medium, and urged exhibitors to reverse the direction of the film through the projector after first playing it in chronological sequence. As exhibited, the spectacle of the miraculous "building up" of the theater could follow its demolition.

"Demolishing and Building Up the Star Theatre" sensationally pictures the slow demolition, over many days, of a large theater. This display of the capability of film as a medium contrasts with the obsolescence of a particular

---

1. See Armitage, *Star Theatre*. Descriptions of the "Star Theatre," including mine, owe much to the scrupulous clarity of Kemp R. Niver, whose catalog of the Paper Print Collection of the Library of Congress is an important resource and whose labors made access to the collection possible. For the entry on "Star Theatre," see Niver, *Early Motion Pictures*, 310.

stage and a particular built structure. How to read this self-reflexive exhibition of the force of film is, however, not self-evident. How, in particular, should one understand the "building up"? The exhibition of the rebuilding of the theater is only virtual: spectators, however amused or dazzled they might have been, probably understood that they were witnessing a special effect.[2] In all too easy retrospect, it is hard not to see the film as harbinger of the cinema's international hegemony over the disintegrating theater. In this way, the Star Theatre film might seem an early, spectacular promise of film's colonization of what had been the aesthetic terrain of the theater. Speed things up and a cinematic lapse in time can show the decline of the theater; the trick of rebuilding what theater did is only a special effect, one made possible by the new medium.

At the time of this early twentieth-century demolition, film's triumph was itself only a distant potential. Broadway was not permanently in ruins but moving uptown to the more vibrant theatrical hub growing around Times Square, leaving Union Square to a new industry that had not yet discovered the permanent sunshine of the Los Angeles basin. The film might allegorize the inevitable dismantling of the theater, of theater as such. And yet the building up of this phantasmatic theater, made possible by the medium of film in reverse, also suggests an alternative allegory: the destruction of a theater, caught on film, lays the groundwork for a new theater, a theater made in part of the effects of film. My argument will move in this second direction, suggesting that film's catastrophic effects on theater were, in a scenario no less paradoxical if also more enduring than the building up of the collapsed Star, also a source of the remarkable experiments of postwar theater.[3]

2. Assertions about what audiences understood are most often speculation. See, however, the critiques of the tenacious myth of credulous audiences running in terror from the train entering the station in Tom Gunning, "An Aesthetic of Astonishment" (114–18) and Martin Loiperdinger and Bernd Elzer, "Lumière's 'Arrival of the Train': Cinema's Founding Myth."

3. Cinema had, of course, had a massive impact on theater before the middle of the twentieth century. "If there is one thing on which cultural historians agree," writes David Savran, "it is that Hollywood has been the 'largest single force' shaping the American theater since at least 1912, when 'the first full-length commercial film was shown in America,' *Queen Elizabeth*, starring (not by accident) the most famous stage actor in the world, Sarah Bernhardt" (*Highbrow/Lowdown*, 43–44). Savran cites Robert McLaughlin's dissertation, *Broadway and Hollywood*, 9. My argument is that a formal response to the impact of film, while not without precedent in the earlier twentieth century, shaped theater in new ways after 1945.

[FIVE]

Residual Becomes Emergent

To many now, theater seems the most embarrassingly residual of media, sustained only by the undead force of petrified distinction in a mediascape where it will never again be new. Where, implicitly or explicitly, the subject is a historical progression of media, theater is very often relegated to the ragged company of antiquated forms long since transcended by technological progress. Following some accounts, succinctly captured, but also challenged, by J. Hoberman's title, *Film after Film*, theater is now cinema's predecessor in another way: an exemplar of a pattern of unplanned obsolescence to which film, too, now falls victim.[1] More typically still, theater simply has no place in contemporary discussions of media theory or history, except sometimes as a metaphor for more important shifts happening elsewhere. Scholars of theater, meanwhile, most often focusing on contemporary theater, have been at pains to stress theater's newly intermedial condition; it is rarer for media theorists or historians whose specialty is not theater to pay attention to it.

A familiar solution to this predicament of arrested development common to scholars of theater has been to claim that as a medium it returns us to forms of experience that other media cannot match. In particular, theater scholarship invokes the importance of co-presence as the factor that makes theater a form or a practice or even a medium unlike others. Theater becomes, among other things, the medium of an abstract "ritual," belonging to no particular religion, somehow secularized, but nevertheless imbued with

---

1. Hoberman's discussion of Tsai Ming-Liang's stunning *Goodbye, Dragon Inn* is especially relevant: the film, writes Hoberman, examines "the inner life of the Fu-Ho theater, a since-demolished poured-concrete cavern in the heart of Taipei" (*Film after Film*, 215). More generally, the book discusses the cinematic consequences of the "digital turn" (vii) away from film as medium that *Goodbye, Dragon Inn* allegorizes. On filmic nostalgia for the movie house itself, see also Gabriele Pedullà, *In Broad Daylight*, 4–5, 15.

a sacral air. If, on the one hand, a too-simple diachronic scheme relegates theater to the sphere of the outmoded, on the other hand a form of synchronic thinking that asserts the importance of theater because of some unchanging, valuable essence ignores the historicity of the form entirely. The choice between triumphalism in which theater is one of the spoils carried by the victors in an inevitable march toward the crowning of the newest of new media and a wishful celebration of theater's special difference from other media is a false one. What's needed are considered and historically alert accounts of theater as a medium among other media—or, more accurately, theater as a set of mediums among media.

The work of Peggy Phelan and Philip Auslander in the 1990s accelerated critical discussion of the status of theater as medium and its relation to mass media. The disagreement between Phelan and Auslander about the status of performance in contemporary culture continues to illuminate theater's medial status, now and also in earlier periods in the continually unfolding age of mass media. I agree with Phelan that there is a peculiar difference to performance, and by extension to theater, though I do not think of this difference as an ontological one.[2] I agree with Auslander that the prestige of liveness is a historical development that followed from the development of mass media—that liveness is discernible only in a historical context when there is something not live to oppose to it—but I don't think that the historicity of liveness means that it simply dissolves into a generalized soup of media, as Auslander sometimes (though not always) seems to suggest. Nor do I think that the only media or aesthetic forms that matter, as he also sometimes (though not always) seems to suggest, are those that are "dominant." To recognize the historicity of liveness emphasizes the importance of its actuality; that this actuality has no essence or ontological quality doesn't mean that it doesn't matter or that it makes no difference.

In *Unmarked*, Phelan starts her influential chapter on the ontology of performance with a claim so resonantly startling (and so often quoted) that the subtlety of the chapter that follows has often been overlooked: "Performance's only life is in the present. Performance cannot be saved, recorded, documented, or otherwise participate in the circulation of representation

---

2. Indeed, I frequently find that I do not understand what "ontology" and its variants mean in writing on literature and the arts, and take some comfort in Alasdair MacIntyre's wry comment in an encyclopedia entry. Writing on late scholastic "division of metaphysics into ontology, cosmology, and psychology," MacIntyre writes: "Along with this division, there persisted the view that being constitutes an independent subject matter over and above the subject matter of the special sciences. The persistence of this view is perhaps to be explained by cultural rather than by intellectual factors" (MacIntyre, "Ontology," in *The Encyclopedia of Philosophy*, 5:542).

of representations: once it does so, it becomes something other than performance. To the degree that performance attempts to enter the economy of reproduction it betrays and lessens the promise of its own ontology."[3] Phelan's chapter inspired discussion in theater studies.[4] Her chapter also provided a critical summation of intensely felt convictions about performance art as a challenge to the art market and to commodity culture more broadly that were part of debates in New York City and elsewhere from the 1970s onward.[5] While translation of its claims from performance art to theater was perhaps inevitable, little in the chapter invites this wholesale adaptation. That said, the intensity of Phelan's argument, grounded equally in feminism, psychoanalysis, and anticapitalist thought, stimulated reflection on the "ontology," and also the phenomenology, of other performance practices, including experimental theater and show business. Her stress on the disappearance of performance, on the irreducible difference between the "maniacally charged present" of performance and the forms of recording—writing, photography, video—that strive to document it, has provoked an immensely constructive debate about what we are talking about when we talk about performance.[6] One important strain of her chapter concerns performance's resistance to the circulation of capital: "Performance resists the balanced circulations of finance. It saves nothing; it only spends. While photography is vulnerable to charges of counterfeiting and copying, performance art is vulnerable to charges of valuelessness and emptiness. Performance indicates the possibility of revaluing that emptiness; this potential revaluation gives performance art its distinctive

3. Phelan, *Unmarked*, 146.

4. See, for instance, Rebecca Schneider, *Performance Remains*, esp. 91–92, where Schneider considers points of disagreement—but also sites of intellectual continuity—between Phelan and Auslander. Schneider's fine-grained institutional history of the emphasis on ephemerality in the Department of Performance Studies at New York University is also relevant here (94–96).

5. In an interview given in 2003, Phelan comments on the reception of *Unmarked* as "a psychoanalytic text" and, while granting the correctness of this reading, insists it was "also about the way in which capital works," linking this to her concentration on performance art: "Much of the energy and inspiration of performance art in the 1970s derived from an attempt to dissolve the materiality of the art object, and to create, in the moment of performance, something of value that did not have an object" (Phelan, "Performance, Live Culture, and Things of the Heart," 293). Decades of correspondence and conversation with the artist and critic Gretchen Faust have informed my own understanding of this milieu.

6. Phelan, *Unmarked*, 148.

oppositional edge."[7] Against photography as the technological medium most closely linked to capital, Phelan opposes performance. For Phelan, performance does not escape the capitalist economy so much as point toward another possible economy that opposes it. To revalue the emptiness at the heart of performance challenges the logic of finance, but what remains is also not without value. With an extravagance that recalls Georges Bataille's accursed share, performance, revalued, "only spends," drawing on the maniacal, always renewed charge account of the present.

In *Liveness*, Auslander objects: "I doubt very strongly that any cultural discourse can actually stand outside the ideologies of capital and reproduction that define a mediatized culture or should be expected to do so, even to assume an oppositional stance."[8] This inexactly summarizes Phelan's argument: performance, in her account, is not in itself discursive but "becomes something other" when it takes discursive forms. This becoming "something other," as her essay acknowledges, may be an inevitable departure from performance, but she insists that performance is different from discursive forms, from the ways it is "saved, recorded, documented"—from the ways, that is, in which it is represented. In Phelan's argument, it is as a practice, and not as discourse, that performance stands outside the reproductive circuits of capital, refusing to "enter the economy of reproduction." For Auslander, such a refusal is an impossibility—even to the extent that "an oppositional stance" seems a critical fantasy. (Similarly, for Auslander, the distinction between discourse and practice might seem almost to deconstruct itself.)

Given the intensity of his objections to Phelan, it may appear that for Auslander "liveness" is simply a critical mystification. Auslander does not, however, finally argue that "liveness" does not exist, or even that it is not a useful category. His argument deconstructively reverses the priority of the live over the reproduced: "Live performance cannot be said to have ontological or historical priority over mediatization, since liveness was made visible only by the possibility of technical reproduction."[9] He does argue that liveness has no "distinctive ontology": "Any distinctions," he writes, "need to derive from careful consideration of how the relationship between

7. Phelan, *Unmarked*, 148. The question of whether "performance art" and "performance" are synonyms in this passage indicates one rhetorical trait of the chapter that invites generalization.

8. Auslander, *Liveness*, 40.

9. Auslander, *Liveness*, 54. Stanley Cavell had anticipated this argument about liveness as an effect of the recorded in *The World Viewed* (182), but to say this risks simplifying his reflections on the live and the recorded (see, for instance, 182–84).

the live and the mediatized is articulated in particular cases, not from a set of assumptions that constructs the relation between live and mediatized representations *a priori* as a relation of essential opposition."[10] The critical task, then, becomes not how to establish a definitive ontology of liveness but instead how to track the articulation of liveness and its others in particular circumstances. In *Postdramatic Theatre*, a book first published in German in the same year as *Liveness*, Hans-Thies Lehmann similarly argued that film was crucial to theater's realization of "the live process (as opposed to the reproduced or reproducible appearances) as a *differentia specifica* of the theatre."[11] Lehmann argues that this discovery of "the live process" as theater's medium led to "retheatricalization": "It was not just a matter of a retheatricalization immanent to theatre, but at the same time of an opening of the theatrical sphere to others: to cultural, political, magical, philosophical, etc. forms of practice, to gathering, feast and ritual."[12] With Phelan, I stress the difference that performance can make in a mass-mediated culture. With Auslander, I swerve away from the idea that this difference is an ontological one and stress the historical quality of theater's response to the hegemony of media and mass culture—especially film—in the decades following 1945. With Lehmann, I stress the ways that twentieth-century theatrical experimentation followed from a "media-historical caesura: the emergence of film."[13] But the theatrical experiment I trace here is neither the development of some potentiality that was always immanent nor an opening outward to other forms of practice—especially not ritual ones. Twentieth-century theater poached from such practices in a process that Lehmann politely calls the "productive reception of (European and non-European) non-literary theatre traditions in the historical avant-gardes."[14] The theater makers I consider here did not see such appropriation as an answer to the dilemma of the contemporary predicament of theater in the wake of the consolidation of film. Rather than drawing from existing traditions or from the store of the "primitive," seeking to address a contemporary predicament with repurposed ritual or resurrected carnival, they wrote plays designed for the theatrical situation of their historical present.

10. Phillip Auslander, *Liveness*, 54. In "Theater and Media Before 'New' Media," I misrepresented Auslander's emphasis on the particularity of the relationship between the live and the mediatized (see esp. 11).

11. Lehmann, *Postdramatic Theatre*, 50.

12. Lehmann, *Postdramatic Theatre*, 51.

13. Lehmann, *Postdramatic Theatre*, 50.

14. Lehmann, *Postdramatic Theatre*, 51. Lehmann cites Fischer-Lichte's *The Show and the Gaze of Theatre*.

Tennessee Williams used one of his favorite quotations, from a letter from August Strindberg to Paul Gauguin, as the occasional epigraph to *Orpheus Descending*: "I, too, am beginning to feel an immense need to become a savage and create a new world."[15] This impulse toward modernist primitivism, complexly mediated as it is in the form of quotation from a message from playwright to painter, did not preclude writing a play in three acts to be staged on Broadway. The peculiar and historically specific forms of theatricality I consider here did not constitute an elemental discovery of theater as medium, and were not the unveiling of something that had been always immanent but only hidden and awaiting its moment of emergence or emergency: they represented one historical development of what theater could become after film, just as the movement toward the theatrical desire to achieve the condition of ritual was another. The desire to dissolve the divide between participant and spectator—a desire for which an idealized form of ritual or festivity had long been the model—was always a fantasy of overcoming the complexities of mediation.[16] The plays considered here do not imagine that the difference between spectator and performer can be overcome; they also do not imagine that such overcoming would be the only possible form of critique inside the theater. Samuel Beckett's adherence to the frame of the proscenium is a particularly clear example of this project of undoing spectatorship inside the theater (an argument I pursue at greater length below). Instead of pursuing the project of dissolving that divide between the spectator and performer, if anything these plays accentuate it, producing divisions inside the practices of spectatorship.[17] Theatrical spectatorship was not cinematic spectatorship, and working inside the difference between theater and film—producing negative versions of cinematic experience inside the theater—contributed to the force of experimental drama in the 1960s and 1970s.

15. The quotation appears, for instance, on the cover of the Dramatists Play Service edition.

16. That one can trace this desire to texts that well predate cinema, including Rousseau's *Letter to d'Alembert* of 1758 and Nietzsche's *Birth of Tragedy* of 1872, suggests those philosophers' perceptiveness to the mediation of experience and a longer history informing the notion that modernity has made experience less transparent. Early in his *Transparency and Obstruction*, Starobinski isolates this essential formulation: "We must live in opacity" (11). His account of Rousseau is one complex account of a struggle with this necessity.

17. See my dialogue with Julia Jarcho, "Dividing the Audience."

[SIX]

Medium/Media/Remediation
in Reverse

Auslander would not be alone in insisting that *medium* makes no sense without considering *media*: the conditions of a medium are not ontological, but, instead, historical and relational, and important among these relations is a relationship to media. Marshall McLuhan's classic formulation bears repeating:

> The instance of the electric light may prove illuminating in this connection. The electric light is pure information. It is a medium without a message, as it were, unless it is used to spell out some verbal ad or name. This fact, characteristic of all media, means that the "content" of any medium is always another medium.[1]

Pairing this quotation with a passage from Lisa Gitelman's *Always Already New* emphasizes the historical quality of the relationship between media:

> it is as much of a mistake to write broadly of "the telephone," "the camera," or "the computer" as it is "the media," and of—now somehow, "the Internet" and "the Web"—naturalizing or essentializing technologies as if they were unchanging, "immutable objects with given, self-defining properties" around which changes swirl, and to or from which history proceeds. Instead, it is better to specify telephones in 1890 in the rural United States, broadcast telephones in Budapest in the 1920s, or cellular, satellite, corded, and cordless landline telephones in North America at the beginning of the twenty-first century.[2]

1. Marshall McLuhan, *Understanding Media*, 19.
2. Lisa Gitelman, *Always Already New*, 8.

The scare quotes with which McLuhan surrounds that most suspect word, "content," open up a space Gitelman illuminates. McLuhan's punctuation acknowledges that "content" is necessarily a provisional term. Nevertheless, McLuhan's simple copulative—"the 'content' of any medium *is* always another medium"—appears to assert an identity: we may not know what word should take the place of "content," but we know what that the thing that takes the place of content "*is* always another medium." The promise here is that we know what a medium, or "another medium," is, that once we recognize which medium provides the "content" for another medium, we will be able to recognize the second medium. The force of Gitelman's critique, by contrast, lies in her insistence that a technology is not a stable entity that could, in some unproblematic way, provide the "content" for another technology. There is a vanishing point implicit in Gitelman's theorization beyond which it would be impossible to speak of a technology or a medium at all; as Meredith McGill pointed out, Gitelman's approach still requires, however provisionally, a certain abstraction or reification of historically disparate practices into something called a medium or a technology.[3] In a particular historical moment and geographical site, a medium and its attendant practices become recognizable: this abstraction of "medium" will have required the separating out of unusual or residual uses of the medium. Gitelman's revision of McLuhan offers one way to read his scare quotes around the word "content." That interrogative punctuation alienates any simple notion of a given content provided by one medium that another medium might adopt or translate. Gitelman's emphasis on the historicity of that content suggests a modification of McLuhan's thesis: the "content" provided by one medium to other media will not remain constant. Even if one accepts McLuhan's formulation, one will need to recall that the content provider must itself be seen as changeable, as not a stable medium at all.

McLuhan's formulation seems to me enduringly provocative, and especially for the sphere of the aesthetic, where the question of the influence of media on mediums has long been subject to provocative speculations. As noted above, *Theater after Film* alludes to and reverses the titles of two important studies published almost fifty years apart: A. Nicholas Vardac's *Stage to Screen* (1949) and Ben Brewster and Lea Jacobs's *Theatre to Cinema* (1998). What has *not* changed in Brewster and Jacobs's revision of Vardac is telling: the preposition "to" remains. Of course, historically stage and theater preceded screen and cinema: both books demonstrate how theater provided certain kinds of content for film, with special attention to the development of melodrama from medium to medium. Both books revise

---

3. I owe this point to conversation with McGill.

overly simple accounts of historical relationship between theater and film. Nevertheless, teleology remains.[4] This is especially true in Vardac's account, which, as Brewster and Jacobs comment, relies on a kind of *Kunstwollen* to explain how film satisfied desires for realistic effects first created by nineteenth-century theater.[5] The point of my "after," then, is to stress two things: first, and most simply, that theater has, despite every announcement of its unplanned obsolescence, continued after film and, second and more complexly, that theater's interaction with film shaped this afterlife in important ways.

To return to the familiar sentence from McLuhan: "This fact, characteristic of all media, means that the 'content' of any medium is always another medium." What this does not say is that a new medium will take its content from an old medium. Some of McLuhan's examples may be taken to suggest this, but he does not explicitly limit his larger claim to that form of appropriation. The "old" medium, that is, may take the newer one as its content just as surely as the reverse. Indeed, the letter of McLuhan's claim would be that such taking is necessarily a feature of every medium in every situation, no matter the "age" of that medium. (The question of the age of a medium is also a complicated one. Virtually no theater historian would claim an unbroken history for theater, and yet it is not uncommon to encounter overviews of a singular history of one medium unfolding from an origin in Greece.) Complicated questions circle around that questionable term, "content." In *Remediation*, Jay David Bolter and Richard Grusin return to McLuhan's declaration about medium and content and observe: "As his problematic examples suggest, McLuhan was not thinking of simple repurposing, but perhaps of a more complex kind of borrowing in which one medium is itself incorporated or represented in another medium. Dutch painters incorporated maps, globes, inscriptions, letters, and mirrors in their works." In the same paragraph, Bolter and Grusin remind the reader:

---

4. "All the 'from . . . to' histories have for too long been, as we now realize, deeply flawed," writes Thomas Elsaesser ("Early Film History and Multi-Media," 22). Thinking of the familiar movement from page to stage, Jennifer Buckley levels an especially acute critique of a similar "from-to formulation" in *Beyond Text*, 10–11. Julian Olf challenges this teleology from a phenomenological direction: "That the play is a *moving picture* is a truism, not a hypothesis in need of validation" (Olf, "The Play as a Moving Picture," 12). This can be a truism only with the erasure of any historical specificity to "the moving picture."

5. Brewster and Jacobs, *Theatre to Cinema*, 6. Brewster and Jacobs, indeed, are at pains to undo a history of teleological thinking within film history, where early film with its debts to theatrical practice inevitably gives way to later, more sophisticated filmmaking—"genuine" cinema—built around montage.

"Again, we call the representation of one medium in another *remediation*, and we will argue that remediation is a defining characteristic of the new digital media."[6] A detail here is telling: in paraphrasing McLuhan, Bolter and Grusin think of the form that content takes as a matter of *incorporation* or representation. Their example of Dutch painting is a resonant one. Their definition of remediation, however, drops "incorporation" to isolate "representation" as the mode of remediation. With all their elaboration of what "representation" can mean, this reliance on representation is consequential. Here, Phelan's insistence on the difference between a performance and its representation resonates: this reduction of all forms of content to representation is particularly suggestive for the meeting of, and missed connections between, media studies and aesthetics. In the particular field that occupies this book, postwar theater—a field marked by a particularly generative crisis of a medium among other media (if, indeed, it makes sense to think of theater as a medium at all)—representation is exactly the wrong concept to describe what happens when a medium becomes part of the "content" of another medium, when film in all its totalizing force, perceived or real, becomes part of the substance of theater.

Bolter and Grusin's vocabulary for the modalities of remediation is suggestive. "Dutch painters," they write, "*incorporated* maps, globes, inscriptions, letters, and mirrors in their works." *Incorporation* is an odd figure for the mimesis in painting of these earlier inscriptive forms and media, but it accords with their insistence that the force of Dutch painting lies in its combination of the persuasive illusion of immediacy characteristic of painterly perspective with the simultaneous attention to the modes of inscription that characterize what they call hypermediacy.[7] The example of the instruments and documents in Northern European painting is exemplary here: Hans Holbein's *Ambassadors*, for instance, simultaneously appears to have incorporated objects of a lavishly equipped early capitalist world and, especially through its fatal anamorphic blot—the skull that becomes visible from an oblique angle—obliges the viewer to contemplate the painting's mode of representation. This model of the representation of earlier media or technologies inside later ones tells us a lot about the history of media and about the history of various arts. It can't, however, account for the theatrical examples that interest me. Indeed, an insistence on the *mimesis* of a medium as the signal of the incorporation of that medium explains why the response of postwar theater to mass media has been misrecognized. Here

---

6. Bolter and Grusin, *Remediation*, 45.

7. See, for instance, Bolter and Grusin, *Remediation*, 33–34.

I offer an account of aesthetic responses to a mass-mediated environment that is not about incorporation or representation or remediation. That is, these responses are *not* traceable because of their explicit repetition of mass-mediated "content" inside works of art—for example, letters inside paintings, or television monitors on stage, and so on. Nevertheless media shape aesthetic fields.[8]

Andreas Huyssen, in his study of what he has dubbed the "modernist miniature," has decisively altered the terrain of this debate by arguing that these miniatures are the result of what he calls "remediation in reverse": "moments when an older medium reasserts itself by critically working through what the new medium does and does not do."[9] Twentieth-century theater is a crucial site of such reassertion, and this is especially true after World War II. Huyssen argues "that the old medium, in this case literature, can remediate the newer ones, creating new and unexpected hybridities of cultural articulation."[10] Huyssen's work has long stressed the interdependence of mass culture and modernism without dissolving the differences between different aesthetic forms.[11] His emphasis on "differential specificity" without hierarchy or teleology is a model for thinking about mutually entangled histories: "It is always premature to declare the obsolescence of literature or any other medium."[12] Nothing in the sorts of linear trajectories of aesthetic forms that simply assume, or confidently predict, such obsolescence can explain why drama and theater were so urgently a part of the "cultural articulation" of the postwar years. They cannot explain the ways that theater in this period revivified itself in part through its response to the challenges and limits of the new media of film and of mass culture.

Theater's remediation in reverse of film was not primarily a matter of the migration of content from medium to medium: the adaptation of movies to the stage, which has in recent decades been a prominent part of the

8. In an earlier version of this argument, I proposed *dismediation* as a term for certain aesthetic responses to mass media ("Theater after Film, or Dismediation"). The term no longer strikes me as needed.

9. Huyssen, *Miniature Metropolis*, 8.

10. Eric Bulson, "Literature and Close Reading."

11. It is also no accident that, different from so many of the most prominent critics of modernism, drama has always been among the forms to which he pays attention. See, for instance, his chapter "Producing Revolution: Heiner Müller's *Mauser* as Learning Play," in *After the Great Divide*, 82–93.

12. Huyssen, *Miniature Metropolis*, 22.

work of the director Ivo von Hove, for instance, is not what is at issue.[13] The works I consider here for the most part respond to film not through adaptation; they do not integrate cinematic plots, settings, or acting styles. (Adrienne Kennedy will be the striking exception, but her remediations of Hollywood cinema are more complex than any model of the migration of content from one medium to another might suggest.) The "differential specificity" of theater followed from its distance from a set of techniques understood to be typical of cinema. The specificity of this difference required a certain abstraction—a certain lack of specificity—in the conception of cinema. A generalized conception of film, of its effects, and of its powers of interpellation produced certain very definite, very specific, experiments on stage.[14]

13. Von Hove's version of John Cassavetes's *Opening Night* is particularly interesting here. By building the film around an opening night in a theater that goes comically wrong, Cassavetes reflects on the improvisational practice that was essential to his movie-making; von Hove's adaptation, then, is a literal-minded return to relative looseness of the theatrical space to which the film aspires. And yet this theatrical remediation of Cassavetes seemed to me, in performance at the Brooklyn Academy of Music in 2008, curiously petrified. Tom Sellar reported that von Hove had never seen Cassavetes's film: "His innocence helped rather than hindered him, he said, in imagining his stage version based on Cassavetes' original screenplay" ("Theater Director with a Filmmaker's Eye"). It may be that this "innocence," the choice to treat Cassavetes's work as pure content rather than as a film with its own challenging address to the spectator, contributed to a certain inertness in the remediated version for the stage.

14. I have learned from critics who have anticipated this book's argument. George Szanto, in *Theater and Propaganda*, places Beckett's theater in relation to mass media (145–77) but comes to very different conclusions: "The final effect of a Beckett play," writes Szanto, "is to disallow the perspective necessary to critique it" (155). Martin Puchner's emphasis on the work of the negative in modern drama in *Stage Fright* and, in particular, his argument about Beckett's plays as a necessary negative response to "theatricalized mass politics" has been crucial (170). Sarah Bay-Cheng's chapter on Gertrude Stein and "the origins of Stein's drama in cinema" in *Mama Dada* (27–45) is exemplary in thinking about the formal relationship between a body of experimental work for the theater and the influence of cinema. Christopher Grobe's "Why It's 'Easier to Act with a Telephone than a Man'" is acutely alert to the historical specificity of the telephone on stage. While her focus is on later drama, Elizabeth Klaver's coordination of drama and media in *Performing Television* has affinities with my argument; see also her "Spectatorial Theory in the Age of Media Culture."

[SEVEN]

Theater/Film

Claims about theater's relationship to film have a history almost as long as cinema itself. As early as 1918, Alexander Blok declares: "In my opinion cinema has nothing in common with theatre, is not attached to it, does not compete with it, nor can they destroy each other; those once fashionable discussions 'on cinema and theatre' seem quite unreal to me."[1] Blok already thought the vogue for discussions "on cinema and theatre" was passé. Blok's admirably clear position, however, was exceptional. Despite his confidence in the datedness of this fashion, proclamations, arguments, and strong claims about the nature of the difference between theater and cinema punctuate film theory from Hugo Münsterberg's *The Photoplay: A Psychological Study* (1916) to Stanley Cavell's *The World Viewed: Reflections on the Ontology of Film* (1971) and beyond.[2] For this book, an especially significant moment in this long history occurred in the 1960s. In the first half of that decade, the issue of theater as medium became a live one for critics from Michael Fried to Susan Sontag. This debate concerned the problem of what the essential medium of theater might be: for Fried "*What lies* between *the arts is theater*" because it has no medium to which it can be specific.[3] Sontag also addresses another question, that is, whether theater, like film, can "encapsulate" another art form: "One *can*," she asserts, "film a play or ballet or opera or sporting event in such a way that film becomes, relatively speaking, a transparency, and it seems correct to say that one is seeing the event filmed. But

---

1. Alexander Blok, quoted in Jay Leyda, *Kino*, 130.

2. Two anthologies survey the problem: James Hurt's *Focus on Film and Theatre* and Robert Knopf's *Theater and Film: A Comparative Anthology*.

3. Fried, "Art and Objecthood" (1967), in *Art and Objecthood*, 164.

theatre is never a 'medium.'"[4] Sontag's claim underlines the aspiration of experimental postwar theater: its project was in part to reject this model of medium as transparency.[5] If this theater made a claim to the prestige of medium in the sense important to Fried, the specificity of the medium belonged to its repudiation of a medium's transparency in Sontag's sense. This is also to say that in important ways this theater constituted itself as the reverse remediation of cinema. Surely these theorizations of the first half of the 1960s involved a phantasm of film itself as hypnotic and hegemonic medium few critics or theorists would now endorse. And yet understanding postwar theater, and potentially the postwar arts more generally, requires registering how a persuasive conception of film as medium became part of a structure of feeling or horizon of expectation. In this context, it's significant that Raymond Williams first sketched his notion of "structure of feeling" in "The Dramatic Tradition," his long contribution to the short book *Preface to Film*, published in 1954.[6] The power of film as an instrument in the production of fascist publics; the paired notion of Hollywood as a machine of capitalist hegemony; the wider and widespread sense of mass culture as an unprecedented tool for the production of docile subjects: such beliefs were simply central to postwar discourse, elements of which remain remarkably tenacious even now.[7] The focus on the inevitable psychic effects of the cinematic apparatus in somewhat later theories of the 1970s may have been a paranoid idealization of the moviegoer's experience, but it did accurately summarize a

4. Sontag, "Film and Theatre," 25. In *Theatricality as Medium*, a collection of essays, Samuel Weber revives the argument about theater as medium. Weber consistently argues that to claim a singular medium for theater is to risk the error of imagining that an aesthetic entity might be self-identical. Often but not everywhere in Weber's text, theatricality is precisely what theater cannot attain.

5. That theater, from Broadway to the Brooklyn Academy of Music, has now often become a mode for the remediation of cinema and television is fascinating, but not my topic here.

6. Williams and Michael Orrom, *Preface to Film*, 21–22. See the illuminating discussion of structures of feeling in Williams's *Politics and Letters*, 156–74. In that interview, Williams points out his use of the phrase in *Preface to Film* (158–59). For a useful overview of the place of drama to Williams's thought, see Jim McGuigan's chapter, "Drama in A Screen Age," in *Raymond Williams: Cultural Analyst* (61–82).

7. Andrew Ross's *No Respect* remains a valuable critique of postwar intellectuals: see especially chapter 2, "Containing Culture in the Cold War" (42–64).

conception of film that helped to shape postwar theater negatively even as that theater worked to negate it in practice.[8]

Theodor Adorno's model of negation would be more helpful were it not for its insistence on social totality as what art negates. The sameness against which Adorno constantly argues returns in the consistency with which he describes "the" work of art. And yet that model's theorization of aesthetic negation as simultaneously the incorporation and undoing of the logic of what it negates is essential.[9] The conception of the force of film in theorizations of the apparatus relied on a particular sense of the spectator in the dark movie theater as passively manipulated: Jean-Louis Baudry's translation of Plato's allegory of the cave from ancient puppet show for the forcibly restrained to cinema may stand in for a larger body of theories and assumptions.[10] Postwar theater, in short, worked to negate a model of the spectator associated with mass culture. Theater's remediation in reverse of cinematic spectatorship is not so much a matter of representation as a concerted dramaturgical insistence on the *absence* of the incorporated medium. If, to use Adorno and Max Horkheimer's phrase, culture was now "administered," many saw film as central to the apparatus of that administration. For theater to come after film, then, was for theater to come after the belief in the cultural force of cinema and mass culture had become a commonplace, part of the postwar cultural imaginary.

The contrast between cinema's international power as an apparatus of subjection after 1945 and the slender means of postwar theaters is glaring. Remediation in reverse, to be sure, very often becomes the project of a

8. The importance of Brecht to the *Screen* collective is significant in this context: it was partly through a theory of theater as the other of a stultifying mass culture that the *Screen* group conceptualized a potential for film that broke with cinematic norms. For a particularly representative issue of the journal, see *Screen* 14, no. 2 (Summer 1974). This issue includes a translation of Roland Barthes's "Diderot, Brecht, Eisenstein" (33–39), a dossier on Brecht's *Kuhle Wampe* (41–73), and Stephen Heath's "Lessons from Brecht" (103–28). For another representative publication, see Martin Walsh, *The Brechtian Aspect of Radical Cinema*.

9. For an important study of twentieth-century and contemporary theater in relation to Adorno's conception of negation, see Julia Jarcho, *Writing and the Modern Stage*.

10. See Jean-Louis Baudry, "The Apparatus: Metapsychological Approaches to the Impression of Reality in the Cinema," in Philip Rosen, ed., *Narrative, Apparatus, Ideology*, 299–318. Gabriele Pedullà, in *In Broad Daylight*, summarizes the Platonic analogy, and asserts that "American cognitive film theorists" such as Noël Carroll have proved it wrong (11). What interests me here is not the analogy's empirical accuracy but its persuasive force, along with that of analogous pictures of cinematic experience in the period.

relatively marginal avant-garde. And yet the importance of theater between 1950 and 1970—to give very rough dates—lies in part in its alienation of assumptions about the spectator. To an unprecedented degree, from Brecht and Beckett to Jerzy Grotowski and the Living Theatre to Peter Handke and Adrienne Kennedy, scrutiny of the spectator and disruption of its place became central to theatrical experiment. The cinematic spectator became, to adopt McLuhan's formulation, the "content" of theater after film. That this theater to a large degree also dispensed with more familiar forms of dramatic storytelling points not so much to some transhistorical suspicion of "narrative" as to the reverse remediation of the pleasures of cinematic narration in particular. Displaced as the preeminent medium for narration using human bodies, theater remade itself as a medium for reflection on such narration and on the structures of identification that made that cinema so powerful a force of subjection.

In the period when "mass culture" became solidified, this model of cinematic spectatorship and its power to form subjects shaped the plays I study here. This is not to say that there were no alternative theories of cinema. There were also patterns of spectatorship that did not conform to the theories of docile spectatorship that the mass culture model might have predicted. The premise of this book relies on the possibility of resistance to the power of cinematic interpellation. No matter how overwhelming the playwrights might have sensed cinema's power to be—and there is plenty of evidence that they did—their plays are evidence of various modes of distance from the pleasures and passions of cinema. They were also not entirely isolated, a few postwar philosophers of the stage who managed to tear themselves away from the cave to see the light. I have been interested in tracing and valuing—without, I hope, fetishizing—the tracks of their moviegoing. In 1951, for instance, Beckett writes to Georges Duthuit that he has been in Paris for a few days, where it is "impossible to sleep": "Naturally we made straight for the cinema yesterday evening, *Les Chaînes du destin*, with Barbara Stanwyck. [. . .] I have never seen her so good, a few looks that showed extraordinary pathos."[11] How many times had he seen her? Granting a certain puckish humor in that "naturally," nevertheless this passage attests to

---

11. Beckett, letter to Georges Duthuit, August 1, 1951, trans. George Craig, *Letters*, 2: 274. A few days earlier, he had written in another letter to Duthuit: "Envie de cinema et de terrasse de café" ("Feel an urge to go to the cinema, to sit at a café terrace") (Beckett, letter to Georges Duthuit, July 26, 1951, trans. Craig, *Letters*, 2: 269; 270). Writing about roughly this period in Beckett's life, Deirdre Bair observes: "He still had a passion for movies, which [his wife] Suzanne shared; it was one of the few things they did together" (Bair, 417).

moviegoing as habit, with at least a few points of comparison by which to judge the "extraordinary pathos" of Stanwyck's performance.

Habitual moviegoing created new audiences, but no apparatus entirely determined what they made of that habit. With their fine-grained and richly historical arguments about particular gendered and raced audiences, Miriam Bratu Hansen's *Babel and Babylon* and Jacqueline Stewart's *Migrating to the Movies* are especially compelling challenges to zombie theories of cinematic interpellation. Hansen recognizes the "ideological objective of constructing a unified subject of—and for—mass-cultural consumption" but she also insists that, however strong this "normative aspect," that "there remains, even in the ceaseless repetition of this process, a margin of autonomous interpretation and reappropriation."[12] Stewart's thick description of Black audiences and spectatorial practices in Chicago in the early decades of the twentieth century emphasizes the public dimensions of cinematic experience, reading "Black spectatorship as the creation of literal and symbolic spaces in which African Americans reconstructed their individual and collective identities in response to the cinema's moves toward classical narrative integration, and in the wake of migration's fragmenting effects."[13] Stewart's constellation of migration from the South and urban cinematic experience is especially relevant to Kennedy: a similar constellation structures *A Movie Star,* and Kennedy's experiment in autobiographical writing, *People Who Led to My Plays,* could be one source for a study of Black moviegoing and performance culture in Cleveland in the late 1930s and 1940s.[14] Together, Hansen and Stewart inform my approach here because of the ways their work at once considers cinema's general structures of solicitation and audience address while also considering, in rich detail, deviations from those structures, what Hansen calls "a tension, at least during the silent era, between the cinema's role as a universalizing, ideological idiom

12. Hansen, *Babel and Babylon,* 16–17.

13. Stewart, *Migrating to the Movies,* 94.

14. A book on the model of Hanns Zischler's *Kafka Goes to the Movies* could be written about any of the playwrights considered here. For instance: Kennedy writes that she saw Lena Horne "on the stage at the Palace Theatre at age eleven—a Negro woman, a beautiful, vital spectacle"; she links this to Horne's "hypnotic glamour" in MGM films (*People Who Led to My Plays,* 61). Edward Albee II, the playwright's grandfather, opened that theater in 1922 ("Palace Theater"). Lena Horne played the Palace Theatre on September 8, 1944, just before Kennedy's thirteenth birthday. Horne performed with an impressive band led by Cootie Williams with what a prose advertisement called "a combine of perfectionists," including Eddie "Cleanhead" Vinson on saxophone and the young Bud Powell on piano ("Two Bands Please Young Bugs").

and its redemptive possibilities as an inclusive, heterogeneous, and at times unpredictable horizon of experience."[15]

As Hansen's stress on the silent era emphasizes, these studies both focus on early cinema, when that "classical narrative integration" had not yet solidified. The plays I consider here all occupy a space after such narrative had become the dominant mode of commercial cinema. After the caesura of World War II, the weight of that mode had become heavier.

15. Hansen, *Babel and Babylon*, 19.

[EIGHT]

Apparatus

A return to the most familiar narrative of an apparatus and its force will help to situate the historicity of the postwar revision of theater as medium. Louis Althusser, it's worth stressing, insistently describes his "theoretical scene" in theatrical terms: he calls the policeman's hailing of the subject "my little theoretical theatre" and further calls his account "this *mise en scène* of interpellation." Theater figures the apparatus that makes possible the narrativization *in time* of the ideological formation of the subject that has "always-already" happened, as Althusser stresses, that is, outside of time.[1] Such a translation from unthought, timeless ideology into aesthetic medium is necessary in order to recognize how ideology works: the model of the theater makes it possible to imagine in temporal sequence something that does not belong to the order of time at all.

Althusser's account of ideological apparatuses, that is, illuminates the ambitions of the postwar theater and in particular its negative relation to film imagined as a powerful, quasi-official ideological apparatus. The exercises in theatrical reflexivity critics were beginning to call metatheater—a term invented, symptomatically, by Lionel Abel only in 1963, and in part in response to Beckett[2]—was not, then, simply another chapter in the long history of a medium's calling awareness to its own artifice. Against cinematic experience insistently figured as a warm bath in the sleep of ideology or the "Hollywood dream factory," theater insistently returned to reflection on its own medium.[3] Such exposure of a medium as medium, however, pointed not to some late modernist project of the reduction of a medium to its essentials but to theater as a place where, through negation, processes of subjection through interpellation could be made visible. Emphasis on

1. Louis Althusser, "Ideology and Ideological State Apparatuses," 174, 177, 175.

2. Lionel Abel, *Metatheatre*.

3. See Hortense Powdermaker, *Hollywood, the Dream Factory*.

the relative poverty of theater as medium—alas, poor theater!—also, that is, underlined its *inefficiency* as ideological apparatus. The richness of film as a medium for realist narrative, and consequently its power as conduit for ideology, had made theater's relative poverty especially visible. If film was an apparatus of subjection, theater as medium could make that formation visible through metatheatrical techniques. These techniques were at once inside stage traditions of address and arose specifically in negative reaction to what was understood to be cinema's immense power to form subjects.

Stories of the demolition of the theater over the course of the twentieth century and its relegation to the junkyard of media history neglect the ways theater rebuilt itself as a medium formed in relation to other media. This rebuilding happened in part through remediation in reverse, through the formal negation of modes of spectatorship associated with the cinema. Such remediation in turn, in the work of Jean-Luc Godard and others, fostered cinematic experiment designed to counter the Hollywood apparatus. My aim here, however, is not to argue for the importance of postwar theater because of its effects later or elsewhere or because of some other rebuilding project—for instance, inside the history of film—to which it might have contributed. This theater becomes newly visible because of its relation to other media. The forms of remediation in reverse I have in mind have not wholly died out, but they are no longer so central to the making of experimental theater as they were between the mid-1950s and the mid-1970s or so: Adrienne Kennedy's *A Movie Star Has to Star in Black and White*, first staged in New York in 1976, is one important theatrical sublation of and endpoint to the period of remediation in reverse I have in view. After the splintering in the belief of film as medium of mass subjection, and consequent changes in conceptions of spectatorship—that is, *after* film, in an important sense—theater became, again, a different medium.

[NINE]

Williams, Beckett, Kennedy

Canonical though each playwright is, there is nothing inevitable about the trio of Tennessee Williams, Samuel Beckett, and Adrienne Kennedy. Scholarship largely treats them separately: considering them together at once illuminates the work of each playwright and points to a larger argument about the theatrical culture around them. They form a historical and even dialectical sequence. Williams forthrightly acknowledges the affective power of mass culture inside his plays. Furthermore, several of his early plays had great success when adapted for film. Beckett's dramaturgy carries this acknowledgment further, but his plays register the force of mass culture negatively, by mostly (but by no means entirely) excluding it. While his plays were broadcast on radio and television more often than some characterizations of his work and his resistance to adaptation would suggest, his only film, *Film*, played festivals and art houses. Kennedy, like Williams, acknowledges the power of mass culture, and especially movies, to shape subjectivity and to train desires. Her work, like Beckett's responds to this power by shaping dramatic structures that neither mainstream cinema nor mainstream theater has ever assimilated.

This historical and intertwined sequence matters to the structure of this book, but I do not claim to offer a history, nor would I assert that a more capacious theatrical history would necessarily map onto the contours of my accounts here. It is not the case that when Williams began registering the shaping effects of mass culture inside his work, everyone was doing it, and so on. Williams, Beckett, and Kennedy represent moments in the history of theatrical responses to the hegemony of mass culture, but I will not argue that each playwright is somehow typical of their moment in theatrical history. Just as their lives and careers overlapped, so the range of ways that theater came after film in their plays might, with variations, represent a range of potential positions available to drama in the period—available, that is, variously and discontinuously, to different makers of theater at different times. Indeed, these positions are ones contemporary artists still occupy.

To describe these theatrical strategies as positions should not suggest, however, that these are anything like invariant maneuvers that contemporaries can imitate by observing what was done before. My central examples are few here. This is in part the result of my commitment to stressing the importance of the particularities of given aesthetic objects: only close attention can answer the questions I am asking. And yet such an approach must justify itself beyond a circular argument about method. These playwrights exemplify a set of possible responses to film and mass culture in drama; their experiments are also not reproducible. Their plays remain strange, and fascinating because of their strangeness.

The very different lives of the three figures on whom I focus here no doubt marked their work in important ways. It is demonstrable that each produced writing that drew from lived experience. Their experiences were immensely different. Beckett, born in Ireland in 1906, lived in Paris for most of his working life, a more-or-less straight white man whose work was celebrated even while audiences found it confounding. Williams was born in 1911 in Columbus, Mississippi, and, largely based in New York City, lived peripatetically as a celebrity whose queer life was, to some, an open secret. Born five years after Beckett, Williams died six years before him, in 1983; Beckett died in 1989. Kennedy, born in Pittsburgh twenty-five years after Beckett, is a Black woman whose experimental plays match Williams's attention to the pathologies of American life and Beckett's challenge to theatrical conventions while foregrounding race, and alienating conventions surrounding race and its representation on stage, in ways neither Williams nor Beckett ever did. My abbreviated accounts of complex lives are meant at once to stress the differences between them and where these lives intersect: in making challenging theater. Williams and Beckett helped shape the Off-Broadway world in which Kennedy began to write plays. The products of the studio system—"classical Hollywood cinema"—were also crucial to her work. The disruption of dramaturgical and especially spectatorial norms in the plays of Williams and Beckett variously illuminate Kennedy. The clarity and complexity with which she lays out how cinema determines the conditions for theatrical spectatorship also makes the mass cultural context for the work of the other two playwrights more legible. The plays of Williams and Beckett already dislocated the putatively unmarked spectator of a cinematic apparatus dedicated to the interpellation of every last soul. Their plays were also addressed to an anonymous audience and to anyone who might see them. These theatrical forms of address were designed, however, to question the apparatus of interpellation associated with cinema, to discomfort the audience rather than to provide something like the cinematic solace of unified subjectivity through intensely pleasurable identification and abstracted spectatorship. Reading Williams with Beckett with Kennedy illuminates how this project of questioning cinematic interpellation through theatrical experiment was racialized from the start. This is not to say that Williams or Beckett anticipated Kennedy's radical commitment to investigating and alienating the power of cinematic identification through theatrical refunctioning (to use a Brechtian term I will discuss at greater length below) or her attention to how such identification intersects complexly with race. I am, in short, not claiming that these playwrights did the same thing. Indeed, I strive to discuss them in their particularity. Even as they share in the general project of the disruption of norms of cinematic and mass cultural interpellation through theatrical experiment, the point of grouping them arises also from attention to their singularities. All three are exemplary of a project central to theater in the decades after World War II—the theatrical challenge to mass cultural interpellation—but they are exemplary in their strangeness and in what remains recalcitrant.

I should acknowledge that Beckett takes up more space in this book than the other two. This imbalance reflects my conviction that Beckett's plays remade theater. I could wish this were more controversial: my worry is not that this claim will seem outlandish but that it will seem all too familiar, practically a given. I can hope, however, that even while my insistence on Beckett's importance to theater in this period may seem unsurprising, my argument will disrupt ways we think about that importance. Beckett here is not the laureate of the human condition or the theatrical champion of the absurd or the deconstructive rebel who at last dynamited an oddly sturdy Cartesian subjectivity. In their circulation such arguments tend to reproduce an ahistorical Beckett. Indeed, Beckett in this book is not our contemporary. Beckett's plays were so powerful because they responded to a historical moment in which mass media were seen as hegemonic and theater, in however qualified and unequal a form, could answer that hegemony.

[TEN]

Walter Benjamin's Work of Art Essay

Walter Benjamin's artwork essay continues to open up questions about the way new technological media changed older aesthetic forms, and this theoretical and historical opening shaped some of my questions here. His conception of the intertwined histories of the aesthetic sphere and media technologies, and the subsequent development of this conception in his successors in the Frankfurt School, are crucial to my argument. The Frankfurt School's dialectical understanding of the place of art in capitalist culture, and the critical examples of Benjamin and Adorno, have proved the most useful theoretical template for the problems this book grapples with. Benjamin's essay also includes claims about theater that have been relatively neglected. I do not offer a rereading of the essay as a whole, and instead concentrate on Benjamin's suggestions about theater in the aesthetic terrain transfigured by mass reproducibility.[1]

The question of how the argument of the artwork essay applies to theater is a complicated one. To make sense of this, a brief return to the essay's initial arguments is crucial. Benjamin describes the fate of an object—of a thing called an artwork:

> These changed circumstances may leave the artwork's other properties untouched, but they certainly devalue the here and now of the artwork. And although this can apply not only to art but (say) to a landscape moving past the spectator in a film, in the work of art this process touches on a highly sensitive core, more vulnerable [*verletzbar*] than that of any natural object. That core is its authenticity [*Echtheit*]. The authenticity of a thing is the quintessence of all that is transmissible in it from its origin

---

1. Readings of the essay that have been especially important to me include Susan Buck-Morss, "Aesthetics and Anaesthetics"; Miriam Bratu Hansen, "Benjamin's Aura"; and the chapters on Benjamin in Hansen's *Cinema and Experience* (75–204).

31

on, ranging from its physical duration to the historical testimony relating to it.[2]

The authenticity of that thing is "vulnerable" to alteration or, as the German word suggests, even to injury: it changes in the wake of reproduction. Tradition is thoroughly disrupted:

> It might be stated as a general formula that the technology of reproduction detaches the reproduced object from the sphere of tradition. By replicating the work many times over, it substitutes a mass existence for a unique existence. And in permitting the reproduction to reach the recipient in his or her own situation, it actualizes that which is reproduced. These two processes lead to a massive upheaval [Erschütterung] in the domain of objects handed down from the past—a shattering [Erschütterung] of tradition which is the reverse side of the present crisis and renewal of humanity.[3]

It is not that manifold reproductions—photographs of a painting, for instance—are detached from the "sphere of tradition": these reproductions cannot be detached to a sphere to which they never belonged. Instead, the original object, the thing that has been reproduced—the painting itself—is detached from this tradition. This removal from tradition constitutes the injury to which artworks are vulnerable. The artwork's aura, that "quintessence of all that is transmissible in it from its origin on," gives way to "*a mass existence.*"[4] If a "quintessence" occupied that "core," now that core is evacuated: "mass existence" takes the place of the quintessential.[5] Benjamin's humble figure for this historical situation—the destruction of tradition as the "reverse side" of crisis and renewal—is deceptively complex:

2. Walter Benjamin, "The Work of Art in the Age of Its Technological Reproducibility: Second Version," 22; Benjamin, "Das Kunstwerk im Zeitalter seiner technischen Reproduzeirbarkeit," in *Gesammelte Schriften*, 7:353.

3. Benjamin, "Work of Art," 22; "Kunstwerk," 353. Unless otherwise noted, emphasis in quotations from Benjamin is original.

4. Benjamin, "Work of Art," 22.

5. The phrase in question here—"*it substitutes a mass existence for a unique existence*"—translates Benjamin's "setzt sie an die Stelle seines einmaligen Vorkommens sein massenweises" ("Kunstwerk," 353). This might alternately be translated: reproducibility "puts a mass occurrence in the place of its singular one." It is not clear, that is, that Benjamin has forms of *existence* in mind here. It is true that Benjamin pictures the artwork as subject to injury, but he also stresses that this vulnerability is one *not* shared by "natural" objects ("Work of Art," 22). His model is not that of organic life.

with shattering on one side, the other side contains both crisis and renewal. The result of a certain dialectical but also topological compression, the figure also suggests remnants of a confidence in historical progress in the mid-1930s—crisis and renewal as a conjoined pair—that Benjamin would fully abandon by the time of the "Theses on the Philosophy of History" in early 1940.[6] The crucial point here, however, is that for Benjamin the crisis in the traditional sphere of the aesthetic is part of a larger historical predicament.

The "most powerful agent" of this "shattering of this tradition" and actualization of "that which is reproduced," Benjamin goes on to insist, "is film." Liquidating tradition, film reaches "the recipient in his or her own situation," and "actualizes that which is reproduced." From an untouchable core to manifold transmission, from a "here and now," to which the art pilgrim must travel, to a form that moves from town to town, from theater to theater, from spectator to spectator: the situation of art has changed. Benjamin's claim here is worth stressing: the development of film, unthinkable without the reproduction that makes possible its mass social force, alters the situation of visual art, unthinkable—before the advent of mass reproduction—without the "here and now" of the unique, authentic object. Even when there is no question about the provenance of that object—institutions and traditions still guarantee that the original remains the original—that object is no longer what it was: its core emptied out, its aura withered.

This rehearsal of Benjamin's argument underlines two aspects of it: its initial reliance on the artwork as object, as unique thing, and its subsequent emphasis on film's impact across media. A thing with no aura, no uniqueness in any particular here and now, fundamentally changes the thing that had an aura, an aura now at least partly "withered." This destruction of aura by the non-auratic, however, also has as its counterpart the migration of aura into places, practices, and creatures that, given the initial definitions in the essay's opening sections, would seem never to have possessed aura at all. Benjamin's argument radiates around the model of the artwork as object, as a thing that perseveres over time. Theater is not an artwork in the sense that a painting might be: it is not clear if these early stages of Benjamin's argument touch theater at all. If theater is not an object, might it escape the logic of this exposure to historical vulnerability? And yet a strange multiplication of the auratic precisely as it withers is a notable feature of the essay

---

6. Hansen argues that Benjamin was consistently suspicious of narratives of historical progress throughout his career (*Cinema and Experience*, 305n4). One might argue that moments of utopian anticipation do not constitute faith in progress: utopia is precisely not what is inevitable.

and becomes especially clear when Benjamin considers the relationship between theater and film:

> The situation can also be characterized as follows: for the first time—and this is the effect of film—the human being is placed in a position where he must operate with his whole living person, while forgoing its aura. For the aura is bound to his presence in the here and now. There is no facsimile of the aura. The aura surrounding Macbeth on the stage cannot be divorced from the aura which, for living spectators, surrounds the actor who plays him. What distinguishes the shot in the film studio, however, is that the camera is substituted for the audience. As a result, the aura surrounding the actor is dispelled—and, with it, the aura of the figure he portrays.[7]

If the aura of the artwork depends not only on the artwork's "presence in the here and now," but also on a quintessence belonging to the object that survives over time despite changes in function, location, and ownership, and also on the "historical testimony" that authenticates this quintessence, then it is unclear in what way a person, onstage or otherwise, possesses aura. What "historical testimony" or other expertise could verify the performer's authenticity? The possibility of the "facsimile" would seem to belong to the domain of reproducible objects: some auratic original, in its here and now, might be copied, and in the process lose its aura. Nevertheless, in the comparison of the stage actor and the screen actor, presence in time and place alone—the actor together with the "living spectators"—seems to produce aura; the historicity of the thing, the question of tradition, is no longer essential to aura. Aura is no longer peculiar to the work of art but a quality shared by artworks and people: artworks and people alike lose aura in the wake of reproduction.

The artwork essay suffers from an incoherence that cannot be internally reconciled. Miriam Bratu Hansen's superb scholarship has demonstrated that its definition of aura is "deliberately restrictive": "The exemplary linkage of aura to the status of the artwork in Western tradition, whatever it may have accomplished for Benjamin's theory of modernity, was not least a tactical move designed to isolate and distance the concept from the at once more popular and more esoteric notions of aura that flourished in contemporary occultist discourse (and do to this day)."[8] Hansen suggests that, however restrictive his tactical move may have been, Benjamin did

---

7. Benjamin, "Work of Art," 31.

8. Hansen, *Cinema and Experience*, 113, 104.

not fully exclude from the essay "the more common understanding (now as then) of aura as an elusive phenomenal substance, ether, or halo that surrounds a person or object of perception, encapsulating its individuality and authenticity."[9] One place where this "common understanding" overcame Benjamin's attempts to restrict his definition to a more acceptably materialist one is around the problem of theater and the actor. "The aura surrounding Macbeth on the stage" evidently draws on the understanding of aura as a halo made of an "elusive phenomenal substance," and this more familiar conception of aura helps to make sense of contradictions outlined above.

The aura abandoned by the film actor, then, is not precisely the aura possessed by the artwork, and yet the two definitions also inform each other. The aura is at once the artwork's vulnerable "core"[10] and, implicitly, a halo that surrounds it; the actor's aura surrounds him, and this halo is, implicitly, an emanation from and guarantee of the actor's authentic core. As photographs and other reproductions injure the core of the artwork, so film forces actors to perform while abandoning their auras. Benjamin describes an unprecedented situation: the actor "must operate with his whole living person, while forgoing its aura." The potentially redundant emphasis on the status of the person as "living" is complemented by the equally striking emphasis on the audience as "living spectators." This emphasis on the living stresses a divide between the living actor and the camera, the apparatus that produces the sense of estrangement described by Pirandello in one of Benjamin's exemplary quotations: the silent film actor "senses an inexplicable void, stemming from the fact that his body has lost its substance, that he has been volatilized, stripped of his reality, his life, his voice."[11] Volatilization— the dissolution of a solid into vapor—is a vivid figure for the vanishing of what Hansen calls "the elusive phenomenal substance" of aura. The quotation most startlingly suggests that the loss of aura is death for the actor's "whole living person."

Benjamin's repeated evocations of the living—the living actor, the living audience—anticipate more recent discussions of the historical predicament of liveness in relation to media discussed above. Benjamin recognizes the precarity of this liveness, the speed with which the living actor may be subsumed by the film or the camera substituted for the living audience. He does not, however, produce a strict dichotomy with the living and efficacious linked to the theater and the deadly and politically inert linked to cinema.

9. Hansen, *Cinema and Experience*, 106.

10. Benjamin, "Work of Art," 30.

11. Benjamin, "Work of Art," 31.

In the section immediately preceding his discussion of the film actor's loss of aura, Benjamin discusses the film as a test of the film actor. In one of the most utopian of his scenarios for the political work of mass culture, the actor's successful performance in the face of the cinematic apparatus becomes a victory for the film's audience:

> To perform in the glare of arc lamps while simultaneously meeting the demands of the microphone is a test performance of the highest order. To accomplish it is to preserve one's humanity [*Menschlichkeit*] in the face of the apparatus. Interest in this performance is widespread. For the majority of city dwellers, throughout the workday in offices and factories, have to relinquish their humanity [*Menschlichkeit*] in the face of an apparatus. In the evening these same masses fill the cinemas, to witness the film actor taking revenge [*Revanche*] on their behalf not only by asserting *his* humanity [*Menschlichkeit*] (or what appears to them as such) against the apparatus, but by placing the apparatus in the service of his triumph.[12]

Benjamin writes in the midst of what he has called the "crisis and renewal of humanity."[13] Fascism and the threat of another and more devastating war are not the only features of this crisis: for Benjamin the threat does not belong to the future. The city, with its apparatuses—its factories and offices—is already the scene of a crisis in which most workers "relinquish their humanity in the face of an apparatus." (Who among this "majority" does not?) The cinematic apparatus, analogous to these institutional ones, threatens, like them, to force the actor to relinquish his humanity, but the actor takes the audience's vicarious revenge on the apparatus through his performance. Cinema, then, provides the site of a certain preservation or defense against dehumanization.

In parentheses, Benjamin seems to qualify his claim: it *appears* to the masses that the film actor takes his revenge against the apparatus "on their behalf." The force of his qualification remains unclear and raises questions central to the unresolved antinomies of Benjamin's thought. The apparent revenge, it would seem from the subsequent section, involves relinquishing the very aura that one might count as part of the humanity that is lost in performing for the apparatus. This problematic nexus of humanity, technology,

---

12. Benjamin, "Work of Art," 31; "Kunstwerk," 365.

13. Benjamin, "Work of Art," 22. The words in question here are not identical. When Benjamin describes the crisis of humanity, the word is "Menschheit" ("Kunstwerk," 353): humanity in general. The actor takes revenge on behalf of "Menschlichkeit," which includes a suggestion of an ethical claim.

and art leads in many directions, inside and beyond Benjamin's thought. Its importance for my argument lies in the paradigmatic status Benjamin grants the theater: it is in the theater that the force of film is most vivid. The force of film's liquidation of aura becomes visible as an issue concerning not artworks alone but also humanity *in the theater*, in the place where the "human being"—or so it seems—continues to "operate with his whole living person," but *without* "forgoing its aura." Benjamin continues: "It is not surprising that it should be a dramatist such as Pirandello who, in reflecting on the special character of film acting, inadvertently touches on the crisis now affecting the theater. Indeed, *nothing contrasts more starkly* with a work of art completely subject to (or, like film, founded in) technological reproduction than a stage play [*Schaubühne*]."[14] Pirandello, without knowing it, "touches on" a crisis. While Benjamin does not elaborate on its nature or extent, the next sentence implies that this crisis follows from the fact that "a stage play," more than anything else, contrasts with a work of art that can be reproduced or that is inseparable from "technological reproduction." The crisis, then, might lie in the extreme vulnerability of a form so completely in contrast with the dominant, reproducible aesthetic modes.

Such a conception of the potential death of theater in the face of reproduction is true, however, neither to Benjamin's theory of art nor to his understanding of crisis. Film is, to recall the earlier formulation, the agent of the "present crisis and renewal of humanity." As the pairing of crisis and renewal suggests, in the artwork essay Benjamin continues to harbor hope that the crisis confronting humanity might hold emancipatory potential. The "stage play," then, is the index of the crisis precisely because it is the other of the technological sources of that crisis: it is not "completely subject to (or, like film, founded in) technological reproduction." On the one hand, theater's archaic freedom from technological reproducibility means that it does not take part in the changes wrought by reproduction: it remains, in short, in the "here and now" where the actor still performs without surrendering his aura. And yet, not being "completely subject to . . . technological reproduction" does not mean escaping its sovereignty completely. Just as painting becomes subject to reproduction even while, strictly speaking, no particular painting can be reproduced, so the "stage play" is in the orbit of reproduction's power of subjection. Partially subject to technological reproduction, theater may be the last place "where the human being is placed in a position where he must operate with his whole living person" *without* "forgoing its aura." But even if this survival of the performer's aura is the exemplary condition of the theater, this exception to the rule of aura's

---

14. Benjamin, "Work of Art," 32; "Kunstwerk," 366–67 (my emphasis).

withering would mean that theater puts this loss in relief even as it does not, perhaps, partake in it. Theater's distinct untimeliness would lie in its making the historical situation of aura visible precisely by being the zone where the human being does not forgo "its [sic] aura."

The "stage play," then, emerges as the historical form that most contrasts with the "mass existence" that increasingly characterizes modernized life. Here, Benjamin's famous thesis on the politicization of political life becomes especially relevant. Fascism, Benjamin argues, "sees its salvation in granting expression to the masses—but on no account granting them rights."[15] Some of the venues of this expression resemble exploded theatrical forms: "In great ceremonial processions, giant rallies and mass sporting events, and in war, all of which are now fed into the camera, the masses come face to face with themselves."[16] The masses, having given up aura in order to amass themselves for the camera, "come face to face with themselves" but this form of "face to face" contact resembles the way the reproduced artwork can "meet the recipient halfway"[17]: it is a new human configuration, where the camera mediates the "face to face." At least two suggestions are at work in the work of art essay: on the one hand, Benjamin suggests that this relinquishing of a shared "here and now" means that some damage has been done to the human being and to humanity. On the other hand, the text also implies that this destruction, or forgoing, of aura is the necessary prelude to politicizing of art that will contribute to a more just culture: humanity, to remain human, must work in the world of withered aura.

The question of an aestheticized mass politics is germane here. The more pressing issue, however, concerns more immediately theatrical issues. In the work of art essay, Benjamin raises the question of the theater's vulnerability, but that vulnerability remains a kind of lacuna in that text: theater is a vivid point of contrast, but Benjamin does not pursue the question of theater's response to mass reproduction. Benjamin does, however, directly address this response in related essays: in short, if the problem is the survival of theater in the face of mass culture, the answer is Brecht. To a degree not yet widely enough acknowledged, Benjamin's argument in the artwork essay owes much to Brecht's essays as well as to his plays. More important, for Benjamin, Brecht's theatrical practice answers the demands of an epoch changed by technologies of reproduction. In his succinct discussion of Brecht in "The Author as Producer," for instance, Benjamin draws from

15. Benjamin, "Work of Art," 41.

16. Benjamin, "Work of Art," 54n36.

17. Benjamin, "Work of Art," 21.

Brecht's discussion of the professional theater as an apparatus that possesses those who work inside it, and, quoting Brecht, describes theater's contemporary dilemma and Brecht's response to it:

> This theater, with its complicated machinery, its gigantic supporting staff, its sophisticated effects, has become a "means against producers" not least in seeking to enlist them in the hopeless competitive struggle in which film and radio have enmeshed it. This theater (whether in its educating or its entertaining role; the two are complementary) is that of a sated class for which everything it touches becomes a stimulant. Its position is lost. Not so that of a theater that, instead of competing with newer instruments of publication, seeks to use and learn from them—in short, to enter into debate with them. This debate the Epic Theater has made its own affair. It is, measured by the present state of development of film and radio, the contemporary form.[18]

Theater does not enter the debate with film and radio, that is, by emulating or incorporating it, by becoming a simulacrum of these gigantic apparatuses. Nor is there any question of a meaningful competition: the hopelessness here does not mean that the situation of theater is hopeless, but that film and radio will win any competition gauged by the size of the audience or profit. Theater gains its position not by entering into this futile competition but by using and learning from these "newer instruments of publication." Theater, that is, develops its own form of publication and becomes contemporary by acknowledging radio and film, and also by establishing its difference from them.

Benjamin's discussion of Brecht in "The Author as Producer," seen in the light of the slightly later artwork essay, describes a range of responses to the crisis facing theater. The professional theater seeks to adapt by producing an apparatus of a complexity to rival that of the technological media. Brecht, quite differently, "fell back on the most primitive elements of the theater. He contented himself, by and large, with a podium. He dispensed with wide-ranging plots. He thus succeeded in changing the functional connections between stage and public, text and performance, director and actor."[19] For Benjamin, Brecht's theatrical response to the challenge of film and radio is paradigmatic: it at once engages with their new modes of "publication" and, equally crucially, develops a new and contemporary

18. Benjamin, "Author as Producer," in *Writings on Media*, 90. Benjamin takes the quotation from Brecht from *Versuche 4–7* (Berlin: Kiepenheuer, 1930), 107.

19. Benjamin, "Author as Producer," in *Writings on Media*, 90.

mode of theatrical publication that neither denies nor imitates those of the newer media. Benjamin's particular argument is that the Epic Theater incorporates cinematic montage into theater: montage is the model for the interruptions that are central to Brechtian dramaturgy. This argument is fascinating in itself, but what is most crucial here is the larger import of his argument. The force of the artwork essay has proven to lie as much in its suggestiveness for subsequent periods as for its illumination of Benjamin's time. Benjamin's argument about the relationship between aesthetic forms with long histories and the newer media of film and radio is crucial because of his dialectical understanding of this relationship: the Epic Theater's adaptation of montage to the stage and Brecht's falling back on "the most primitive elements of the theater" are equally responses to the force of film.

Theater after Film considers theater that Benjamin did not encounter in the aftermath of a war he did not survive. Benjamin's thinking about the force of mass culture remains foundational, however, and for several reasons. To move from Benjamin's language to terms of a more recent vintage, Benjamin's focus falls on mediatization. Mediatization—always an elusive concept—describes complex forms of interaction and influence between media; it can also name social effects of the rise of mass media that extend beyond media. The density of the artwork essay stems in part from its insistence on tracking both of these processes, both the impact of mass media on earlier aesthetic forms and their rearrangement of the conditions of social life. Benjamin's phrase, "mass existence," may seem melodramatic.[20] Benjamin anticipates playwrights and theorists of the period I consider in this book, however, in seeing the changes within the aesthetic field as coterminous with larger alterations of the human.

20. See Samuel Weber's discussion of Benjamin's language of the "mass" in *Mass Mediauras*. 84–107.

[ELEVEN]

Benjamin's Medium

Benjamin's most sweeping claim: *"Just as the entire mode of existence of human collectives changes over long historical periods, so too does their mode of perception. The way in which human perception is organized—the medium in which it occurs—is conditioned not only by nature but by history."*[1] Tobias Wilke has convincingly argued that Benjamin's definition of medium does not align with the most familiar current one. Not simply a "technological medium of reproduction," the "medium names the comprehensive force field that links human sensorium to world and that is constituted in doing so by the interplay between natural (physiological, physical) and historical (social, technological, and aesthetic) factors."[2] Film is an important part of that linking of sensorium to world in the 1930s, but it is not in itself, in Benjamin's sense, the medium in which the organization of perception occurs. No single technological medium could play, or has ever played, that role. No medium, in the more current sense, can be, in Benjamin's sense, *the* medium. This does not mean, of course, that film was not immensely powerful: it was, Benjamin claimed, the "most powerful agent" of the social transformations he linked to the decline of aura.[3] As Erwin Panofsky wrote in "Style and Medium in the Motion Pictures," an essay reprinted with a frequency that rivals the republication of Benjamin's work of art essay and, like that essay, dating from the mid-1930s:

> The "movies" have reestablished that dynamic contact between art production and art consumption which, for reasons too complex to be considered here, is sorely attenuated, if not entirely interrupted, in many other fields of artistic endeavor. Whether we like it or not, it is the movies

1. Benjamin, "Work of Art," 23.

2. Wilke, "Tacti(ca)lity Reclaimed," 40.

3. Benjamin, "Work of Art," 22.

that mold, more than any other single force, the opinions, the taste, the language, the dress, the behavior, and even the physical appearance of a public comprising more than 60 percent of the population of the earth. If all the serious lyrical poets, composers, painters, and sculptors were forced by law to stop their activities, a rather small fraction of the general public would become aware of the fact and a still smaller fraction would seriously regret it. If the same thing were to happen with the movies the social consequences would be catastrophic.[4]

Later in the essay, Panofsky writes that "in modern life the movies are what most other forms of art have ceased to be, not an adornment but a necessity."[5] Benjamin writes of the organization of perception, and Panofsky of the molding of opinion, taste, language, dress, behavior and appearance, but they agree that film plays an unequaled role in these processes.

The postwar moment marks a historical shift, a moment where the perception of the saturation of consciousness by film becomes common, even, to use Raymond Williams's term, a structure of feeling. The range of celebration and dismay, elite, middlebrow, populist, and otherwise, in the face of this structure of feeling is familiar, but also, in my view, not dismissible. And I mean that is not dismissible not in the sense that we are in a position now to endorse or to condemn or to celebrate it, but in the sense that to think about aesthetic forms historically will require recognizing the force of this structure of feeling. The power of film as an instrument in the production of fascist publics; the allied notion of Hollywood as a machine of capitalist hegemony; the wider and massively widespread sense of mass culture as an unprecedented tool for the production of docile subjects: such beliefs were simply central to a postwar common sense, elements of which remain remarkably tenacious in critical and not-so-critical discourses. Adorno was not entirely alone, only blunter than some of his contemporaries, when he wrote in *Minima Moralia*: "Every visit to the cinema leaves me, against all my vigilance, stupider and worse."[6]

Understanding this widespread apprehension of the hegemony of cinema also illuminates the question of the poverty of theater as medium, and, for that matter, it has implications for the postwar situation of any "traditional" art. If we understand medium in Benjamin's expanded sense—as

4. Panofsky, "Style and Medium in the Motion Pictures," in *Three Essays on Style*, 94. For a fascinating and thorough consideration of Panofsky's essay, as well as an account of its publication history, see Thomas Y. Levin, "Iconology at the Movies."

5. Panofsky, "Style and Medium in the Motion Pictures," 120.

6. Adorno, *Minima Moralia: Reflections*, 25.

the ensemble of apparatuses that produce perception—then it becomes clear that the role of these arts in the production of perception was relatively meager. This is neither to say that they had no role, nor that their role in the production of perception would have been, or is now, easily measurable. To say that theater was important to mass subject formation in the decades after 1945 would be to misrecognize it, to misunderstand both what theater aspired to do and also what it achieved. Just as uninteresting would be to dismiss theater as not worth consideration because of this diminished power. To make the power to shape subjects the criterion of aesthetic interest would be to surrender to the hegemony that theater countered. Indeed, the importance of theater in this period would be measurable (if it were measurable) in inverse proportion to its limited power to shape perception. It was precisely because theater had so little power to shape subjects that it could so powerfully stage how subjects were shaped.

Theodor Adorno's dialectical theorization of the postwar situation of art informs my understanding of theater in the period. In the wake of his heated debates with Benjamin in the 1930s, but also informed by wartime catastrophes Benjamin partly anticipated but the full horror of which he did not witness, Adorno's conceptualization of the aesthetic as the negation of a wholly administered world illuminates the negations peculiar to postwar theater. Below, I will address my points of departure from Adorno; first I will acknowledge my debts. A section of *Minima Moralia*, despite its contempt for the products of the culture industry, is illuminating:

> *Pro domo nostra.*—When during the last war,—which like all others, seems peaceful in comparison to its successor—the symphony orchestras of many countries had their vociferous [*bramarbasierende*] mouths stopped, Stravinsky wrote the *Histoire du Soldat* for a sparse, shock-maimed chamber ensemble. It turned out to be his best score, the only convincing surrealist manifesto, its convulsive, dreamlike compulsion imparting to music an inkling of negative truth. The pre-condition of the piece was poverty: it dismantled official culture so drastically because, denied access to the latter's material goods, it also escaped the ostentation that is inimical to culture. There is here a pointer for intellectual [*geistige*] production after the present war, which has left behind in Europe a measure of destruction undreamt of by even in the voids of that music. Progress and barbarism are today so matted together in mass culture that only barbaric asceticism towards the latter, and towards progress in technical means, could restore an unbarbaric condition. No work of art, no thought, has a chance of survival, unless it bear within it repudiation of false riches and high-class production, of colour films and television,

millionaire's magazines and Toscanini. The older media, not designed for mass-production [*nicht auf Massenproduktion berechneten Medien*], take on a new timeliness [*Aktualität*]: that of exemption [*Unerfaßten*] and improvisation. They alone could outflank the united fronts of trusts and technology. In a world where books have lost all likeness to books, the real book can no longer be one. If the invention of the printing press inaugurated the bourgeois era, the time is at hand for its repeal by the mimeograph, the only fitting, the unobtrusive means of dissemination.[7]

Given the perspicacity with which this passage appears to have anticipated a range of postwar art practices from Yoko Ono's event scores to Jerzy Grotowski's *Towards a Poor Theatre* to *Arte Povera*, not to mention the mimeograph revolution of the 1960s, it is worth pausing over a caution within it: this soldier's tale could not have dreamed of the destruction of the war still ongoing at the time Adorno was writing. The brutality of the Second World War makes that of the First seem like peace. Similarly, the very exemplarity of *Histoire du Soldat* may be deceptive: the negative truth of the art that will respond to this unanticipated destruction may distantly resemble that of Igor Stravinsky's "best score," but it will necessarily be different from that of that work. The passage, that is, undercuts the authoritative prognostication about the future of art "after the present war."

The fiddler's "repudiation of false riches" in the scenario of Stravinsky's piece exemplifies the postwar reconfiguration of art. Adorno's argument about the new "timeliness" of forms of media "not designed for mass-production" recalls Benjamin's work of art essay, but Adorno emphasizes not the ways that early media have lost their aura but the new forms of actuality they come to possess. The passage recalls Benjamin's argument that the reproduction reaches "the recipient in his or her own situation" and thereby "actualizes that which is reproduced."[8] As Adorno echoes the terms of this argument, however, he also marks his difference from it. It is not through a mobility granted by reproduction that these works gain a new timeliness or actuality, but precisely through their resistance to reproduction, through the force of what the English translation calls "exemption." The poverty of the *Histoire du Soldat* models the rejection of the sophisticated apparatuses of mass culture that for Adorno is crucial to the prospective overcoming of barbarism that the postwar arts may achieve. Here it is important to note both the wholesale contempt for mass culture that marks

---

7. Adorno, *Minima Moralia: Reflections*, 50–51; *Minima Moralia: Reflexionen*, 57–58.

8. Benjamin, "The Work of Art," 22.

this passage, which is on its surface anything but dialectical, and the way that this contempt does not precisely map onto the episode with which the section begins or the logic of the section as a whole. The *Histoire du Soldat* does not reject the "high-class production" of Technicolor and so on, but the bloviating excesses of the putatively high culture of the European symphony orchestra.[9] This repudiation does not, that is, map easily onto some given division between high and low. Andreas Huyssen's fundamental contribution here is illuminating. In "Adorno in Reverse," a chapter that focuses not coincidentally on Adorno's *In Search of Wagner*, Huyssen synthesizes his complex account of Adorno's understanding of the relationship between art and mass culture: "Adorno's bleak description of modern mass culture as dream turned nightmare has perhaps outlived its usefulness and can now take its place as a historically contingent and theoretically powerful reflection on fascism. What has not outlived its usefulness, however, is Adorno's suggestion that mass culture was not imposed on art only from the 'outside,' but that art was transformed into its opposite thanks precisely to its emancipation from traditional forms of bourgeois art. In the vortex of commodification there was never an outside."[10] Similarly, in "Pro doma nostra," there is no false choice between absolute dependence upon reproduction and freedom from reproduction: the mimeograph, after all, is a device to produce copies, though maybe not in the numbers that would count as "mass-production." (But what *does* count?) Further, *Minima Moralia* was published, by Suhrkamp in 1951, as a book: Adorno, writing during the war, might not have felt confident in a world in which his books would again be published; nevertheless, his writing as disseminated relies on media and apparatuses that produce even his prose as commodities. To observe this is not naively to accuse Adorno of hypocrisy but to underline that his thought is valuable here precisely for its articulation of the connections between art and commodity. Or, in another register of this passage, it is only a barbaric renunciation of barbarism that could make the unbarbaric imaginable. Adorno acknowledges Benjamin's dictum that there "is no document of culture which is not at the same time a document of barbarism," but he also complicates Benjamin's thesis by suggesting that the way to culture leads through barbaric rejection of its progress.[11]

In *Aesthetic Theory*, Adorno returns to similar concerns and writes: "Even given the most extreme reductionism in art's consciousness of needs,

---

9. Thanks to Lisa Harries Schumann for suggesting "bloviating" as an alternative translation of "bramarbasierende."

10. Huyssen, "Adorno in Reverse," in *After the Great Divide*, 42.

11. Benjamin, "On the Concept of History," in *Selected Writings*, 4:392.

the gesture of self-imposed muteness and vanishing, art persists, as in a sort of differential. Because there has not yet been any progress [*Fortschritt*] in the world, there is progress in art; *'il faut continuer.'*"[12] Or, in Beckett's self-translation: "I can't go on, I'll go on": the final words of Beckett's *The Unnamable* serve as the ironic motto for the progress that a reduced art makes. The period between the composition of *Minima Moralia* in the mid to late 1940s and that of *Aesthetic Theory* in the late 1960s is not only coincidentally the period at the heart of this book. Beckett's importance to the culmination of Adorno's writings on aesthetics is well known.[13] And yet it is the earlier formulation that is more telling for the purposes of this book. Adorno's complex attention to media in "Pro domo nostra" stresses the way those not designed for mass reproduction gain, though their very anachronistic qualities, the timeliness of what he calls the *Unerfaßten*: exemption, perhaps, but also that which has not yet been grasped or understood. Progress in art happens through the negation of progress in media.

Adorno returns to the concerns and language of "Pro doma nostra" in a later section of *Minima Moralia* titled "Bequest":

> If Benjamin said that history had hitherto been written from the standpoint of the victor, and needed to be written from that of the vanquished, we might add that knowledge must indeed present the fatally rectilinear succession of victory and defeat, but should also address itself to those things which were not embraced by this dynamic, which fell by the wayside—what might be called the waste products and blind spots that have escaped the dialectic. It is in the nature of the defeated to appear, in their impotence, irrelevant, eccentric, derisory. What transcends the ruling society is not only the potentiality it develops but also all that which did not fit into the laws of historical movement. Theory must needs deal with cross-gained [*sic*], opaque, unassimilated [*Unerfaßte*] material, which as such admittedly has from the start an anachronistic quality, but is not wholly obsolete since it has outwitted the historical dynamite. This can most readily be seen in art.[14]

Adorno extends his thinking about the value of what appears to be outmoded in "Pro doma nostra," but he links it to larger problems of

---

12. Adorno, *Aesthetic Theory*, 208; *Ästhetische Theorie*, 309–10.

13. For one succinct and excellent account, which focuses on *Endgame*, see Jay Bernstein, "Philosophy's Refuge: Adorno in Beckett." See also Adorno's "Notes on Beckett."

14. Adorno, *Minima Moralia*, 151 *Minima Moralia: Reflexionen*, 200.

historiography, again meditating particularly on the seventh of Benjamin's theses on the concept of history. The historical framework here places the "unassimilated" or *Unerfaßte* inside a historical dynamic larger than that of the succession of media, but in both sections Adorno privileges art as the site where these historical changes become visible.

It may seem odd to concentrate on these earlier passages from *Minima Moralia* rather than turning to Adorno's later and most authoritative statement on art, *Aesthetic Theory*. *Minima Moralia* is important here precisely because of its difference from the later book. Like *Aesthetic Theory*, it describes a dynamic of negation. *Minima Moralia*, however, provides a fragmentary model for a different modality of negative thought, one perhaps foreclosed by the later development of Adorno's aesthetic theory. *Minima Moralia* offers a minimal aesthetics. Against the massive stakes of negation in *Aesthetic Theory*—the artwork as negation of the world as it is—in such sections as "Pro doma nostra," *Minima Moralia* points the way to a narrower conception. The idea of an anachronistic timeliness attached directly to a critique of the idea that there is progress in media points to ways to think about negation that pair, not artwork and world, but artwork and the apparatuses that drive the culture industry. The paired examples of the *Histoire du Soldat* and the mimeograph exemplify the dialectical claim that a "poor" artwork in a reduced medium can provide a critique of an apparatus and its techniques. Just as "shock-maimed chamber ensemble" succeeds the ostentation of the symphony orchestra and the mimeograph may succeed the book, so theater comes after film.[15]

In the Hegelian tradition Adorno at once criticizes and continues, the theoretical question here is one of determinate negation: as Christoph Menke puts it, this is a matter of negations "grounding in the negated."[16] My difference from earlier scholarship concerns how one locates this ground. Julia Jarcho's *Writing and the Modern Stage* has brilliantly read modern texts and plays, including Beckett, in terms of negation:

> Adorno's work is dedicated to theorizing the ways in which art and thought, while utterly implicated in and conditioned by historical reality, imaginatively exceed that reality by negating it. The prospect of thus exceeding what is real motivates philosophy's "contradictory effort to say, through mediation and contextualization, what cannot be said *hic et nunc*" (Adorno, *Lectures* 74), as well as art's "determinate negation of the

15. On this topic, see Joel Burges, "Adorno's Mimeograph."

16. Menke, *The Sovereignty of Art*, 25.

existing world order" (*Aesthetic* 344). Adorno's insistence that art must be understood in this way, as a determinate negation that gestures beyond the real through a recognition of itself as *within* the real, will be the central theoretical premise of this book.[17]

In this account, art is grounded in, and negates, "the existing world order." The disproportion between the fragile, maimed artwork and the world order to which it belongs and yet negates is central to Adorno's later thought and to Jarcho's book. So thoroughly has that order organized everything that it is only through the aesthetic that any utopian possibility emerges: "When Adorno says that 'utopia is essentially in the determined negation, in the determined negation of that which merely is' (Bloch and Adorno 12), he thus emphasizes that utopia is never entirely detached from the present reality; on the contrary, the present reality remains utopia's 'content,' to use Hegel's term, alongside that reality's negation. Utopia, then, is not simply nowhere, or elsewhere; its 'u-' is saturated with its actual 'topos,' the site that it rejects."[18] The question here concerns *how* "present reality" saturates theatrical works. Is negation an all-or-nothing proposition? Is totality the only ground for negation? Theater is "utterly implicated in and conditioned by historical reality"; this raises the question of how that implication and that conditioning become knowable. Could this premise be something one could know something about? If present reality becomes part of the content of every artwork in the same way, this would seem to lead to a sameness across the artworks themselves to rival the sameness of the world that they negate. In Adorno's account, there is a kind of sameness in that which is negated that may not track the ways that different forms of art and different artworks respond to different forms of determination. In *Aesthetic Theory*, it is as though any negation that does not negate everything is no negation at all. I want to suggest that there can be perhaps more minor but also specifiable negations. The language of negation helps to describe the way that the world becomes part of the artwork—through a negative incorporation that does not always name what has conditioned or determined the artwork.

To adapt Adorno's thought more directly to my central concerns here: there is no escaping the rectilinear history that narrates the twentieth-century triumph of cinema, and no denying its far greater power (to recall Panofsky's word) to "mold" far larger audiences. Its triumph left theater by

17. Jarcho, *Writing and the Modern Stage*, 15.

18. Jarcho, *Writing and the Modern Stage*, 74.

the wayside, a poorer medium, more eccentric and more derisory, with none of the cultural centrality it possessed in the nineteenth century or, even, earlier in the twentieth. There is also no denying—and this may be an only slightly more controversial claim—that the postwar period in Europe and America was a remarkable period for theater and drama, a period of resonant experiment and achievement. The argument of this book is that these two facts are tied, that the most compelling drama of the postwar period "outwitted the historical dynamite" by studying the explosions and imagining ways to defuse them: possessing nothing of mass culture's power to form subjects, theater staged forms of the power it did not possess. Sometimes its experiments are legible as the "repudiation of false riches and high-class production, of colour films and television": the austerity of Beckett's plays derives in part from something like this repudiation, which saturates those plays to the level of technique. Tennessee Williams, however, is another central example because his work engages with mass culture in ways that are dialectally opposed. The precondition for the austere repudiation of mass culture in Beckett is the recognition of how it thoroughly it had remade consciousness, and Williams's plays are, among other things, a layered site of this recognition. The recognition of mass cultural hegemony inside drama is complex: to stage the force of mass culture is not to take on its shaping power. Further, the rapid migration of Williams's plays from Broadway to Hollywood sometimes makes it difficult to remember that his plays belonged first to the stage. This also means, however, that the dynamic of theater after film enfolds Williams's work in an unusual way: plays after 1951 follow the success of the film of *A Streetcar Named Desire*. That his plays had become templates for mass entertainments contributed, sometimes through negation, to Williams's subsequent technique as a playwright. No film of Beckett's work ever became a smash hit, and his insistence on the specificity of the media in which he worked (however often various radio and television presentations in fact violated this code) stands in striking contrast to Williams's success on stage and on screen. The divide between Williams and Beckett is real: the vividness of the pairing makes for their collective exemplarity. They are, however, exemplary of contrasting aesthetic and theatrical responses to a historical dynamic that included them both. Theater came after film.

The passages from *Minima Moralia* are also important because of Adorno's sense of the break marked by World War II. Most urgently, that break requires facing the Holocaust: "The idea that after this war life will continue 'normally' or even that culture might be 'rebuilt'—as if the rebuilding of culture were not already its negation—is idiotic. Millions of Jews have been murdered, and this is to be seen as an interlude [*Zwischenspiel*] and not the catastrophe itself. What more is this culture waiting for?"[19] The necessity and impossibility of thinking about the consequences of the Holocaust are of immeasurable significance to Adorno's work. Here, it is important to stress that his notorious suspicion of mass culture is entwined with the critique of fascism. His critical view of mass media followed from his conviction that they bore some responsibility for genocide. The historical caesura marked by the war is not primarily an event in the history of media, but it is also that.

All twentieth-century theater came after film, but 1945 marked a profound difference in the perception of what that succession meant. Fred Turner's summary of the historical situation after 1945 suggests the degree to which Adorno was not an outlier. Worries about the power of mass culture had been common since the end of the nineteenth century, but the war had changed these concerns:

> Now analysts worried that mass media drew individual citizens into protofascistic relationships with the centers of political and commercial power and with one another. In the one-to-many communication pattern of mass media they saw a model of political dictatorship. In mass media audiences, they saw the shadows of the German masses turning their collective eyes toward a single podium and a single leader. To enter into such a relationship with media, many worried, was to rehearse the psychology of fascism. The rise of National Socialism in Germany demonstrated that such rehearsals could transform one of the most cultured of nations—and perhaps even America itself—into a bastion of authoritarianism.[20]

What more was this culture waiting for? On the one hand, the damage had already been done: mass media had contributed to totalitarian disasters. On the other hand, thinkers saw that history as, to use Turner's so resonant word, a rehearsal of possible futures. The problem here was at once a matter of medium in Benjamin's expanded sense of that word, a problem of the mediascape that produced perception, and at the same time a problem of media in the narrower sense—that is, of particular technologies: radio, film, and, increasingly, television. The most powerful media that produced perception were, whatever their very real differences, all forms of "one-to-many communication," and this trajectory of communication seemed not accidentally but intrinsically protofascist.

19. Adorno, *Minima Moralia*, 55; *Minima Moralia: Reflexionen*, 65.
20. Turner, *The Democratic Surround*, 16.

The idea that a medium of mass communication includes a politics by design is no longer tenable. So compelling are the arguments against such political determination by technological design that it can be difficult to recognize historical junctures when many believed that indeed a dangerous politics was part, so to speak, of the hardware of a technology or set of technologies. Media theorists have largely abandoned the idea that a medium contains a politics immanent to it. Nevertheless, certain histories will require attention to other convictions about media. Whether accurate or not, in the postwar period the conviction that "one-to-many" media tended toward the politically dangerous, or even fascist, interpellation of subjects was common. This belief contributed to the shape of postwar art in many media.[21]

21. For studies that variously consider the impact of mass culture on postwar art forms, see David Joselit, *Feedback*; Carrie Noland, *Poetry at Stake*; and Judith Rodenbeck, *Radical Prototypes*.

[TWELVE]

Modernism

Shaw, Lorca, Brecht

Film and mass media did not begin to matter to theater only after 1945. The first issue of *Theatre Arts Magazine*, in 1916, began with a foreword that concluded with this exemplary postscript: "P.S.—We intend not to be swallowed by the movies."[1] It was, then, early in the century that theater makers began their attempts to evade the voracious maw of the movies. Attempts to vie with film's mass audiences through theatrical gigantism or to integrate film as part of the mise en scène, for instance, were important to interwar modernism.[2] Consciousness of cinema became part of the texture of plays across the spectrum, from dramas by the most established playwrights to far less visible experiments. In George Bernard Shaw's *Heartbreak House*, for instance, Captain Shotover, the cantankerous paterfamilias, objects when Mangan, the supposed captain of industry, announces that he will marry Ellie Dunn, who has found refuge of a kind in Shotover's house:

MANGAN: I'm going to marry her all the same.

CAPTAIN SHOTOVER: How do you know?

MANGAN [*playing the strong man*]: I intend to. I mean to. See? I never
made up my mind to do a thing yet that I didnt bring it off. Thats the

1. Foreword, *Theatre Arts Magazine* 1, no. 1 (November 1916): 1. Subsequent issues frequently include variations on this motto. See, for instance, the "Foreword to Volume Two": "And finally we repeat: 'We intend not to be swallowed by the movies'" (*Theatre Arts Magazine* 2, no. 1 [December 1917]: 1).

2. Jeffrey Schnapp's "Border Crossings" is an especially fine synopsis of interwar attempts to create "theaters of totality"; see also Schnapp's *Staging Fascism* for a detailed case study of one failed theater of totality. John Willett's descriptions of the use of film in Weimar political theater by Erwin Piscator and his collaborators suggest that its value lay in the efficiency with which it could, for instance, evoke the battlefields of the First World War: "living scenery," as Piscator called it (quoted in Willett, *Theatre of Erwin Piscator*, 60). That film might bring an inassimilable ideological burden along with that efficiency does not seem to have concerned Piscator and company very much.

52

MODERNISM: SHAW, LORCA, BRECHT > 53

sort of man I am; and there will be a better understanding between us when you make up your mind to that, Captain.

CAPTAIN SHOTOVER: You frequent picture palaces.

MANGAN: Perhaps I do. Who told you?

CAPTAIN SHOTOVER: Talk like a man, not like a movy. You mean that you make a hundred thousand a year.[3]

As *Heartbreak House* was first published in 1919 and first performed in 1920, Shotover's command that Mangan should "talk like a man, not like a movy" is especially delicious: given that movies then included no recorded dialogue, Shotover paints Mangan's speech on stage as the imitation of macho intertitles of the "strong man" or of the talk one might associate with moving lips accompanying the vociferous gestures of the silent star. Despite being "silent," the movies had produced a discourse that Mangan could volubly imitate and, at least in passing, the play associates Mangan, who proves to be a fraud, with the falseness of "picture palaces."

At the other end of the spectrum, Federico García Lorca's wonderful, surreal play *Buster Keaton's Outing*, despite its brevity, is an exceptionally intriguing meditation on theater and film. Again meditating comically on the basic divide between silent cinema and the talking theater, Lorca's Keaton exclaims, "I have nothing to say. What can I say?"[4] The film star, structurally unable to speak on screen, declares, on stage, that he has nothing to say there—although this is neither the beginning nor the end of the dialogue that Lorca gives him. Toward the end of the piece, Buster Keaton encounters a "wasp-waisted YOUNG WOMAN" riding a bicycle, who has "the head of a nightingale":

YOUNG WOMAN: Whom do I have the honor of meeting?

BUSTER KEATON [*bowing*]: Buster Keaton.

The YOUNG WOMAN faints and falls of her bicycle. Her striped legs tremble on the grass like two dying zebras. A gramophone played simultaneously in a thousand movie-houses: "In America, there are no nightingales."[5]

Symptomatically, the standard Spanish edition of Lorca's works has ignored or overruled the negative in the manuscript and so the gramophone

3. Shaw, *Heartbreak House*, 74–75.

4. Lorca, *Buster Keaton's Outing*, in *The Unknown Lorca*, 46. On *Buster Keaton's Outing*, see also Willard Bohn, "Lorca, Buster Keaton, and the Surrealist Muse."

5. Lorca, *Buster Keaton's Outing*, in *The Unknown Lorca*, 48.

delivers a different message in that version: "In America there are nightingales."[6] Wrong as ornithology, the affirmation could be correct as metaphor. Pairing the overdetermination of the nightingale as emblem in the history of poetics with the fact that the bird is not native to the Americas, Lorca links the fabulous expressivity of the nightingale to his imagination of a simultaneous soundtrack across a thousand movie theaters. Lorca's play is a kind of closet drama, no doubt, describing in laconic stage directions things difficult to stage in any theater.[7] The many gramophones mimic a broadcast medium, however, and so the cinema does not offer a solution, either. The scenario might seem to affirm or to deny the possibility of a new mass-produced poetic medium "in America," as embodied by the young woman with the head of nightingale: there *is* this nightingale, this chimera on a bicycle, who swoons when introduced to Buster Keaton.

Buster Keaton's Outing precedes Lorca's major plays: its surreal tangling with the question of the relationship between theater and film, an issue that engaged many in the 1920s, might be considered the preliminary experimentation that made plays such as *Blood Wedding* and *Yerma*, with their evacuation of modernity, possible. A negative registration of mass culture, that is, might contribute to the power of those plays, just as their poetic qualities might respond to the nightingales generated by mass culture. The example of Lorca emphasizes that in the interwar period even or especially the most compressed theatrical worlds, seemingly insulated from the pressures of mass reproduction, might negatively bear the imprint of the media they seem to resist. The break represented in my argument by 1945 is by no means an absolute one. There is nevertheless a divide.

More vividly than that of any other figure, Bertolt Brecht's engagement with theater and media in the 1920s and 1930s anticipates the postwar dynamic of theater after film. Brecht produced a substantial body of writing that speculates about media, and he worked in theater but also in radio and film.[8] And yet the difference between his understanding of mass media and

6. Xon de Ros points this out in "Cinema," in *A Companion to Lorca*, 106.

7. Consider the long stage direction describing Buster Keaton's bicycle, which begins: "The bicycle has only one dimension. It can fit inside books and lie flat in bread ovens" (*Buster Keaton's Outing*, in *The Unknown Lorca*, 46). That this bicycle can fit inside books stresses its connection to print: as Martin Puchner stresses, long stage directions are one of hallmarks of the closet drama's "productive resistance to the theater" (*Stage Fright*, 27).

8. For a valuable overview of these aspects of Brecht's work, see Roswitha Mueller, *Bertolt Brecht and the Theory of Media*.

that of the figures on whom I concentrate is substantial. Simply put, Brecht imagined that mass media, whatever the form of their actually existing subservience to capital, might at some point be remade to serve other political and aesthetic ends. His concept of "refunctionalization" (*Umfunktionierung*) describes this potential. Walter Benjamin described his friend's term: "To signify the transformation of the forms and instruments of production in the way desired by a progressive intelligentsia—that is, one interested in freeing the means of production and serving the class struggle—Brecht coined the term *Umfunktionierung* [functional transformation]."[9] As Roswitha Mueller observed, the concept was marked by "an anticipatory if not utopian move": "What makes this project hard to realize is the primacy of the theater and the cultural apparatuses in general, whose aims are in conformity with the 'old drama.' Essential, therefore, to the 'refunctionalization' of the theater is the appropriation of the apparatuses by the producers, to achieve control over their means of production."[10] Brecht and Benjamin alike were aware of the challenges facing such efforts at refunctionalization and alert to the imperturbable resilience of "the bourgeois apparatus of production and publication," which, as Benjamin wrote, "can assimilate astonishing quantities of revolutionary themes—indeed, can propagate them without calling its own existence, and the existence of the class that owns it, seriously into question."[11] Benjamin accordingly emphasizes the importance of technique, a question that may become clearer by taking a brief detour through Brecht on radio.

In his 1932 essay "The Radio as a Communications Apparatus," Brecht lampoons proposed humanitarian uses of the radio, imagining the installation of receivers under bridges so that the homeless can take in Richard Wagner's *Meistersinger*, and arrives quickly at the heart of his critique of the medium: "the radio is *one-sided* when it should be two-sided." This technological deficiency of the radio, Brecht implies, has political and social consequences. Brecht imagines a technical solution: "Radio must be transformed from a distribution apparatus into a communications apparatus. The radio could be the finest possible communications apparatus in public life, a vast system of channels. That is, it could be so, if it understood how to receive as well as to transmit, how to let the listener speak as well as hear, how to bring him into a network instead of isolating him." In parenthesis, Brecht delivers what sounds like an adage:

9. Benjamin, "The Author as Producer," trans. Edmund Jephcott, in *Writings on Media*, 85.

10. Mueller, *Bertolt Brecht and the Theory of Media*, 21, 25.

11. Benjamin, "The Author as Producer," 86.

"He who brings much, brings no one anything."[12] This aphorism clarifies what is at stake: the problem with radio is that it is a broadcast medium at all, rather than a two-way form of communication like the telephone. To Brecht, broadcasting is simply a form of distribution, and distribution is not communication. The fantasy of the "vast system of channels" pictures not the multiplication of stations broadcasting different programs but a public "network" of sound and of speech in two directions. Radio's indiscriminate dissemination, bringing much to many while failing to register how listeners respond, is a flaw to be fixed rather than a feature of the medium. Brecht concedes that his "fundamental suggestion that a communications apparatus for the general benefit of the public should be made out of radio" is "utopian."[13] This concession, however, by no means constitutes surrender: the utopian refunctioning of radio is a potential of the apparatus that would transform radio into a valuable medium.

In a 1942 diary entry written during Brecht's exile in Los Angeles recounting a conversation with Adorno, Brecht records a similar objection to cinema: "Mechanical reproduction makes everything appear final, unfree, inalterable. this brings us back to the basic objection: the public no longer has a chance to adjust the actor's performance, it is not faced with a production but with an end product that has been produced in its absence."[14] As Ben Brewster points out, reading this passage requires some caution, as it is not clear where Brecht's paraphrase of Adorno begins, or where it ends: the positions described are not necessarily Brecht's.[15] In any case, the passage is most striking for its rejection of the political potential that Benjamin, their mutual friend and interlocutor, had perceived in mass culture. The invocation of "mechanical reproduction," for Brecht and Adorno alike, would have conjured the artwork essay, which both of

12. Brecht, "The Radio as a Communications Apparatus," in *Brecht on Film and Radio*, 42.

13. Brecht, "The Radio as a Communications Apparatus," 45.

14. Brecht, *Journals*, 214. Ben Brewster's incisive essay "The Fundamental Reproach" builds an argument about Brecht's objections to cinema around this passage.

15. "It might thus seem," writes Brewster, "that Brecht here is adopting Adorno's pessimism vis-à-vis the mass media, going back on the positions he had taken in the *Dreigroschenprozess* in 1931." Brewster argues, however, that the position Brecht takes here "is not an Adornoan one" ("The Fundamental Reproach," 192).

them knew intimately.[16] It is clear, however, that Brecht does believe that there is a basic difference between theater and film: "i myself do not believe that *all* technical problems are in principle soluble. above all, i think that the effect of an artistic performance on an audience cannot be independent of the effect of the audience on the artist. in the theatre the public regulates the performance."[17] This "regulation" of the theater by its public contrasts with the cinema, in which the audience can have no effect on the film: "The public no longer has a chance to adjust the actor's performance." Brecht is taking part in what was, by 1942, a substantial critical tradition of attempting to establish the essential differences between theater and cinema. Brecht's position may have shifted, but this diary entry is in general accord with much of his theoretical writing in seeing the potential for the public to change the theater as a model for its potential to change the social world outside the theater. By contrast, "mechanical reproduction makes everything appear final, unfree, inalterable." That the audience cannot change the film has political implications: the rigidity of the culture of "mechanical reproduction" produces the correlative appearance of an unchanging, and unchangeable, social totality.

The point here is not whether Brecht held a consistent position about cinema: his writing at different moments registered contradictory positions, and this embrace of contraries is a mark of Brecht's dialectical thought. Further, this thinking about cinema, radio, and mass media, whatever its contradictions, shaped his work for the stage. *The Measures Taken* and his other learning plays of the early 1930s collectively constitute an especially remarkable predecessor to those I consider here. Brecht's challenge to the theatrical apparatus in those plays not only undoes the conventions of the bourgeois stage and the ability of that stage to swallow works like *The Threepenny Opera* whole: the learning plays also exist in an agonistic relationship to the apparatuses of mass culture in which Brecht invested hope,

16. For Brecht's involvement with the artwork essay, see the detailed and philologically precise account in Wizisla, *Walter Benjamin and Bertolt Brecht*, 160–62. As other entries in the journals demonstrate, the shock to Brecht of life in Los Angeles did inspire a more sweeping condemnation of mass culture, at least in its American incarnation; see, for instance, the journal entry of December 27, 1941: "I tell [Oskar Homolka] about GALILEO. and it is as if I were remembering a strange, sunken theatre in ancient times on a submerged continent.—here all they are concerned about is selling an evening's entertainment" (*Journals*, 185). See also, however, the valuable correctives to tales of mandarin Germans in Los Angeles in Nico Israel's *Outlandish*, David Jenemann's *Adorno in America*, and Stathis Gourgouris's "The Lyric in Exile."

17. Brecht, *Journals*, 214.

while also being suspicious of their current manifestations. The learning plays, however, also belong to a particular conjuncture at the beginning of the 1930s. The relationship to the audience and the apparatuses those plays assume, and the possibilities of their refunctioning, belong to a moment of relative optimism on the left that could not be sustained after 1933, or 1945.

The "effect of an artistic performance on an audience cannot be independent of the effect of the audience on the artist": what did this actually mean? A crucial moment in Brecht's learning play *The Measures Taken* crystallizes the problem. First performed in Berlin in December 1930, *The Measures Taken* has been at the heart of arguments about the politics of Brecht's theater. Reporting the killing of the young comrade to the Control Chorus, the four agitators turn to the audience:

> Pressed for time, we found no way out.
> Just as animals help their own kind
> We also wished to help him who
> Fought with us for our cause.
> For five minutes, in the face of our persecutors
> We deliberated in hope of finding a
> Better possibility.
> Now it's your turn to deliberate.
> And find a better course of action.
> *Pause.*
> And so we decided: we now
> Had to cut off a member of our own body.
> *It is a terrible thing to kill.*
> We would not only kill others, but ourselves as well, if the need arose.
> For violence is the only means whereby this deadly
> World may be changed, as
> Every living being knows.[18]

The German verb here translated as "deliberate" is the everyday *nachdenken*: "Auch ihr jetzt denkt nach über | eine bessere Möglichkeit."[19] The pause that follows this appeal to the Control Chorus, or to the audience, or to the Control Chorus in its capacity as a stand-in for the audience, is difficult to read. Its awesome, awful theatricality dilates that pause in incalculable ways. For not the least of the alienating aspects of this passage is the way

18. Brecht, *The Measures Taken*, 32.

19. Brecht, *Die Maßnahme*, 132. (This is the text of the *Gesamtausgabe*, or collected works, of 1937/38.)

that it estranges time: the time that thinking takes, the time that decisions take, but also the time that things take to happen in the theater and the disproportion between the time of lived experience and time on stage—all of this punctuated by the insistent repetition of "now." The five minutes the four agitators report they devoted to their decision to murder the young agitator might seem horribly rushed; an equivalent silence in the theater— five minutes for the audience to think—would seem intolerably long. The pause for deliberation during which the audience can think about, think over, a possibility better than murder: how long should this be? How long was it? In a remarkable live recording of *The Measures Taken* in performance in Dresden in 1998, about ten seconds pass, during which one can hear that familiar awkward punctuation to silence in the theater: someone coughing.[20] Measured, those ten seconds are no time at all, and yet it takes a long time to listen to that silence. Times passes, but in no simple sense does the response of the audience change the performance: after the pause, the performers continue with the text. If, that is, the audience has had an effect on the performance, it is unclear how to discern that.[21]

Here it is important also to stress the particular moment in which Brecht was writing:

> Die Vorführrenden (Sänger und Spieler) haben die Aufgabe, lernend zu lehren. Da es in Deutschand eine halbe Million Arbeitersänger gibt, ist die Frage, was im Singenden vorgeht, mindestens so wichtig wie die Frage, was im Hörenden vorgeht.[22]

> The presenters (singers and actors) have the task, to teach while learning. Given that there are a half million worker-singers in Germany, the questions of what happens in the singers is at least as important as the question of what happens in the hearers.

---

20. For this recording, see Eisler and Brecht, *Die Maßnahme*.

21. The five German versions of *Die Maßnahme* over the course of the 1930s treat this pause variously. The first version delivers a long silence (*"Langes Schweigen"*) (Brecht, *Die Maßnahme*, 32). In a version printed to accompany the first performance, these lines follow the pause: "Klagend zerschlugen wir uns unsere Köpfe mit unseren Fäusten | Daß sie uns nur den furchtbaren Rat wußten: jetzt | Abzuschneiden den eigenen Fuß vom Körper" ["Lamenting we beat our heads with our own fists | That they could acknowledge only the terrible judgment: now | We must cut off our own foot from our body" (my translation)] (Brecht, *Die Maßnahme*, 63).

22. Brecht, "Einübung der "Maßnahme,"" in Brecht, *Die Maßnahme*, 242 (my translation).

The learning plays were written, so to speak, with a historically specific apparatus in mind: the working-class choruses of Weimar were a precondition for their composition.[23] And yet Brecht also wanted to re-function, or at least to radicalize a potentiality, of these choruses. As Brecht conceived of the learning plays, they would work not as a one-way transmission from stage to audience, but as a self-reflexive performance that was also a process of learning for the singers themselves. Roswitha Mueller has stressed that the *Lehrstück* aimed to erase "the central contradiction—that between producers and means of production."[24] Mueller quotes Reiner Steinweg: "The great pedagogy changes the role of acting completely: it annuls the system actor/audience; it recognises only actors who are at the same time students."[25] The learning play, then, is part of the long history of the desire to undo the separation of performers and audience, a history that extends at least from Jean-Jacques Rousseau's *Letter to d'Alembert* to *Paradise Now* and beyond. One does not need to be overly skeptical to wonder whether Steinweg has conflated the aspiration that helped to produce a form with its achievement. On the one hand, there is the question of whether *The Measures Taken* in performance, in December 1930, succeeded in annulling "the system actor/audience." On the other hand, there is the larger theoretical and historical question of whether this system has or can be annulled, or what the conditions of this annulment might have been.

23. On these choruses, see Bodek, "Red Song."

24. Mueller, *Bertolt Brecht and the Theory of Media*, 32. For a synthesis of Mueller's argument about the *Lehrstück*, see her "Learning for a New Society."

25. Steinweg, *Das Lehrstück: Brechts Theorie einer politischästhetischen Erziehung*, 23–24, quoted in Mueller, *Bertolt Brecht and the Theory of Media*, 32.

[THIRTEEN]

Participation in Postwar Theater

The desire for such an annulment is one of the abiding, contradictory projects of theater in the postwar period: it may be that the dissolution of the divide between audience and performer, whether in an erotic or political form or some combination of the two, will always remain phantasmatic, but as an ideal it had a powerful effect. There is something elegiac now in reading Jacques Rancière's challenge to that ideal in his 2007 essay, "The Emancipated Spectator," with its defense of distanced spectatorship in a mode that rejects the grand antinomies associated with the names of Brecht and Antonin Artaud. Rancière's assertions that performances "verify . . . the capacity of anonymous people, the capacity that makes everyone equal to everyone else," and that this verification happens across "irreducible distances," compellingly challenges the logic of the desire to undo the divide between audience and performer. "Being a spectator," Rancière writes, "is not some passive condition that we should transform into activity. It is our normal situation."[1] Rancière folds spectatorship into his larger argument about equality as premise rather than outcome, and disarmingly finds a way beyond an agon that has been central to thinking about drama: "The theatrical stage and performance thus become a vanishing mediation between the evil of spectacle and the virtue of true theatre."[2] Restoring

1. Rancière, "The Emancipated Spectator," 17.

2. Rancière, "The Emancipated Spectator," 7. At the start of the essay, Rancière stresses that its impetus emerged from the publication of *The Ignorant Schoolmaster*; his critique of explication and mastery as pedagogical modes provides the groundwork for his sense of spectatorship as activity. Rather than being the passive recipient of the lessons of whatever is staged—a situation Rancière calls the "stultification whenever one intelligence is subordinated to another" in *The Ignorant Schoolmaster* (13)—the spectator translates "what she perceives in her own way." Rancière directly links this free translation to the notion of the "shared power of the equality of intelligence" ("Emancipated Spectator," 17), precisely the theory of equality developed in *The Ignorant Schoolmaster*.

spectatorship to a position outside of this melodrama—his emphasis on distanced spectatorship as a fact of "our normal situation"—is Rancière's vital contribution to contemporary thinking about the politics of art.

Challenging the philosophical basis of an argument between "the evil of spectacle" and "true theatre," however powerful an intervention in the contemporary politics of art, does not necessarily illuminate the history of those who made theater and thought of the situation of the spectator—and the spectator's perceived passivity—as a vexatious problem to be solved. Rancière not only explicitly names Brecht and Artaud as figures for the poles of the inherited antinomy he dissects and hopes to dissolve: Guy Debord, too, is an antagonist here. True theater's evil other hypostasizes Debord's target in *The Society of the Spectacle*, a book first published in France in 1967.[3] Debord stresses that what the spectacle produces is separation or distance. "Distance," objects Rancière, "is not an evil to be abolished, but the normal condition of any communication."[4] Rancière's insistence on distance as a norm essential to communication has a satisfyingly pragmatic debunking force, but it also simplifies the historical situations of theater by representing all distances and all communications as alike. The slippage from "the spectacle" in Debord to "spectacle" in Rancière erases a difference that matters here. For Debord, mass media are only the "most stultifying superficial manifestation" of the spectacle.[5] The spectacle is *not* "a product of the technology of the mass dissemination of images": "It is far better viewed as a weltanschauung that has been actualized, translated into the material realm—a world view transformed into an objective force."[6] How important the mass media, however "stultifying superficial," might be to this actualization and translation "into the material realm" remains somewhat enigmatic in Debord's text. It is notable that "apparatus" in Debord's text recalls Brecht's use of the term and that he also echoes Brecht's critique of the direction of mass communication: "If the social requirements of the age which develops such techniques can be met only through their mediation, if the administration of society and all contact between people now depends on the intervention of such 'instant' communication, it is because this 'communication' is essentially *one-way*."[7] Debord's scare quotes under-

---

3. Two useful anthologies illuminate the work of the Situationists that led to Debord's book: see McDonough, *Guy Debord and the Situationist International* and Knabb, *Situationist International Anthology*.

4. Rancière, "The Emancipated Spectator," 10.

5. Debord, *The Society of the Spectacle*, 19.

6. Debord, *The Society of the Spectacle*, 12–13.

7. Debord, *The Society of the Spectacle*, 19–20.

mine both the idea that this communication is instantaneous and the claim that such "instant" messaging is communication at all. As with Brecht, it seems that communication would require the rejection of such "one-way" apparatuses and would also demand duration outside of the temporality of the instantaneous.

Debord follows the implications of this passage to a relevant aesthetic conclusion:

> The fact that the language of real communication has been lost is what the modern movement of art's decay, and ultimately of its formal anni-hilation, expresses *positively*. What it expresses *negatively* is that a new common language has yet to be found—not, this time, in the form of unilaterally arrived-at conclusions like those which, from the viewpoint of historical art, *always came on the scene too late*, speaking *to others* of what had been experienced without any real dialogue, and accepting this shortfall of life as inevitable—but rather in a praxis embodying both an unmediated activity and a language commensurate with it. The point is to take effective possession of the community of dialogue, and the playful relationship to time, which the works of the poets and artists have here-tofore merely *represented*.[8]

As in the earlier passage, Debord here links the two poles of an ideal of "real communication" to the problem of temporality: "the playful relationship to time" would be a feature of the truly communicative praxis of some other form of life. This ideal of the utopian invention of an "unmediated activity" is one of the objects of Rancière's later skepticism: in his account, as in those of many of his contemporaries, there will be no language outside of the circuits of mediation. Nevertheless, Debord's importance for my argument lies both in the clarity with which he defines the dilemma of the spectacle and in his typicality for a certain long historical moment. Debord does not conflate the spectacles of the aesthetic with the spectacle; nor does he imagine that the aesthetic—theatrical spectacle, for instance—could be wholly separate from the spectacle. Debord articulated a project that had special force for theater. The desire to take "effective possession of the com-munity of dialogue" and to seize a "playful relationship to time," and even more the ideal of escaping representation through this effective possession: Debord supplies a contemporary language for a range of theatrical projects that were dedicated precisely to the project that Rancière scrutinizes. The dissolution of the divide between audience and performer was one of the

---

8. Debord, *The Society of the Spectacle*, 133 (emphasis in original).

most intensely pursued undertakings of theater makers and of artists working in related forms, especially in the 1960s. Further, this project was often explicitly understood as a political and theatrical response to the apparatus (or medium, in Benjamin's sense) that Debord called the spectacle. From Allan Kaprow's *18 Happenings in 6 Parts* in New York City in 1959 to the Living Theatre's *Paradise Now*, which was first performed at the Avignon Festival in 1968, undermining or destroying the distinction between audience and spectacle was an aesthetic and political project.[9]

In her revisionary *Radical Prototypes*, Judith Rodenbeck argues that Kaprow's happenings must be understood in relation to (among other things) mass culture. Her exemplary investigation of the discursive position of those happenings models how scholars might at once theorize and historicize the relation between avant-garde performance practices of the 1960s and the larger mediascape. Particularly refreshing is her deep consideration of the links between practices narrowly understood as visual art *or* theatrical ones. Defending later formations against Peter Bürger's notorious critique, she argues that for the neo-avant-garde "the recuperation of an effective criticality necessarily lay in a reassessment of the dialectics between elite and mass culture, and between autonomy and alienation, and required addressing cultural production and consumption in a new way."[10] The remaking of theatrical practices in light of these reassessments led to challenges to the basic conditions of performance, to a critique of the apparatus of theater and to a movement of theater outside traditional theater spaces, to continually rethought strategies for dissolving the divide between performers and audience—to *Paradise Now* and a number of other experiments.

This critique did not happen all at once. As early as July 25, 1948, Judith Malina, already imagining what the Living Theatre would be—though the company had yet to stage anything—copied a passage from André Gide's journal of 1914 into her diary:

9. Situationists were also skeptical of actually existing attempts to dissolve the divide between spectator and performance. See "Editorial Notes: The Avant-Garde of Presence," a text from 1963: "To the degree that participation becomes more impossible, the second-class engineers of modernist art demand everyone's participation as their due" (in McDonough, *Guy Debord and the Situationist International*, 144).

10. Rodenbeck, *Radical Prototypes*, 21. For Bürger's critique of the neo-avant-garde, see *Theory of the Avant-Garde*, 58.

Dramatic art must no more seek to create the illusion of reality than does painting: it should work through its own special means and aim towards effects that belong to it alone.

Just as a painting is a space to set in motion, a play is a space of time to animate.

Malina's commentary on this passage provides a capsule survey of theatrical experiment in the years between Gide's diary entry and her own:

In looking for those "special means" and those "effects that belong to it alone" many means and effects have been devised: the bioconstructivism of Meyerhold, the expressionism of Kaiser, the Dadaist antilogic, the superrealism of David Belasco, or Reinhardt's sentimental grandeur. All efforts to theatricalize the theater.

But today all these structures have been debased into superficial devices.

Broadway buries itself under a sugary realism and experimental theater devotes itself to various forms of fantasy; Hollywood inserts surrealistic dream sequences into banal love stories.[11]

"To theatricalize the theater": Malina's phrase summarizes a wide range of twentieth-century attempts to find the effects that belong to theater alone.[12] Her diagnosis also symptomatically, and without needing to remark on the logic of the transition, shifts from avant-garde experiment to Broadway and then to Hollywood, as though cinema were the inevitable destination of a process of debasement, via Broadway, as experimental "structures" become "superficial devices." Superrealism becomes sugary realism; antilogic becomes fantasy. There is no need to remark on this transition because, in the imaginary that grounds much postwar theatrical experiment, the idea of Hollywood as the antithesis and dead end of that experiment was well established. Malina's comment, however, also suggests that some attempts to "theatricalize the theater" were already regressive in their moment: Reinhardt's "sentimental grandeur," as embodied in his elaborate simulations of religious effects and affects in mass spectacles from *The Miracle* to

11. Judith Malina, *Diaries*, 50.

12. That this phrase anticipates Hans-Thies Lehmann's better-known formulation—retheatricalizing the theater—emphasizes that the response to mass media that he associates with the later movement of postdramatic theater was at the very least anticipated well before 1970, the date he offers for its advent. For retheatricalization, see Lehmann, *Postdramatic Theatre*, 50–52.

Everyman, were the antithesis of the political theater of Malina's teacher, Erwin Piscator. "Broadway," meanwhile, is itself marked as a step on the way to the fully commodified entertainment of Hollywood.

Far from a record of the absolute rejection of Broadway, however, Malina's diaries are marked by an ambivalence about New York's theatrical entertainment center. Malina saw everything possible, on all stages, and the diaries document her continued engagement with Broadway plays and her work in television. One entry records her making "the rounds of theatrical offices" while her mother watches her child: "I have an inordinate love for the crowds and for the racetrack atmosphere of Broadway, so distasteful to Julian. After a time I'll despise it again, but right now it's a refuge."[13] The diaries rarely contain any suggestion, however, that Broadway might provide a venue for her own theatrical project. In an extensive and aspirational entry from 1951, she writes:

> There is a need for spontaneity. Everything else has been replaced by the film and other mechanical media.
>
> Theater work is now so specialized that no one is permitted knowledge of another's activity. The stagehands paint the flats; the actors stand in front of them.

Broadway's restriction of work to guilds that possess specialized knowledge damages the theater: "There can be a *living* theater only in the work of small groups of people interested neither in effect nor success—except for the successful action." The specialization that mars Broadway is an aspect of those "mechanical media" to which Malina opposes the living theater; indeed, the passage implies that such specialization turns theater into one of these "mechanical media."[14] The solution:

---

13. Judith Malina, *Diaries*, 86.

14. Judith Malina, *Diaries*, 169. In his influential *Growing Up Absurd*, Paul Goodman, who had been Malina's therapist (her diaries record a tortured friendship), attacks valueless work as "boondoggling": "The $64,000 Question and the busy hum of Madison Avenue might certainly be called boondoggling. Certain tax-dodge Foundations are boondoggling. What of business lunches and expense accounts? fringe benefits? the comic categories of occupation in the building trades? the extra stagehands and musicians of the theater crafts?" (30). His exposure to the orbit of the Living Theatre, which produced four of his plays between 1951 and 1959, might have inspired the otherwise surprising inclusion of union labor in the theater here. Malina records that "even" Goodman helped construct the set for his *Faustina* in 1952 (*Diaries*, 226). For a list of the Living Theatre's New York productions, see Biner, *The Living Theatre*, 228–29.

Attain the perfection of production through the perfection of immediacy.
The Noh is a perfect medium, but the Noh is too rigid.[15]

This passage captures the paradoxical foundation of this Living Theatre, as of so much aesthetic experimentation in the period Malina's diaries introduce, in at once imagining the perfection of a medium for immediacy while also complaining that the perfect extant medium is nevertheless "too rigid." Or is the problem that the Noh is the perfect medium, only for an experience more rigid than that of the desired immediacy? And yet this desire for a stage apparatus that might better produce the conditions for more intimate theatrical experiences was also widespread: her diaries record Malina and Beck's consideration of a whole range of possible and less possible spaces for their theater, including a quonset hut.[16]

Malina's sweeping claim is important: "Everything else has been replaced by the film and other mechanical media." Many asked questions similar to Malina's: if "film and other mechanical media" had replaced everything, what was left? If one-way broadcast media and cinema had remade subjectivity, how could theater respond? A similarly characteristic passage appears in Herbert Blau's *The Impossible Theater*, first published in 1963: "The instruction of the citizenry is largely dependent on the mass media; so, we are reading the shadows on the wall. The result is public hallucination."[17] The claim that the mass media were now the most important force in the "instruction of the citizenry" was simply common sense. Blau's blindingly rapid translation of this mass instruction into the scene of Plato's cave and his insistence that the result of that instruction is necessarily "public hallucination" certainly locates him on the more skeptical end of the spectrum, but even—or especially—the comparison to Plato's cave was not unique.[18] Blau claims that this culture of mass hallucination—a culture fostered by the apparatuses of the mass media, including newspapers—produces the "atmosphere" in which he made theater, and he writes further: "What we have been trying to develop in our theater is a counter-atmosphere in which

15. Malina, *Diaries*, 169.

16. For the genesis and collapse of the idea of the quonset hut, see Malina, *Diaries*, 90–92.

17. Blau, *Impossible Theater*, 107.

18. Blau connects the mass media to Plato's cave in similar terms in a critique of the cult of experts earlier in the book: "As for the electorate, having very little to say in its own right, and informed—as Arthur Schlesinger said to his fellow historians—by media that have as much relation to reality as the shadows in Plato's cave, it is also full of experts" (*Impossible Theater*, 61).

the special properties of the dramatic form, devoted to crisis, are enlisted against the epidemic of mystifications." Blau simultaneously suggests that the mystifications against which his theater struggled were particular to the Cold War and yet somehow also eternal, modeled on the structure of Plato's cave. Similarly, he suggests that the function of theater in this era is simultaneously particular to the mass-mediated culture in which it developed, and also something essential to "dramatic form" itself because of its devotion to crisis. That formal devotion to crisis in his view makes drama peculiarly well suited to the Cold War plague of mystifications. His work should have some concern with "social issues," he writes, "but our main dedication, in an era of weird bureaucracy and statistical miasma, is to the spirit of theater itself—communal, playful, protestant, and life-giving."[19] "Statistical miasma" exemplifies Blau's disorienting braiding of the contemporary and the ancient: Greek "pollution"—*miasma*—takes its twentieth-century form in a welter of statistics. The particular forces of the Cold War period cause Blau and his company to rededicate themselves to the permanent "spirit of theater," pitting theater's classical, even permanent devotion to crisis (Blau may again be alluding to the term's Greek roots) against modern mystifications. No detail of these passages is more telling that than the lowercase "p": this theater will be "protestant," in general revolt, not taking take part in any particular doctrinal controversy. In Blau's quartet of affirmative terms—"communal, playful, protestant, and life-giving"—the first resonates most with *The Impossible Theater* as a whole, and also with the larger discourse of theater in the era in which he wrote. For all the real peculiarity of Blau's unmistakable idiom, his claim typifies a strain of the celebration of theater as the communal negation of an alienating mass culture. Further, this ideal of community is linked to a desire to return to or to reawaken powers attributed to classical theater.

Blau's "statistical miasma" condenses a larger dynamic of the ancient and modern in his work. Blau respectfully considers the poet Karl Shapiro's stoical advice to his students, in Shapiro's words, "to cultivate an ignorance of contemporary political and military events because they do not matter." Blau writes: "Refusal to participate is a risk worth argument. But the trouble with the drama is that it always comes back to those risks which cannot, for all the argument, be argued away. Which may be what we mean when we call it a social form, whose specialty is crisis, haunted by paradox."[20]

19. Blau, *Impossible Theater*, 107.

20. Blau, *Impossible Theater*, 98. The quoted passage appears in Shapiro's tribute to Henry Miller, "The Greatest Living Author," which had been reprinted as an introduction to the Grove Press edition of Miller's *Tropic of Cancer* in 1961 (xv).

Crisis and paradox: terms with Greek roots again signal Blau's conception of theater's transcendence of historical contingencies and roots in ancient practice. That twentieth-century theater might be continuous with ancient theater is hardly a claim unique to Blau: projects for restoring or reinventing that link are part of modern theater's history. The particular form this claim takes here, however, is less familiar. Blau implicitly concedes that for the poet "refusal to participate" might be possible. Drama, however, makes the evasion associated with the poet's potential principled ignorance of the contemporary impossible: drama cannot evade the risks that come with engaging contemporary social and political conflicts because its permanent and transhistorical essence is to embrace argument, crisis, and paradox. Paradox meanwhile also structures Blau's argument: precisely because of its ineluctable, historically unchanging "specialty" in crisis, the history of drama consists of a series of encounters with the contemporary—for instance, with those aspects of "contemporary political and military events" that argument cannot argue away. There may be a further paradoxical suggestion here that the aspect of these contemporary events that cannot "be argued away" itself belongs to the ahistorical core of a conception of human nature that, in Blau's rhetoric, is tied up especially with "blood" and all that that word conjures.[21] The heart of the contemporary, according to this conception, then, is itself not contemporary.

Confronting the Cold War paradoxes of "maximum deterrence and massive retaliation," Blau argues with Reinhold Niebuhr. Blau quotes Niebuhr's rejection of "the strategy of fleeing from difficult problems by taking refuge in impossible solutions." Niebuhr's disavowal provokes one of Blau's meditations on the relationship between theater and the key word of his book's title: "One impulse, however, of every major drama is to take refuge in impossible solutions. Or, to put it another way: to refuse to recognize the impossible as impossible until the solution is shown not to be a solution. The Utopian solution may fail, but in the maturest drama it is, somehow, represented, whatever may be true of politics."[22] The "lunatic" principles that guide the logic of deterrence concern Blau, but he is also—and maybe especially—determined to think about where the forces that produce these ideologies leave theater: "One of the prices our theater has to pay for such a world is that no illusion it can create—even by anti-illusion—can

21. For a review of Blau's later work that is especially alert to his rhetoric of blood, see W. D. King, "Blau-Blooded Thought."

22. Blau, *The Impossible Theater*, 96. See Elin Diamond's discussion of Blau's work in "Re: Blau, Butler, Beckett" and, in particular, her linking of Blau's theorization of the theater and the Cold War to his later work (34–35).

comprehend the illusions we live by."[23] The predicament of "our theater" is, Blau suggests, not entirely new—and yet the concatenation of Cold War "illusions we live by" produces a new and more acute dilemma of comprehension. The price theater pays is that it can no longer produce the paradoxical illusion that makes sense of a culture's illusions. The chapter in which these reflections appear meditates on Brecht, particularly *Galileo*: one argument is that the "anti-illusion" of Brechtian dramaturgy can no longer sustain the force it might have had. To phrase the question in a different idiom: What happens when ideological apparatuses produce an illusion that theater cannot comprehend through its strategies of demystifying illusion? That theater's demystifying powers are lessened does not mean that Blau thinks it has no political role. He describes a culture in which complexity renders expertise moot: "If experts can't judge, how can the theater presume? In actuality, it doesn't. The theater doesn't so much judge as take 'a reflective gape' (Henry James' phrase) at the flow and disruption of human purpose. And it documents that gape in action. It embraces the shape of crisis—kisses the Medusa's lips. The theater enables by re-enacting; it renders and it stands in awe. This may be a rude reawakening, woe producing wonder, but energy is restored and inertia overcome. We *feel* less powerless."[24] To feel less powerless, Blau's italicization implies, is better than the reigning Cold War sensation of absolute powerlessness. And yet the passage's density, so characteristic of Blau's prose throughout his career, underlines the problem of what forms his power might actually take. The logic of the prose (equally characteristic of Blau's practice as a writer through his career) is hard to follow because it aspires to embody theater's escape from the discursive paradigms that surround it while also remaining committed to struggling with language. Theater "takes" a gape, rather than the more idiomatic look, and this gape is a "reflective" one. (The association with Henry James further authorizes this reflection, even if the context of the original phrase might seem to undermine it.) But this gape does not consist in a stance of open-mouthed astonishment: theater at once gapes while also self-reflexively documenting its own "gape in action." This action, further, is an embodied,

23. Blau, *The Impossible Theater*, 96–97.

24. Blau, *The Impossible Theater*, 97. The fascinating origin of the interior quotation is Henry James's description of his childhood experience of Paris and of Parisian puppet shows: "It was the social aspect of our situation that most appealed to me, none the less—for I detect myself, as I woo it all back, disengaging a social aspect again, and more than ever, from the phenomena disclosed to my reflective gape or to otherwise associated strolls; perceptive passages not wholly independent even of the occupancy of two-sous chairs within the charmed circle of Guignol and of Gringalet" (James, *A Small Boy and Others*, in *Autobiography*, 188).

even erotic encounter: that embrace of "the shape of crisis," kissing "the Medusa's lips." The chapter from which these passages are taken is called "The Balance of Terror": as with a few other chapters, especially in the first part of Blau's book, catchphrases belonging to the vocabulary of the Cold War structure *The Impossible Theater*. Blau is pondering the psychic strain of the encounter with the destructive potential of the era: the Cuban missile crisis haunts him. Blau knows that his mass-mediated sources of knowledge are the only sources of the news he has, and he also knows that he distrusts them: the mediated source of his knowledge of these crises sets up theater as an alternative mode of communication. Theater reenacts the shape of such crises, but in an enabling form. Theater, Blau suggests, represents its own counterbalance of terror.

That in the Medusa this enabling reenactment takes the form of a male fantasy of a dangerous yet survivable erotic encounter with a feminized embodiment of danger and spectacular doom suggests Blau's investments in what I have elsewhere called a twentieth-century fantasy of destructive spectatorship.[25] Blau imagines the collective work of theater as heroic action, and this emphasis on action is important. Writing in the early 1960s, Blau participates in the gendered and sexualized promotion of performative efficacy that Stephen Bottoms has analyzed so tellingly.[26] The fleeting but significant fragment of the narrative of the Medusa suggests that, instead of being stunned into petrified passivity by the sight, our newly empowered hero makes a sexual conquest of the effeminizing spectacle that would otherwise have fed his inertia and immobilized him. As Bottoms's analysis would predict, it is telling that this victory for the theater is also the heterosexual vanquishing of a sexuality imagined as perverse and destructive. As

25. Harries, *Forgetting Lot's Wife*.

26. Bottoms, "The Efficacy/Effeminacy Braid: Unpacking the Performance Studies/Theatre Studies Dichotomy." In *The Impossible Theater* (38–43), Blau engages with precisely the debate around Edward Albee's *Who's Afraid of Virginia Woolf?* which provides an important example for Bottoms's argument. Indeed, Blau quotes a line from a *TDR* editorial by Richard Schechner also singled out by Bottoms: "The lie of his work is the lie of our theater and the lie of America." Schechner, as Bottoms demonstrates, links this to decadence and to homosexuality; Blau neither fully endorses nor clearly rejects this logic, and he addresses the homophobia of Schechner's account only obliquely. The "quality" of Albee's work, Blau writes, "suggests he has to live through the lie to go beyond it. Moreover, if we accept—as Albee's most intellectual critics tend to do—the 'ontological speculation' of Genet, we may have to seek reality by acting over its provisional lies, including our own" (42). The interior quotation cites Schechner's essay: "Genet can raise sexual perversion to the level of ontological speculation—he is a poet and a mighty intellect" ("Who's Afraid of Edward Albee?," 9).

Bottoms would also predict, theater's implicit other here is entertainment, the passifying and mystifying atmosphere to which an efficacious theater must offer a "counter-atmosphere."

Malina, writing roughly a decade earlier, was not immune to this sexualized rhetoric of theatrical action. Attending a Ballet Theater benefit performance with Paul Goodman, her friend and analyst, she records the response of a "dignified matron" when "a crazy crank loped by in red satin": "Why, it's a drag!" The entry continues: "Paul said: 'We have taken over.' But what we want to change must be changed by revolution and not by camp."[27] That camp and drag might be subversive practices is not thinkable for her. Another long entry on her ideas about theater complements Blau on the overcoming of inertia. The visit of Jean-Louis Barrault's company to New York in November 1952 inspired thoughts that include intimations of the later work of the Living Theatre:

> Participating in eternity I am only a part of things, therefore I am immortal.
>
> In the theater, this urge toward participation leads to eliminating the line between the reality of the theater and the reality of the world outside the theater.
>
> Barrault's production of *The Trial*, adapted by Gide, like Piscator's production, externalizes K's persecution.
>
> Art itself is an externalization of the unspeakable cry.
>
> If I did this play I would try to make it unbearable for the audience. Only when the audience realizes its impotence will it rebel. If I could drive them to such extremes of exasperation in the theater that their restrained outcries began to materialize in their throats, then I might drive them to enact their needs when they hit the air outside the theater.
>
> The act of sitting in the theater is an agreement to tolerate the action as a demonstration and an enlightenment. The energy to change the unbearable situation mounts in the theater. Then we will go out and destroy the outer law and the inner chains: the state's yoke and the spirit's harness.[28]

From its spirituality without doctrine at the entry's start to its confidence that theater might produce an anarchic destruction of the state's coercion at its end, this entry anticipates the Living Theatre's work of the 1960s and

---

27. Malina, *Diaries*, 305.

28. Malina, *Diaries*, 253.

especially—even though that apotheosis of Malina's ideas would first be staged only sixteen years later in Avignon in July 1968—the final "action" of *Paradise Now* out of the theater and onto the streets.[29] In this 1952 diary entry, Malina does not somehow foresee that future project; she does imagine a production of *The Trial* that would have a different effect on its audience than those by two directors she admires, Piscator and Barrault. Barrault and Piscator externalize K's persecution; art externalizes "the unspeakable cry." It would appear, then, that Malina argues that by externalizing persecution, they have evaded the task of art and the externalization of the cry: this is what her production would achieve. And the logic here makes clear why Malina thinks of this as a matter of "externalization" instead of, for instance, expression. She imagines a theater that makes the passivity of the theatrical situation, "sitting in the theater"—that is, Rancière's norm for spectatorship—unendurable. As Blau does, Malina meditates on the ability of the audience to act. His audience feels "less powerless"; her audience experiences itself, in the theater, as impotent, and this "unbearable situation" leads to an externalization in the form of an outcry, which, "outside the theater," the audience no longer restrains and, further, to rebellion against "the outer law and inner chains."

Although Malina does not make this explicit in this entry, a context for this utopian desire for an efficacious and potent theater that leads to revolutionary social and personal change is a mass culture perceived as designed to manipulate its audiences into passivity. Without yet having read Artaud, Malina anticipated the collision of Brechtian alienation with ideas derived, however loosely, from the theater of cruelty that would form one important theatrical strand in the 1960s.[30] For both Malina in her diary entries from the 1950s and Blau in his book-length "manifesto" from the early 1960s, an urgency to renew theatrical practice emerged in part out of its resistance to the stultifying effects of mass culture. Malina's passionate anarchism was more utopian than Blau's qualified belief in the potential political force of theater, but for all their differences they embody one important strand of the response to the perceived pressures of mass culture: the ritual efficacy of theatrical practice as local rebellion against the global hegemony of mass

29. A heading in the text of *Paradise Now* marks the movement toward "the rear of the theater" and into the street as the eighth and final "Action" of the piece (Malina and Beck, *Paradise Now*, 139).

30. In one of the sparse notes Malina supplies to her diaries, she implies that she had indeed taken in something like Artaud's influence through the "dancer and actress" Valeska Gert: "Her pre-Artaudian 'outcry' (*Schrei*) had a profound influence on Julian and me and, consequently, on the Living Theatre" (*Diaries*, 463).

culture. In "The Theatre's New Testament," an interview with Eugenio Barba from 1964 republished in *Towards a Poor Theatre*, Jerzy Grotowski described one of the impulses for his research: "In our age when all languages are confused as in the Tower of Babel, when all aesthetical genres intermingle, death threatens the theatre as film and television encroach upon its domain. This makes us examine the nature of theatre, how it differs from the other art forms, and what it is that makes it irreplaceable."[31] Grotowski restates the desire to understand the specificity of theater as medium that Malina discovered in André Gide's journals, but with the difference that he understands this project as directly related to the encroachments of film and television.

The impulse in theatrical practices of this period to imagine theater as action, even ritual, was not unprecedented, and its many manifestations could be the topic of a separate book.[32] Mass culture in part determined this impulse. To imagine a theatrical efficacy that would provide a "counter-atmosphere" in the context of this mass-mediated "atmosphere," to use Blau's terms, was never, however, the only form that thinking about theater in the context of mass media took. Consider, for instance, a book that continues to provide at the very least one of the most persistent labels for dramas of this period: on the first page of the preface of *The Theatre of the Absurd* Martin Esslin writes that "the theatre, in spite of its apparent eclipse through the rise of mass media, remains of immense and growing significance—precisely because of the spread of the cinema and television." Esslin's planetary realignment, where the "rise of mass media" eclipses theater, anticipates an aspect of my argument in that it is "precisely" this eclipse that produces the "immense and growing significance" of theater. At the very start of *The Theatre of the Absurd*, Esslin points to "the spread of the cinema and television" to the formation of that drama. Esslin's understanding of this dynamic is, however, very different from that of Malina or Blau or Grotowski: "These mass media are too ponderous and costly to indulge in much experiment and innovation. So, however restricted the theatre and its audience may be, it is on the living stage that the actors and playwrights of the mass media are trained and gain their experience, and the material of the mass media is tested. The avant-garde of the theatre is, more likely than not, the main influence on the mass media of tomorrow. And the mass media, in turn, shape a great deal of the thought and feeling of people throughout

---

31. Grotowski, "The Theatre's New Testament," trans. Jörgen Andersen and Judy Barba, in *Towards a Poor Theatre*, 27–28.

32. See, for instance, Erika Fischer-Lichte, *Theatre, Sacrifice, Ritual.*

the Western world."[33] The importance of theater, for the moment, lies in the influence that it will have, as a site of training and testing, on the media that have eclipsed it. Many examples, looking both backward and forward from the time of the first publication of Esslin's book in 1961, could attest to the truth of this argument: one could compile a substantial catalog of actors and playwrights whose careers began in experimental theater and ended, sometimes with an occasional return to theater, in movies and television. Esslin's opening argument about the latent force of theater as the practice that shapes the media that, in turn, "shape a great deal of the thought and feeling of people throughout the Western world," however, is more in the way of an introductory gambit than an argument central to his work. Esslin more often values theater for its present importance: "The theatre, an art more broadly based than poetry or abstract painting without being, like the mass media, the collective product of corporations, is the point of intersection where the deeper trends of changing thought first reach a larger public." Here, indeed, the temporality of his argument reverses itself: rather than a pioneer of forms that will shape the mass culture of the future, the theater under consideration, as unnamed others have noted, "represents trends that have been apparent in the more esoteric kinds of literature since the nineteen-twenties (Joyce, Surrealism, Kafka) or in painting since the first decade of this century (Cubism, abstract painting)." Esslin responds: "But the theatre could not put the innovations before its wider public until these trends had had time to filter into a wider consciousness."[34] The present moment of theatrical experiment, then, arrives between its staging of "trends" that had already been legible in aesthetic experiment in other art forms and its latent potentiality in shaping a future mass culture.

One way to translate Esslin's observations about the theater and its transmission of "trends"—a term that for Esslin has no connotations of triviality—would be to say that theater disseminates modernist discoveries to a wider audience and prepares the way for still wider dissemination of these discoveries in the mass media for which the theater is the training ground. "Modernism" is not, however, an important term for Esslin: in the preface, the interest lies in theater as the mediator between the "esoteric" literature and painting of the early century and the mass media of the future. Theater is significant now, he writes, "as an expression—one of the most representative ones—of the present situation of Western man."[35]

33. Esslin, *Theatre of the Absurd*, xiii.

34. Esslin, *Theatre of the Absurd*, xiv.

35. Esslin, *Theatre of the Absurd*, xiv.

Implicitly, the literature and fine art of the early century sensed something of this situation in advance: drama now communicates this to more people, and mass media will, in time, catch up. The question of when the "situation of Western man" became an absurd one is not one Esslin attempts to pinpoint. In any case, the central argument of *The Theatre of the Absurd* does not concern drama's intermediary position in the history of media; Esslin argues that in drama the absurd is no longer a philosophical position but becomes part of the form of drama in an unprecedented way: "While Sartre and Camus express the new content in the old convention, the Theatre of the Absurd goes a step further in trying to achieve a unity between its basic assumptions and the form in which it is expressed."[36] No longer content or thesis, absurdity becomes a formal principle.

Neither absurdism as formal and philosophical principle nor the reenchanted aesthetic of the Living Theatre and similarly ritual-minded theater makers exhausted theatrical negotiations with the problem of mass culture. A very different, indeed almost dialectically opposite, understanding of how theater might reorient its audience in the wake of mass culture, for instance, inspired makers of documentary theater. Peter Weiss's pages toward a "definition of documentary theatre" stress the roots of the movement in an effort to counter the mass media's slant "towards the point of view of dominant interests": "Although the means of communication have now reached maximum extension and bring us news from all over the world, the causes and relationships of the decisive events which shape our present and our future remain hidden from us." Weiss's diagnosis of "the artificial fog behind which the world's rulers hide their manipulations" recalls Blau (and many others) on the media's mystification of the causes and effects of political decisions.[37] Neither Blau nor Weiss argues that theater can provide unmediated access to an otherwise concealed political or historical truth. Weiss does argue that one of the central tasks of the documentary theater is the "critique of concealment"; he does not, however, suggest that such a critique will make visible what has been concealed but that it will raise the question of the interests behind that concealment. In his conception, the documentary theater produces a model that makes judgment possible:

36. Esslin, *Theatre of the Absurd*, 6. This argument echoes that of Adorno's essay on *Endgame*: "For Beckett absurdity is no longer an 'existential situation' diluted to an idea and then illustrated. In him literary method surrenders to absurdity without preconceived intentions" ("Trying to Understand *Endgame*," in *Notes to Literature*, 1:241).

37. Peter Weiss, "The Material and the Models: Notes towards a Definition of Documentary Theatre," in Brandt, *Modern Theories of Drama*, 248, 249.

The strength of the Documentary Theatre lies in its ability to shape a useful pattern from fragments of reality, to build a model of current events. It does not stand at the centre of events, it adopts the position of the spectator and analyst. By means of its montage technique, it emphasizes significant details in the chaotic material of external reality. Through the confrontation of contradictory details it shows up an existing conflict to which, on the basis of the assembled documentation, it then brings a suggested solution, an appeal, or a point of principle. All that which in open improvisation, in politically coloured 'happenings,' leads to diffuse tension, to emotional sympathy, to an illusion of participation in current events, is in Documentary Theatre dealt with attentively, consciously, and reflectively.[38]

Paul Goodman complained in 1961 of "our wretched universal reporting and spectatoritis"; an allied critique of spectatorship with its accompanying desire for participation is a leitmotif of Malina's diaries and was central to the dramaturgy of the Living Theatre from the 1950s onward.[39] The contrast here with Weiss is stark: long before Rancière's emancipated spectator, Weiss had questioned the division of the universe of experimental theater into the camps of Artaud and Brecht. His emphasis on spectatorship and analysis surely had roots in Brecht's theories, but the inclusion of "choric chants" points toward a different dramaturgical mode. Weiss conceives of Documentary Theatre not as "direct political action" but as "an image of a segment of that actuality torn out of its living context."[40] It is striking that Weiss imagines this theater as other than "living." It is also striking that it is by adopting a technique central to the practice and theorization of the

38. Weiss, "The Material and the Models," 248, 250.

39. Paul Goodman, "Notes on the Underworld," 215. "Spectatoritis" was not Goodman's neologism: Jay B. Nash had published a book, *Spectatoritis*, in 1937. Participation as ideal was so important to the Living Theatre that tracing the term fully through their work might amount to a history of the company. Concentrating on the importance of this term inside the collaboration between the Living Theatre and Goodman would be itself revealing. At the ending of Goodman's *Faustina*, which the Living Theatre produced in 1952, an actress berated the audience for its passivity in the face of violence. A debate between Malina and Goodman about revolution spanned decades. In a letter to Malina written in May 1972, the last year of his life, Goodman wrote: "I agree that there is no political truth except in participation." He continued: "But there is also the question of *who* participates" (quoted in Taylor Stoehr, "Paul Goodman, the Living Theater, and the Great Despair," 18). Goodman, that is, challenged the idea of participation in itself as ideal.

40. Weiss, "The Material and the Models," 249.

cinema, montage, that Weiss imagines that documentary theater might cut through the "artificial fog" of the mass media. Theater would counter the spectacle by adopting one of its devices.

That a cinematic device might support the theatrical undoing of spectacle was not an unknown logic in the period. A particularly vivid exhibit in this history is the Fall 1966 issue of the *Tulane Drama Review*, which gathered articles on the confluence of film and theater, forming a compelling predecessor to more recent volumes on intermediality and theater. In an introductory essay, Richard Schechner writes:

> Theatre, it seems to us, is expanding. Cubic space, film images, multifocus—everywhere old frames are breaking. It is no longer easy to distinguish between theatre and the other performing arts. It is already difficult to say when a painting is a painting and when it is a performance. The literary model is passing away and it is being replaced by a performance model whose shape, happily, is not yet fixed. The World of Murray the K and the World of Gunther [*sic*] Grass overlap; flickadisc at the Circle-in-the-Square and Erik Vos's production of *Prometheus* at Stanford converge. Many theatres are actively seeking new audiences.[41]

Well before the appearance of Gene Youngblood's *Expanded Cinema* in 1970, Schechner imagined an expanded theater. Well before Henry Jenkins theorized convergence culture in 2006, Schechner noted the convergence of rock and roll on the radio, high literary ambition, multimedia dance parties, and new productions of classical drama. There are also intimations of the formation of performance studies as a discipline here, as theater and the other performing arts become hard to distinguish and painting (and everything else) verges on performance.

Where Schechner saw euphoric convergence, Susan Sontag and Michael Fried (to return to an earlier pairing) saw conflict, real or potential. Sontag's "Film and Theatre" (the first full-length essay in that Fall 1966 issue of *TDR*) begins: "The big question is whether there is an unbridgeable division, even

---

41. Richard Schechner, "The New Look," 22–23. Murray the K, the self-proclaimed "Fifth Beatle," was an influential New York disc jockey. An English translation of Günter Grass's play, *The Plebeians Rehearse the Uprising*, appeared in 1966. For "flickadisc," which appears to have been a club environment roughly like Andy Warhol's Exploding Plastic Inevitable, see Sam Zolotow, "'Village' to Get an Unusual Show"; for his own account of his production of *Prometheus*, see Erik Vos, "*Prometheus* as Total Theatre: Production Notes."

opposition, between the two arts."[42] For Fried, who has never hesitated to decide "when a painting is a painting and when it is a performance," "*What lies* between *the arts is theater*" because it has no medium to which it can be specific. Sontag, too, recognizes a conflict between two "radical positions," one that "recommends the breaking down of distinctions between genres" and one that "recommends the maintaining and clarifying of the barriers between the arts, by the intensification of what each art distinctively is."[43] Her essay begins with a "big question" about an opposition between theater and film; it ends with another question about the need for a new idea: "Will we be able to recognize it?"[44] The essay is a document of the division of Sontag's sympathies between something resembling Fried's stringent modernism and her appreciation of art forms that result from the "breaking down of distinctions between genres" such as the happening. There is opposition, struggle, and war if one occupies one or the other of the "radical positions" she describes; if not, not so much. The essay recognizes the power of each of these positions while finally endorsing neither, concluding instead with that open-ended question.

At the end of the period on which this book concentrates, Raymond Williams offered one solution—in its way, quite a radical one—to the problem of theater's relationship to film. His lecture of 1974, "Drama in a Dramatized Society," begins by proposing that the "problems of drama, in any of its many perspectives, are now serious enough to be genuinely interesting and indeed to provoke quite new kinds of questions."[45] What interests Williams is a "transformed situation": "Drama is no longer, for example, coextensive with theatre; many dramatic performances are now in film and television studios. In the theatre itself—national theatre or street theatre—there is an exceptional variety of intention and method. New kinds of text, new kinds of notation, new media and new conventions press actively alongside the texts and conventions we think we know, but that I find problematic just

42. Susan Sontag, "Film and Theatre," 24.

43. Sontag, "Film and Theatre," 35.

44. Sontag, "Film and Theatre," 37.

45. Raymond Williams, "Drama in a Dramatized Society," 11. The implication here that earlier these problems were not "genuinely interesting" is curious coming from the author of *Drama from Ibsen to Brecht*, and yet this might also explain why I suspect I am not alone in feeling that the lecture of 1974 has more of interest than the book. Very much in the spirit of Williams, the film historian Charles Musser proposes "a history of 'theatrical culture', which includes both stage and screen" ("Towards a History of Theatrical Culture," 3). Musser cites Kenneth Macgowan as a predecessor in refusing the scholarly impulse "to separate theatre from film" (16n11). On the intersection of theater and cinema histories, see also Hans-Christian von Herrman, "Stimmbilding."

because these others are there."[46] While Williams allows that "the theatre itself" remains a meaningful category, more striking is his insistence—from his title onwards—on drama as a mode that crosses formats and media. The movement from stage to television is not simply a question, Williams stresses, of vaster audiences, but of watching drama after drama after drama as part of daily life: "What we have now is drama as habitual experience: more in a week, in many cases, than most human beings would previously have seen in a lifetime."[47] Williams insists repeatedly that drama has become a *need*:

> Yet our lives are still here, still substantially here, with the people we know, in our own rooms, in the similar rooms of our friends and neighbours, and they too are watching: not only for public events, or for distraction, but from a need for images, for representations, of what living is now like, for this kind of person and that, in this situation and place and that. It is perhaps the full development of what Wordsworth saw at an early stage, when the crowd in the street (the new kind of urban crowd, who are physically very close but still absolute strangers) had lost any common and settled idea of man and so needed representations—the images on hoardings, the new kinds of sign—to simulate if not affirm a human identity: what life looks like beyond this intense and anxious, but also this pushed and jostled, private world of the head.[48]

Because we now lack "any common and settled idea of man," there is a need for representations "to simulate if not affirm a human identity." The turn to Wordsworth's encounter with advertisements on hoardings as a model for the "new kinds of sign" people need might in other contexts be a vast one: the divide between simulation and affirmation could be more troubling. It should perhaps be surprising that it is not. Williams looks back toward his own work on advertising—and, further still, to "the fury against advertising in Leavisian practice" that Jennifer Wicke analyzes in *Advertising Fictions*.[49] He also anticipates, in the idea of simulation, a key term of Jean Baudrillard's apocalyptic meditations on similar themes in *Simulacra and Simulations* of 1981. What is striking here is that Williams elides differences

46. Williams, "Drama in a Dramatized Society," 11.

47. Williams, "Drama in a Dramatized Society," 12.

48. Williams, "Drama in a Dramatized Society," 14–15.

49. Jennifer Wicke, *Advertising Fictions*, 11. The *Scrutiny* group around F. R. Leavis was important to Williams's professional formation: see McGuigan, *Raymond Williams: Cultural Analyst*, 9–10.

between advertising's representations and those of drama without anything resembling that earlier fury or that later apocalyptic note.[50] The contemporary "need" for drama resembles the need the London crowd had "at an early stage" for the "new kinds of sign" that would at the very least simulate "a human identity." And "need" emerges as a keyword for this essay: having "lost any common and settled idea of man," representations become necessary. Advertising in Wordsworth's London satisfied this need; drama in Williams's present—very often on television, sometimes in the cinema, and occasionally in the theater—satisfies this need.

The collapse of theater and film into drama and the suggestion that drama may share a function with advertising as a discourse that plugs the empty space once occupied by a "common and settled idea of man" challenge the avant-garde belief that a genuine theater would disrupt the ideological structure of the mass-mediated culture surrounding it. In that avant-garde discourse, advertising as the degree zero of mass culture is the evil twin of the desire for participation: advertising does make you do something, but what it makes you do only increases the alienation that the ideal of participation is designed to combat. The plays on which I focus here are not so sanguine about what participation might achieve; they are also marked by the knowledge, as Wicke writes, that modern literature "has its reading parameters determined by the linguistic horizon of advertising—a language that emanates from everywhere and nowhere."[51]

In a long new foreword to his *Critique of Everyday Life* completed in 1957, Henri Lefebvre, probably in part informed by the excitement around the visit of the Berliner Ensemble to Paris in 1955, meditates on the power and the contradictions of Brechtian dramaturgy and asks whether the ambitions of Brecht's theater had been justified. Lefebvre stresses Brecht's association of participation with identification in the classical theater and its "espousal of accepted norms and values," its consecration of a "negative" aspect of everyday life: "the magic of participation and ritual." Lefebvre flatly notes one basic shortcoming: "Nowhere—even in Germany—does it seem to have become truly popular." Lefebvre implicitly contrasts Brecht with Charlie Chaplin, the other performing artist to receive extensive attention in the foreword. A more expansive discussion concerns Brecht and the spectator:

50. Wicke writes of Williams's article, "The Magic System," that it "provides a sense of the global importance of advertising, while nonetheless shrouding this discovery in the apocalyptic garb often featured by highly conservative commentators on modern culture" (*Advertising Fictions*, 8).

51. Wicke, *Advertising Fictions*, 53.

The spectator wavers between an externalized judgement—an intellectual state which implies high culture—and an immersion in the image proposed. Perhaps this is what the dialectic of the *Verfremdungseffekt* is. The spectator is meant to *disalienate* himself in and through the consciousness of alienation. He is meant to feel wrenched from his self but only in order to enter more effectively into his self and become conscious of the real and the contradictions of the real. Unfortunately, there is a risk that this process will take on the disturbing form, worse even than classic identification, of *fascination*. Whether it be to compare them or contrast the two, French partisans of Brecht's theatre nearly always refer to Antonin Artaud's theatre of cruelty. The violence of dramatic effects, of the lighting, of the images, make it even more impossible for the spectator to relax his mind and momentarily resolve his inner tension by identifying with the hero or by escaping into a kind of dream. There is a danger that unity will be re-established momentarily in the spectator's disoriented mind, caught up as he is by the image; for tension needs moments of respite; expectation demands to be satisfied, if only fleetingly. Unable to find this in a 'classic' completeness, there is a danger that he will look for them in a sort of bloody ecstasy. Therefore generalized strangeness entails a danger (which was avoided by Brecht, but not necessarily by the people who produce his plays or write about them). An art based on alienation must struggle against alienation; if not it sanctions it.[52]

Like Williams, Lefebvre is concerned with the force of the image: his understanding of a dialectic within the *Verfremdungseffekt* rests on his reading of Brecht's dramaturgy as based not on a rejection of immersion or identification but on that spectatorial wavering: immersion, identification, capture by the image; then withdrawal. The moment of capture is one kind of alienation: a wrenching away of the self that can be ecstatic or thrilling but which, in the next movement of the spectatorial dialectic, is followed by consciousness of "the real and the contradictions of the real." That Lefebvre associates that moment of "externalized judgement" with "high culture" may imply that immersion, identification, and, even worse, fascination are the results not only of misbegotten Brechtian or Artaudian theatrical projects but also of a mass culture that similarly alienates but prevents that swerve toward judgment: "fascination" here returns to its magical roots and names the enchantment of the undialectical and unceasing immersion in "generalized strangeness." The danger, that is, is the society of the spectacle, and Lefebvre's question is whether drama can be made to struggle against it.

52. Henri Lefebvre, *Critique of Everyday Life*, 23–24.

With the exception of Raymond Williams, each of the arguments surveyed so far in this section preserves a divide between mass culture and theater, and imagines that theater might counter the force of mass culture. This belief was crucial to a range of avant-garde and experimental practice. In 1965, LeRoi Jones / Amiri Baraka implicitly countered this: "Art is method. And art, 'like any ashtray or senator,' remains in the world. Wittgenstein said that ethics and aesthetics are one. I believe this. So the Broadway theatre is a theatre of reaction whose ethics, like its aesthetics, reflects the spiritual values of this unholy society, which sends young crackers all over the world blowing off colored peoples heads."[53] For Baraka, the aesthetic of Broadway was complicit in the colonial warfare of an "unholy society," and the revolutionary theater would counter this. Baraka, then, would seem to subscribe to something like the argument this section has traced: the ethical methods of the avant-garde against Broadway and the other apparatuses that perpetuate wars "all over the world." There is no trace in this essay, however, that Jones believes that any other actually existing theater, Off-Broadway, Off-Off-, or anywhere else, would survive the accusations he levels at Broadway. The basic division between hegemonic spectacle and theater as "counter-atmosphere," again to invoke Blau's term, does not survive because theater has never yet been revolutionary in Baraka's sense: it is part of the racist atmosphere that genuinely revolutionary theater would destroy. "Clay, in *Dutchman*, Ray in *The Toilet*, Walker in *The Slave*, are all victims. In the Western sense they could be heroes. But the Revolutionary Theatre, even if it is Western, must be anti-Western. It must show horrible coming attractions of *The Crumbling of The West*. Even as Artaud designed *The Conquest of Mexico*, so we must design *The Conquest of White Eye*, and show the missionaries and wiggly Liberals dying under blasts of concrete. For sound effects, wild screams of joy, from all the peoples of the world."[54] Like so many of his contemporaries, Baraka invokes Artaud, but few of these contemporaries matched Jones in his pointed endorsement of the necessity of theatrical violence or in his echo of Artaud's desire to produce theater, with its "horrible coming attractions" and "sound effects," as transcendently violent mass culture.

The desire to produce a theater that might undo the social separation and alienation produced a series of experiments in, or proposals for, or fantasies of the dissolution of the divide between performer and audience.

---

53. Jones, "The Revolutionary Theatre," in *Home*, 212.

54. Jones, "The Revolutionary Theatre," in *Home*, 211.

The history of this desire, of which the preceding section is one fragment, is fascinating. That rapturous dissolution, at once political and erotic, sometimes remains the goal of a theater of declared radical intentions. The case studies that follow focus on a different kind of theater and a different kind of politics.

[FOURTEEN]

Artaud's Voice against Radio

In the last year of his life, Antonin Artaud worked toward a radio broadcast, *To have done with the judgment of god*. It was, notoriously, cancelled.[1] In the aftermath of its cancellation, Artaud protested vehemently, often invoking the vast public that awaited it. In a letter to the head of French radio, who was responsible for the decision, Artaud refers to "the great majority of the public [*la grosse masse du public*] | who looked to it for a kind of deliverance."[2] In related letters, Artaud frequently invokes that phantom majority who had so eagerly awaited the broadcast. The same phrase appears when Artaud writes to Fernand Pouey, the supportive producer who had commissioned the broadcast: Artaud considers the "unsophisticated listener" and affirms that

the truth is that
never
has a broadcast been ANTICIPATED with greater curiosity and impatience by the great mass of the public [*la grosse masse du public*] who were specifically waiting for this broadcast to help form an attitude to confront certain aspects of life.[3]

1. For a succinct account of the circumstances of the broadcast's cancellation, see Weiss, "From Schizophrenia to Schizophonica: Antonin Artaud's *To have done with the judgment of god*," in *Phantasmic Radio*, 12–13. The indispensable collected French edition of Artaud's work provides material for a broader picture. It includes not only texts relevant to the broadcast but also a dossier including contemporary press responses to the broadcast and its cancellation alongside letters from Artaud and others (*Œuvres complètes*, vol. 13). The first publication of the text of the broadcast, by the publisher K in 1948, already includes a similar, if smaller, dossier of texts: the broadcast as print object has long existed alongside texts about the controversy.

2. Artaud, letter to Wladimir Porché, February 4, 1948, in *Selected Writings*, 578; *Œuvres complètes*, 13:130.

3. Artaud, letter to Fernand Pouey, February 7, 1948, in *Selected Writings*, 581; *Œuvres complètes*, 13:134.

The broadcast, Artaud believed, would, at last, have achieved that mass impact that was one of the aspirations of his conflicted project:

> I mean that this broadcast [*émission*] was a search for a language which the humblest road-mender or coal-seller would have understood, a language which conveyed by means of bodily transmission [*émission*] the highest metaphysical truths.[4]

The transmission of a bodily language over the airwaves recalls but also differs from the dream of transparent hieroglyphic bodily speech in Artaud's earlier texts, including *The Theatre and Its Double*. The erasure of the radio as medium, where its *émission* becomes bodily, is part of a long project of Artaud's attempts to undo mediation. Artaud imagines that his own radio project might uniquely short-circuit the technology's mediation of the body, that his voice might overcome radio's most basic limitation and potential: the absence of the body.

How did those in theater rethink their relation to audiences in the light of cultural forms that were addressed at once to everyone and to no one in particular? The example of Artaud suggests how the *idea* of radio and the direction of its address to an unspecified mass of auditors shaped postwar experiments in the theater. In postwar France, the media historian Hélène Eck has shown, radio articulated itself as a medium for the formation a genuinely popular national culture. Radio would be the forum where, according to an official proposal of 1946, "in all the realms of art and of thought, the conceptions of the spirit [or mind or intellect: '*les conceptions de l'esprit*'], may be made public [*puissent être exposés*]."[5] The radio would be, in short, "the voice of France."[6] Before dismissing this last formulation as empty cliché, an idiom made all too familiar by the Voice of America (or by a 1935 film about the BBC, *The Voice of Britain*), it's worth emphasizing how, in such projects for state radio, the unitary voice of the radio should become the medium for a multiplicity of conceptions: one voice conveys all there is to convey. Is it impossible to imagine that we might have spoken since 1942, for instance, of the Voices of America? Such a plural form also carries on the fantasy of full democratic representation, a confidence that the voice of state radio might bring all the products of the spirit to the open ears of the public.

4. Artaud, letter to René Guilly, February 7, 1948, in *Selected Writings*, 583; *Œuvres complètes*, 13:137.

5. Eck, "Radio, culture et démocratie en France," 55 (my translation).

6. Eck, "Radio, culture et démocratie en France," 58.

To have done with the judgment of god challenged this ideal in virtually every possible way. If the ideology of state radio holds that its voice builds the very public it addresses—builds it by addressing it—Artaud's broadcast challenges the logics of voice and of publics that underwrite this ideology. The status of address is especially problematic in texts Artaud produced while in various asylums during World War II and in the years before his death in March, 1948. Among these are a number of quite remarkable "spells," as they have been called in English: scrawled by hand and punctured by burns, addressed to individuals ranging from Artaud's friends to, most notoriously, Hitler, these "spells" seem to be at once intended for their named addressees and to be marked by the logic of any incantation, broadcast to a particular named addressee and to invisible powers alike. *To have done with the judgment of god*, a work for radio in five loosely related parts and performed by Artaud in collaboration with Roger Blin, María Césares, and Paule Thévenin, was likewise a generic experiment with medium, voice, and problems of address. More bluntly, it was Artaud's experiment in radio against radio. It was also a satire on the situation of, and fantasies about, media in the postwar world.

To have done with begins with Artaud's voice speaking with idiosyncratic and choppy deliberateness, his voice a hybrid of argumentative crank in a café and Sarah Bernhardt. Artaud speaks the opening of the address:

> I learned yesterday
> (you must think that I'm very slow, or perhaps it is only a false rumor, some of the dirty gossip that is peddled between the sink and the latrines at the hour when the buckets are filled with meals once again regurgitated),
> I learned yesterday
> about one of the most sensational official practices of the American public schools
> which no doubt make that county consider itself at the head of progress.
> Apparently, among the examinations or tests that a child has to undergo on entering a public school for the first time is the one called the seminal liquid or sperm test,
> which consists of asking this newly-enrolled child for a little of his sperm in order to put it in a glass jar
> and of thereby keeping it ready for all the attempts at artificial insemination which might eventually take place.
> For more and more the Americans find that they lack manpower and children,
> that is, not workers

but soldiers,
and at all costs and by all possible means they want to make and
manufacture soldiers
in view of all the planetary wars which might subsequently take place,
and which would be destined to *demonstrate* by the crushing virtues of
force
the superexcellence of American products,
and the fruits of American sweat in all the fields of activity and potential
dynamism of force.[7]

Listening to or reading that opening, or shuttling between recording and
text, it may be that the chief historical surprise surrounding Artaud's last
effort for radio is not that the broadcast was cancelled, as it was the day
before the scheduled transmission, but that it was ever scheduled at all. The
rhetoric surrounding Artaud's broadcast is, however, important here. This
rhetoric illuminates a moment in the history of what Gregory Whitehead
and Edward Miller call "radiovoice."

Two points from Miller's treatment of the radiovoice in his *Emergency
Broadcasting* are important to stress here. First, that voice is acousmatic;
that is, a radio voice is detached from any particular body. Second, that
voice, in the United States in the 1930s, tended to be male. Both claims
might also safely be made of France in the immediate postwar period. So
Artaud's recorded voice overturns one of the hegemonic features of the radiovoice. Ambiguously gendered, cutting across the grain of the comfort-
ably trained and authoritative male voice of the radio, Artaud's seems at
once in the tradition of the grandly mannered enunciation of the French
classical stage and to claim an authority precisely on the basis of its undoing
of the normative conditions of the radio or, for that matter, of everyday
speech. As Miller also stresses, for the radio listener a voice may conjure a
body: "Depriving an auditor of the source of the voice provokes a fantasy
of the originary body."[8] If, to borrow Allen Weiss's word, the experience of
radio is almost inevitably "phantasmic," if it involves the construction of an
imagined body out of the grain of the broadcast voice, then one might ask
what sort of body Artaud's voice conjures.

7. Artaud, *To have done with the judgment of god*, in *Watchfiends and Rack Screams*,
284–85; *Œuvres complètes*, 13: 71–72. My source for Artaud's broadcast is the Sub Rosa
CD; at the time of this writing, the recording remains available on *UbuWeb*. The UCSB
Cylinder Audio Archive includes a recording of Sarah Bernhardt as Phèdre from 1910.

8. Miller, *Emergency Broadcasting*, 6.

In considering Artaud's introductory monologue, this question immediately divides itself into a pair of questions, for not only might his voice invoke the phantasm of his body, of the body invoked by his strained, weirdly formal, oddly formalized enunciation, but this opening passage invokes a series of other disturbing bodies: the bodies of the American schoolchildren who must submit to the "seminal liquid or sperm test" and the bodies of the soldiers produced through artificial insemination. That is, Artaud's broadcast begins, one might say, as an allegory of radio's phantasmic power, of its production of artificial bodies out there among the cherished listeners of radio land, what the French dubbed *les cherzauditeurs*. This compound noun, which occurs a few times in the newspaper accounts of the cancellation of his broadcast, itself marks a group produced precisely by its listening, by its being addressed by voices on the radio.[9] While the pun on "emission" is not as neat in French as in English, surely the system of state-mandated ejaculations Artaud imagines in the schools also rhymes with the control of diurnal and nocturnal radio emissions by the French state. This introductory section, then, is not only a fierce, comic critique of the new political alignments of the Cold War—Artaud will soon warn his listeners about "Stalin's Russia" as well[10]—but also, and perhaps more immediately, an undermining of radio's logic of mass dissemination. Artaud's experiment with a voice that cannot be incorporated—or, maybe more accurate, a voice that incorporates itself painfully—announces itself explicitly as the voice of an anti-American critique. But the very outlandishness of that critique, with its story of the harvesting of sperm from pubescent kindergartners, points to an object at once less distinct and closer to hand:

Because there must be production,
nature must be replaced wherever it can be replaced by every possible means of activity,
a major field must be found for human inertia,
the worker must be kept busy at something,
new fields of activity must be created,
where all the false manufactured products,
all the ignoble synthetic ersatzes will finally reign . . . [11]

9. For "cherzauditeurs" (variously spelled), see Artaud, *Œuvres complètes*, 13:330; 336.

10. Artaud, *To have done with the judgment of god*, in *Watchfiends and Rack Screams*, 286.

11. Artaud, *To have done with the judgment of god*, in *Watchfiends and Rack Screams*, 285.

The first phrase here, it seems to me, marks a break. If the opening scenario describes a freakish United States, itself a creation of rumors, or "noise," the command that "there must be production" is not limited to the American example. Artaud's satire of the rule of production marks this reign of "ignoble synthetic ersatzes" as universal. In short, while the text never names France, its subject is at least as much France as it is the United States, and France's "artificial insemination factories"—that is to say, in the tenor of Artaud's satire, its radio, where the ear exposes itself to "false manufactured products."

In the fall of 1947, Artaud wrote several texts for the broadcast that were not, in the end, included, largely because of limitations on time. Artaud intended one of these texts as an introduction to the section on America that I have been discussing. After seventeen lines of glossolalia, the text addresses its would-be auditor:

> Whoever is sick to the bone like me
> need only think of me,
> he will not meet me in spirit along the route through spaces
> because what's the good of meeting in spirit
> and not meeting in body?

A few lines later, Artaud again invokes a listener:

> whoever has pain in the gums like me and who thinks of me, the space
> that has separated us turns to dust,
> it dwindles and becomes smaller, and it's that, space, which becomes
> blind and not me ... [12]

Artaud would die only months after writing and recording the broadcast: one can read this fantasy of corporal connection with a similarly ailing addressee as Artaud's working through fears about his own dying body. Artaud projects blindness and diminution onto the body of space that separates him from an audience, and Artaud and audience alike are made anew in the reunion of their radiophonic bodies without organs. And yet this utopian language also invokes one of the more familiar rhetorics for the workings of radio and mass communication more generally. What is the force of radio supposed to be but that of overcoming the power of space? That is to say, Artaud's invocation of a phantasmatic union with his addressee has a peculiar poignancy given the state of his singularly blasted body, with its history

12. Artaud, *Œuvres complètes*, 13:247–48 (my translation).

of addictions and shock treatments, but the melancholy iconicity of that body alone does not describe how this passage works.

An altered public required a remade theater. Michael Warner's *Publics and Counterpublics* offers theoretical clarification of the historical problem theater faced in these years. "Much of the art of writing, or of performing in other media," Warner writes, "lies in the practical knowledge that there are always many different ways of addressing a public, that each decision of form, style, and procedure carries hazards and costs in the kinds of public it can define. The temptation is to think of publics as something we make, through individual heroism and creative inspiration or through common goodwill."[13] Surely the career of *To have done* is a vivid illustration of what can happen when the rhetoric of a particular text collides with a historically concrete, if also changeable, organization of media. Fernand Pouey, who commissioned Artaud's broadcast, was not in some simple way "wrong" to have done so; it is conceivable that things might have gone the other way: the transmission might have been broadcast. A scant two years after the end of the war, French state radio was itself an apparatus in the process of becoming an institution, testing ideologies of listening and the restrictions on the freedom of speech that radio seemingly demanded. (The broadcast had been scheduled for 10:45 p.m., an hour when, commentators observed, children and old maids would be asleep.[14]) One way to describe Artaud's career might be to say that the self-extinguishing power of his texts comes from his belief that he could make—or, just as important, destroy—a public through individual heroic effort.

In a review that provoked an outraged response from Artaud, René Guilly wrote in the newspaper *Combat* that he approved of the decision to ban Artaud's recording. Guilly sums up his objections: "This brilliant madman [*Ce fou génial*] is not—and should not be—by nature a public figure [*un homme public*]."[15] The two antagonists agree that *To have done*, had it been broadcast, would have had a mass audience. Guilly imagines the million protest letters that would have followed the broadcast; Artaud imagines the "mass audience" that would have greeted it: "hairdressers, / laundresses, / tobacconists, / ironmongers, carpenters, printers, / in short, all people who earn their living by the sweat of their elbows, / and not certain capitalists of dung / grown rich in secret / who go to mass every Sunday and who

13. Warner, *Publics and Counterpublics*, 14.

14. See, for instance, Pierre Joffroy, "Une émission fait du bruit," in Artaud, *Œuvres complètes*, 13:329.

15. René Guilly, "Antonin Artaud: Sera-t-il l'auteur radiophonique maudit?," in Artaud, *Œuvres complètes*, 13:356 (my translation).

desire above all the respect of ritual and of the law."[16] Artaud understands the cancellation as the sin of forbidding "a human voice that was addressing itself for the first time in this age to the best in man / to speak out." That is to say, Guilly's declaration that Artaud could not be a public man directly contradicts Artaud's understanding of his broadcast as an address to a mass working-class audience, as quintessentially public, or, that is, thoroughly counterpublic:

THE DUTY

of the writer, of the poet
is not to shut himself up like a coward in a text, a book, a magazine from
which he never comes out
but on the contrary to go
into the world

to jolt [*pour secouer*],
to attack [*pour attaquer*]
the mind of the public [*l'esprit public*],
otherwise
what use is he?[17]

According to Guilly, Artaud's brilliant madness excludes him from the ranks of the public figures and, indeed, almost from the public itself; for Artaud, his principled attack on "mind of the public" defines the *public* value of his or any writer's work. It is not clear that this formulation is sufficiently strong: depending upon how one understands Artaud's "*esprit public*," one might say that he understands his assault to be one upon the "public spirit" itself, on the very notion of a transcendent essence that defines the public. That is to say that, in France, in 1947–48, Artaud imagined radio against radio.

In one of Artaud's last, pained, and most poignant letters, lamenting the suppression of his radio work, he describes once more his aspirations for a true theater of cruelty and proclaims: "*Cela se fera*": "This will happen."

Wherever the *machine* is
there is always the abyss and the void [*le néant*],
there is a technical intervention that distorts and annihilates what one
has done.
[...]
this is why I am through with Radio

16. Artaud, *Selected Writings*, 582; *Œuvres complètes*, 13:135–36.
17. Artaud, *Selected Writings*, 582–83; *Œuvres complètes*, 13:136–37.

and from now on will devote myself
exclusively
to the theater
as I conceive it,
a theater of blood,
a theater which with each performance will have done
something
bodily
to the one who performs as well as to the one who comes to see others
perform,
but actually
the actors are not performing,
they are doing.[18]

18. Artaud, letter to Paule Thévenin, February 24, 1948, *Selected Writings*, 585;
Œuvres complètes, 13:146–47.

[FIFTEEN]

Publics

Over the first pages of their *Public Sphere and Experience*, Oskar Negt and Alexander Kluge make a fundamental distinction:

> The public sphere denotes specific **institutions,** agencies, practices (e.g., those connected with law enforcement, the press, public opinion, the public, public sphere work, streets, and public squares); however, it is also a general social **horizon of experience** in which everything that is actually or ostensibly relevant for all members of society is integrated. Understood in this sense, the public sphere is a matter for a handful of professionals (e.g., politicians, editors, union officials) on the one hand, but, on the other, it is something that concerns everyone and that realizes itself only in people's minds, in a dimension of their consciousness.[1]

The public sphere is, then, at once a plural set of apparatuses and a singular "general social horizon of experience" that integrates the effects of these various apparatuses in the minds of those who are part of the public sphere. This distinction between various apparatuses and the horizon of experience seems to me useful and important to thinking about the place of theater and about the large question of the politics of theater. A primary question concerns the definition of this sphere, and more particularly theater, in relation to this basic division in the public sphere. Is theater part of the public sphere? Theater scholars have long been somewhat chagrined that Jürgen Habermas, in the book that accelerated the debate about the public sphere, seems to exclude theater precisely because it gathers people bodily rather than contributing to the abstraction and disembodiment of persons that the public sphere requires.[2] Newspapers and the novel are crucial to the public

1. Negt and Kluge, *Public Sphere and Experience*, 1–2.

2. See Habermas, *The Structural Transformation of the Public Sphere* and Christopher Balme's revisionary account, *The Theatrical Public Sphere*. Other works important

sphere, a distinction made also in Benedict Anderson's *Imagined Communities*; the theater, it seems, is not. The question of whether the theater is in itself among the institution of the public sphere may be less useful, however, than the matter of how it relates to it. How do works of drama and theater, in particular periods, respond to those "specific institutions, agencies, practices"? There is a tendency to imagine that theater, itself an apparatus or set of apparatuses, must claim its political force by responding, whether through negation or affirmation, to the public sphere understood as the generalized horizon of experience. Theater, it seems, is that apparatus that must take upon itself the work of constituting a global response to that generalized sphere. This insistence that theater constitute such a counterpublic force in relation to the public sphere as a whole leads, on the one hand, to claims about its political efficacy, or its political failures, that follow logically from the grand initial claims made for theater. Theater's negation of totality in the spirit of Adorno, for instance, allows theater all the power in the world so long as it does not wander from the aesthetic sphere, so long as it abides by the taboo against addressing anything in particular. One faces an antinomy placing theater's direct political force or, more often, its failures against the power of negation, always in reserve, which may nevertheless contain the kernel of a utopian potential to be realized in some other time and in some place other than the theater.

Returning to discussions of the public sphere has the potential to be useful for theater studies, I think, if we ask other questions. What if, rather than asking whether theater somehow negates the whole of the public sphere, one were to allow a set of more particular questions? These questions would assume that while theater very often engages with apparatuses of the public sphere, and especially with media of the public sphere, it is nevertheless distinct from those apparatuses and media. This relationship is, further, a historical one: no transhistorical generalization about theater as medium can be assumed, as the relationship between theater as medium and the media of a changing public sphere is not constant.

Such questions might include:

- How might theater respond not to the public sphere as generalized horizon but to particular apparatuses that produce that horizon?
- How do the apparatuses of theater work like other apparatuses in the public sphere?

---

to my sense of theater's relation to its publics include Michael Warner's *Publics and Counterpublics* (which does not concentrate on theater) and Nicholas Ridout's *Theatre and Ethics, Passionate Amateurs,* and *Scenes from Bourgeois Life* (which do).

- How might attending to homologies between theatrical and other apparatuses allow for a more nuanced account of the politics of theater?
- How does the embodied critique of technologies of abstraction in the public sphere allow for theorization of a specifically theatrical politics?

Versions of these questions will circulate through discussions of playwrights and plays below. A result of asking questions along these lines will be that rather than invoking "the" media, there will be attention to particular media and to particular objects. Tracking the historical character of theater's engagement with the public sphere—of its uneasy place within and partial alienation from that sphere—will mean tracking specific objects, specific intersections, specific contradictions.

[SIXTEEN]

Handke's *Offending the Audience*

Peter Handke continues to offend. The controversies surrounding his *A Journey to the Rivers: Justice for Serbia*, first published as a set of articles in a German newspaper in 1996, and his speech at the funeral of Slobodan Milošević in 2006 have had the effect of a peculiar *Nachleben*, dragging everything written before these provocations along with them.[1] And yet what Rainer Nägele wrote in 1980, well before these controversies, remains true of *Offending the Audience* and Handke's other early plays: despite his seemingly "apolitical" rhetoric, "his texts participate objectively in the political and social movements of the period."[2] Those earlier plays belong to a context that his later commitments should not wholly erase. There are also, however, continuities between the earlier theater and the logic of *A Journey to the Rivers*. The later book even shares, in a rough way, a structure with *Offending the Audience*, beginning with sections that confront the media; continuing with the longest section, which strives to transcend those mediated representations; and ending with a re-immersion in the critique of mediated representations. There are even, late in the text of 1996, untranslatable German invectives that recall the long, various, and contradictory catalog of insults over the last pages of the play of thirty years before: Handke condemns a German journalist as "Reisswolf and Geifermüller."[3]

1. For a superb discussion of Handke's engagement with the wars in Yugoslavia, see Branislav Jakovljević's "Fording the Stream of Conscience."

2. Nägele, "Peter Handke: The Staging of Language," 328.

3. Handke, *A Journey to the Rivers*, 77. The translator gives a literal version of these insults and explains a reason for them: "slashing wolf and vicious-tongued miller—a play on the last name of Johann Georg Reismüller, an editor of the *FAZ* [the *Frankfurter Allgemeine Zeitung*]" (77). This explanation exemplifies how deeply the text (at least at this juncture) belongs inside the discourse of German journalism that Handke attacks. Handke's German text does not name the editor but the allusive expectation is that the reader will know the target of these invectives. A connected pair of examples may suggest the freedom, and also the political stakes, of Roloff's 1969 translation. Roloff

97

No play better exemplifies the dialectic of theater and mass culture in the period I am concerned with than *Offending the Audience*, first performed on June 8, 1966, at the Theater am Turm in Frankfurt.[4] The play's staging of theatrical spectatorship, from the behavior of ushers to the attention of the audience, transpired as a response to and negation of the dominant forms of spectatorship in the period. One of the work's remarkable paratexts, *"Rules for the actors,"* makes something about the conditions of theatrical engagement in these years absolutely clear: immersion in a larger mediascape was the condition for rethinking theater. Handke's play presents immersion in the larger medium, in Benjamin's sense, as the prerequisite for the play's distillation of theatrical constraints and conventions. Handke's rules convey imperatives concerning a variety of publics, media, technologies, and behaviors. The rules list things the actors should listen to and watch, beginning with Catholic litanies and ending with "the behavior of bums and idlers [*Tagediebe und Nichtstuer*] as they amble on the street and play the machines in the penny arcades."[5] The list is remarkable for the contrast between the specificity of these rules and the silence about what the reasons for them might be.

One example: "Listen to 'Tell Me' by the Rolling Stones."[6] There are several ways to think about this listening. By June 1966, the Rolling Stones had already released several long-playing records, and the song appeared on the first of these; "Tell Me" had also been released as a single in Germany in 1964, as the B-side to "It's All Over Now." The song, the Stones' second hit in Germany, was on the German charts for four weeks in 1965, peaking at 22.[7] (Handke, that is, might well have listened to it frequently while writing

---

transforms Handke's "Genickschußspezialisten"—specialists in shots to the neck—into "napalm specialists" and "Nazischweine"—Nazi pigs—into "killer pigs," thus erasing the specificity of terms associated with Nazi murders and connecting the audience instead to war crimes in Vietnam and, maybe, to homicidal American policemen (Handke, *Publikumsbeschimpfung*, in *Stücke 1*, 45; *Offending the Audience*, in *Kaspar and Other Plays*, 30). In a note, Roloff slyly claims that he was merely seeking "new acoustic patterns" in English (*Kaspar and Other Plays*, vii), disavowing the deliberate redirection of Handke's insults into a US context.

4. For a detailed account of the first performance and of the play's subsequent stage history, see Defraeye, "You! Hypocrite Spectateur."

5. Handke, *Offending the Audience*, in *Kaspar and Other Plays*, 3; Handke, *Publikumsbeschimpfung*, in *Stücke 1*, 13.

6. Handke, *Offending the Audience*, in *Kaspar and Other Plays*, 3. The full list of rules appears on this page.

7. See Offizielle deutsche Charts, https://www.offiziellecharts.de, accessed July 11, 2024. Wikipedia has also been very helpful about discographical matters.

the play.) How might docile actors have followed this rule? Would they have sought out an LP or 45? Visited a bar with a jukebox? Waited for it to come round on the radio? These questions emphasize the very different media-historical moment in which Handke devised his rules, but one might also ask: Why *this* song? Another of Handke's rules might provide a clue: "Listen to the hit parade [*Hitparade*] on Radio Luxembourg." Radio Luxembourg was one of Europe's first commercial radio stations, with aspirations to reach the whole continent, and these songs are hits, not rarities: "Tell Me" is in the mix precisely because it was widely heard. And yet this doesn't yet tell us anything about why the actors should listen to *this* song: there were, after all, many hits.

"Tell Me" is an imperative; the song appears in Handke's list of imperatives. (This is especially striking in English translation: the verbs that appear at the beginning of each rule in English appear, less urgently, at the end of each rule in German.) Further, the force of this imperative is unclear. The song's fuller title suggests the problem: "Tell Me (You're Coming Back)." The record's insistent repetition of this phrase could convey persuasive force, or, more convincingly, rhetorical failure: in the space of the song, anyway, repetition suggests that you are not coming back, that you have not come back, that you will not come back. The increasingly desperate imperative, in turn, links the particular romantic situation of this song to larger questions of mass cultural address: the singer addresses an intimate listener over the radio waves. This address, in turn, illuminates problems of address in Handke's play. Handke writes of his so-called *Sprechstücke*, or speaking plays: "They need a vis-à-vis [*eines Gegenübers*], at least *one* person who listens; otherwise, they would not be natural but extorted by the author."[8] Mick Jagger, again and again, sings, "You gotta tell me you're coming back to me": is this an example of failed address, of would-be extortion? The song is *about* mediation, and in particular the mediation of desire: "I hear the telephone that hasn't rung." The radio listener has no way to reply, and the song's words imagine the sound of this non-reply. The Stones take advantage of the very feature of radio that Brecht thought of as a flaw: that there was no channel through which the listener could reply. The song imagines a situation of mediated, intimate non-communication in a broadcast medium that violates the dyad of a point-to-point medium. (That the voice of Mick Jagger can bear an intimate charge complicates this. A particular listener may think: oh, but *I* will, I would come back.)

---

8. Handke, *Offending the Audience*, in *Kaspar and Other Plays*, ix; Handke, *Stücke 1*, 201. Roloff's translation of *Sprechstücke* as "speak-ins" is one of several moments where a desire for contemporary connotations overtakes accuracy.

"Tell Me" illuminates a problem for postwar drama: what is theatrical address? What had it become? *Offending the Audience* ends with explicit insults, but the play's laconic address to its audience, delivered not by "actors," as the rules would suggest, but instead by "four speakers," as the skeletal dramatis personae specifies, offends from the start by describing the situation of the theater instead of representing a drama:

> You will hear what you usually see.
> You will hear what you usually don't see here.
> You will see no spectacle [*Schauspiel*].
> Your curiosity [*Schaulust*] will not be satisfied.
> You will see no play [*Spiel*].
> There will be no playing here tonight. [*Hier wird nicht gespielt werden.*]
> You will see a spectacle without pictures [*Schauspiel ohne Bilder*].[9]

The presumption here is that the audience desires what it does not get, that the piece does not satisfy all the complex spectatorial desires suggested by the words (and variants of) *Schau* (the root of *schauen*, to look) and *Spiel* (play): the pleasures of seeing and desiring to see and to be seen, in short, of scopophilia, of watching impersonation, of drama, of images. This *Schauspiel* will satisfy no *Schaulust*. Roloff's translation of *Schauspiel* as "spectacle" is tendentious—the standard rendition would be, simply, "play"—but this translation does capture the mass cultural context of those desires the work engages while it refuses to satisfy them. Meanwhile, his translation of *Schaulust* as simply "curiosity" avoids important connotations of this word, which has a complex history in English translation. Sigmund Freud's authoritative translators, so enamored of turning more or less familiar words in German into technical and Latinate terms, rendered his *Schaulust* as "scopophilia," capturing the condition's potential kinkiness but not its everyday currency. In a comment that illuminates the difficulty Roloff faced as translator, Jean Laplanche remarks, "We use the word 'scoptophilia,' even though it is a fairly recherché translation of a term that is very common in German: *Lust*, combining as it does both desire and pleasure, is almost

---

9. Handke, *Offending the Audience*, in *Kaspar and Other Plays*, 7; Handke, *Publikumsbeschimpfung*, in *Stücke 1*, 19. I have added "here" to the second line of Roloff's translation of this passage. In German the line reads: "Sie werden hören, was Sie hier sonst nicht gesehen haben." While Roloff may have excised the word to avoid the awkward homophone of "hear" and "here," the explicit location of the place where this seeing and hearing happens is important.

untranslatable in either French or English."[10] *Schaulust*, that is, has at once an everyday familiarity and is part of a psychoanalytic discourse about the pleasures and desires associated with looking, a discourse that has been especially pervasive in thinking about film. The announcement of what will and what will not happen here on this stage violates the convention that the audience should not be addressed and also the expectation that the theater will offer a drama that will satisfy some of the pleasures of *Schaulust*. The denial of these pleasures and desires does not take place in a vacuum, but inside the space that Handke's rules for the actors, with all their ambiguities, open up. The phrase imagines the theater as usually a space that produces the pleasures of *Schaulust*—plays or spectacles *with* pictures—but that affirmation that here we will see "a spectacle without pictures" is also a negation of film's spectacular production of *Schaulust* on a mass scale.

Returning to the specificities of Handke's rules, and to his particular fascination with rock and roll, illuminates his idiosyncratic attention to mass culture. The Beatles also appear in these rules and, in another paratext, John Lennon appears as the last in the play's list of dedicatees, along with a cluster of German theater artists, including Claus Peymann, the director of the first production. There are many signs of Handke's identification with disruptive white male rock stars: the dedication includes Lennon, not McCartney.[11] Three of Handke's rules belong to a subset that asks the actor to notice something very particular in a movie. One of this set involves the Beatles: "In 'A Hard Day's Night' watch Ringo's smile at the moment when, after having been teased by the others, he sits down at his drums and begins to play." Once again, it is worth thinking about the work that following this rule would have required in 1966: seeking out a screening or, more

10. Laplanche, "To Situate Sublimation," 13.

11. Peymann writes that "the formal structure of this play . . . resembled in an astonishing way the musical structure of the first Beatle records" and writes that the text gave the company "the opportunity to bring the Beatle beat onto the stage" ("Directing Handke," 49). Anja Pompe begins her book on Handke and "pop as poetic principle" with lines from his first, unpublished radio address, "Der Rausch durch die Beatles." Handke celebrates the Beatles as "those who have made the earth unsafe [*die Erde unsicher gemacht haben*]" and those who "have allowed themselves to become unsafe through the Beatles [*welche durch die Beatles sich unsicher machen ließen*]" (Pompe, *Peter Handke: Pop als poetisches Prinzip*, 7). Handke's U.S publishers play along with the cover image with their cover for *Kaspar and Other Plays*, introduced by Farrar, Straus, and Giroux in 1969 and still in print: Handke, photographed apparently in a photo booth, wears dark shades and not by coincidence resembles the Beatles' German friend and collaborator, Klaus Voorman. The same strip appears on the cover of the 1970 Suhrkamp collection, *Prosa Gedichte Theaterstücke Hörspiel Aufsätze* and (altered in the manner of Warhol) on the cover of Pompe's book.

implausibly, finding a print and screening it in private. Imagining these efforts illuminates a certain initiation into a practice of attention. The rules, that is, ask for disciplines of attention unusual in the face of the usual seductions of visual pleasure, to use Laura Mulvey's phrase. It is symptomatic, however, that the longest and strangest of the rules belongs inside the nexus of gendered spectatorial desire that Mulvey analyzed: "Listen to the dialogue between the gangster (Lee J. Cobb) and the pretty girl [*der Schönen*] in 'The Trap,' when the girl [*die Schöne*] asks the gangster how many more people he intends to kill; whereupon the gangster asks, as he leans back, How many are left? and watch the gangster as he says it." Handke names Lee J. Cobb, while the actor Tina Louise, who plays "the pretty girl," loses her name and disappears into her role as "*die Schöne*," the beautiful one, a cipher of what Mulvey calls "*to-be-looked-at-ness*."[12] Strictly speaking, Handke's rule specifies that the actors should *listen* to this dialogue and *watch* the gangster's reply, with all its genocidal overtones. This division between sight and sound recalls the line in the passage from the text quoted above: "You will hear what you usually see." Muddying the difference between hearing and seeing a movie is at once completely colloquial and an estranging pattern inside *Offending the Audience*, which suggests that one can isolate particular senses, separating listening from hearing, in ways that do not conform with usual ways that spectatorship or the senses work. This rule is itself a trap, at once affiliating itself with the most familiar appeal to a gendered *Schaulust* and suggesting that the actor who follows the rules will watch not the beautiful one but instead the gestures of the gangster as he speaks.

In a small way, the rules resist a standard picture of the relationship to mass culture as passive seduction, as all receptivity without selection or will. On the one hand, Handke's rule asks the actor to behave in a way contrary to the training in attention that mass culture inculcates, to pay extraordinary attention to a passing moment, to a gesture. Of course, fans pay such attention all the time, but the trick here is that the actor should pay attention to a moment to which Handke has paid attention and then demands that the actor should pay the same attention: the actor should focus on this moment Handke has isolated. The rules might be seen as an exercise in producing what Pierre Hadot has called the long tradition, dating

---

12. Mulvey, "Visual Pleasure and Narrative Cinema," 62. Handke approximates the dialogue. As Linda Anderson, Tina Louise asks, "How many do you have to kill? How many do you want?" Lee J. Cobb, as the gang leader Massonetti, replies: "How many are there?" It's probable that Handke saw a dubbed version of the film, and the dialogue he reports may more closely resemble that of the dubbed version.

to antiquity, of the spiritual exercise: particular forms of attention to mass culture become a way of life that prepares the actor to offend the audience. The question all of these rules leave open is how they prepare for the performance of *this* play. The rules sketch a cross section of a mediascape, but that mediascape enters into the play itself largely through negation.[13] In this way, Handke's play exemplifies a strand of experimental drama in the period. Contrary to theories of media convergence in the mode of Henry Jenkins or remediation in the mode of Jay David Bolter and Richard Grusin, the media surround determines *Offending the Audience* through its absence: "You recognized that we negate something [*verneinen*]. You recognized that we repeat ourselves. You recognized that we contradict ourselves. You recognized that this piece is conducting an argument with the theater. [*Sie haben erkannt, daß dieses Stück eine Auseinandersetzung mit dem Theater ist.*] You recognized the dialectical structure of the piece. You recognized a certain spirit of contrariness. The intention of the piece became clear to you. You recognized that we primarily negate. You recognized that we repeat ourselves. You recognize."[14] One might re-translate: "You have recognized that this piece is a confrontation with the theater." A confrontation through negation: Handke invokes one of the most famous passages in the German theater, when Goethe's Mephistopheles tells Faust that he is the spirit who negates: "Ich bin der Geist der stets verneint!" (No wonder the audience recognizes this.) And yet this negation also needs to be understood in relation to the play's "confrontation with the theater." Further, the prefatory rules become differently legible around this confrontation. They frame *Offending the Audience* and its confrontation with "the" theater as a matter having to do with a preparatory confrontation with, and an aesthetic negation of, the mediascape. *Offending the Audience* is exemplary of a strand of drama that prevailing media-historical models, because of their reliance on the idea of content or narrative that adapts to changes across media, cannot explain very well. Handke's play announces from the start that it belongs in a particular media surround, but it also challenges its audience and its readers to ask how it belongs to this surround. "Belonging" is itself a metaphor, and my aim is to think about the formal and historical qualities of works that locate themselves in relation to mass culture through negation, and that incorporate—to play with the word—that negation.

13. This media surround arguably infiltrates Roloff's at times very loose translation even more than Handke's German text.

14. Handke, *Offending the Audience*, in *Kaspar and Other Plays*, 14; Handke, *Publikumsbeschimpfung*, in *Stücke 1*, 27.

To gather a small convolute of quotations:

But each further step leads us to remarkable differences between the stage play and the film play. In every respect the film play is further away from the physical reality than the drama and in every respect the greater distance from the physical world brings it nearer to the mental world.

Hugo Münsterberg, 1916

The realism of the cinema follows directly from its photographic nature. Not only does some marvel or some fantastic thing on the screen not undermine the reality of the image, on the contrary it is its most valid justification. Illusion in the cinema is not based as it is in the theater on convention tacitly accepted by the general public; rather, contrariwise, it is based on the inalienable realism of that which is shown.

André Bazin, 1951

On the stage a horse or dog that is not plaster or cardboard causes uneasiness. Unlike cinematography, looking for truth in the real is fatal in the theatre.

Robert Bresson, 1975

The contrast between theatre and films is usually taken to lie in the materials represented or depicted. But exactly where does the difference lie? It's tempting to draw a crude boundary. Theatre deploys artifice while cinema is committed to reality, indeed to an ultimately physical reality which is "redeemed," to use Siegfried Kracauer's striking word, by the camera.

Susan Sontag, 1966

In the cinema as in the theatre, the represented is by definition imaginary; that is what characterises fiction as such, independently of the of the signifiers in charge of it. But the representation is fully real in the theatre, whereas in the cinema it too is imaginary, the material being already a reflection.

Christian Metz, 1977

I see no difference between the theater and movies. It is all theater. It is simply a matter of understanding what theater means. That is not generally understood. I mean, what do you call the place where a movie is made if not a theater?

Jean-Luc Godard, 1968[15]

One could go on. Small wonder, then, that for Handke the urge to compare theater to cinema, stage to screen, becomes the ground of a complaint about comparison as such. Comparison as social practice—a practice closely allied, Handke argues, to the constant and invidious assignation of value and to understanding everything as a commodity—results in the abstraction of objects into "possibilities for comparison."[16] If there is *Schaulust*, scopophilia, there is another, allied compulsion: *Vergleichslust*, the drive to compare, the pleasure in comparison.[17] This drive to compare erases the specificity of objects; their quiddity disappears in the mechanical process of comparison. Comparison, in Handke's essay, indeed becomes a form of defense against recognition of the "incomprehensible, strange, and complicated."[18]

Handke's counterdrive to concentrate on objects in their separateness and strangeness illuminates his rules for actors, which encourage not contemplation of some undifferentiated mass cultural surround but the discipline of attention to particular moments. Handke's work continues to thematize the aesthetics of attention to the particular. On the one hand, this strand leads to

15. Münsterberg, from *The Film: A Psychological Study*, in Mast, Cohen, and Braudy, *Film Theory and Criticism*, 356; Bazin, "Theatre and Cinema," in *Film Theory and Criticism*, 383; Robert Bresson, *Notes on the Cinematographer*, 63; Susan Sontag, "Film and Theatre," in *Film Theory and Criticism*, 363; Christian Metz, *The Imaginary Signifier*, 67: Sterritt, *Jean-Luc Godard: Interviews*, 14. I have chosen to gather these quotations largely from an influential anthology to make the point that the attempt to distinguish cinema from theater has been a central, if changeable, aspect of the canon of film theory. Charles Musser, naming the work of Münsterberg, Bazin, and Metz, remarks: "A central purpose of these meditations on film and theatre was to differentiate the two forms of expression, to show how each was its own distinct art form" ("Towards a History of Theatrical Culture," 4). For succinct historical account of the changing relations between theater and cinema, see Charlie Kiel, "'All the Frame's a Stage'" and Thomas Kuchenbuch, "Theoretical Approaches to Theatre and Film Adaptation: A History," in Chapple and Kattenbelt, eds., *Intermediality in Theatre and Performance*, 169–80. For intriguing comments on the quotation from Godard, especially in relation to *Contempt*, see Dutoit and Bersani, *Forms of Being*, 44–48.

16. Handke, "Theater and Film," 185.

17. Handke, "*Theater und Film*: Das Elend des Vergleichens," in *Ich bin ein Bewohner des Elfenbeinturms*, 66. Handke links this desire to that of the "Kauflustiger" or consumer (66).

18. Handke, "Theater and Film," 186.

Once Again for Thucydides, a series of very closely observed prose vignettes. On the other hand, it informs Handke's idealization of Serbia with its "sharpened and almost crystalline everyday reality."[19] Handke's work makes for a compelling and contradictory chapter in what Rei Terada calls phenomenophilia, the cultivation of *"particularly ephemeral perceptual experiences*, perceptions that seem below or marginal to normal appearance." "To be told what to perceive," writes Terada, "is to be told what not to look at, and when to cut a look short; it's also to be told where to look—to maintain one's focus on the things that matter."[20] Terada does not need to signal that the final phrase—"the things that matter"—carries the censorious endorsement of a norm the phenomenophile resists. This formulation also raises a question about Handke: what phenomenophile would institute rules instructing actors where to look? Handke's rules, it may be, cultivate a resistance to the massified force of something called mass culture: the point, then, would not be dogged obedience to this list but a model for everyday practices of looking away, to use Terada's phrase—a practice that makes possible a theater that does not give in to the massed norms of spectatorship. This practice of looking away would be a *detournement* of the very force that regularly tells you where to look, a modest form of disobedience in the face of an apparatus designed to tell you where to look, a refusal of the things that matter.

On the one hand, this practice of phenomenophilic resistance to mass culture could lead to a celebration of the idiosyncratic folkways of fandom that are a theme of cultural studies: we are all always already poaching mass culture in ways no program can control.[21] On the other hand, Handke's work raises the question of how a representation of phenomenophilia or a list of "rules," however ironically designed, can lead to the pleasurable errancy that that representation describes or those rules seem to proscribe. Let's say I follow the rule to the letter and watch "Ringo's smile at the moment when, after having been teased by the others, he sits down at his drums and begins to play." Given that, by looking for Ringo's smile, I am following this rule, can this be the uncoerced pleasure of the true phenomenophile? Am I seeing what I should see? "Let us imagine a rule intimating to me the way I am to obey it;" writes Ludwig Wittgenstein, "that is, as my eye travels along the line, a voice within me says: '*This* way!' What is the difference between this process of obeying a kind of inspiration and that of

19. Handke, *A Journey to the Rivers*, 69.

20. Terada, *Looking Away*, 3; 200–201.

21. See Certeau's great chapter "Reading as Poaching" in *The Practice of Everyday Life* (165–76). On Handke and popular culture, see also Lutz Koepnick, "Negotiating Popular Culture."

obeying a rule?"[22] Handke's rules intimate that a resistant practice of mass cultural perception—a practice that is, in many of its forms, peculiar in its attention to evanescent detail—is the basis for a new theatrical aesthetic: "This stage [*Bühne*] is no world, just as the world is no stage."[23] The obverse of the close, resistant attention to the passing phenomena of mass culture is a theater that refuses the illusion of appearances: "This is neither make-believe [*Lokalaugenschein*] nor a maneuver. On the one hand we do as if. We do as if we could repeat words. We appear to repeat ourselves. Here is the world of appearances [*Welt des Scheins*]. Here appearance is appearance. Appearance is here appearance."[24] *Lokalaugenschein* is an Austrian idiom for a "visit to a scene of a crime," and so Handke is referring not to "make-believe" in general but to that convention of drama (as of film) that makes the spectator intimately privy to scenes of violence. The insistence on appearance as appearance rejects the convention that theatrical appearance must become something else, the illusion of another, fictional world. This rejection of dramatic illusion is not unique to Handke, although the thoroughness with which the play rejects the trappings of drama—plot, character, fictive space—was arguably unprecedented. Here, it is important to remember the frame *Offending the Audience* does not break and, indeed, insists upon: "The usual theater atmosphere [*gewonhte Theaterstimmung*] should prevail."[25] Handke's elaborate instructions, including the demand that "inappropriately dressed ticket holders should not be admitted," strenuously maintain the habitus of the bourgeois theater, particularly in its postwar German version.[26] The insistence on the decorum of the theater is the

22. Wittgenstein, *Philosophical Investigations*, §232.

23. Handke, *Offending the Audience*, in *Kaspar and Other Plays*, 18; Handke, *Publikumsbeschimpfung*, in *Stücke 1*, 31.

24. Handke, *Offending the Audience*, in *Kaspar and Other Plays*, 17; Handke, *Publikumsbeschimpfung*, in *Stücke 1*, 30.

25. Handke, *Offending the Audience*, in *Kaspar and Other Plays*, 5; Handke, *Publikumsbeschimpfung*, in *Stücke 1*, 15.

26. As June Schlueter notes in this context, "For this nation of state-subsidized theaters, theatergoing was still very much a social event; the participation of the well-dressed audience in the intellectual and emotional life of the drama was often subordinate to participation in the ritual of theater attendance" (*The Plays and Novels of Peter Handke*, 17). An invaluable Hessischer Rundfunk film of the second night of the first production in Frankfurt (sporadically available in a pirated version online) documents the demure, formal attire of the audience—thin dark ties, unostentatious dresses—and more generally the habitus of theatergoing in that place and time. (On the probable date of the recording, see Defraeye, "You! Hypocrite Spectateur," 413–14.) The uproar the performance produces makes that habitus all the more glaringly

obverse of the studious and insistent dismantling of the conventions of drama. This second set of instructions—rules for the director and stage manager?—even specifies that one might produce the illusion that behind the curtains preparations are under way for a drama with a set: "Or, even better, use tape recordings of other performances in which, before the curtain rises, objects are really shifted about. These noises should be amplified to make them more audible, and perhaps should be stylized and arranged so as to produce their own order and uniformity [*Ordnung oder Gesetzmäßigkeit*]." The actors prepare through a practice of deliberate engagement with the technologically reproducible, while a recording might fool the audience. The play's paratexts establish a dynamic with mass culture and reproducibility, first closely observed by the actors and then, behind the curtain, the source of the deception of an unwitting audience. The drive to remake theater happens through the technologies it negates.

---

visible. Thanks to Nick Ridout, whose *Scenes from Bourgeois Life* informs these observations, for drawing this video to my attention.

∴

TENNESSEE WILLIAMS

∵

[SEVENTEEN]

Williams's Material

The cover of a typescript of the screenplay of *The Glass Menagerie* bears Tennessee Williams's handwritten inscription: "I have never read this thing, word of honor!"[1] He may not have read the screenplay but he had seen, and disliked, the Hollywood film made from his first stage success, judging it "horribly mangled."[2] The mock gallantry of the inscription captures the spirit of a disavowal that hovers over many accounts of the process of adaptation from stage to screen: the precious play becomes a "thing" that the erstwhile author vows he has not read. The disavowal is also a joke. (*"Read* it? I didn't even write it!")[3] Very often a rearguard defense of the older medium against the effects of the newer medium, perceived as inevitably coarsening, is folded into such proclamations. In the case of Williams and *The Glass Menagerie*, however, this disavowal is particularly complex. A "film treatment and unproduced screenplay for MGM, titled 'The Gentleman Caller'" preceded the stage play.[4] The screenplay for the film of 1950—the document Williams swears he has not read—is, then, is an adaptation of a stage play of 1945, which itself an adaptation of a screenplay and treatment. And the story doesn't end here: before his time at MGM, Williams had already adapted a short story, "Portrait of a Girl in Glass," for the stage, and this play, too, was called "The Gentleman Caller."

The point here is not to seek an origin in one or another piece of writing or to claim (as the title of this book might seem to do) that work in one medium precedes the other. In Williams's own writing from the summer of 1943, when he was employed by MGM and working on versions of the

---

1. This typescript was on display as part of an exhibition, *This Is: Tennessee Williams & Friends*, at the Columbia University Library in 2011. The document is from the library's Tennessee Williams papers, box 9, folder 6.

2. John Calendo, "Tennessee Talks to John Calendo."

3. With apologies to Andrew Parker, from whom I have stolen the form of this joke.

4. See Thomas Adler, "The Glass Menagerie."

story in different genres, all of these iterations return not to a written origin but to what he calls "material." On June 12, 1943, he writes to Audrey Wood, his agent: "I have completed a long short story, 28 pages, which is another use of the material of 'The Gentleman Caller' and may give you a clearer impression of what will be in it, the stage version."[5] On June 29 he writes, again to Wood, again of "Portrait of A Girl in Glass," that it is a "minor excursion into the same material," and anticipates her response: "I am sure you will think this material too slight for a long play, but the play will necessarily embody a good deal more than the story would suggest, and the character of Amanda should sustain it."[6] Williams is using a term with a long historical and philosophical pedigree here: material as the thing that takes form, particularly aesthetic form. A certain, more local Hollywood connotation—writing as raw material in the process of industrial production—also informs these passages from 1943. There is an implication that the "material" should, at least to some degree, determine that form and that "material too slight for a long play" might be perfect for a short one, or for a short story. Amanda, as "character," will, however, compensate for any apparent slightness in the material. Finally, however, for Williams, since material has a plenitude beyond this or that literary form, the story cannot even suggest what the play "will necessarily embody." Williams's relentless process of revision means that it remains impossible ever to determine the definitive text of a play: his work exists with significant variations across printed editions that no criterion should rationalize. And this is not an editorial matter only. What mattered to Williams was the "material" as the promise of an ongoing embodiment through writing and staging and filming. That material could always be put to "another use." Practically, this potential for other uses meant that Williams left the possibility of revision and adaptation across media open. Equally important, "material" as not yet literary and not yet formed potentiality drives Williams: "material" is at once the stuff that writing takes as its source, and an ideal outside of writing and outside of genre and outside of medium that no writing can ever quite attain.

In an essay first published in the *New York Times* in 1957 and then republished in editions of *Orpheus Descending*, a play central to the following pages, Williams considers the long genesis of that text—unusually long, even for him: "And so you see it is a very old play that *Orpheus Descending* has come out of, but a play is never an old one until you quit working on it and I have never quit working on this one, not even now. It never went into

5. In Williams, *Notebooks*, 370.

6. In Williams, *Notebooks*, 374.

the trunk, it always stayed on the work bench, and I am not presenting it now because I have run out of ideas or material for completely new work. I am offering it this season because I honestly believe that it is finally finished."[7] That unnecessary "honestly" underlines the contradiction central to this passage. Williams, the humble laborer at his bench, has not "quit working"—"not even now"—even though he believes the play is "finally finished." That the play is finished offsets defensiveness around the question of new "ideas or material." *Orpheus Descending*, even though it is done, contains the promise of ongoing writing and remains material.

In a foreword to his memoirs, Williams continues to think of material in this way. He writes that his theater is "in a state of revolution," rejecting the "kind of play that established my early and popular reputation," and he insists that he is pursuing "a different thing which is altogether my own." And yet he also emphasizes that he has not changed: "My thing is what it always was: to express my world and my experience of it in whatever form seems suitable to the material."[8] Once again, contradictions mark Williams's vocabulary for his trade. His more recent plays are a "different thing," and yet his "thing," a word that has taken on something of the post-hippie connotations of the era in which he is writing, "is what it always was." The mode has changed, but he keeps doing his thing. The world and his experience of it have also changed, but in all this change an idea of what finds comes before form—that is, material—remains a constant. On the one hand, this leads to a conception of writing as gesture toward an ideal it can only approximate: revision is constant because it never gets where it is going. On the other hand, this sense of writing as never quite adequate to its material underwrites Williams's openness to the profusion of media forms his work might take. Williams's relative receptiveness to remediation needs explanation, just as one needs to explain Beckett's resistance to it. "Material" in Williams's sense is not medium-specific. And genre has not yet shaped it.

7. Williams, "The Past, the Present, and the Perhaps," in *Plays 1957–1980*, 7.

8. Williams, *Memoirs*, xvii.

[EIGHTEEN]

Learning Sexual Violence
with Tennessee Williams, or
Streetcar in Pictures

A Streetcar Named Desire exists permanently as the film from 1951. Productions since work with, or against, or inside of that permanence: the usual situation of a stage play with a substantial performance history—its being a "memory machine," haunted by previous performances, as Marvin Carlson has stressed—becomes unusually charged.[1] The performances of Marlon Brando, Vivien Leigh, Kim Hunter: to stage the play is to deal with those ghosts. Beyond the confines of the stage, in everyday life their performances fueled identification, provided the stuff of comedy, became the source of veneration and pastiche. What member of a dying generation has not, in a moment of mock or even real agony, cried "Stella!"? The effects of the film's power are also, however, legible inside Williams's work. The naturalized path from stage to screen turns back on itself, in a feedback loop with far-reaching consequences for Williams's writing, so that, after *Streetcar*, his theater comes after film in a particular way. Williams had to reclaim his own theater, remake it after the film that had remade and petrified his play. His theater, as memory machine, had to deal with the recent memory of what the Hollywood machine had done to his play. And the loop continued, of course: while none of the others attained quite the iconic status of *Streetcar*, the several films based on his plays were both a sign of his eminence and a spectacular constraint with which he needed to cope as he continued to write for the stage.

It was never simply an anomaly that Hollywood took to Williams so devotedly; the fit was also never perfect. Working within and expanding the possibilities and pleasures of identificatory structures associated with theater, and especially melodrama, cinema produced an unprecedented machinery for mass identification. Williams, like other playwrights, wrote inside the force of this machinery. Rather than writing against or outside the codes of identification, however, he challenged the familiar repertoire of

1. See Carlson, *The Haunted Stage.*

identificatory objects. Does any of his protagonists resemble a familiar leading type? Laura Mulvey's classic discussion of Hollywood cinema clarifies Williams's experiments within and against the grain of its familiar dynamics: "The scopophilic instinct (pleasure in looking at another person as an erotic object), and, in contradistinction, ego libido (forming identification processes) act as formations, mechanisms, which this cinema has played on. The image of woman as (passive) raw material for the (active) gaze of man takes the argument further into the structure of representation, adding a further layer demanded by the ideology of the patriarchal order as it is worked out in its favorite cinematic form—illusionistic narrative film."[2] Williams abandoned neither scopophilia nor identification. Indeed, his plays extravagantly generate scopophilic possibilities and put identificatory processes in motion. These plays, however, offered a gallery of transgressive erotic objects and nonbinary opportunities for identification. If films of these plays always feel odd, it may be because they translate plays that partially subverted the codes of "illusionistic narrative film" back into these codes as if the texts put up no resistance. Following the lead of a commentator like Gore Vidal, one could see the plays as a queer reversal of Hollywood cinema: "The male is his obsession and male sexuality the benchmark. Females are principal characters in his plays because it's through them that you're going to view the male, which is the playwright's objective."[3] Translated into Mulvey's terms: Williams's audience identifies with the gaze of the female protagonist and indulges in the scopophilic pleasure of viewing the male. Such a potentially feminist, potentially queer reengineering of Hollywood was in itself a substantial renovation. And yet Williams does not simply keep the structure of identification and scopophilia in place while altering the genders of viewer and sexual object or challenging the heterosexual logic of that gaze. The technologies of film, in Mulvey's argument, focus and direct the male gaze: the close-up is a clear example of this focus. Williams seems more dedicated to the polymorphous multiplication of identifications rather than to directing or determining them.

Mulvey points to the ways that the dramatic situation of female characters underwrote their status as erotic objects in Hollywood cinema: "In their traditional exhibitionist role women are simultaneously looked at and displayed, with their appearance coded for strong visual and erotic impact so that they can be said to connote *to-be-looked-at-ness*."[4] Williams is con-

---

2. Mulvey, "Visual Pleasure and Narrative Cinema," 67.

3. Lahr, from an interview with Gore Vidal, in *Mad Pilgrimage*, 146.

4. Mulvey, "Visual Pleasure and Narrative Cinema," 62.

stantly alert to this encoding, and by no means abandons it: what character is not to be looked at? Shonni Enelow's incisive analysis of the theatricality of Williams's female characters illuminates his mischievous incorporation of this dynamic: "Self-conscious theatricality is often his way of representing the bottomless and formless passions that course through these plays, and, like his female characters, Williams embraces it, even as he recognizes its inevitable inadequacy."[5] Enelow's argument that the self-consciousness of this mode of theatricality registers rather than negates the power of that passion clarifies the relationship between Williams's plays and Hollywood. If a historical chain seemed to lead in one direction—stage melodrama to cinematic melodrama—Williams's plays take up this tangled inheritance, at once theatrical and cinematic, never trying to disguise mass-mediated sources of desires that play out on his stage. That films based on his plays then reincorporate this theatrical response to cinema makes for that feedback loop—a loop that spins further as Williams responds to what cinema has made of his plays.

Arthur Miller considered the impact of the first production of *Streetcar* in an essay published in 2004: "Along with Williams the other great revelation of the performance was of course Brando, a tiger on the loose, a sexual terrorist. Nobody had seen anything like him before because that kind of freedom on the stage had not existed before. He roared out Williams' celebratory terror of sex, its awful truthfulness and its inexorable judgments, and did so with an authority that swept everything before it. Brando was a brute but he bore the truth."[6] "Tiger," applied to Brando, strangely echoes the equally strange appearance of the word in the play itself: very soon before the curtain drops on the unseen rape, Stanley exclaims: "Tiger–tiger! Drop the bottle-top! Drop it!"[7] That this repetition recalls the opening of William Blake's "The Tyger" suggests something of the moment's aestheticized primitivism. Stanley's "Tiger" describes the vehemence of Blanche's self-defense. He has also translated her potential to wound him and the force of that defense against his threat to "interfere with" her into a libidinal impulse.[8] For Miller, Brando as Stanley speaks on behalf of Williams, roaring out his "celebratory terror of sex, its awful truthfulness and its inexorable judgments." In Miller's account, sex terrifies Williams, and he celebrates this terror; indeed, this terror is in itself a celebration. And the

5. Enelow, *Method Acting and Its Discontents*, 49.

6. Arthur Miller, introduction to Williams, *Streetcar*, xii.

7. Williams, *Streetcar*, 162.

8. Williams, *Streetcar*, 161.

celebration marks something like sex itself as overpowering legal judgment, sex as truth, sex as violent and inexorable, and, most of all, authoritative: he "was a brute but he bore the truth." Bore the truth? Brando's emblems are the mark of a brutal judge: with his "freedom" as "sexual terrorist," he is the "revelation" of the brutal truth of sex. We've all had this date with the truth of sex from the beginning.

A Streetcar Named Desire has been an important vehicle of a peculiarly US American notion of the conjoined beauty and violence of male desire. More than implicit, I think, is the notion that the "truth" of this male passion *produces* consent, that in its sublime form it overwhelms any woman subject to it. That Miller, along with Shakespeare and Thornton Wilder, was for a long time a secular sage bound to the place of drama in US high schools is no accident.[9] His reading assures the reader of the truth of Williams and of the truth of sex and of the truth of Williams's representation to sex. And yet we are, Miller suggests, in danger of forgetting these truths. "Caricature can be the fate of plays as successful as *Streetcar*," writes Miller, "ironically because they have been so well-mined in drama schools and acting classes."[10] That critique of this understanding of *Streetcar* is immanent in the play itself. The play does contain something like this theory of the inexorable violence of genuine male desire. But a comedy balances and militates against this fable ending inevitably in rape, a comedy that Miller registers when he slips the name of the great screwball comedy starring Irene Dunne and Cary Grant into one of his most grandly portentous (if also self-immolating) phrases—that is, when he describes *Streetcar*'s "awful truthfulness." Enelow has described a related dynamic: though Jessica Tandy's performance in the original production appeared theatrical, Brando seemed an agent of truth in performance that permanently marked common conceptions of Method acting: "If *Streetcar* is a play about the work of performance, it is also a play about contrasting performance styles that asks how one comes to stand for truth and authenticity and another for falsity and lies."[11] Enelow argues that this contrast is not only a relic of the first production but a conflict interior to the play—a conflict in which Blanche bears a truth that is at least equal

---

9. Miller's *The Crucible* last appeared on the Educational Theater Association's list of plays most performed in high schools in 2018–19. David Savran's pathbreaking discussion of Miller together with Williams in *Communists, Cowboys, and Queers* remains a crucial work on these two playwrights. My account is indebted to his revisionary reading of Williams as revolutionary playwright.

10. Arthur Miller, introduction to Williams, *Streetcar*, xiv.

11. Enelow, "Sweating Tennessee Williams," 139.

to the "awful truthfulness" of Stanley. Enelow also suggests that Williams knew he would be misread.

The misreading began early. The play became what the ads used to call a "major motion picture," but even before the release of the film and not long after its premiere, it circulated as a set of massively distributed photos. The play opened on Broadway on December 3, 1947. In its issue of December 15, 1947, *Life* magazine introduced the play with an anonymous short article and a set of captioned photos.[12] (*Life*, if read against the grain, is a valuable source for theater history.) This form of mass remediation—the introduction of the play into a wider public sphere far beyond the audience that would have had exposure to the play in New York City—supplemented live performance on Broadway. I'd guess that no account of what happens in the play has been more widely read. A work of interpretation inevitably accompanied this process of re-narration and remediation. These captions form a peculiar, mass-circulated form of what Bertolt Brecht, who took captions seriously and used them on stage, called literarization. This was Brecht's word for acknowledging that images do not speak for themselves, that the stage, for instance, might need titles in order to produce the "complex seeing" and complex thinking that he wanted to produce in the theater.[13] As the example of *Streetcar* shows, the presentations of theater in *Life* illustrate the range of ideological designs captions can serve. *Life* first presents the author and the play: "His gift for poetic showmanship in *Streetcar Named Desire* imbues with warmth and compassionate perception the story (*next page*) of a girl who retreats from reality to find consolation and final sorrow in sex and alcohol."[14] "Final sorrow": how else would a retreat from reality end? From the start, this account implies that it can identify who remains inside the reality from which Blanche flees. *Next page*: the journal assures us that the story treated with such warmth and compassion is the story recounted here in captions, with photographic evidence, in the pages of *Life*:

THE HEROINE, Blanche Du Bois, is a Southern girl who lives in a make-believe world of grandeur, preens in faded evening gowns and makes herself out to be sweet, genteel and delicate. She comes to visit her sister Stella and brother-in-law in the French quarter of New Orleans. In this

---

12. A lavishly illustrated online in-house history identifies the photographer as Eliot Elisofon, but erases the captions (Cosgrove, "Brando Takes Broadway").

13. Brecht, *Brecht on Theatre*, 82.

14. "'A Streetcar Named Desire': Tennessee Williams has Written the Broadway Season's Best New Play."

role English Actress Jessica Tandy, who is on stage most of the time, won high praise from the critics, sharing it with brilliant Director Elia Kazan.

IN HER SISTER'S FLAT Blanche and Stella (Kim Hunter) undress in a bedroom which is divided from living room by partly closed curtains. Though Blanche complains about the noisy poker party which is going on in the adjoining room, she purposely stands so she can be seen by Mitch (Karl Malden, *third from left*). Her sister's happy, sensual married life disturbs and offends Blanche. She tells Stella that it is vulgar and revolting.

HER SISTER and her sister's Polish husband Stanley (Marlon Brando), after a fierce quarrel brought about by Blanche's endless meddling, are reconciled in a touching love scene on stairway of their ramshackle little flat.

ACTING THE COQUETTE, Blanche curtsies to Mitch, whom she has lured into courting her. Mitch proposes marriage but jilts her when he discovers that in her home town Blanche was practically a prostitute.

"WE'VE HAD THIS DATE with each other from the beginning," says Stanley to Blanche. For weeks she has been insulting and trying to attract him. When his wife is in the hospital having a baby, Blanche hysterically attacks him with the top of a broken bottle. In a half-drunken fury, Stanley rapes her.

THE DRAMA ENDS when Blanche, clinging to her pitiful delusion that she is a grand lady, is pronounced insane, is led away by asylum attendants. Her sister and husband can now resume their happiness, proving Williams' thesis that healthy life can go on only after it is rid of unwholesome influence.[15]

Life's account is partial, outrageous, misogynist, and stupid. *Streetcar* is not reducible to a thesis, and certainly not the one ascribed to Williams at the end here. It is true that Blanche describes Stella's marriage as an abusive one and harshly criticizes Stanley as "bestial," and Stella defends her choice to remain with Stanley by explaining the "things that happen between a man and a woman in the dark."[16] Blanche does describe their life as "vulgar and revolting," but she also recognizes in it the actuality of a domestic violence that may grow more dangerous—as it does, with her as the victim. And here it is important to emphasize the genesis of domestic

15. Captions from "'A Streetcar Named Desire': Tennessee Williams Has Written the Broadway Season's Best New Play."

16. Williams, *Streetcar*, 82, 81.

FIGURES 1 AND 2. "'A Streetcar Named Desire': Tennessee Williams Has Written the Broadway Season's Best New Play." From *Life* (December 15, 1947). For many readers, *Life* and other magazines provided mediated access to the theater. And how might magazines have shaped the reception even of those who saw the plays *Life* covered in the theater? These pictures of plays were everywhere the plays could not be. Photograph: Courtesy *Life* and Shutterstock.

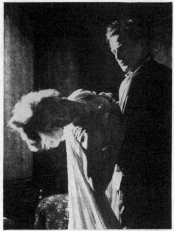

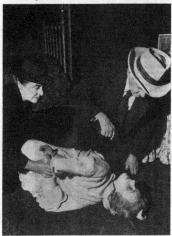

FIGURES 1 AND 2. (*Cont.*)

violence in the play as imagined by *Life*. The summary consistently pictures violence as the regrettable but also maybe inevitable result of what the anonymous authors of the captions call Blanche's "endless meddling." Throughout, it suggests that Blanche is delusional, hypocritical, and crafty: she claims to dislike the poker game, yet "purposely" exposes herself; she poses as a genteel girl, yet tries to attract Stanley; she tries to fool Mitch, whom she "lures into courting her," but he discovers that she "was practically a prostitute." This is especially notable in its description of the actions leading to Stanley's rape of Blanche. In the magazine's paraphrase, she has been insulting him and trying to attract him; she "attacks him with the top of a broken bottle"; he rapes her "in a half-drunken fury." The clear implication is that, yes, alcohol has impaired his judgment, but his violence is reciprocal, a response to her brandishing of the broken bottle. Having tantalized Stanley, it is, it would seem, Blanche's fault that Stanley rapes her while Stella is in the hospital giving birth. Furthermore, the summary sets up this moment of violence by describing Mitch's discovery that "that in her home town Blanche was practically a prostitute." In the sexual logic of this re-narration, this description, even with the uncertain qualification provided by its adverb—"*practically* a prostitute"?— leads directly to the next frame and to the rape. The description implies an opposition between acting and actuality, the division Enelow has incisively criticized: having acted as "coquette" while being in fact "practically a prostitute" increases her vulnerability but also assures that she all the more accurately fits the bill of victim to be blamed. The adverb also echoes Stanley's narration to Stella of what he has heard from "our supplyman down at the plant" about her life in Laurel: "she's practically told by the mayor to get out of town."[17] Blanche interrupts a "happy, sensual married life"; only when she is "led away by asylum attendants" can that happy life resume. No reader of this 1947 account would guess that the asylum is the solution to Blanche's narration of the truth of the rape. As Eunice says to Stella: "Don't ever believe it. Life has got to go on."[18]

My aim cannot be simply to correct the emphases of *Life*'s re-narration, as if it were a question of correcting the force of this retelling in the present, but instead to suggest that its understanding of sexual violence is wrapped up with the reception of the play. And does *Life* simply get it wrong? It would be comforting to be able to claim that there is no basis in the play for its account, that a better reading of *Streetcar* will distance us from the antiquated sexual politics of the mid-century magazine. The play is certainly not any simple fable of moral hygiene through the expulsion of the dirty and sexually deviant. The summary in *Life*, however, is attuned to one powerful strand in the text of the play: its representation of sexual violence in the domestic setting as inevitable. In *Streetcar*, this domestic violence is not

17. Williams, *Streetcar*, 119, 121.

18. Williams, *Streetcar*, 166.

separable from male sexuality and is, indeed, lodged there as an aspect of its beauty and "terror." Furthermore, this representation of male sexuality as at once violent and beautiful has resonated in American culture—and Williams responded to this resonance.[19] The lone quotation from *Streetcar* in *Life*'s literarization perfectly captures the sexual logic in question: "We've had this date with each other from the beginning!"[20] The line is the last of the play's penultimate scene, which leads to the offstage rape of Blanche. Given something of the finality of the lines that very often brought scenes to an end in melodrama, it is also a strangely metadramatic pronouncement. The word "date" hovers uncertainly between its everyday social meaning and some grander insinuation of historical inevitability, as in pompous or semi-official announcements of dates with destiny. Mitch and Blanche have had, a few scenes before, a desultory "date," but the previous scene ends as this one does not and Mitch flees rather than insisting on what he's "been missing all summer."[21] As the magazine intuited, Stanley's pronouncement is itself already a kind of caption, an interpretation, a defense in advance of the rape that is, as everyone knows, about to happen. He encodes his encounter with Blanche as a "date," a romantic rendezvous, while also implying more grandly that he and she have had a "date" with date rape "from the beginning." This phrase, too, needs scrutiny: what "beginning" does Stanley have in mind?

Like "date," this "beginning," too, oscillates uneasily, referring at once to the moment of their first meeting and to something more transcendental—a beginning containing that inevitability and everything that follows from it. The text, indeed, installs this more transcendental sense of "beginning" into the moment when Blanche and Stanley first meet. The dramaturgy of this scene is complicated: every important character in the play appears in it, even if only fleetingly. Stanley has returned from a night out with friends, including Mitch; they plan a poker game. Blanche's accusatory tale of the dissolution of the family home leaves Stella in tears: Stella withdraws to

---

19. Leo Bersani's insistence on the cruelty of sexuality, "at least in the mode in which it is constituted," complicates this picture. Writing of the child's "vulnerability to be shattered into sexuality," Bersani observes, "The *mystery* of sexuality is that we seek not only to get rid of this shattering tension but also to repeat, even to increase it" (*Freudian Body*, 39, 38). Or, as Bersani writes in "Is the Rectum a Grave?," "the self which the sexual shatters provides the basis on which sexuality is associated with power" (218). Williams at once recognizes the masochism that Bersani insists is constitutive of sexuality and alienates the "mode in which it is constituted."

20. Williams, *Streetcar*, 162.

21. Williams, *Streetcar*, 149.

the play's one private space, the bathroom, to wash her face. As Stanley's friends disperse, this famous stage direction appears:

> [*He is of medium height, about five feet eight or nine, and strongly, compactly built. Animal joy in his being is implicit in all his movements and attitudes. Since earliest manhood the center of his life has been pleasure with women, the giving and taking of it, not with weak indulgence, dependently, but with the power and pride of a richly feathered male bird among hens. Branching out from this complete and satisfying center are all the auxiliary channels of his life, such as his heartiness with men, his appreciation of rough humor, his love of good drink and food and games, his car, his radio, everything that is his, that bears his emblem of the gaudy seed-bearer. He sizes women up at a glance, with sexual classifications, crude images flashing into his mind and determining the way he smiles at them.*]
> BLANCHE [*drawing back involuntarily from his stare*]:
> You must be Stanley. I'm Blanche.
> STANLEY
> Stella's sister?[22]

In the space of a sentence, a certain sex positivity—his pleasure in the "giving and taking" of pleasure—dissolves into barnyard hierarchies: "*the power and pride of a richly feathered male bird among hens.*" The transparent elision of "rooster" or, more simply, "cock"—what other male bird would be "among hens"?—leads to that celebration of the beauty of phallic power in the "gaudy seed-bearer."[23] The stage direction also traces a kinship structure that leads first to Stanley's homosocial bonds and to pleasure in eating and then to property as such: amid all the metaphor of this passage, the simplicity of the phrase, "everything that is his," stands out. The passage imagines his sexual pleasure as the basis of every affect associated with property and the pleasure of owning things, and the play will go on to associate eroticism and property, in part by linking sexual violence to Stanley's right to destroy what he owns, including his radio. So this is one beginning: we hear that,

22. Williams, *Streetcar*, 24–25. Despite Stanley's having appeared earlier, this is Williams' first extensive description of the character.

23. The chicken coop finds its way into the dialogue: Steve tells a fable of a lustful roster distracted by feed (*Streetcar*, 48–49); Blanche asks Stella about Mitch: "Is he a wolf?" (52); Stanley demands of Stella and Blanche that "you hens cut out the conversation in there" (54). And the "gaudy seed-bearer" wears "gaudy" (70) a.k.a. "brilliant silk pyjamas" (160).

in general, Stanley *"sizes women up at a glance, with sexual classifications, crude images flashing into his mind,"* and so we do not need to be told—and the stage direction does not bother to stress—that he looks at Blanche in this way. The contrast between the prose of the stage direction and the simplicity of Blanche's identification of Stanley and her introduction of herself stresses a failure of etiquette—Stanley has stared rather than introducing himself—but also establishes the kinship relations that mean, for Blanche, that Stanley shouldn't be looking at her or smiling at her as he has done. Later Blanche will tell Mitch: "The first time I laid eyes on him I thought to myself, that man is my executioner!"[24]

The last lines of the first scene bring this beginning to a close and also look forward to the end of the rape scene. Not for the first and (of course) also not for the last time, Stanley calls the name of his wife:

> Hey, Stella!
> STELLA [*faintly, from the bathroom*]:
> Yes, Stanley?
> STANLEY:
> Haven't fallen in, have you? [*He grins at Blanche. She tries unsuccessfully to smile back. There is a silence*] I'm afraid I'll strike you as being the unrefined type. Stella's spoke of you a good deal. You were married once, weren't you?
> [*The music of the polka rises up, faint in the distance.*]
> BLANCHE:
> Yes, when I was quite young.
> STANLEY:
> What happened?
> BLANCHE:
> The boy—the boy died. [*She sinks back down.*] I'm afraid I'm—going to be sick!
> [*Her head falls on her arms.*][25]

Stanley knows the answers to all of the questions he asks here: he knows that Stella hasn't fallen into the toilet, just as he knows that Blanche was once married and that her husband died. This "grin" might be the smile Stanley adopts for his sister-in-law, but her failed attempt to smile in return suggests that that she senses that the aim of the questions is to establish,

---

24. Williams, *Streetcar*, 111.

25. Williams, *Streetcar*, 27–28.

whatever her marital status and whatever the kinship structures that bind them, that he sees her as sexually available. She is going to be sick.

The rape scene concludes with this stage direction:

> [*She moans. The bottle-top falls. She sinks to her knees. He picks up her inert figure and carries her to the bed. The hot trumpet and drums from the Four Deuces sound loudly.*][26]

Loud music drowns out the sight and sound of rape. The text insists on the repetition of the first scene at the end of the tenth. "*She sinks back down*"; "*She sinks to her knees*": both scenes ends with Blanche's sinking into inertness. (She also "*falls to her knees*" at the end of the ninth scene.)[27] This sinking is the translation of the tragic fall into the tragedy of domestic violence, of the date rape as the inevitable result of terror of male sexuality.

Against this current of sexual violence and "final sorrow," there is another trajectory. An anecdote from Gore Vidal's memoirs illuminates what I have in mind. Vidal once served as "interpreter" for the English actress Claire Bloom and Williams when Bloom was preparing to play the role of Blanche. Williams asked her if she had any questions about the play:

> "Yes." Claire pulled herself together. "What happens *after* the final curtain?"
>
> The Bird [Vidal's nickname for Williams] sat back in his chair, narrowed his eyes. "No actress has ever asked me that question." He shut his eyes; thought. "She will enjoy her time in the bin. She will seduce one or two of the more comely young doctors. Then she will be let free to open an attractive boutique in the French Quarter..."
>
> "She wins?"
>
> "Oh, yes," said the Bird. "Blanche wins."[28]

(Had *every* actress asked?) The aim of this fabulation would have been to affect a performance in the play as written: Williams was guiding Bloom away from understanding Blanche as tragic victim. And there is nothing definitive about Williams's improvisation, one of the myriad rewritings that are scattered across his published and unpublished work. But his response

26. Williams, *Streetcar*, 162.

27. Williams, *Streetcar*, 150.

28. Vidal, *Palimpsest*, 156.

to Bloom does point to a critique of the tragic or terroristic allure of sexual violence that a reader like Miller attributes to the play.

Early in the play, Blanche confronts Stella about Stanley and Stella's attraction to him, and Blanche suggests that she will do all she can to rescue herself and Stella from their shared predicament. Blanche is shocked, for instance, that Stella on her wedding night was "sort of—thrilled" by the spectacle of Stanley's smashing the lightbulbs in their apartment with her slipper. Stella corrects Blanche's assumption that she is in something she wants "to get out of." Stella explains:

> But there are things that happen between a man and a woman in the dark—that sort of make everything else seem—unimportant. [*Pause.*]
> BLANCHE:
> What you are talking about is brutal desire—just—Desire!—the name of that rattle-trap street-car that bangs through the Quarter, up one old narrow street and down another . . .
> STELLA:
> Haven't you ever ridden on that street-car?
> BLANCHE:
> It brought me here.—where I'm not wanted and where I'm ashamed to be.[29]

This discussion of the streetcar is striking because of the deliberateness with which Williams has installed the play's title within the dialogue: nothing could announce itself more obviously as a key to interpretation. (The *Life* story recognizes this by providing a photo: "A STREETCAR NAMED DESIRE actually exists in New Orleans.") The elaboration of the figure of the streetcar is, however, striking for its contradictions. On the one hand, Blanche insists that Stella doesn't understand that those things that happen between men and women in the dark are just "brutal desire." She grants that one might "go out" with a man like Stanley when "the devil is in you. But live with? Have a child by?"[30] On the other hand, Blanche's version of the figure has nothing of what Miller would call the "inexorable." One could rationalize this failure of the streetcar to figure overpowering eros by emphasizing the divide between the men you have sex with when possessed by the devil and the men you settle down with: the streetcar as a figure for the everyday "rattle-trap" obverse of inexorable passion. Such a reading, however,

29. Williams, *Streetcar*, 73, 80, 81.

30. Williams, *Streetcar*, 81.

ignores Blanche's insistence that the name for what happens in the dark is "Desire." This streetcar is not the vehicle of "Williams' celebratory terror of sex, its awful truthfulness and its inexorable judgments." When Blanche and Mitch return from a date late at night, with Mitch *"bearing, upside down, a plaster statuette of Mae West, the sort of prize won at shooting-galleries and carnival games of chance,"* she asks how he will get home:

> MITCH:
> I'll walk over to Bourbon and catch an owl-car.
> BLANCHE [*laughing grimly*]:
> Is that street-car named Desire still grinding along the tracks at this hour?
> MITCH [*heavily*]:
> I'm afraid you haven't gotten much fun out of this evening, Blanche.
> BLANCHE:
> I spoiled it for *you.*
> MITCH:
> No, you didn't, but I felt all the time that I wasn't giving you much—entertainment.[31]

One can imagine the backstory, with all its gendered clichés: Mitch wins a prize, leaving the choice to Blanche. (Stella brings her to "Galatoire's for supper and then to a show"; Mitch brings her to an amusement park.)[32] As with the sexy French sentences he cannot translate, as with so much of what Blanche says in his presence, the statuette belongs to a code Mitch cannot begin to crack.[33] And any image of West is in any case overdetermined: an exemplar of cinematic sexual frankness and gay icon, she was also Williams's predecessor in bringing such frankness to the American stage.[34] What kitschy icon of an icon could better puncture the myth of sex and its "awful truthfulness," not to mention the myth of what Stanley calls "this Hollywood glamor stuff," than an upside-down Mae West?[35]

The statuette introduces the play's sixth scene, in which in the midst of awkward steps toward romance Blanche narrates her love for, and rejection of, her gay husband, Allan Gray, and his suicide. There is no key to this scene. On the one hand, Blanche describes the intensity of her first love, her having been "deluded," her certainty that Allan committed suicide because she told him he disgusted her. The violent end of an impossible love

31. Williams, *Streetcar*, 100–101.

32. Williams, *Streetcar*, 29.

33. The Smithsonian has such a statuette of Mae West in its collection of "carnival chalkware."

34. See Bak, "'May I Have a Drag . . . ?'"

35. Williams, *Streetcar*, 39.

in betrayal and suicide points toward the play's tragedy of queer desires that this world cannot assimilate. On the other hand, the scene moves toward recognition of the possibility of love despite past betrayals and carnage. The parallel—Mitch has earlier also sketched a "sad" romance and the loss of "very strange girl"—suggests a chance for something different.[36] If the scene feels like a sad compromise, this is in part because of a sentimental logic of the first as the only love. Under the sign of the statuette of Mae West, a different, comic, Kleinian logic of the good enough becomes visible. Blanche's descriptions of the streetcar named Desire unmistakably figure it as a vehicle for sex—it bangs and grinds—but, just as unmistakably, this "rattle-trap" figure has nothing of the inexorable masculine terror of sex.

Williams did see the play celebrated as an event along these lines: "Among the play's many narrative sensations," writes John Lahr of the impact of the first production, "was the first sighting on the American stage of a sexual male."[37] Lahr can make this claim because *Streetcar*, onstage and especially on film, contributed to the construction of the model of male sexuality that some imagine it unveiled. After *Streetcar*, Williams's plays were in part engaged with a rare kind of success: they had to struggle with a successful intervention in the machinery of the social imaginary based on a one-sided understanding of *Streetcar*. His theater had to deal, after *Streetcar*, with the alienating spectacle of its impact as film.

36. Williams, *Streetcar*, 58.

37. Lahr, *Mad Pilgrimage*, 146. Would this have been a *narrative* sensation? Lahr relies heavily here on an interview he conducted with Gore Vidal in which Vidal claimed that Brando "played with his cock onstage and that excited people."

[NINETEEN]

Lead Belly's Guitar
and Williams's Counterpublics

Orpheus Descending, a work Williams labored over for many years and, indeed, seems never to have really finished, had its premiere under this title in March 1957, roughly a decade after *Streetcar*.[1] The title proclaims an engagement with Greek myth, and critics have been more than willing to chart the play's debts to and revisions of the story of Orpheus.[2] What has been less visible, in part because of the kinds of questions asked, is how the play's declared engagement with Greek myth should be read also as an encounter with myth in the sense that decades of critical theory have illuminated it— myth, that is, as a product of the apparatuses of a mass culture.[3] Yes, we are supposed to remember Orpheus when a singer seems for a time to rescue a woman who says she is in hell, and again when the singer is murdered and dismembered at the end of the play. The play, however, consistently insists on aspects of the mass cultural surround: on the power and contradictions of counterpublics built around Black music, on the ways massively mass-reproduced images mediate desire, on "exhibitionism" as a symptom of a culture that pathologizes the desire to be seen that it also cultivates. The play is typical of Williams's work in its staging of a dialectic between kitsch

---

1. For a detailed account of the path from the 1940 *Battle of Angels* to the 1957 *Orpheus Descending*, see Jeffrey B. Loomis, "'Cassandra, Meet Leadbelly'": Loomis's painstaking scholarship on the various drafts of this play—or these plays—is, however, more compelling than his reading of this process of revision as a movement from Nietzsche to Christ.

2. Parker Tyler faults Williams for celebrating "the degeneration of a great human motif such as the ultimate sublimity attainable by love through music" (review of *The Fugitive Kind*, 49).

3. Classic statements include Horkheimer and Adorno's "The Culture Industry: Enlightenment as Mass Deception" in *Dialectic of Enlightenment* (94–136) and "Myth Today," the long essay with which Barthes concludes *Mythologies* (217–74). A premise here is that a lively vernacular version of this debate was happening in the public sphere and inside Williams's work.

and authenticity—the signature of the statuette of Mae West—and the play's still startling power lies in part in its refusal to value one over another. Nothing precludes the inauthentic as a site of real desire. Williams's plays in this period were a remarkable barometer of debates over authenticity in US culture. The terrain in *Orpheus Descending* is not, however, Mae West's camp but Black music. *Orpheus Descending* understands Black music as, in Paul Gilroy's words, "the principal symbol of racial authenticity."[4] But what does it mean to stage a debate about music and authenticity mostly in the absence of Black characters?

The one non-white character in *Orpheus Descending*, Uncle Pleasant, a "conjure man," is frequently identified as "The Negro" in stage directions, while the text insists on his mixed Black and Choctaw descent. Carol Cutrere, the type of the rebel daughter of a wealthy Southern family and a representative of what she will dub "the fugitive kind," consistently claims familiarity with him and with Choctaw practices. She explains early in the play: "He's part Choctaw, he knows the Choctaw cry." Against the wishes of the other white women in the room, she encourages him to give the cry:

> Come on, Uncle Pleasant, *you* know it! ([. . .] *She starts to cry herself. He throws back his head and completes it: a series of barking sounds that rise to a high sustained note of wild intensity.* [. . .] *Just then, as though the cry had brought him, Val enters the store* U.C. *He is a young man, about 30, who has a kind of wild beauty about him that the cry would suggest. He does not wear levis or a T-shirt, he has on a pair of dark serge pants, glazed from long wear and not excessively tight-fitting. His remarkable garment is a snakeskin jacket, mottled white, black and grey. He carries a guitar which is covered with inscriptions. Looking at the young man.*) . . . Thanks, Uncle . . . (*Val observes with a calm interest. Carol smiles. Uncle Pleasant waits for his dollar.*)[5]

This is, of course, nuts. Carol responds—and the potential for comedy here is worth noting—as though the cry had satisfied her wish, producing out of nowhere the wildly beautiful man of her desires. The suggestion that the "wild" cry has conjured this "wild beauty" only emphasizes the whiteness

---

4. Gilroy, *The Black Atlantic*, 96.

5. Williams, *Orpheus Descending*, 11. Quotations are from the Dramatists Play Service edition unless otherwise specified. Drewey Wayne Gunn calls this the "far superior" text ("The Various Texts of Tennessee Williams's Plays," 373). Certainly its qualities speak to issues that interest me. I thank Elizabeth Bonapfel for her clarifying thoughts about the question of the unique edition.

of that beauty and the contrasts between the conjure man who cries and what he conjures.[6] Uncle Pleasant never speaks; Val is a "peculiar talker."[7] On the one hand, this is part of a long and all-too-familiar practice of marginalizing Black characters. On the other hand, *Orpheus Descending* is a play full of words featuring a voluble protagonist; as its title alone implies, the play values the inarticulate power of music. And, as in this portentous opening introduction of Val, *Orpheus Descending* associates that power with Black and, much less consistently, with indigenous music and expressive culture. This cry aside, however, that power is purely a matter of talk: there is nothing like the "blue piano" of *Streetcar* or the Delta blues of *Cat on a Hot Tin Roof*.[8] The play harnesses an idea of Black music in the absence of Black musicians—and of the sounds of Black music. There is instead, as this spectacular entrance suggests, Valentine Xavier, Williams's hybrid of hipster and Elvis, with his "wild beauty," his snakeskin jacket, and his precious guitar.[9] In his biography of Elvis, Peter Guralnick writes that he "wanted to save Elvis Presley from the dreary bondage of myth": *Orpheus Descending* does something like the reverse: extravagantly, hyperbolically building up

6. "Wild" is a keyword in the afterlife of *Orpheus Descending*. Cinematic landmarks in this afterlife include an incoherent movie about the taming of Elvis, *Wild in the Country* (1961), in which he falls in love with his therapist, who grooms him for a writing career and for college; David Lynch's *Wild at Heart* (1990), in which Nicholas Cage's Sailor announces, "This is a snakeskin jacket! And for me it's a symbol of my individuality, and my belief . . . in personal freedom"; and Wong Kar-Wai's *Days of Being Wild* (1990), which includes a revision of Val's speech about a legless bird that "has to stay all its life on its wings in the sky" (*Orpheus Descending*, 29).

7. Williams, *Orpheus Descending*, 26.

8. Some texts of *Orpheus Descending* do include a stage direction at the end of the penultimate scene: "Music fades in: 'Dog Howl Blues'—minor—guitar" (*Orpheus Descending* in *Plays 1957–1980*, 81). I have found no other trace of this song. On the use of Black music in *Streetcar* and *Cat*, see McGinley, "Reconsidering 'the American Style.'" Nicholas Moschovakis's "Tennessee Williams's American Blues" traces Black music in Williams's early career.

9. The link to Elvis had been noted from the start: see, for instance, Edwin Schallert's review in the *Los Angeles Times* in November of 1957: "This is the story of a wandering minstrel whose proudest possession is a guitar that has enabled him to earn a meager living in cafes. If anybody detects a resemblance to a present-day rock 'n roll singer this will not be remarkable. However, any comparison must be termed purely coincidental" ("Sex Problems"). Parker Tyler's review of *The Fugitive Kind* offers the sketch of a psychoanalytic account of play's refraction of Elvis. The fullest account of this aspect of the play is Charles Goldthwaite's "All Shook Up."

myth as a way to explore and expose it—which does not mean that the play escapes myth.[10]

In 1963, Marion Magid, in a symptomatic essay about Williams as symptomatic, outlined a composite version of the United States in the image of Williams's myth. Her piece begins:

> A European whose knowledge of America was gained entirely from the collected works of Tennessee Williams might garner a composite image of the U.S.: it is a tropical country whose vegetation is largely man-eating; it has an excessive annual rainfall and frequent storms which coincide with its mating periods; it has not yet been converted to Christianity, but continues to observe the myth of the annual death and resurrection of the sun-god, for which purpose it keeps on hand a constant supply of young men to sacrifice.

Magid's comic catalog continues in this hyperbolic and yet perceptive vein. She then observes, however: "A culture does not consistently pay the price of admission to witness a fable which does not ensnare some part of the truth about it." She continues to think about contradictions between Williams's representational extremes and his knowledge: "His imagination, magnetized though it is by the outlandish and the outré, is a kind of fever chart of our national ailments."[11] Her example alludes to the ending of *Orpheus Descending*, among other examples: "the beautiful young man at bay, the quarry ringed by his pursuers."

> The mind, the sensibilities, the stomach, all recoil from this image when it is served up with obvious relish in a darkened theater, snakily choreographed by Kazan or distended on wide screen in all the glory of MGM technicolor. Yet that image is frighteningly akin to the one emblazoned not long ago on all the front pages of the land: Meredith ringed by the Mississippi National Guard on the campus at Ole Miss; and in the background, blurred figures with clenched fists. Who knows what goes on behind those flat faces with steel-rimmed eyeglasses and slits for mouths? One has a sense that Williams dwells closer to that knowledge than other dramatists writing about us, for us, today.[12]

---

10. Guralnick, *Last Train to Memphis*, xiii.

11. Magid, "The Innocence of Tennessee Williams," 34.

12. Magid, "The Innocence of Tennessee Williams," 34–35.

Magid's parallel registers without directly commenting upon the racial logic that substitutes the beautiful white sacrifice for the Black subject of racial violence.[13] The link between the stories of Val and James Meredith, a Black man surrounded by racist hatred while integrating the University of Mississippi, has to do not with a racial identity they share but with the hateful, inhuman men who hunt them. Williams's "fever chart of national ailments" registers the "outlandish and the outré," but this outlandishness turns out not to be a measure of the bizarre, Magid suggests, but instead a sign of how Williams's mythical method is alert to a central dynamic of American life. What if the point of this method, here, is the glaring obviousness with which Williams asks his audiences to accept the white protagonist as surrogate for a history of racial violence that the plays insist on and yet do not directly represent?

An earlier dialogue foreshadows the climax to *Orpheus Descending* in which Val is thrown naked to "chain-gang dogs"—an event that happens, despite Magid's allusions to Elia Kazan's snaky choreography, offstage.[14] Val is speaking with Vee, the play's "visionary" artist, about the sources of her art:

> You lived in Two River County, the wife of the county sheriff. You saw awful things take place.
> VEE: Awful! Things!
> VAL: Beatings!
> VEE: Yes!
> VAL: Lynchings!
> VEE: Yes!
> VAL: Run-away convicts torn to pieces by hounds! (*This is the first time she could express this horror. The lights are fading slowly.*)
> VEE: *Chain-gang dogs!* Tear fugitives to *pieces!*
>   [...]
> VAL: But violence ain't quick always. Sometimes it's slow. Some tornadoes are slow. Corruption—rots men's hearts and—rot is slow. . . .
> VEE: —How do you—?
> VAL: Know? I been a witness, I know!
> VEE: *I* been a witness! *I* know!
> VAL: We seen these things from seats down front at th' show.[15]

---

13. On the question of Williams and sacrifice, see especially Clum, "The Sacrificial Stud and the Fugitive Female."

14. Other texts more strongly emphasize the sadism of the murder of Val and include references to a blowtorch: see *Orpheus Descending* in *Plays 1957–1980*, 96.

15. Williams, *Orpheus Descending*, 46.

The awful things they have seen directly foreshadow what the audience in their seats will not see, twice: Lady and Val listen to dogs chase and capture a convict and, also offstage, the audience watches as Carol Cutrere listens *"in vicarious agony"* as dogs pursue and capture Val.[16] The call-and-response of the first part of this passage points to an evangelical mode of worship very different from that of the Episcopal Church that Vee has just described as "ours."[17] The metatheatrical insistence on this witnessing as taking in a show reminds the audience of their own spectatorship at a show about the quick and the slow violence of Two River County. This insistence also recalls the publicness of spectacles of lynching that Jacqueline Goldsby has emphasized. Goldsby corrects previous accounts of lynching by demonstrating that rather than some survival of atavistic violence, lynching was a measure not only of racism but also of "mass culture's impact."[18] *Orpheus Descending* exists in the space of that impact. Val and Vee's dialogue draws a distinction between simply being part of the audience for racial terror—a mass audience through its mass cultural dissemination, as Goldsby stresses—and being a *witness*: "Before you started to paint, it didn't make sense," Val says to Vee. The scene implies that for Val, as for Vee, making art is a way of making sense of what they have witnessed and in itself a form of witness. (Both Vee and Val have had audiences in the metropolis of New Orleans.) And this art transforms rather than simply documenting: Vee paints a steeple red because she paints "a thing how I feel it instead of always the way it actually is."[19]

This preference of feeling over "always the way it actually is" recalls Magid's "fever chart": Williams as one who *feels* "our national ailments," the plays as a way of making sense—that is, the plays as work on the material of myth. Williams as barometer of social and political affect recalls his own account of his work as expression of "my world and my experience of it in whatever form seems suitable to the material."[20] The idea that Vee's art—and, by implication, Val's and also that of Williams—is a way to "make sense" accords with a modernist tradition exemplified by T. S. Eliot's essay of 1923, "Ulysses, Order, and Myth." Franco Moretti's argument that Eliot "tried to obtain with poetry results that would

16. Williams, *Orpheus Descending*, 47–48; 78.

17. Williams, *Orpheus Descending*, 44.

18. Goldsby, *Spectacular Secret*, 23.

19. Williams, *Orpheus Descending*, 46; 44.

20. Williams, *Memoirs*, xvii.

be attained only with *mass culture*" illuminates Williams.[21] These plays know that drama cannot aspire to order the world through the force of some synthesis of a disordered world in art. Williams's plays rework mass cultural myth on stage—as myth. (*Streetcar* emblematizes how complicated this becomes: Williams contributes to the mass cultural production of myth to which his plays then respond.) This working-through mass cultural myth on stage makes for (some of) the hyberbolic excesses of Williams's work.

From its title forward, with allusions to the Greek myth as just one of the layers of its overdetermined mythical content, *Orpheus Descending* does pile it on. A crucial carrier of that myth is Val's guitar, signed by mostly Black musicians. In his first scene together with Lady, the owner of the small-town mercantile store from whom he seeks a job and with whom he will have the affair that leads to their deaths, she "*stares at him softly*" and takes an interest in his guitar. Williams's beautifully preposterous dialogue:

> I can do all kinds of odd jobs. Ma'am, I'm thirty today and I'm through with the life that I've been leading. I lived in corruption but I'm not corrupted. Here is why. (*Holds up his guitar.*) My life's companion! It washes me clean like water when anything unclean has touched me. . . .
>
> LADY: (*Coming back downstairs.*) What's all that writing on it?
>
> VAL: Autographs of musicians.
>
> LADY: Can I see it?
>
> VAL: Turn on that light over you. (*She switches on green shaded bulb over counter. VAL, holding the instrument tenderly between them as if it were a child, his voice soft, intimate, tender.*) See this name? Leadbelly?
>
> LADY: Leadbelly?
>
> VAL: Greatest man ever lived on the twelve-string guitar! Played it so good he broke the stone heart of a Texas governor with it and won himself a pardon out of jail. . . . And see this name Oliver? King Oliver? That name is immortal, lady. Greatest man since Gabriel on a horn. . . . .
>
> LADY: What's this name?
>
> VAL: Oh. That name? That name is also immortal. The name Bessie Smith is written in the stars!—Jim Crow killed her, John Barleycorn

21. Moretti, "From *The Waste Land* to the Artificial Paradise," in *Signs Taken for Wonders*, 210.

and Jim Crow killed Bessie Smith. She bled to death after an auto accident, because they wouldn't take her into a white hospital. . . . See this name here? That's another immortal!

LADY: Blind Lemon Jefferson? Is his name written in the stars, too?

VAL: Yes, his name is written in the stars, too. . . . (*Her voice is also intimate and soft: a spell of softness between them, their bodies almost touching, only divided by the guitar.*)

LADY: You had any sales experience?[22]

Lady's comic deflation of this moment's intimacy also punctures this mythical constellation of love and theft. The signatures guarantee a direct connection between Val and those musicians: he was in their presence without the mediation of recordings or broadcast. The guitar's cathartic effect is partly a matter of a life of "corruption" in New Orleans: while never fully explicit, the play implies that Val's entertainment involved selling sex as well as songs. This dialogue, however, also suggests that the guitar itself, as object, redeems Val from the corruption of the culture that incarcerates Lead Belly and lets Bessie Smith die for want of care. He has been a witness, not a participant. In 1957, at a moment in which one of the most sensational manifestations of mass culture was the appropriation of Black music by white musicians—in short, Elvis as phenomenon—*Orpheus Descending* imagined Val as inheritor of this constellation of immortals.

But when can all this Orphic activity be happening? One date is more or less clear: this scene occurs on Val's thirtieth birthday. Relevant dates in the lives of the musicians who have signed his guitar are as follows:

Lead Belly: January 20, 1888–December 6, 1949
King Oliver: May 11, 1885–April 10, 1938
Bessie Smith: April 15, 1894–September 26, 1937
Blind Lemon Jefferson: September 1893–December 1929

Let us stipulate for a moment that you can be alive and yet your name may already be "written in the stars." Given that, whenever these events transpire, Bessie Smith has already died, then the play must happen after September 26, 1937—and probably not on September 27, 1937: the news of the

---

22. Williams, *Orpheus Descending*, 25–26. One example of why this text is preferable surfaces in the passage quoted here: where, in the Dramatists Play Service edition, Val sketches the circumstances surrounding the death Bessie Smith, in others a phrase simply elides these details: "but that's another story. . . ." See, for instance, *Orpheus Descending* in *Plays 1957–1980*, 35.

death of Bessie Smith is already known. This stipulation, however, doesn't explain other evidence, including Val's description of Lead Belly: "Greatest man ever lived on the twelve-string guitar!"[23] The posthumous suggestion here is clear. Continuing for now with this chronology, this puts the play squarely post-1950, after the death of Lead Belly. While the play resists any clear date, the milieu, however mythologized, belongs to the decade in which it was first performed. Later in the play, the men who are about to kill Val read aloud the names of the signatures of "musicians dead and living": "*Men read aloud the names printed on the guitar: Bessie Smith, Leadbelly, Woody Guthrie, Jelly Roll Morton, etc.*"[24] The "etc." implies that those performing the play will know how to adlib the correct proper names and not to add Perry Como to the list. Additional names surface here:

Woody Guthrie: July 14, 1912–October 3, 1967
Jelly Roll Morton: September 20, 1885–July 10, 1941

Guthrie, the only white artist whose name appears, was also the only musician still living at the time of the play's first production. His own guitar had also been famous for the words written on it, the resonant "THIS MACHINE KILLS FASCISTS."[25] Modern myth, too, happens through bricolage. The play happens after the death of Lead Belly in 1949; Val is near his thirtieth birthday; Blind Lemon Jefferson died in 1929. So: Val happened to run into Blind Lemon Jefferson, here or there, some time before Val's tenth birthday.

This unlikelihood of this encounter is not a mistake, but a strategy.[26] The play, that is, exaggerates the fantastic quality of the affiliations between Val and the musicians who have signed his guitar. Even without the addition of the particularly implausible name of Blind Lemon Jefferson, the play maps a constellation that resembles the musical canon of counterpublics

23. On preferring "Lead Belly" over "Leadbelly," see Filene, *Romancing the Folk*, 246n15. I retain Williams's "Leadbelly" in quotations.

24. Williams, *Orpheus Descending*, 65.

25. This phrase was widely reported. See, for instance, Wanda Marvin's review of two hours of CBS television on the night of Friday, August 25, 1944, including *They Were There*, a half hour with Guthrie: "The guitar with which he accompanies his singing carries the painted slogan, *This Machine Kills Fascists*. Producer-Director Leo Hurwitz deserves kudos for either choosing a natural or rehearsing him and his hostess to letter perfect."

26. As if in a half-hearted attempt to rationalize the chronology, other versions of the text drop Jefferson and substitute Fats Waller (1904–1943): see, for instance, the Library of America edition (*Plays 1957–1980*, 35).

around the burgeoning folk music revival.[27] With the addition of Jefferson, who was, among other things, known in those circles as a teacher of Lead Belly, that canon becomes at once historically all but impossible (where the signatures on the guitar are concerned) and pointedly marked as the sign of that counterpublic's utopian elective affinities. The historical impossibility is, so to speak, the point: the non-coincidence of lived lives emphasizes the active choice of inheritance. But these elective affinities only emphasize the whiteness of the Orpheus whose guitar testifies to an inheritance the play insists on but does not represent.

But why is the guitar signed at all? Val's explanation is perfectly vague: "Autographs of musicians I run into here and there." The word "autographs" suggests the fan: these are the writing of the musicians themselves, collected not in an autograph book but on the surface of the guitar the fan plays. There is also a suggestion, however, that these signatures are also a kind of sponsorship, a sign that the musicians have recognized and endorsed a fellow musician, as the scene with Lady emphasizes. Immediately following the discussion of the names on the guitar, Val pulls out a "character reference," which Lady reads aloud, concluding with "Yours truly"—excluding, that is, any mention of a name following the closing: "Huh!—Some reference!" she comments.[28] The names of the musicians, that is, testify in advance for the lack of the name in the character reference. Great Black musicians vouch for Val. Inside the world of the play, these references count for nothing: the white people who encounter the names evince no glimmer of recognition. There is a kind of insider's dramatic irony here, where some of the audience recognize what the characters in the play do not.[29]

If the names on Val's guitar serve as a counterpublic service announcement, understanding their place in the larger play involves putting them in the context of other names and other constellations in the play. Val's

27. For an admirably dialectical account of the historical engagements of the folk revival, see Cantwell, *When We Were Good*. See also Sonnet Retman's valuable discussion of the production of "folk" as commodity and its relationship to mass culture in the 1930s in *Real Folks*.

28. Williams, *Orpheus Descending*, 26.

29. Paige McGinley links Williams to the folk revival and stresses the presence of Black performers in Williams's previous Broadway production, the 1955 *Cat on a Hot Tin Roof* ("Reconsidering 'the American Style,'" 10–11). These performers included the blues duo, Brownie McGhee and Sonny Terry. She also notes that reviews by Brooks Atkinson in the *New York Times* and by Eric Bentley in *The Nation* overlooked the Black performers, who, she argues, "were cast by [director Elia] Kazan as representatives of an authentic, nostalgic South—but also of a politicized antiracist and antifascist coalition" (14).

familiarity with the legend of Lead Belly's winning his freedom from prison through song is typical of the hybrid mythological work inside *Orpheus Descending*. On the one hand, Val's autographs trace fragments of a recognizable canon of American music. On the other hand, the story of Lead Belly's redemption from prison resonates with the Orphic frame. This translation of the mythological stratum the play invokes through its title and through a tale from the history of Black music is deeply typical of the play's hyperbolic and yet compelling navigation of various logics of American authenticity. This story of Lead Belly's winning his freedom was not the arcane property of a folkie counterpublic, but something that had been reported, for instance, in that surprising source, *Life*. *Life*'s report begins with this confident reading of the meaning of Lead Belly's popularity: "The easiest way to avoid or at least to mitigate the consequences of sin is to entertain your fellow man. Amuse the public, and you can get away with almost any crime. Prime example of the great American appreciation of criminal talent is the case of Huddie Ledbetter, better known as Lead Belly. Twice imprisoned for murder or attempted murder, he has twice strummed and sung his way to gubernatorial pardons, is celebrated today at the country's No. 1 Negro minstrel."[30] Val, that is, has the endorsement of the greatest of the blues singers, the singer whose voice and guitar freed him from not one but two sentences in prisons, including the Louisiana State Penitentiary, a notorious hub of the US prison system, popularly known as "Angola" and operating still. For *Life*, the legend is about getting away with something. For Williams, Lead Belly's breaking the warden's stone heart is cathartic, even Ovidian: where Orpheus moves the "bloodless spirits"—even the Furies weep—Lead Belly's music is so good that it breaks the "stone heart" of the governor.[31] Benjamin Filene's reflections on the place of Lead Belly in public memory after his death are relevant here: "Successive cohorts of middle-class, almost exclusively white audiences could become entranced by the Lead Belly myth, revel in the bracing foreignness of his songs, and, eventually, reinterpret the songs as their own. After his death, then, Lead Belly himself became an authenticating agent, one who could bestow legitimacy

30. The magazine's article, appallingly titled "Lead Belly: Bad Nigger Makes Good Minstrel," was published in April 1937. For the context of this article, and especially the way that the article disseminates stories from *Negro Folk Songs as Sung by Lead Belly*, see Wolfe and Lornell, *The Life and Legend of Leadbelly*, 194–99. Wolfe and Lornell are alert to the ideological work of *Life*'s captions, pointing out that "a beautiful photo of Huddie's hands fingering" his guitar has these words beneath it: "THESE HANDS ONCE KILLED A MAN" (197).

31. Ovid, *Metamorphoses*, 343. In Ovid, Orpheus's "stupor" after he looks back makes him "no different" from other mythical figures who become stone (343).

on performers and fans searching for a sense of roots in the midst of ephemeral pop culture."[32] In *Orpheus Descending*, Williams staged the myth of a transmission of "bracing foreignness" from Black musician to white acolyte, without the music. Scenes of such transmission were central to American mass culture in those years, and to fantasies of such transmission in artifacts ranging from Norman Mailer's *The White Negro*, first published in 1957, the year of the premiere *of Orpheus Descending*, to Elvis's starring role in *King Creole*, which opened in 1958. These local instances speak to the contemporaneity of Williams's engagements with mass culture, but also to the larger history of minstrelsy and its centrality to the history of American performance and mass culture.[33] With Val as the white face of Black music, appropriation resembles erasure. The very insistence on racial division, however, might also reify the category of "Black music" by ignoring the hybridity of American music. Where are we on the spectrum of Eric Lott's dialectic of love and theft? *Orpheus Descending* does not make coherent these complex and contradictory histories.

Black musical deities may have signed Val's guitar, but the song he sings is his own—or, that is, Williams's —signature piece:

> My feet took a walk in heavenly grass.
> All day while the sky shone clear as glass.
> My feet took a walk in heavenly grass,
> All night while the lonesome stars rolled past.
> Then my feet come down to walk on earth,
> And my mother cried when she gave me birth.
> Now my feet walk far and my feet walk fast,
> But they still got an itch for heavenly grass.
> But they still got an itch for heavenly grass.[34]

The song's title appears three times; Val's performances are interrupted twice before he finally finishes the song.[35] Its title appears in stage directions as if it were a hit single or a standard everyone would know. The song did have a life across media, but it was never a hit, and never became a standard, and its most durable life has been as an art song. Like the play in which

32. Filene, *Romancing the Folk*. 75.

33. Central contributions to the scholarship on minstrelsy include Eric Lott's *Love and Theft* and Daphne Brooks's *Bodies in Dissent*.

34. Williams, *Collected Poems*, 63.

35. Williams, *Orpheus Descending*, 16; 25; 47.

Williams included it, "Heavenly Grass" has had a strange career. As the editors of Williams's *Collected Poems* explain, the lines surface in a draft dated Key West, 1941. "Heavenly Grass" first appears, in 1946, in one of a set of four music sheets published by Schirmer "in the series *Blue Mountain Ballads*." Further, a recording on the 1952 Caedmon LP, *Tennessee Williams: Selections from His Writings, Read by the Author*, appeared in advance of the lines' first publication as a printed poem in *In the Winter of the Cities*, in 1956. This strange print and recorded history suggests a certain resistance to print—or a certain kind of print—and printed texts of the play, in which the words to the song never appear, continue this trajectory. That "Heavenly Grass" first appeared in a collection of "ballads" is especially suggestive. Meredith McGill succinctly calls the category of the ballad "the literary form of non-literary verse."[36] It is, then, doubly interesting that Williams also collected "Heavenly Grass" with eleven other pieces in a "bound typescript" dated 1942 "under the title 'BLUE MOUNTAIN BLUES/(A collection of folk-verse)," to which Williams appended this note: "This collection is written primarily as lyrics for blues music or a folk opera but no music has been composed for them yet."[37] So, to summarize: lines written in 1941 get collected as "lyrics for blues music" in 1942, published as words for a setting by Paul Bowles in 1946, printed as a lyric poem in 1956, and sung on stage by Cliff Robertson, who originated the role of Val— Williams's white mythological descendant of Orpheus, Lead Belly, and Elvis—in 1957. "Heavenly Grass," that is, variously aspires to the condition of folk music, pop song, art song, and printed "lyric." The poem is, then, the perfect icon of *Orpheus Descending*: the play is at once a staging of a genealogy of "poetry" luxuriating in the tensions between mass and high culture and a conflicted monument to the genealogy it stages.[38] Williams strives, to borrow a phrase from Jonathan Freedman, to autocanonize his own words and to render them anonymous.[39] And this

36. McGill, "What Is a Ballad?," 161.

37. For a meticulous discussion of the dissemination of "Heavenly Grass," on which I rely here, see the editors' note in Williams, *Collected Poems*, 236. The editors point out that the lines appear in an unpublished play also titled "Heavenly Grass" and again, sung by Kilroy, at various places in drafts of *Camino Real*. Tom Mitchell discusses the unpublished play—a Black nativity story set in the Mississippi Delta—in "Tennessee Williams Wrestles with Race in Three Unpublished Works" (65–67).

38. In this context it is notable that in *Battle of Angels*, Val isn't a musician, but a writer, and that one of the aliases the young Williams considered was Valentine Sevier, a notable ancestor (Lahr, *Mad Pilgrimage*, 18). Val may be seen, as Lahr suggests, as a barometer of Williams's shifting identifications.

39. See Jonathan Freedman's discussion of Barry Manilow's "I Write the Songs" in "Autocanonization."

LEAD BELLY'S GUITAR AND WILLIAMS'S COUNTERPUBLICS > 143

describes the movement of the pop-cultural archive that the song, in its place in *Orpheus Descending*, at once resists and imitates: what Parker Tyler called "the Elvis Presley tradition of folk music gone bobby-sox."[40] That is, the truest form of autocanonization would be to achieve the state of sublime anonymity that this hybrid of folk and mass culture might embody. The mercantile store Orpheus sings a song only paratexts assign to Williams.

That segue from ballad to blues to "folk-verse" is suggestive of the ways these genres speak a particular jargon of authenticity, a jargon with etymological roots at least as deep or as shallow as those collection of folk songs that entranced the Romantics and those other collections of folk songs that entranced the original hipsters of the 1930s and 1940s. Williams channeled this jargon. *Orpheus Descending*, staged about a decade after the success of *A Streetcar Named Desire*, achieved nothing like it on stage or in the film adaptation, *The Fugitive Kind*, which appeared in 1959. *Streetcar* is relevant here, however: Williams is at pains to distance Val from Brando's Stanley Kowalski and specifies in the stage direction introducing Val: "*He does not wear levis or a T-shirt.*"[41] More important, *Orpheus Descending* belongs among Williams's meditations on the shaping of the social imaginary through his own mass cultural work. Williams had become a figure in the very mass solicitation of cathexes against which the legitimate theater is reputed to provide an anecdote.

Williams's staging of the first sexual encounter between Lady and Val signals the play's awareness of the dialectic between public spheres. Lady has secretly set up a room for Val in an alcove in the back of the store. After examining the space in which she proposes he should sleep, he immediately understands her invitation as seduction:

> I never been in a position where I could turn down something I got for nothing in my life. I like that picture in there. That's a famous picture, that September Morn picture you got on the wall in there. Ha ha! I might have trouble sleeping in a room with that picture. I might keep turning the light on to take another look at it! The way she's cold in that water and sort of crouched over in it, holding her body like that, that—might—ha ha!—sort of keep me awake. . . .
>
> LADY: You with your perfect control of your functions, it would take more than a picture to keep you awake!

40. Tyler, review of *The Fugitive Kind*, 47.

41. Williams, *Orpheus Descending*, 11. Michael Cadden, in an undergraduate lecture at Princeton in the 1990s, observed that this stage direction registers the impact of *Streetcar*.

VAL: I was just kidding.

LADY: I was just kidding too.[42]

Lady jokes about proud claims of self-control that Val makes when they first meet, and these jokes are also part of an encrypted debate about the power of mass-reproduced images. *September Morn* had indeed been a "famous picture," massively reproduced and re-circulated, caricatured, spoofed and parodied. For some, the painting is an icon of kitsch. The painting had inspired censorship in the early twentieth century, but it was, by the 1950s, considered rather tame and that controversy a relic of a transcended puritanism.[43] Val reads Lady's use of the image correctly. What matters here is that for Lady the reproduction of the painting is not kitsch, and that the painting's massive popularity does nothing to temper its force for her as the expression of an emotion otherwise unspeakable. If the structure of the play places Val squarely with music and an emerging hipster counterpublic, it just as squarely places Lady with a ubiquitous visual culture as the lingua franca of desire. Carol Cutrere, near the end of the play, "*crosses downstage and speaks to the audience and to herself*": "Something is still wild in this country! This country used to be wild, the men and women were wild and there was a wild sort of sweetness in their hearts, for each other, but now it's sick with neon, it's broken out sick, with neon, like most other places. . . ."[44] The blocking might suggest that this familiar critique of mass culture is authoritative, that Carol's condemnation of neon as the synecdoche for advertising embodies the play's implied appeal to some genuine, authentic, anti-commercial myth as the privileged outside of debased mass culture. This moment, however, needs to be read alongside *September Morn* and the play's refusal to condemn mass-mediated desire. Carol's nostalgia for an old wild country also emphasizes ways that the play distances itself from the myth-making tendencies this speech exemplifies: when was this sweet, wild time? A prime locus of nostalgia within the play is the wine garden Lady's father established and ran: the first scene includes the narration of the collapse of that idyllic space when a thinly veiled KKK ("the Mystic Crew")

---

42. Williams, *Orpheus Descending*, 49.

43. See Paul Chabas, *September Morn*, ca. 1912, now in the Metropolitan Museum of Art, New York. The substantial annotated bibliography provided by the museum on its website tracks a history from scandal and censorship to benign acceptance. A remarkable online resource, "The *September Morn* Archive," made a trove of ephemera inspired by the painting available: the Internet Archive's Wayback Machine preserves thumbnails from this archive.

44. Williams, *Orpheus Descending*, 69.

burns down the garden and murders her father because he has sold liquor to Black customers.[45]

Carol is, alongside Val, the play's exemplum of an alternative to the racist order of the town. Early on, she declares herself to be an "exhibitionist" and compares herself to Val, who vehemently rejects any likeness between them. In a long speech, she narrates her history from her days as "a Christ-bitten reformer"—a "kind of benign exhibitionist"—to her current identity as a "lewd vagrant." She moves from speeches and "letters of protest, about the gradual massacre of the colored majority in the county" through "pellagra and slow starvation":

> And when that Willie McGee thing came along—he was sent to the chair for having improper relations with a white whore—(*Her voice is like a passionate incantation.*) I made a fuss about it. I put on a potato sack and set out for the capitol on foot. This was in winter. I walked barefoot in this burlap sack to deliver a personal protest to the Governor of the State. Oh, I suppose it was partly exhibitionism on my part, but it wasn't completely exhibitionism, there was something else in it, too.

After walking for six miles surrounded by abuse, she is arrested for "lewd vagrancy."[46] The vernacular self-diagnosis of exhibitionism here implies that the cause of racial justice gave her a motive to display herself: the spectacle of the scantily clad woman announces itself as protest but cannot disguise the real, pathological need to be seen: now, she owns her identity as simply a "lewd vagrant." But was there "something else in it, too"? As with the names on the guitar, Williams pointedly includes the name of a real figure: Willie McGee was convicted of rape in Mississippi and murdered by the state, after appeals and protests, in 1951. This episode, then, exemplifies a strategy of surrogation in which the visibility of white characters stands in for the unseen Black victims of racial violence.

Orpheus Descending closes with Val's offstage murder: Carol Cutrere "*crouches over in vicarious agony as the sound of pursuit reaches a climax.*" The Conjure Man emerges with Val's snakeskin jacket, which he has somehow rescued from the scene, and Carol exchanges it for a gold ring: "*a simple ceremony.*" Carol once again crosses down center: "Wild things leave skins behind them, they leave clean skins and teeth and white bones behind them, and these are tokens passed from one to another, so the fugitive kind

---

45. Williams, *Orpheus Descending*, 8.

46. Williams, *Orpheus Descending*, 19–20.

can always follow their kind." The sheriff enters and orders her to stop; she ignores him and exits. As the Conjure Man looks up "*with a secret smile*," the curtain falls.[47] Imagining the "fugitive kind" who will know how to receive these tokens and how to follow "their kind," *Orpheus Descending* prepares for its own afterlife explicitly. This reflection on the passing of "tokens" from one to another emphasizes Carol as a figure for the transmission of an insider's knowledge about outsiders, an unusual way for a Broadway play to divide its audience: the downstage speech, before the curtain falls, as an appeal to the elective affinities of some part of that audience.[48] Or a utopian appeal to everyone: this place does not need to be, in Vee's words, "always the way it actually is." To understand this—and this what the play wants everyone to understand—should be an induction into the fugitive kind.

Vee's phrase and the play's final utopian gesture recall the argument of Julia Jarcho's *Writing and the Modern Stage*: "Beckett," Jarcho writes, "registers the present in recoiling from it, and this preserves a longing for something else through its very refusal to make the 'something else' manifest."[49] For Jarcho, the preservation of this longing and the refusal to stage an alternative to the present is a utopian mode. Williams, too, recoils from the present—but not as thoroughly, not from all of it. In *Orpheus Descending*, Williams generates intimations of a counterpublic that could become something more than simply underground and fugitive out of the contradictory materials of Black music and mass culture. The play does not, however, stage this counterpublic. There are only fragments: the cry of the Conjure Man, "Heavenly Grass," Vee's visionary painting. And furthermore the idea that the fugitive condition can be a matter of elective affinity stresses the play's invocation of Black popular culture through erasure. From his second play, *Fugitive Kind*, to *Camino Real* to the reemergence of *The Fugitive Kind* as the title of the film adaptation of *Orpheus Descending*, "fugitive" is a keyword across Williams's work, and his concern with the possibility of

---

47. Williams, *Orpheus Descending*, 78.

48. One piece of evidence of the force of this appeal to a counterpublic is the letter Judith Malina and Julian Beck of the Living Theatre wrote to the "Drama Mailbag" of the *New York Times*, published on April 7, 1957: "It seemed to us that in the case of 'Orpheus Descending' there is an important element to which at least passing notice should be given. 'Orpheus Descending' powerfully illustrates the principle that hatred breeds hatred; and we are shown how hatred in the South for one segment of the population multiplies until corruption is rampant and evil prevails. As a piece of social writing, it is unsurpassed in the contemporary American theater."

49. Jarcho, *Writing and the Modern Stage*, 74.

counterpublics of outsiders is a pervasive ideal.[50] That fugitivity is also a key concept in contemporary Black studies points to a point of contact, but also to a divergence. Fred Moten's phrase, "the possibility and the law of outlawed, impossible things," resonates with Williams's concern with those who are essentially alien to the social order and yet obliged somehow to make a life inside it. Moten's interest in limning the "fugitive law of movement that makes black social life ungovernable" marks the decisive difference between an elective position of outsider liminality, however little that position might seem like a choice, and a structural position, however fugitive that position might be.[51] Williams's drama of white protagonists cannot illustrate what Moten calls the case of Blackness.

In the opening scene of *The Fugitive Kind*, Sidney Lumet's film of 1960, Marlon Brando, as Val, stands before a judge's desk in New Orleans, framed by an unwavering camera as he speaks hesitantly and softly. Questioned by this invisible judge, Val describes his agony because his guitar is in hock at a pawnshop: the guitar is, he says, "a gift from a very great man, Lead Belly." The play's signatures are no longer enough: the film needs the fantasy of the guitar as Lead Belly's gift to Val to imagine a counterpublic durable enough to withstand the movement from theater to film.[52] "It is a heavy burden to be made to stand as the racial-sexual embodiment of the imagination in its lawless freedom," writes Moten in a different context.[53] In *Orpheus Descending*, Val is one of Williams's embodiments of this burden. This embodiment rests on a set of mass cultural fantasies: of Elvis as the hot white center of a

---

50. *Fugitive Kind*, performed in 1937 but published only in 2001, already explicitly thematizes Williams's concern with the fugitive. Leo, the son of the Jewish owner of a "flophouse," announces a "cordial welcome to gentlemen of the nomadic disposition, the fugitive kind" and later declares that "we're outcasts, lunatics, criminals—the Fugitive Kind" (*Fugitive Kind*, 34; 133). Terry, a bank robber and so in that literal sense a fugitive, riffs on the label: "Fugitives from justice? Naw, we're fugitives from *in*-justice, honey!" (138; see the similar passage on 121). A fuller reading of this play might begin with that word "disposition" and its suggestion that fugitivity is somewhere between fate and choice. In *Camino Real*, the airplane that, like the plane in *Casablanca*, might rescue those stranded in the play's mythical city, is a "non-scheduled thing" called the Fugitivo (see *Camino Real* in *Plays 1937–1955*, 799).

51. Moten, "The Case of Blackness," 178; 179.

52. In an ironic echo of this scene, Kurt Cobain, introducing Nirvana's version of Lead Belly's "Where Did You Sleep Last Night?" for *MTV Unplugged*, drolly narrates: "This guy representing the Lead Belly estate wants to sell me Lead Belly's guitar for 500,000 dollars. . . . I even asked David Geffen personally if he'd buy it for me." This may mark an endpoint in what Joel Dinerstein, in a discussion of *The Fugitive Kind* in *The Origins of Cool in Postwar America*, calls "existential cool as a myth for rebels" (383).

53. Moten, "The Case of Blackness," 212.

set of mass cultural fantasies about race and about sexuality; of Black music as portable, representable as a signifier in the absence of Black performers and the sounds of Black music; of alterity as elective rather than as a fact of structure. Williams makes Val stand as such an embodiment, but that position is not that of those who are "*made* to stand" in that place.

∴

SAMUEL BECKETT

∵

[TWENTY]

Beckett, Cinema, Politics

Beckett does not aspire to the condition of the moving picture. His stage pictures, decreasingly mobile, increasingly pictures of stasis, proceed away from the direction of cinema. Even *Film* seems determined to swerve away from film's potential for movement, the thrill of speed, which, in such different forms as the chase and montage, has been fundamental to film. This is not to say that there is a single orientation to movement in Beckett's work, nor that some cinema has not countered the general tendency toward greater and greater speed, toward more frantic action and more frequent cuts. The comparison between cinema and Beckett's work is also not only descriptive. The argument of what follows is that in substantial ways Beckett's theater exists and existed in relation to film, in relation to the mass cultural surround in which his plays were first performed. The comparisons that matter are not between something called film, or the larger category of mass culture, and an idea of Beckett's theater, but ones driven by historical questions such as those I have discussed above: What was cinema, and how did Beckett's theater respond to it? Or to phrase this differently: What was cinema, such that Beckett's theater *had* to respond to it?

This form of the question emphasizes the ways film established the conditions of possibility for theater in the postwar world. And yet nothing determined the particular form of the relationship between theater and film. Beckett's theater is exemplary of one response: theater's condition of possibility as the negation of cinema. This is true at one relatively trivial if also revealing level: no character in a theater piece ever talks about going to the cinema or alludes directly to an experience of moviegoing. Many episodes of more-or-less modern life do appear: bicycles, tourism, a reel-to-reel tape recorder, even, as I will discuss later, familiar brand names. In *Happy Days*, Winnie remembers fragments of verse and Willie reads the newspaper, but she never mentions a moment together at the cinema, and he reads aloud phrases from want ads, not coming attractions. The absence of the pastime of going to the cinema, for decades so common a feature of the everyday life of Europe and America before *Waiting for Godot* first appeared onstage in 1953, is significant, as if these characters occupied some time anterior to cinema or to the side of cinema, some time or place outside cinema.

[TWENTY-ONE]

Film and Its Audiences

In an article published in June 1954 in *France-Observateur*, Roland Barthes reflected on what it meant that *Waiting for Godot*, a play seemingly destined for those small audiences accustomed to attending avant-garde productions, had, after roughly a year and a half, gained a cumulative audience of roughly a hundred thousand spectators. Barthes anticipated many strands in later criticism of Beckett. He anticipated, for instance, the argument of this book—only in reverse. To explain the audience *Godot* had gained, Barthes pointed to the play's refusal to flatter its audience, to its toughness, and its plainness:

> The secret of such consistency linked to such accessibility, that's one of theater's great secrets: a literal language with no double and no connivance. Criticism, always careful to reassure us, has struggled from the beginning to supply the keys to *Godot*: Pozzo, that's capitalism, Godot, that's God, etc. And then what? All of these allegories take part in a theological order that is not at all that of theater. Theater is an immediate act: all that matters is what is said and seen in the precise density of that act: the rest is the stuff of diaries. Put otherwise, the language of *Godot* leaves every allegory at the entrance to the theater: it is a sufficient language, perfectly plain, of the kind that concedes nothing to symbolic commentary.[1]

Barthes's critique of the drive toward the reassuring palliatives of allegory in the critique of Beckett remains bracing; his emphasis on the literal—in the theater, in Beckett—foreshadows the work of other critics. The "precise density of that act": the phrase captures the drive toward a theatrical event that does not imagine that its importance lies elsewhere, in the satisfactions

---

1. Barthes, "*Godot* adulte," 89. I thank Derek Miller for sharing Barthes's essay with me, and Carrie Noland for her generous collaboration in the translation of these passages.

of allegorical decoding or "symbolic commentary." And yet the literality Barthes links to the theater and to Beckett is not at all specific to the medium of theater, as his phrase may seem to suggest:

> I think that the new public of *Godot* only hears one language, and it is right to do so because what is remarkable in *Godot,* as in Adamov, as in Ionesco, is precisely that it supplies nothing but a language. I think there is there a certain literality, plain and hard, that might recall that of cinema. The general public follows *Godot* insofar as it is a public that has been trained [*dressé*] by the similar exteriority of cinematic language, and thus able to grasp the surface mobility of that language and find there an immediate and sufficient plenitude.[2]

Barthes solves the problem of *Godot*'s popularity: audiences take to the play's "language" because the cinema has trained them for it: they already know the language, or at least something very similar to it. That training in the literality of cinema means that the audience of *Godot* does not need that other plenitude that allegory might provide. (Other critics, trained in other languages, taking the literal language of the play as insufficient, and that insufficiency as the sign of something missing, reach for that allegorical plenitude.) And yet Barthes's analysis of the success of *Godot* provokes the question of why, if the experience it provided was so close to that of cinema, audiences nevertheless sought out the play in such numbers. Why not simply attend another movie to continue one's cinematic training? What difference might the audience's presence in the theater, rather than the cinema, make to an encounter with a literality similar to that of film?

To say that audiences were trained in the language of cinema was one way to picture the saturation of consciousness by film. Even while Barthes here appears to admire the ways that *Godot* follows cinema in its emphasis on surfaces and exteriority, there is also at least a trace of a familiar critique of mass culture in his formulation. Barthes's word here, "*dressé*," or "trained," recalls the training of animals. (The root perseveres in English in the word *dressage*.) The question of what it meant, in and around 1954, to be trained in the language of cinema—to be trained *by* the language of cinema—is a historical question that drives this book. Further, the question of the relationship between this training and Beckett's drama is at the core of *Theater after Film.* This training might include, simply, recognition: *Godot,* for instance, contains the wonderful sequence of hat-swapping that

2. Barthes, "*Godot* adulte," 89–90.

recalls a similar sequence in the Marx Brothers' *Duck Soup*.[3] In 1953 Jean Anouilh famously called the play the "music-hall sketch of Pascal's 'Pensées' as played by the Fratellini clowns," and many have since echoed this erudite tribute to the play's roots in popular performance.[4] Hugh Kenner's insistence on the entwining of these strands remains important: Beckett's debts to slapstick cinema and popular performance are at the same time philosophical commitments, just as his critique of philosophy can appear at the most burlesque moments.

Tracing the intermingling of the strands of popular performance and philosophy in Beckett's plays remains crucial to understanding his work, and especially to understanding how it assumed an audience trained in cinema. I will record my debts to scholars who have traced these strands: my argument partly rests on, but however is not ultimately about, the investigation of the afterlives of popular culture in the plays. These afterlives are the more apparent traces of an engagement with mass culture that goes much deeper than, for instance, the persistence of slapstick on stage, significant and delicious though that persistence is. As I argue above, postwar theater requires rethinking how we picture mass culture's determination of dramatic form. Beckett is exemplary of that strand that registers the force of mass culture through its absence and negation. Beckett does not, like Peter Handke, frame his plays with explicit rules for actors that—to sustain Barthes's metaphor—train theater makers in a particular attunement to the mass cultural surround. That surround is nevertheless an important element of the horizon against which Beckett's plays stood out.

Beckett's work for performance, that is, belongs at the center of this book because it registers and responds to the intricate mass-mediated surround determining the conditions of spectatorship with unique complexity. It is probably no longer necessary to debunk arguments that Beckett depicts the absurd plight of an ahistorical humanity.[5] Despite a general suspicion of any idea of an essential human nature, arguments that Beckett represents

3. Deirdre Bair, for instance, makes this connection in *Samuel Beckett* (388), but the debt is simply there to be recollected, and many spectators have.

4. Jean Anouilh, *Arts Spectacles* (February 27–March, 5, 1953: 1), trans. Ruby Cohn, in Graver and Federman, *Samuel Beckett: The Critical Heritage*, 92.

5. Indeed, it may be more important for me to acknowledge the persuasiveness of Julia Jarcho's defense of "the power of the universalizing impulse in reading Beckett": "The universalizing tendency of so much Beckett reception, then, is not merely an artifact of mid-century chauvinism; rather, such readings respond to an anxiety within the work itself, which forces the prospect of a life that could not offer any resistance to our generalizations—a life for which what happens on one stage for two hours could, horrifically enough, be valid everywhere and always" (*Writing and the Modern Stage*,

permanent conditions of looking remain common. There are several reasons for this. The general absence of pronounced historical markers in his plays has led critics and audiences to imagine that his work aspired to the condition of transhistorical truth. The glamour of such truth was especially appealing to his early critics but has not fully lost its luster. More specific to my concerns here, the historicity of mid-century theories of, or assumptions about, spectatorship that continue to buttress many of these responses is, very often even now, equally overlooked. The allure of ideas concerning the permanent truth of watching has not passed away. Many see demonstrations of these truths in Beckett's plays, his film, and his works for television. Philosophical and theoretical claims about what "the" theater does—what it does in the present, what it has done since the Greeks—can be startlingly illuminating, but in this context such claims sometimes also disguise the conditions that made Beckett's work so powerful in the first place. Or, indeed, these philosophical claims may be valuable precisely for the eloquence with which they describe, without intending to, historically specific conditions as permanent facts of life.

Beckett's stage plays are the sites where the force of film and mass culture leaves its most complex traces on his work.[6] As the following sections will show, negative traces of that force determine many of the characteristic techniques of the plays. I nevertheless begin my discussion of Beckett not with a play, but with *Film*, the twenty-four-minute movie first sketched in 1963, filmed in Manhattan in 1964, and first screened in 1965. *Film* opens up many of the questions important to my discussion of Beckett, including arguments about medium, media, and postwar theories of spectatorship. Critical discussion of *Film* is especially remarkable for the contrast between the historical specificity of the object and transcendent claims made for it. *Film* has inspired a great deal of commentary concerning spectatorship: much of this assumes that the conditions of seeing and of being seen that

---

83). For another recent and resonant anti-historicist reading of Beckett, see Gabriele Schwab, *Moments for Nothing*.

6. I am, then, drawing attention to the ways that the plays for the stage perform a remediation in reverse of the conditions of mass cultural spectatorship. And so my emphasis here swerves away from Beckett's plays for radio and television, which have garnered so much valuable critical attention. Milestones in this scholarship include Clas Zilliacus, *Beckett and Broadcasting* (1976), Martin Esslin, *Mediations: Essays on Brecht, Beckett, and the Media* (1980), Linda Ben-Zvi, "Samuel Beckett's Media Plays" (1985), and Peter Seibert's collection, *Samuel Beckett und die Medien*. Balazs Rapcsak and Mark Nixon's introduction to *Beckett and Media* expertly surveys the state of this field circa 2022 (1–11). Although our conclusions differ, my reasons for concentrating on stage plays resembles that of Stan Garner in his excellent *Bodied Spaces* (see esp. 61n25).

Film investigates are permanent ones. I think this is wrong, and that *Film* makes visible the historicity of Beckett's engagement with spectatorship. The movie belongs to a postwar terrain remade by cinema, and it signals its place so insistently that it is a wonder that this signal has, as a rule, been so thoroughly lost in transmission.

The most glaring index of this historicity is also the most commonly known fact about *Film*: Buster Keaton performs in it. Scholarly accounts such as Michael North's *Machine-Age Comedy* have begun to track the complexity of this collaboration and to acknowledge that Keaton's silent comedies are an important precursor to Beckett's work; Ross Lipman's "kino-essay" *Notfilm* makes a similar argument cinematically. Further, the collaboration of Beckett and Keaton also provides a richly textured window into thinking about Beckett's relationship not to cinema as such, but to the history of film. It was Beckett who suggested that Keaton play the central role in *Film*.[7] This suggestion was a mark of his long-standing interest in silent film comedy in general and Keaton in particular. In early discussions with Roger Blin, the director, about the first production of *Waiting for Godot*, Beckett had mentioned Keaton and Chaplin as models for performance of his plays.[8] Alan Schneider, the director of *Film* who also directed many premieres of Beckett's work in the United States, reports that Keaton had "been offered the part of Lucky in the original American *Godot* some years back, but had turned it down."[9] The reasons for this investment in Keaton bear thought. Keaton's biographer, Tom Dardis, has suggested that Beckett was drawn to the melancholia that marks a film such as Keaton's 1925 *Go West*.[10] Such an affective affinity is indeed remarkable, and the links between the deadpan, recessive humor typical of Keaton's performances in the silents and Beckett's theater are evident: one wishes Keaton had played Lucky.[11] But such a counterfactual wish threatens to reproduce a habit of thinking of Keaton only as a performer appropriate to roles Beckett might

---

7. Schneider, "On Directing *Film*," 67; Dardis, *Keaton, The Man Who Wouldn't Lie Down*, 268. See also Knowlson's valuable pages on the making of *Film* (*Damned to Fame*, 463–67).

8. Bair, *Samuel Beckett: A Biography*, 404.

9. Schneider, "On Directing *Film*," 67.

10. Dardis, *Keaton, The Man Who Wouldn't Lie Down*, 131.

11. Tina Post's remarkable examination of the blackness of Keaton's deadpan resonates here. Via a quotation from Gilberto Perez, a phrase becomes a refrain of her final chapter and coda: "nothing to be done" (Post, *Deadpan*, 184, 203). This phrase, also the first line spoken in *Waiting for Godot*, underlines that affinity between Keaton and Beckett.

have chosen for him. (Schneider's essay on the making of *Film* introduced a certain unfortunate condescension toward Keaton into discussions of the movie's making.) As a filmmaker Keaton anticipated Beckett in thinking about medium—in thinking about the shifting conditions of theater and film together—and it is here that Keaton takes on his real importance. I will focus on how the question of theater as medium—a question at once formal and historical—ties Keaton and Beckett.[12] This investigation, in Keaton as in Beckett, proceeds from the historical predicament of a medium that seems in some ways archaic, left behind by mass culture. Or, to put this in a way at once more dialectical and less tinged by some progressive narrative in which the superior celluloid medium supersedes the stage, Keaton and Beckett both realize in their work that to think the medium of theater must also be to think the medium of film. The reverse also holds: when Keaton and Beckett represent film as medium, theater remains film's dialectical partner.

Critics long argued that Beckett carries on a modernist project—even, by some lights, *the* modernist project—of discovering the material conditions of a particular medium in relation to other media.[13] The formulations of Clement Greenberg, Beckett's near contemporary, continue to set the terms for this discussion. Noting that *Film*, like some of his other experiments in radio and television, came about as the result of an invitation, Hugh Kenner wrote of Beckett: "And since the suggestion has specified a medium, not a subject, he has allowed the novel medium to generate its fit subject."[14] The movement from medium to subject here does not necessarily accord with the logic of seeming inevitability typified by the reduction of painting to the flat surface championed by Greenberg, but Kenner's suggestion that medium generates subject belongs inside the logic of medium-specificity Greenberg inaugurated. Thomas Crow's emphasis on the historical situation out of which the emphasis on medium emerged restores the importance of media history to this argument. Crow synthesizes one strand of Greenberg's early criticism:

> what was occupying his attention was nothing less than a material and social crisis which threatened the traditional forms of nineteenth-century culture with extinction. This crisis had resulted from the economic pressure of an industry devoted to the simulation of art in the form of

12. For a rich discussion of the intersection of theater and film in Keaton, see Henry Jenkins, "'This Fellow Keaton Seems to Be the Whole Show.'"

13. See, for instance, Daniel Albright, *Beckett and Aesthetics*.

14. Kenner, *A Reader's Guide*, 159.

reproducible commodities, that is to say, the industry of mass culture. In search of raw material, mass culture had progressively stripped traditional art of its marketable qualities, and had left as the only remaining path to authenticity a ceaseless alertness against the stereotyped and preprocessed. By refusing any other demands but the most self-contained technical ones, the authentic artist could protect his or her work from the reproduction and rationalization that would process its usable bits and destroy its inner logic. From this resistance came the necessity for modernism's inwardness, self-reflexivity, "truth to media."[15]

Crow's example, modernist painting, remains the privileged field where this project of "truth to media" is most clear; it may be also be the one area where the argument ever had any real purchase. The theater, by contrast, is the form that has proved most troubling to theoretical accounts that link modernism in the arts to "truth to media." What is the medium of theater? Does "theatricality" name the medium to which theater should be true? Or, to put this more historically, the medium to which modernist theater should have been true?

The failure of twentieth-century theater to align with the usual chronology of modernism is well known: somehow Beckett is simultaneously the "last modernist," as Anthony Cronin, the third of his three fine biographers, has called him, and, in theatrical terms, the first—the first, that is, at last to dissolve theater to its medium. It is as if before Beckett theater is not yet quite modernist, and, after Beckett, postmodern. There is some truth to this picture of Beckett's importance. And yet I also think that such formulations miss the challenge of Beckett's theatrical works. Beckett's work demonstrates that no medium as such defines the theatrical. If, as Rosalind Krauss skeptically writes, "a medium is purportedly made specific by being reduced to nothing but its manifest physical properties," theater poses the peculiar problem of a medium where no one can agree what these "manifest physical properties" might be or whether they are "physical" at all.[16] Is theater (to review a debate discussed above) essentially enacted narrative, liveness, a performance with an audience? Beckett's theater emphasizes that if the medium of theater is not a set of "manifest physical properties"

15. Crow, "Modernism and Mass Culture in the Visual Arts," 9. Crow cites two essays in this context: Greenberg's "Avant-Garde and Kitsch" of 1939, and "Towards a Newer Laocoon" of 1940. Shannon Jackson's pages on "theatricality and literality" open up the links between Greenberg and Michael Fried's critique of theatricality in "Art and Objecthood" (*Professing Performance*, 120–26).

16. Krauss, *"A Voyage on the North Sea,"* 7.

but, instead, a relation between performers and audience, then one must face the strangeness—and the historical changeableness—of this relation, a relation that must itself always be seen in relationship to other relations.

Beckett's engagement with the conditions under which one is seen, with what it means, even, to be seen: this problem is fundamental to his work. M, in Beckett's *Play*, repeatedly asks: "Am I as much as . . . being seen?"[17] Beckett frames the text of *Film* with a phrase from another Irish philosopher, George Berkeley, "*Esse est percipi*": to be is to be perceived.[18] (One might then translate and abbreviate M's question: "Am I as much as . . . being?") From Gilles Deleuze's short essay on "The Greatest Irish Film" and his discussion of *Film* in *Cinema 1* to Branka Arsić on Berkeley "via Beckett" to Simon Critchley's essay on *Film*, *Film* has drawn philosophers and philosophically minded critics.[19] Like the related insistence on Beckett's "truth to medium," these philosophical discussions largely treat Beckett's work as though it staged ahistorical problems of ontology. Arsić and Critchley alike write as though particular histories of theater and of film did not exist. Critchley claims that *Film* is "concerned with the genre of *Film* itself, the nature of the cinematic medium."[20] Genre, nature, medium: the rapid slide from one term to another doesn't matter because, whatever this thing might be, it is assumed to be one thing. But *Film* is not a film about film—if, that is, one imagines that film is one medium.

Not only is theater not one thing, and film not some other thing, but each of these is divided: each is several things. A crucial context for postwar theater, I have been arguing, is a conception of cinema as an industry as the apogee of a mass cultural surround; that surround, further, is imagined as what Hans Enzensberger would later call the consciousness industry. The extreme self-containment of Beckett's theater, that is, must be seen in relation to media that seemed to violate all attempts at containment, in relation to those forms of mass dissemination of that, in the 1950s, when Beckett's career in the theater began, already counted as "new media," to quote

17. Beckett, *Play*, in *Collected Shorter Plays*, 160. Ernst Fischer and Simon Critchley are among the critics who have also linked *Film* to this line in *Play* (Fischer, "Samuel Beckett: Play and Film," 102; Critchley, "To be or not to be," 110).

18. Beckett, *Film*, in *Collected Shorter Plays*, 165.

19. Deleuze, "The Greatest Irish Film"; Deleuze, *Cinema 1*, 66–68; Arsić, *The Passive Eye*; Critchley, "To be or not to be." For Deleuze and Beckett, see Garin Dowd, *Abstract Machines* and Audrey Wasser, "A Relentless Spinozism."

20. Critchley, "To be or not to be," 110.

Marshall McLuhan from an essay first published in 1954.[21] But precisely to the degree that those technological challenges demanded an aesthetic response, their shifting status also meant that the "medium" they are helping to determine shifted. Rather than discovering *the* medium of theater, a medium that was always inwardly latent in theater—as the flatness of the canvas was supposedly revealed by modernist painters to have been the medium of painting all along—Beckett's works for performance revealed the historical core of the medium of theater in the postwar period.[22] Telegraphically (to appeal to the ghost of an old medium) one might say that Beckett's works for performance are always shadowed by the rise of that conglomeration then called "the media."

Beckett does follow something like Crow's modernist paradigm. His negations of much of the conventional stuff of drama, as Crow suggests, constituted a response to—and an enacted critique of—film, radio, and other mass cultural forms. That is to say, the seemingly "self-contained" demand arose from the denial or negation of other demands—demands, for instance, that the theater address certain kinds of content or represent the world in particular ways. The paradox of self-containment, here, is that the demand for medium-specificity registered pressures outside the medium: the impulse behind the drive to something one might call medium-specificity was itself not specific to the medium. Beckett's theater is in this sense exemplary: it contains the demand to medium-specificity within itself, and this demand makes legible the exteriority the work resists. That is also to say, the location of this demand cannot be located with any precision: What does it mean to say that such a demand is *within* the work?

Beckett's engagement with this complex problem of medium-specificity becomes especially clear in the early 1960s, when he writes two works that announce their engagement with problems of medium in their titles alone: *Play* and *Film*. *Film* stages the efforts of Keaton's O to escape what Beckett, in his published scenario, calls first an "anguish" and, then, "an agony of perceivedness."[23] E, the eye of the camera, hunts O down and is the chief cause of this agony. In three stages, *Film* moves from the street, to a vestibule and

---

21. "Have four centuries of book-culture hypnotized us into such concentration on the content of books and the new media that we cannot see that the very form of any medium of communication is as important as anything that it conveys?" McLuhan, "Sight Sound, and the Fury," in Rosenberg, *Mass Culture*, 489. This essay was first published in *Commonweal* 60 (1954): 168–97.

22. For a rich and wide-ranging treatment of Beckett and flatness, see Alan Ackerman, "Samuel Beckett's *Spectres du Noir*."

23. Beckett, *Film*, in *Collected Shorter Plays*, 166, 167.

stairs, where O encounters people whose glances he strives to avoid, to a bare room occupied by too many things with eyes: a dog, a cat, a parrot, a photograph "of a Sumerian head of the god Abu" from Baghdad, even an envelope and the back of a rocking chair.[24] In the conclusion of the film, O dozes off in the rocking chair only to find that E is himself.

Beckett's scenario has set the terms for the analysis of *Film*. My account will be no exception, but I will also consider differences between the written scenario and *Film* as completed that critics often disregard. Early in the scenario, Beckett provides these explanatory comments:

GENERAL

Esse est percipi.

All extraneous perception suppressed, animal, human, divine, self-perception maintains in being.

Search of non-being in flight from extraneous perception breaking down in inescapability of self-perception.

No truth value attaches to above, regarded as of merely structural and dramatic convenience.

In order to be figured in this situation the protagonist is sundered into object (O) and eye (E), the former in flight, the latter in pursuit.

It will not be clear until end of film that pursuing perceiver is not extraneous, but self.[25]

Just as many critics have decided that *Film* is about film as such, so critics have often decided, implicitly or explicitly, that Beckett's disclaimer of "truth value" is also a comment to disregard. That decision misses, however, the extent to which the predicament of O in *Film*—his vain attempt to flee from the devouring gaze of E—is not the rule but an exception. The desperate flight from the agony of being perceived is not a universal urge. This attempt to escape being seen is exceptional both in the sense that Beckett's text acknowledges the unusual nature of O's wish not be perceived, and in that *Film* is a document of a culture in which, as Benjamin claimed long

24. According to Knowlson, Beckett's friend Avigdor Arikha suggested the image (*Damned to Fame*, 465). It is curious that accounts of *Film* repeat Beckett's phrase—that O is "disturbed by print, pinned to wall before him, of the face of God the Father"—without considering that this is a very unusual image to illustrate that face (*Film*, in *Collected Shorter Plays*, 169).

25. Beckett, *Film*, in *Collected Shorter Plays*, 165.

FILM AND ITS AUDIENCES > 163

before Warhol, *"Any person today can lay claim to being filmed."*[26] O's question might be whether one can lay claim to *not* being filmed.

Many copies of *Film* have erased the soundtrack's one sound—"sssh!"[27] This revealing technical glitch precisely locates the problem in claiming that *Film* treats film *qua* film. Beckett's film is almost, but not wholly, a silent film, though errors in reproduction sometimes make it one. There are several plausible explanations for Beckett's location of the period of *Film* with what is, for him, a surprising precision: "about 1929."[28] As Michael North notes, one of these reasons might be that this date locates *Film* in the early years of the transition from silent film to sound.[29] *Film*, indeed, undoes this transition in a small way. Made decades into the sound era, its one recorded noise urges the film back into silence. That there might be a continuous life for silent experimental cinema after the hegemony of sound (and, then, color) had been a concern of Beckett's at least since 1936, when in a letter Beckett expressed the hope that "the industrial film will become so completely naturalistic, in stereoscopic colour & gramophonic sound, that a back water may be created for the two-dimensional silent film that had barely emerged from its rudiments when it was swamped. Then there would be two separate things and no question of a fight between them or rather of a rout."[30] This letter imagines a potential remediation in reverse inside a future history of cinema: the technologically produced naturalism of "industrial film" might make possible a new silent era. The "sssh!" acknowledges that *Film* is a creature of a different era: The very refusal of sound happens on the soundtrack, in the mode that put a slow end to the silent era.

Keaton had become an icon of this end: most notably, in *Sunset Blvd.*, that great allegory of Hollywood's abandonment of its silent stars, he appears as one of the "waxworks," the survivors of the silents who gather to play bridge in the house of Gloria Swanson's Norma Desmond while she stews in her lost glory and awaits her return to the screen. ("Pass," is his only line.) As if recalling this scene, Alan Schneider, in a fascinating but

26. Benjamin, "The Work of Art in the Age of Its Technological Reproducibility," 33.

27. Beckett, *Film*, in *Collected Shorter Plays*, 167. Even a gorgeous print of *Film* screened at the Museum of Modern Art on May 13, 2006, erased the "sssh!"

28. Beckett, *Film*, in *Collected Shorter Plays*, 166.

29. North, *Machine-Age Comedy*, 145. Critchley links the year to the economic crash of 1929 ("To be or not to be," 109).

30. Letter to Thomas McGreevy, February 6, 1936, in Beckett, *Letters*, 1:312. During this period, Beckett took an interest especially in Soviet cinema and wrote to Eisenstein to ask for admission to the Moscow State School of Cinematography (letter to Sergei Eisenstein, March 2, 1936, in Beckett, *Letters*, 1:317).

unreliable essay about making *Film*, writes of his melancholy visit to Keaton's home in Los Angeles: "Late one hot night, I arrived at Keaton's house, in a remote section of Los Angeles, to discover that I seemed to have interrupted a four-handed poker game. Apologizing, I was told that the poker game was imaginary (with long-since departed Irving Thalberg, Nicholas Schenk, and somebody else), had been going on since 1927, and Thalberg owed Keaton over two million dollars (imaginary, I hoped). We went on from there, when I suddenly realized that everything in the room harked back to circa 1927 or earlier." A paragraph later, Schneider describes his miffed response to Keaton's offer to doctor Beckett's script: "He'd be glad—for a fee—to supply some ideas. From 1927."[31] For Schneider, Keaton is the pathetic survivor of an earlier period, mummified, like Swanson's Norma Desmond, in the relic of a house lost in an earlier period of film history. There is much to say about this card game and this house, but what most concerns me here is the way this awkward encounter reveals contradictions in the problems of historical representation that surround *Film*.[32] On the one hand, Schneider rejects Keaton's knowledge as sadly dated, and dated to precisely the mythical year of the transition to sound.[33] On the other hand, very soon Schneider describes Beckett's insistence in production meetings—in the company of, among others, the fascinating cinematographer Boris Kaufman, Dziga Vertov's brother, who shot not only *Film* but also *L'Atalante*, *Zero for Conduct*, *On the Waterfront*, and Tennessee Williams's *Baby Doll*—on the use of what Schneider considers outdated techniques: "Sam explained the necessary camera positions and angles to all concerned (nor did he budge from his fundamental position in the face of some highly sophisticated arguments about the new-found flexibility and mobility of the film medium)."[34] Beckett shows no interest in this "new-found flexibility." *Film* is determinedly *not* flexible.

31. Alan Schneider, "On Directing Film," 67; 68.

32. I suspect that Schneider misread the room and got the card game wrong, as *Sunset Blvd.* would also suggest. In *My Wonderful World of Slapstick*, Keaton describes bridge as "Hollywood's favorite indoor sport—well, with one exception" (185). Sidney Feshbach also connects *Film* to *Sunset Blvd.* and assumes that readers will recall Keaton appears in it ("Unswamping a Backwater," 341.) The house in question, which Keaton purchased in 1956, was at 22612 Sylvan Street in Woodland Hills in northern Los Angeles, and torn down in 2020 (Lea Stans, "In Memory of Buster and Eleanor's House").

33. That the transition to sound was not punctual, as the old myth of 1927 and the event of *The Jazz Singer* suggests, is a given in current scholarship on silent film.

34. Alan Schneider, "On Directing Film," 68.

Further, when he made great films Keaton's ideas about cinematic technique were sophisticated ones. In a chapter titled "Camera Men," Michael North argues that Keaton's comedies equal Dziga Vertov's experiments as cinematic reflections on the film as medium; this chapter provides an essential background to North's later argument about *Film*.[35] North rightly stresses Keaton and Vertov's shared concern with the aesthetic possibilities of the mechanical basis of film, and with the anthropomorphized agency of the camera itself. This anthropomorphized camera will become the eye from which Keaton flees in *Film*. Keaton is also one of the great comedians of the psychic element of the apparatus in the "compound" sense of that word that Rosalind Krauss synthesizes in a careful set of negations: "The medium or support for film being neither the celluloid strip of the images, nor the camera that filmed them, nor the projector that brings them to life in motion, nor the beam of light that relays them to the screen, nor that screen itself, but all of these taken together, including the audience's position caught between the source of the light behind it and the image projected before its eyes."[36] The idea that the audience is "caught" echoes the element of spectatorial captivity in the apparatus theory to which Krauss responds. Keaton's films at once picture this captivity and imagine comic forms of escape from it.

A production still from Buster Keaton's *Sherlock Jr.* (1924) shows Keaton's partial emergence from the body of a man in drag. Deadpan as ever, Keaton seems mildly discomfited by his emergence from the frame of the rack of men's ties carried by his loyal assistant, Gillette. Like many production stills, this frame only masquerades as a reproduction of a moment the film. In *Sherlock Jr.*, Keaton eludes the gangsters who are chasing him by jumping into the body of his sidekick, but he emerges otherwise. Keaton is caught in an alley from which there appears to be no escape: Gillette, standing against a wall in drag, gestures to him, pointing to the rack he carries around his neck. With no other option, and with the menacing gangsters watching and ready to pounce, Keaton leaps into the rack—seemingly into Gillette's body—and vanishes. The puzzled gangsters scratch their heads;

---

35. Michael North, *Machine-Age Comedy*, 27–52.

36. Krauss, *Voyage on the North Sea*, 25. Krauss writes further: "Structuralist film set itself the project of producing the unity of this diversified support in a single, sustained experience in which the utter interdependence of all of these things would itself be revealed as a model of how the viewer is intentionally connected to his or her world" (25). *Sherlock Jr.* treats this interdependence comically, suggesting that fantasy is as much part of this apparatus as intention. In *Beckett on Screen*, Jonathan Bignell anticipates linking *Film* and *Sherlock Jr.* (133–38).

Gillette, rubbing his belly as if digesting Keaton, walks away. (A few moments later, the gangsters spot Keaton behind a wooden gate, and chase him; he locks them in behind him. He does not, as in the production still, emerge head first from Gillette.) The perfect visual gag of this impossible disappearance into the body of his sidekick encapsulates and sends up a drive that structures the whole film. *Sherlock Jr.* features a sequence of impossible entries and exits through frames and windows. Jumping through the tray of ties held by his disguised sidekick repeats an escape from the thieves' lair through a window a few moments before. More significantly, this escape recalls Keaton's entry into the space of the film that initiates the film within the film: Keaton as day-dreaming projectionist fantasizes himself into the space of a film melodrama titled *Hearts and Pearls, or the Lounge Lizard's Lost Love.* There is, one can say, escape within escape within escape: the dreamer's identification with the melodrama he screens plunges him into a plot in which he is prey to thieves, and he escapes their clutches by an impossible dive into the body of his sidekick. This dive recalls his initial immersion into the melodrama screened by the cinema at which he works: Gillette, not by accident, has the name of one of the great idols of the American melodramatic stage, William Gillette. Meanwhile, the eagerness his sidekick displays in his invitation to Sherlock to jump into him reverses the initial rebuffs Buster receives when he tries to enter the space of the film: at that earlier point, his rival unceremoniously throws him back over the piano and into the orchestra. In the gag, the body becomes an impossibly permeable screen, precisely as flat as the projected images of the screen: it opens onto the space behind the dead-end alley. These escapes are, that is, comic enactments of the escapism and psychic surrender into the space of fantasy that is a hallmark of theories of the apparatus of cinema.

I have begun to use that semi-technical term "gag," and it's worth pausing over it. Sylvain du Pasquier offers a theory of the gag in which he stresses the gag's power to shock the spectator into the realization of an otherwise unexpected norm: "The hollow character of the original realistic discourse," writes Pasquier, "is revealed in an almost surrealistic shock."[37] In the context of *Sherlock Jr.*, Pasquier's insight points toward the film's frame, in which Keaton's Boy is falsely accused of stealing a watch from the father of the girl he admires (a blocking figure played by Joe Keaton, Keaton's father). Banished from the girl's home, the Boy sets out, with no success, to solve the crime. While the "realistic discourse" of the frame story is already absurd, the gag of jumping through his sidekick's body especially recalls, as I've suggested, the initial entrance into the film. Indeed, this is a gag about

37. Sylvain du Pasquier, "Buster Keaton's Gags," 276.

FIGURE 3. Still from Buster Keaton's *Sherlock Jr.* (1924). The boy contemplates his entry into the glamour of the screen. That entry will be just as difficult as his expression suggests. Photograph: Courtesy of the Everett Collection.

a gag, a gag about the difficulties that beset entering the fiction of the film.[38] The precocity with which Keaton represents, and also sends up, the familiar notion of cinema as regressive escape to a pre-Oedipal space remains startling. On the one hand, the projectionist's fantasy is a fantasy about projection, about the dreamer's desire to install himself into a more elegant and more satisfactory simulacrum of the world in which he lives: identification becomes wish fulfillment. But through a sequence of remarkable gags even the dream marks the difficulty of full incorporation into the space of *Hearts and Pearls*. Asleep, he dreams of entering the world of the film. But even in dreams, the putative state of wish fulfillment, Keaton finds it hard to make the transition: in his first attempt to enter the film, he is simply thrown back into the orchestra pit. In his second attempt, he is successful, but he is tossed from environment to environment in a series of rapid cuts.

38. "That was the reason for making the whole picture," Keaton recalled in 1965. "Just that one situation: that a motion picture projectionist in a theatre goes to sleep and visualises himself getting mixed up with the characters on the screen" (Gillett and Blue, "Keaton at Venice," 30).

FIGURE 4. Production photo from *Sherlock Jr.* (1924). A double fantasy: the moment does not appear in the movie and yet exemplifies Keaton's deeply playful investigation of the psychic lures of cinematic identification. Photograph: Private collection.

Keaton's adjustment to one diegetic space after the other is rapid, but never rapid enough: he dives into water, for instance, only to find his legs splayed upward in a snowdrift. Here, as Robert Stam writes, "the character is made empirically subject to the space of the image and the time of the editing."[39] A certain aggression latent in montage inspires a series of gags. The leap through his sidekick's body reverses the logic of the opening series of this gag: the "empirical" easily, if only temporarily, yields to the desire to escape.

That Gillette's tray contains perhaps the preeminent marker of sexual difference in the male wardrobe—a small array of ready-to-wear ties, set off by the assistant's ribbon—emphasizes the complicated comedy of gender division here. Not only does the gag involve cross-dressing, but it imitates a scene structured around a certain fantasy of gendered spectatorship. That is to say, Keaton's entry into the melodrama is, from the start, marked as feminized. Before the projectionist falls asleep in his booth, the Girl has already solved the mystery behind the theft of the watch, so the dream in

39. Stam, *Reflexivity in Film and Literature*, 39.

which Boy becomes Sherlock Jr. happens in the time between her discovery and her informing him. Strictly speaking, the dream is unnecessary, a compensatory reenactment of a solution already found, but it is as sentimental compensation that the dream has its sense. More generally, intense identification with melodrama was (and is) imagined as a woman's response.[40] Indeed, such putatively feminine spectatorial investment in melodrama has been the type of naive film spectatorship for almost a century.[41]

To return to Pasquier's formulation, then, one can say that Keaton's gag—leaping through the body of the sidekick—illuminates the "hollow character" of a particular discourse of melodrama within and outside *Sherlock Jr.*: this discourse is within the film in that the overall plot of *Sherlock Jr.* sends up melodrama's happy resolution of social and sexual conflict. This discourse is outside *Sherlock Jr.* in the sense that the figure of the overly susceptible spectator of melodrama—a spectator imagined as feminine—was commonplace in the public sphere. A certain fantasy of mass cultural spectatorship shapes *Sherlock Jr.* In a word, Keaton's comic registration of this aspect of a social imaginary anticipates Beckett.

Film begins with a close-up of Buster Keaton's unblinking eye. The second shot pans along a rough brick wall. The eye puts the film's audience in the place of the object that is because it is perceived; this is perhaps more forceful still at the end of the film, where the eye returns. This opening close-up of Keaton's eye initiates the film's sequence of seeing and being seen. The audience is an audience of O's, seen by an eye that is at once Keaton's and its own. But to assert this is already to assert something questionable about the apparatus: To what degree is the audience the object of this eye? Does cinema see us? The lesson of *Sherlock Jr.*: to recognize that we are caught in fantasies about what an apparatus does. Is Beckett's work about these fantasies or wrapped up within them?

40. *Sherlock Jr.* includes a gag that assumes the gendered nature of the melodrama's audience. Sweeping up in the vestibule of the cinema after a showing, three audience members come looking for money they claim to have lost in the cinema. The Boy has found a dollar in the trash, which he returns to the first of the three, a young woman; a second woman arrives, also looking for a lost dollar, and the honest Boy gives her his own dollar, wiping his eyes with her handkerchief. Finally, a large man appears and looks through the trash. The Boy fearfully offers him yet another dollar, but the large man waves it off: he is searching for—and finds—his wallet, which contains a larger wad of cash. Part of the joke is that this hulking man, with a powerful glare caught in a close-up, has been part of the melodrama's audience.

41. Important work on melodrama and spectatorship includes Lauren Berlant, *The Female Complaint*; Miriam Hansen, *Babel and Babylon*; Ben Singer, *Melodrama and Modernity*; and Carolyn Williams, "Moving Pictures: George Eliot and Melodrama."

As startling as the unwavering regard of Keaton's eye is, perhaps more unsettling are the eyelids surrounding it. These eyelids remind the audience of those parts of the eye that do not see, and so potentially of the unseeingness of a close-up of an eye. Later, it emerges that there is a patch over one of Keaton's eyes: one eye cannot see at all. But a visual pun frames the start of *Film*. *Film*'s opening pairing of shots performs a kind of degree-zero experiment in montage: eye and wall. The film opposes eye to wall, the thing that sees to the barrier to sight. As one might expect from the writer who had a one-way correspondence with Sergei Eisenstein, this use of montage is more cunning than simple opposition. The wall has its own history: clearly visible above street level is an area where an opening has been bricked over.[42] The opening sequence aligns the rough, ridged lids of Keaton's eye with the irregular lines of mortar between the bricks of the wall, so it suggests a homology between the eye and this covered opening. This montage at once suggests that the audience is itself seen by the eye that looks out at it and that the eye is no different from this opening that is no longer an opening—that is, that the eye does not see at all and that the audience is not seen. The audience sees an eye that does not see us. But the main action of *Film* involves O's attempts to escape from the glances not only of E but of an increasingly unlikely set of those other "eyes": the eyes of pets, of a window, of figures in photographs, of the filigree of the back of a rocking chair, of an envelope. The anthropomorphic attribution of an eye to the wall invited by the opening sequence is only the first of a whole range of ready-made eyes in *Film*. As Keaton scurries along the wall, he knocks into a man and a woman. He flees the scene of sight; after some awkward business and obscure camera movements, they see the camera, and are horrified. Beckett's scenario describes the encounter: "As they both stare at E the expression gradually comes over their faces which will be that of the flower-woman in the stairs scene and that of O at the end of the film, an expression only to be described as corresponding to an agony of perceivedness. Indifference of monkey, looking up into face of its mistress."[43] The difference between Keaton's gaze and that of the camera is not as clear in the film itself and, sadly, no monkey appears in *Film* (one of the many points of discrepancy between scenario and finished film). These problems aside,

42. Beckett himself found the spot: "Beckett enjoyed hunting for locations, and was childishly delighted when he found the red brick wall of an about-to be-demolished building just under the Brooklyn Bridge, perfect for the opening scene" (Bair, *Samuel Beckett*, 572).

43. Beckett, *Film*, in *Collected Shorter Plays*, 167.

FILM AND ITS AUDIENCES > 171

it is clear that the human response to the direct gaze of the camera in *Film* is always one of dismay, even horror.

North asks a resonant question: "Exactly what is it that so distresses the *other* characters in the film, face to face with E?"[44] Here it's important to note that the first sequence of *Film* does not correspond to the first scene of Beckett's scenario. The scenario begins:

> Dead straight. No sidestreets or intersections. Period: about 1929. Early summer morning. Small factory district. Moderate animation of workers going unhurriedly to work. All going in the same direction and all in couples. No automobiles. Two bicycles ridden by men with girl passengers (on crossbar). One cab, cantering nag, driver standing brandishing whip. All persons in opening scene to be shown in some way perceiving—one another, an object, a shop window, a poster, etc., i.e. all contentedly in *percipere* and *percipi*.[45]

Fragments included in Lipman's *Notfilm* contain shards of a rather different sequence: in any case, because of various technical failures, the related footage was cut. Cutting was, according to Schneider, Beckett's solution to a mutual agreement that this footage, which could not be re-shot, was unusable: "He had never been sure all those people belonged in that opening anyway. They gave it and the film a different texture, opened up another world."[46] And so what might have been a "crowd scene" vanished, replaced by the eye and its lids. The contrasts between what this scene might have contained and the completed film are striking: the solitary figure of Keaton in contrast to the couples; the increasingly unadorned spaces of *Film* in contrast to the street and its shop and poster, advertising and possibilities for consumption; the "agony of perceivedness" against the contentment of seeing and being seen. Beckett was right to say that the scene would have "opened up another world," and also, it may be, right to believe that the film did not require this opening. The world of those content to see and be seen, as the cliché suggests, far from being an unfamiliar world, is an ordinary possibility of everyday life. In the finished film, every human figure is prey to the predatory eye, but the frame for this fear and this predation is a theater of the world in which to be the observed of all observers may also be a pleasure. *Notfilm* includes recordings of production meetings in which

---

44. North, *Machine-Age Comedy*, 145.

45. Beckett, *Film*, in *Collected Shorter Plays*, 166.

46. Alan Schneider, "On Directing *Film*," 77.

Beckett compares the "diseased" forms of perception to be represented in the film against a norm: "The norm is in the spectator's personal experience."[47] Yet in the written scenario even this norm is polymorphously perverse. The logic of the description suggests that the driver with the nag is yet another, interspecies couple among the perceiving and perceived persons: strictly considered, "all in couples" might describe only the workers, but the progression, from workers in couples to pairs on bicycles to the driver and nag, nevertheless suggests a sequence of couples. (The nag might also recall Nagg, one of the couple in trashcans in *Endgame*.) Certainly the passage implies that the driver, as one of the persons "all contentedly in *percipere* and *percipi*," takes visual pleasure in brandishing the whip. Just as the scenario's monkey is indifferent to being seen, so this nag takes no pleasure in "perceivedness," the source of the creature's agony being presumably not (as with some humans) being seen, but the whip.

"The purpose of the monkey, either unaware of E or indifferent to him," Beckett writes, "is to anticipate behaviour of animals in part three, attentive to O exclusively."[48] In the finished film, there is no monkey, but the principle is consistent: while persons find the camera terrifying, animals don't care about it. The nag, another of the scenario's animals, is part of a planned introductory sequence in which all are indifferent to, or take positive pleasure in, seeing and being seen. The driver and the nag disrupt this pleasurable sequence with the surprising inclusion of the man and horse as couple, but also with the incipient everyday violence of the driver's raised whip. The scenario is clear, that is, that this nag and driver are not exceptions to the rule of scopophilia, but included inside it. If, that is, the "norm" that forms the background of O's resistance to being seen is this world of pleasurable sight, the driver and nag disrupt any easy separation of pleasure from violence: the whip the driver brandishes is part of this scene of contentment. Even though there are "no automobiles," there is a driver, a reminder of the use of force—the making another creature move—that lies behind the now domesticated term. The brandished whip in the lost scene suggests a violent potential latent to scopophilia that survives as the only response to being seen in the finished film.

The nag, then, illuminates the question of why *others* might take fright at the gaze of the camera. The driver and the nag conclude the list of contented

47. *Notfilm* includes excerpts of recordings of the conversations. S. E. Gontarski's *The Intent of Undoing* includes a useful transcript of these recordings as an appendix, which, however, symptomatically includes only Beckett's words, as if his collaborators were negligible (187–92; for the "norm," see 191).

48. Beckett, *Film*, in *Collected Shorter Plays*, 172.

scopophilic couples as the embodiment of the latent violence in any exchange of glances. But one doesn't see this violence all at once. Keaton's first encounter with others in *Film*—his collision with the only embodied human couple to survive the cutting-room floor—is exemplary: Keaton walks right into them; they are put out; Keaton walks on; the man adjusts his pince-nez and the woman her lorgnon; they focus on the camera and looks of dismay overcome them; they look away and flee the eye of the camera. In the midst of this action, he "opens his mouth to vituperate. She checks him with a gesture and soft 'sssh!'" "*The film*," Beckett writes in a note, "*is entirely silent except for the 'sssh!' in part one.*"[49] Above, I've noted the irony that the film's one sound reminds the viewer that this is, otherwise, a silent film. As this is the film's only remaining couple, this is the one moment when one person could conceivably have silenced another. Nevertheless, it's significant that the silencing happens here, between this couple. Described as "an elderly couple of shabby genteel aspect," their costumes strand them in some vague pocket of the twentieth century: his collar is oddly liturgical, her floral hat is pointedly unstylish.[50] Most glaringly, their eyewear belongs to another time and place. The business involving the woman's elaborate lorgnon and the man's pince-nez draws attention to their outmoded awkwardness and to the deliberation with which their wearers choose to use them or not to use them: at the moment when they look straight back at the camera and become slowly horrified, she holds her lorgnon up to her eyes, while he does not use his pince-nez. Just as the scenario's driver and nag are features of a modern cityscape mysteriously bereft of cars, so the eyewear is itself anachronistic. These antiquated tools for the correction of vision emphasize the conflicting temporalities at the heart of *Film*. The lorgnon and pince-nez complement the exceptional "sssh!": these are not simply glasses, but tools of a particular kind, of an earlier period, from the days when a piece of eyewear was a fashion accessory with a French name. (Glasses are never a simple matter in Beckett.) The antiquated eyewear, that is, contrasts with the head-on encounter with the camera, with a device that was, in 1929, lodged uneasily between the silent past and future sound: the film at once records the momentary "sssh!" and silences everything else.

The date itself is never mentioned in *Film* itself, and yet this scene affixes the time-date stamp of the transition to sound, and of the historicity of film. When Keaton collides with them, the couple are "peering together at a newspaper," as if to emphasize the contrast between their attempts to keep

49. Beckett, *Film*, in *Collected Shorter Plays*, 167, 165.

50. Beckett, *Film*, in *Collected Shorter Plays*, 167.

current and their anachronistic appearance.[51] The film's only other human actor, an elderly flower seller, is so frightened by the camera that she falls to the floor. *Film* insists on the "agony" with which these figures experience being seen; it also insists on their age. Many have noted that *Film*, in shooting Keaton from behind, fails to take advantage of his famously unsmiling face. The source of the shock of the final moment is not only that the spectator at last sees that face, but also that the deadpan face of the preternaturally youthful comic has become the face of a terrified old man.[52] *Notfilm* includes surviving shots from the abandoned opening sequence: the people in these shots are notably young, and include a mother with her baby. In the finished movie, O views snapshots of the stages of a life, presumably his own, and tears them up: these snapshots, similarly, align the pleasure in being photographed with youth. *Film*, that is, coordinates the fear of being perceived with age.

One could, after Barthes, see this aversion to being seen by the camera as an index of the finitude encapsulated in the photo. The photos Keaton scans, like the reel-to-reel tape recordings in *Krapp's Last Tape*, punctuate the time of performance with the historicity of represented experience. The peculiarly mediated form of this historicity is, however, not incidental: the generational divide in *Film*, especially explicit in the scenario's opening but still powerfully at work in the sequence with the photos in the film as screened in 1965, marks media shifts that are crucial to Beckett's works for performance. *Film*'s silence, a silence made paradoxically more audible by that "sssh!," underlines a divide in the history of film, the historically variable nature of this "medium." Keaton, survivor of black-and-white silents, flees the camera in the age of sound and Technicolor. This divide between silent and sound, this familiar epochal marker in media history, may reify a long and complicated technological change as a break. The generational divide in *Film* does suggest a contrast between those happy to see and be seen, unbothered by the camera, and those who flee from the camera as a threat. A pair of temporalities cross here, almost chiasmatically: on the one hand, *Film* captures a divide of the silent era between those happily

---

51. Beckett, *Film*, in *Collected Shorter Plays*, 167.

52. Did that face not always betray anxiety, if not terror? Tom Gunning seems to me right: "Keaton's reputedly 'blank-faced' expression actually reflects the deadly concentration of someone trying to find his place within a system too large and too intricate for him to control" ("Buster Keaton or the Work of Comedy," 14). See also Jean-Patrick Lebel's description of the face of Keaton as "a face turned in upon itself, concentrating upon itself with a prolonged and unbearable determination" (quoted in Bignell, *Beckett on Screen*, 136).

inside a world of mass-mediated perception and consumption and those alienated from it: the irony that Keaton, so skilled in the manipulation of the apparatus as a director and performer in the 1920s, plays O, fatally afraid of that apparatus, is a striking one. On the other hand, *Film* registers its postwar moment, when the critique of that apparatus saturated elite and popular discourses. *Film* stages a fear of being seen—the fatal apprehension of what it might mean to be "caught" by the apparatus of film, to recall Krauss's word—which was not a fact of a "medium" but a response to historical currents in the understanding of what film and mass culture had become.

The postwar fear of the surveillance and authoritarian control of the visual field can be traced from the pages of mass-market magazines to the *Dialectic of Enlightenment*. More narrowly, it may be that what always seemed the most obvious place to look for Beckett's immediate interlocutors—that is, in French existentialism, and particularly in the work of Jean-Paul Sartre—remains a revealing point of reference. Early in *Being and Nothingness*, for instance, Sartre returns to Berkeley's *"esse est percipi."*[53] More important than the coincidence of the uses of this philosophical formula in both Beckett and Sartre, *Film*'s complicated choreography of the flight from vision recalls Sartre's model of the gaze. "Sartre's primary stories about vision," Stephen Melville writes, "are about the encounter of two persons, one of whom imposes vision on the other, thus rendering that subject object, mortifying and petrifying it through a radical theft of its freedom."[54] At its conclusion, *Film* alters this story by locating the camera's imposition of vision—the seeming externality of E—within O: the subjected O perceives himself, and so there is no escape from eyes or from the imposition of vision or, finally, from self-subjection. Nevertheless, Melville's précis of Sartre's "stories about vision"—an encounter, an imposition of vision followed by objectification, mortification, petrifaction, "a radical theft of freedom"—recalls the aggressive dynamics of sight within *Film*. To see another person, in these stories, is to impose vision; to be seen is dehumanizing objectification. Sartre anticipates later feminist critiques of the male gaze, but here that predatory gaze is marked less by gender than by power, by the divide between the thief of freedom and the objectified other.

53. Sartre, *Being and Nothingness*, 9 ff. It is unclear whether Beckett knew this text; he admired *Nausea* owned a copy of Sartre's *L'Imagination*. See Van Hulle and Nixon, *Samuel Beckett's Library*, 167–68.

54. Melville, "Gaze," 284.

Film's representation of an impossible flight from sight, then, coincides with one of the dominant philosophical accounts of sight in Beckett's milieu. Critics often read Beckett's plays and *Film* as experiments in radicalizing the situation of the subject under the scrutiny of the eye of another, or subject to a more general and more diffuse panoptic surveillance. To say that Beckett's work radicalizes this predicament of uneasy consciousness under the eye of others, or the gaze of the Other, might mean that his work confirms the assumptions about subjectivity and visuality that inform theories of the gaze. And it is no coincidence that these theories were formulated, by Sartre, Jacques Lacan, Michel Foucault, and others, during years that coincided with Beckett's writing for the theater. Nor is it coincidence that this body of thought emerged from the same city, postwar Paris.

There is something embarrassing about linking Beckett to these thinkers. The only thing less compelling than yet another map superimposing Beckett's work onto existentialism, however, might be the equally inadequate account that pretends that his work bears no relationship to intellectual currents that surrounded him. Surely we no longer require Beckett to illustrate philosophical positions, nor can we pretend that this pristine work belongs outside the history that contributed to the formation not only of his work but also to that of the philosophical discourses that have been used to explain that work. Sartre's account of the encounter with the gaze of another begins with this scenario: "Let us imagine that moved by jealousy, curiosity, or vice I have just glued my ear to the door and looked through the keyhole."[55] The fascination with predatory spectatorship that marks *Being and Nothingness*—more accurately, the certainty that vision is, before all else, predatory—is surely not alien to Beckett. Beckett's philosophical contemporaries may seem to gloss his work so well, however, not because they offer declarative formulae that answer to the literary forms of Beckett's work but because they and Beckett were subject to the same history. The problem in such readings is not only that drama, prose, and film meet their fates in paraphrase, but that the historicity of that paraphrase vanishes in its claim to a truth content that it shares, as it were by chance, with Beckett. Sartre's violent account of the look confirms certain aspects of Beckett's investigations of sight, and this coincidence is significant neither as a sign of Sartre's influence on Beckett nor as the symptom of some

---

55. Sartre, *Being and Nothingness*, 347. For discussion of this passage, see Wollen, "On Gaze Theory," 96, and, more generally, Melville, "Gaze" and "Division of the Gaze," and Oliver, "The Look of Love."

shared psychopathology.[56] That philosophical account and Beckett's work alike were formed in the aftermath of apparatuses and practices, political, mass cultural, and everyday, that harnessed sight to violent purposes. And, for a while, these historically dominant purposes became the permanent truth of sight.

In a remarkably compressed, speculative formulation, Thomas Elsaesser has written: "With the multi-media, another age-old dream seems to be coming true: *esse est percipi*—to be is to be perceived. That, too, is of course a thought in the spirit of Foucault. It would make the history of the cinema more like the archaeology of the panopticon, and in the Nietzschean absence of God, the dream would no longer be for humankind's immortal double, but for someone to—once again—watch over you: a specter is, after all, stalking film history—the absence of 'God' as the loss of faith in perception."[57] The "dream" that cinema has been pursuing, in this account, is the dream of cinema's looking back at the spectator, perceiving the spectator who perceives the screen. The realization of this dream in the era of an interactive multimedia environment—near or far, at any rate still to come—looks like the generalization of panoptic space. The prehistory of this perfection of the multimedia suggests, then, that the cinema has always been tending toward this state of seeing those who see it. And if the realization of this promise of an exchange of glances between person and medium looks like the multiplication of the carceral spaces of the panopticon, it also promises something like Jean Starobinski's more benign transparency, a world in which you are watched, and watched over. (Who does not want to be watched sometimes?)

Elsaesser complicates the phrase that critics have taken to be the key to interpretation of Samuel Beckett's *Film*. Rather than considering the phrase as an ontological constant, Elsaesser considers it historically, as descriptive of a period in the past, when to be was to be perceived: Berkeley had faith in perception because he also had faith in God. And Elsaesser also intimates that it might yet be true again: "to be" will, once more, be "to be perceived." For my purposes here, what is crucial is not Elsaesser's speculation

---

56. This is not to say that Sartre may not have influenced Beckett. This is also not to say that biographical accounts might not discover similarities in the place of sight in the psychic lives of Beckett and Sartre: "As early as 1952," Martin Jay points out, René Held had written a psychoanalytic analysis of Sartre's account of sight, arguing that it "demonstrated extreme castration anxiety, a narcissistic fear of splitting the body from the self, and masochistic fantasies about enslavement to dominating figures"; Held also linked this account to "the primitive belief in the evil eye." See Jay, *Downcast Eyes*, 277.

57. Elsaesser, "Early Film History and Multi-Media," 23.

about the futures of multimedia, but his undoing of the ahistorical nature of Berkeley's speculation: When *wasn't* to be to be perceived? This is crucial because Beckett's *Film*—and in my view, his larger body of work for performance—are not stagings of ontological conditions of vision as such, but instead enactments of predicaments concerning the mediated qualities of vision and spectatorship.

Many have claimed that film made itself film—came into its own as a medium—through its negotiation, or repudiation, of its theatrical heritage. The pages that follow argue something like the reverse: Beckett's theatrical practice arises from his engagement with, and his revision of, the conditions of film. In particular, Beckett's theater investigates the conditions of spectatorship as they had been shaped by mass cultural forms, and especially film. This scrutiny of mass-mediated spectatorship characterizes Beckett's theatrical work almost from the start: Estragon, in *Waiting for Godot*, stares out at the audience and calls it a "bog" or, in French, a "*tourbière*," where *tourbe* can mean at once "peat-bog" or "mob."[58] That Beckett carries over into the theater concerns with spectatorship that already mark his prose is also clear. Equally clear is Beckett's characteristically prickly engagement with philosophical debates for which issues of spectatorship are central. Nevertheless, genealogies of Beckett's intellectual debts have disguised the extent to which his scrutiny of the conditions of spectatorship belongs to a particular moment: the aftermath of the discovery of "mass culture" as a cultural formation. Beckett went to the movies, thought about movies: his theater comes after film.

Beckett's *Film* represents his only work in cinema, and in no other work (with the possible exception of *Play*) is his investigation of sight so programmatic or so unremittingly a matter of the eye's predatory designs on those it perceives. Far from confirming our (or, it may be, Beckett's) desire to find in it an object lesson in the nature of a medium, *Film* consistently points to the historicity of cinema and so to that of *Film* itself as an object in this history. That *Film* could for so long, could *still*, be taken as exemplary of film as such is part of the history to which Beckett belongs.

---

58. Beckett, *En attendant Godot/Waiting for Godot*, 34–35. The 1927 *Petit Larousse* defines "tourbe": "*Fig.* Multitude confuse, surtout en parlant du bas people. Foule de gens mèprisables [a confused multitude, especially when speaking of low-class people. A crowd of contemptible types]" (1040) (my translation).

[TWENTY-TWO]

Catastrophe

Fixing the Audience

Catastrophe, a *dramaticule*, as Beckett dubbed it when he collected it with four other short plays for publication in French in 1982, is one culmination of his engagement with mass culture in the theater.[1] Closely contemporary pieces for television from the same late period, *Quad* (1981) and *Nacht und Träume* (1982), mark other endpoints for this long working through the logics of mass culture in Beckett's work for theater, radio, film, and television. My account of Beckett's theater begins with this ending in *Catastrophe* to emphasize the ways Beckett's encounters with mass culture have happened on stage and in the theater. Critical accounts of Beckett and media tend to stress his work in radio, film, and television. Conversely, the scholarship and philosophical writing most attentive to what Beckett called the "rupture of the lines of communication" tends not to concentrate on the media environment of that communication.[2] I hope to combine the attentiveness to the historical conditions of Beckett's surround while attending to how the plays register the disruption of lines of communication or seek

1. There was a precedent for the seemingly Beckettian word "dramaticule": see DeWitt, *Dramaticules for Choric Recitation with Group Movement*.

2. Leo Bersani and Ulysse Dutoit quote the passage containing this phrase from Beckett's 1934 "Recent Irish Poetry" in their brilliant analysis of Beckett's "more general epistemological skepticism about all subject-object relations" (*Arts of Impoverishment*, 26, 25); for its context, see "Recent Irish Poetry" in *Disjecta*, 70. Among the early philosophical essays on Beckett, both Theodor Adorno's "Trying to Understand *Endgame*" and Stanley Cavell's "Ending the Waiting Game" are acutely alert to the play's alteration of the conditions of theatrical relation and they register, without really thinking through, the play's media surround. See, for instance, the moment when Adorno aligns the alienating effect of Beckett's plays with how "people leaving the movie theater seem to see the film's planned contingency continuing in chance events on the street" ("Trying to Understand *Endgame*," in *Notes to Literature*: 1:262) or the rapidly associative paragraph in which Cavell lines *Endgame* up with *Dr. Strangelove* ("Ending the Waiting Game," in *Must We Mean What We Say?*, 134–35).

179

to disrupt those lines. This scholarship has helped clarify my conviction that Beckett's most disruptive and far-reaching work inside and against the twentieth-century media surround happened not on film or in broadcast media but in the theater. *Catastrophe* insists on the metatheatrical situation of the rehearsal of a play inside a theater and yet also emphasizes how this event—here, in the theater—happens inside a larger media surround that partly determines what happens in that theatrical space.

The title of *Catastrophe* plays with the meanings of the Greek root of the ever more common French and English word—"overturning, sudden turn, conclusion"—and in particular with its association with the way some Greek commentators believed tragedies should end.[3] The play stages a minuscule dramatic catastrophe; it represents—or gestures toward—a catastrophic situation. Text and performance pose the question of how to read the play's catastrophe in the narrow sense—its abrupt turn or conclusion—in relation to the larger worldly catastrophe that it so enigmatically stages. The catastrophic culmination of this *dramaticule* would, in many other contexts, be insignificant, nothing but a bodily movement, one of many gestures in a larger drama:

> *Pause. Distant storm of applause. P raises his head, fixes the audience. The applause falters, dies.*

> *Un temps. Lointain tonnerre d'applaudissements. P relève la tête, fixe la salle. Les applaudissements faiblissent, s'arrêtent.*[4]

In every preceding moment of the play, the Protagonist is anything but the instigator of action that the term identifying him—another resonant loan word from ancient discussions of drama—suggests. Largely the passive object of the Director's orders regarding the molding of his body, the Protagonist does one thing that might be taken as an act of will: this gesture is the Protagonist's action. The sequence here is important: a "sudden turn," and so in this literal-minded sense a "catastrophe," the action follows that "distant storm of applause." In both English and French, the clichéd phrases describing the distant audience's enthusiastic responses fit the artificially

---

3. *Oxford English Dictionary*, s.v. "Catastrophe." In a letter to the *New York Review of Books*, Stephen Halliwell notes that Aristotle did not use the term; Daniel Mendelsohn, in a reply, notes: "The technical use of *katastrophe* as the 'final turning-point' in a drama appears in much later Greek authors, for instance in Polybius' Histories 3.48.8 and in Lucian's Alexander, 60" (Halliwell and Mendelsohn).

4. Beckett, *Collected Shorter Plays*, 299; *Catastrophe et Autres Dramaticules*, 81.

reproduced and mechanical nature of this applause.[5] The catastrophe of *Catastrophe* responds to a condensed, technologically reproduced fragment of the mass-mediascape that is no longer only outside the theater. This aural fragment is a significant reminder of the mass audience the Director desires. This reminder can, however, occupy Beckett's theater only at a distance, at once audible inside the theater as recorded sound and yet also outside it as a "distant storm." This intimate externality of the mass cultural response points to a formation that determines the forms of Beckett's theater and marks that theater's difference from the mass culture of which it cannot fully be a part and from which it can also never fully alienate itself. The "distant storm of applause" is elsewhere—where, exactly?—and yet we hear it: the Protagonist's gesture happens in the theater. That raising of the head, at once a culmination and disruption of the play's catastrophe—a response in the theater to the theater's mass cultural doppelganger—belongs to the dynamic of theater after film that this book traces. The applause is the quintessence of a lifetime's registration of the intimately alienating proximity of mass culture.

What have listeners heard in that applause? Reviewing the 1983 New York City production so important to this book, Edith Oliver recorded her response: "Director predicts an enthusiastic response from the audience; a sound effect of applause follows, in which I thought I also heard hoofbeats and the turning wheels of a tumbrel—but maybe not, maybe that was only an aural hallucination from my own spellbound imagination."[6] This account is remarkable for the precision with which Oliver describes her impressions and for the uncanny name she gives the vehicle whose "turning wheels" she thought she heard mixed into the sound effect of the applause: a "tumbrel," a "dung-cart," particularly in reference to carts "used to transport condemned prisoners to execution to during the French Revolution."[7] To her ears the applause became the hallucinatory sound effect of a history of mass culture that sweeps through the French Revolution and reverberates into the play's political moment.[8] The storm or thunder (*tonnerre*) of

---

5. Dictionaries are suggestive about these clichés. The *Petit Larousse* of 1961 includes "*un tonnerre d'applaudissements*" under the entry for "tonnerre." The *Petit Robert* of 1982 contains "*Salve, tonnerre, tempête d'applaudissements*" under the entry for "applaudissement."

6. Edith Oliver. "The Theatre: Off Broadway."

7. *Oxford English Dictionary*, s.v. "Tumbrel."

8. On theater and mass culture in the French Revolution, see Susan Maslan, *Revolutionary Acts*. See also Patrick Brantlinger's discussion of the increasingly common positing of mass culture as the other of tragedy since the French Revolution in *Bread and Circuses* (64–65).

applause, a recording of a mass acclamation that happened elsewhere, or conjured through the ingenuity of a sound designer and then inserted into the theatrical event, typifies a strain in Beckett's work: the concentrated synecdoche of the domain of mass culture.[9] These compressed, synecdochic fragments acknowledge the theater's saturation by mass culture and yet also testify to this theater's difference from the domain of that saturation, encapsulating how, for Beckett, imagining theater after film means imagining a theater that partially negates film. As the presence of these moments suggests, that negation is never total, never the mark of any absolute isolation of some purely theatrical medium from the mass cultural domain. In these monadological and compressed moments, Beckett's theater registers the power of the apparatuses it would resist, expressing at once the hegemonic force of those apparatuses and the intensity of the resistance necessary to make a theater that does not simply redouble or feed their power.

While part of a pattern across Beckett's work, these synecdochic moments are also not simply repetitions. *Catastrophe*, for instance, is in certain ways remarkably unlike Beckett's earlier plays. Consider the first words that follow the title, the remarkable paratext "For Václav Havel."[10] The text's dedication, at the time of its first performance and publication in French in the summer and fall of 1982, and then again when first published in English in *The New Yorker* in January 1983, and in subsequent performances and publications, appeared to signal from the start that *Catastrophe* engaged with politics with a directness that had marked no other play in the corpus.[11] Havel was then in a Czech prison. Public performances of *Catastrophe* reminded the audience that the dedicatee could not see then read or see the play performed. During these initial performances, there was an apostrophic quality to this dedication to Havel, who was in a material way absent from the scene of performance and addressed in his absence. As a public performance celebrating a political figure forcibly sequestered by the state from the scene of political activity, *Catastrophe* juxtaposes the potentiality

9. Marc D. Malamud, the production's sound designer, recalls that he created the effect with an audio engineer "at Westrax studios in New York. We started with a canned audience applause and faded down to Alan [Schneider] clapping in the studio. It took several takes to get exactly what Alan wanted" (Malamud).

10. Beckett, *Collected Shorter Plays*, 293.

11. In February 1984, the text appeared again in *Index on Censorship*, alongside Havel's response to it, the short play *Mistake*. The dedication was also printed in programs for the first New York production. For a nuanced and thorough discussion of the context of the first performance, see Emilie Morin, *Beckett's Political Imagination*, 242–47. See also Morin's "Political Theatre and the Beckett Problem."

of a political theater with the fact of an exemplary public figure's forced isolation.

The dedication to Havel engaged with politics by invoking a figure forcibly removed from political activity by the force if the Czech state. The captivity of *Catastrophe*'s Protagonist, confined to the "*black block*" on which he is displayed, had to be considered in relation to the political imprisonment of Havel.[12] This rough comparison, however, did not and does not lend itself to any obvious political meaning, and the play includes warnings against assigning such meanings with rapidity. The Director rejects his female Assistant's suggestion that the Protagonist should raise his head: "For God's sake! What next? Raise his head? Where do you think we are? In Patagonia? Raise his head? For God's sake!"[13] The rehearsal continues, and the Director approves: "*Distant storm of applause.* [. . .] *The applause falters, dies.*" Many have recognized that this theatrical display of disobedience seemed to be—seems to be—the representation of a political act. Indeed, Ruby Cohn notes that the "protagonist's defiant gesture is always interpreted as a *triumphant* turning point."[14] The text begins with this stage direction:

Rehearsal. Final touches to the last scene.

Répétition. On met la dernière main au dernier tableau.[15]

The dramatic situation concerns the making of a play, or of a climactic moment in a play—its "final tableau," to re-translate the French—its "catastrophe." (This word, *tableau*, will return below.) What, then, to make of the "distant storm of applause"? The canned applause seems the obligatory or programmed response to the Director's confidence in the excellence of his catastrophe:

Terrific! He'll have them on their feet. I can hear it from here.

Formidable! It va faire un malheur. J'entends ça d'ici.[16]

---

12. Beckett, *Collected Shorter Plays*, 295.

13. Beckett, *Collected Shorter Plays*, 298.

14. Cohn, *A Beckett Canon*, 373.

15. Beckett, *Collected Shorter Plays*, 295; *Catastrophe et autres dramaticules*, 71.

16. Beckett, *Collected Shorter Plays*, 299; *Catastrophe et autres dramaticules*, 80.

The French idiom—to have a great success is to "make an evil"—becomes, in English, the anticipation of a standing ovation as the embodied performance of an audience's approbation. At first, then, the applause is the proleptic registration of the director's confidence in how an audience will respond: we hear, in the theater, the response he can already hear, the response he is certain he will hear. As Williams has the audience share in Blanche's aural hallucination of the "Varsouviana," Beckett makes the audience share the Director's in the hearing of a sound effect that mimics the applause he believes is sure to come. Beckett follows many films in troubling the audience's confidence about the divide between the diegetic and the extra-diegetic. With only a little adjustment, Slavoj Žižek's comments on the canned laughter of the television audience appear to be germane: "The Other—embodied in the television set—is relieving us of our duty to laugh—is laughing instead of us."[17] Near the end of the this very short play, which ends almost as soon as it begins, the recorded applause anticipates the applause of the living audience in the theater: the recording relieves us of the duty to applaud, or, maybe more accurately, provides the applause that the living audience, appalled by the manipulation of the Protagonist, refuses, at least at the moment of the recorded response. And yet, somehow, the mechanical satisfaction of the Director's wish goes awry: that phantom audience also registers the Protagonist's raising of his head as upsetting. Applause for the performance of submission "falters" as the Protagonist refuses fully to submit. How can we explain the sound effect's registration of not only the coerced applause, but also of that response to the Protagonist's refusal to comply with direction? This dialectical sound image, which passes so quickly in the theater, nevertheless contains contradictory parts, and these parts require critical attention that divides the moment. The dialectical image, Walter Benjamin observes, "is to be found, in a word, where the tension between dialectical opposites is greatest": similarly, Beckett's sound image contains and generates antinomies that cohere only through contradiction.[18]

The initial, obligatory quality of this applause, as Bert States observes in one of the most searching readings of *Catastrophe*, suggests that the recorded audience "was a group of fools, or sheep": "But what are we, the second audience, applauding: the performance of the outrage or, inadvertently, the outrage itself?" States insists on the continuity rather than the

17. Žižek, *Sublime Object of Ideology*, 35.

18. Benjamin, *Arcades Project*, 475 (N10a, 3). Beckett's sound effect produces the stasis required to read a dialectical image: "Where thinking comes to a standstill in a constellation saturated with tensions—there the dialectical image appears" (ibid.).

distance between the coerced, automatic, canned applause and the applause of the audience in the theater: "Suppose, wanting to honor Beckett for honoring Václav Havel, or wanting—presuming you were so moved—to honor Havel himself for raising his head and 'fixing' his audience in far-off Czechoslovakia—suppose you rose to your feet, as the Director knew you would, and applauded, like the audience in the play. What are you applauding?"[19] States captures the predicament of the audience of *Catastrophe*: the choice to applaud so soon after the alienating canned applause of the complicit audience seems wrong; to remain silent, in violation of all of the protocols of bourgeois theatergoing, also seems wrong.[20] States stresses Beckett's verb: "*P raises his head, fixes the audience.*" All of the many meanings of "fix" are in play here. The word abbreviates a common idiom: to fix your eyes on someone, or something, to attach a fascinated look to a particular object. Beckett's abbreviation also turns the verb, and the fascinated stare, into a transitive process: the Protagonist "fixes the audience"—repairs the audience; or fastens the audience in place; or neuters it, as one fixes a dog. The Protagonist's look does something to the audience. What does the look fix?

First, it fixes the audience's illusion that it sees without being seen. This simple violation of the fourth wall—a violation the play anticipates by placing unseen Luke, the electrician, offstage, and by moving the Director into the house with the audience—raises questions that will be essential to the readings offered in the following sections on Beckett. States calls this moment of fixing through sight a "grim symbiosis of a media society,"[21] and anticipates my argument that this moment must be seen in relation to a larger media surround. States's analysis, however, takes part in a pathos-laden discourse about the subsumption of all art into a single system aimed at the pleasing the consumer; this discourse does not account for the difference between *Catastrophe* and the mass-mediascape to which—as States very rightly stresses—the play bears a relation. The proximity of the canned applause to applause in the theater certainly asks the audience to contemplate continuities between recorded applause and its own. And yet that proximity also points to differences. States's account overlooks the antinomies contained in the moment of applause. That recorded applause, within the fiction of the play, is by definition not the recording of a response to

19. States, "*Catastrophe*: Beckett's Laboratory / Theatre," 19.

20. States discusses these protocols—the curtain call as a "seam in social nature" or "'border category' between aesthetics and manners" in *Great Reckonings in Little Rooms* (198). For wide-ranging studies of the production of the bourgeois audience, see Richard Sennett, *The Fall of Public Man*, and Nicholas Ridout, *Scenes from Bourgeois Life*.

21. States, "*Catastrophe*: Becket's Laboratory / Theatre," 20.

this production, which is still in rehearsal and has not yet been performed in front of an audience.[22] This recording is, instead, sutured to *Catastrophe*, and this suturing emphasizes the malleability of the recorded and the totalitarian habit of imagining or inventing storms of thunderous applause—more generally, that is, of manufacturing consent.[23]

States's phrase, "the grim symbiosis of a media society," consistent with the rest of his argument, implies that theater is one of that society's apparatuses. States draws primarily from what the *Oxford English Dictionary* identifies as a "transferred and fugitive" use of the most familiar biological meaning of "symbiosis": "Association of two different organisms (usually two plants, or an animal and a plant) which live attached to each other, or one as tenant of the other, and contribute to each other's support." "Symbiosis," in States's account, describes the attachment of theater to the media society around it. But is theater a "tenant" in that society, and do theater and "media society" mutually support each other? There a trace of Jean Baudrillard's frictionless picture of absolute subsumption in this summary of what "we" might have known in 1987. My account relies on a different understanding of this "symbiosis": the world is *not* literally a theater; catastrophes happen separate their representation and dissemination through media. States's compellingly subtle account of the dynamic of *Catastrophe* concludes with an account of the spectacularization of politics and the collapse of theater into an undifferentiated mass called "media society."

Through the "storm of applause," *Catastrophe* produces a Brechtian gestus of manufactured consent. But this is only one part of this dialectical sound image: the Protagonist interrupts the tableau by raising his head; the applause "falters" and "dies." The "storm of applause" imagines theater as one of the apparatuses of the production of mass consent; the Protagonist's disobedience—a gesture the Assistant first conceives of as compatible with the overall desired effect—breaks with this scene of consent. This theater admits the power of mass culture while also marking its distance from it. There is no way to make conventional dramatic sense of the sound effect: only a paranoid reading that asserts that the Director and production crew anticipated that the Protagonist would protest by raising his head can

22. For another account of the specific politics of the use of a recording of applause in *Catastrophe*, see Craig N. Owens, "Applause and Hiss," 78–79.

23. It is germane to this context that the phrase, in italics and between parentheses as in stage directions, appears frequently in U.S government translations of Soviet speeches. See, for instance, the transcript of Stalin's speech of February 9, 1946: on one page, the phrase "storm of applause" appears twice, along with "stormy applause," "thunderous applause," and "stormy, prolonged applause" (Stalin, 176).

explain, in anything resembling conventionally realist terms, why the applause registers both the expected mass approbation and the diminution of the applause. Similarly, a cynical reading that explains the effect away with the falsely worldly observation that of course any actual director and production crew will know that they need to design *this* sound effect overlooks the force of the moment in the theater and Beckett's refusal ever fully to suspend the dramatic convention that something, however minimal, is happening onstage. If the first movement of the sound effect registers the audience's submission to the manufacture of its consent, the second resists that. The applause is canned, but—or so this drama suggests—the faltering and dying of applause is not. Inside the drama of *Catastrophe*, this contradictory thing happens: the force of a theatrical gesture, as the Protagonist looks up, disrupts the recording, causing the mechanical applause to falter and die. The Protagonist's action causes the recorded to go live.

In *Beckett's Political Imagination*, Emilie Morin has painstakingly and persuasively documented the history of Beckett's political commitments and debunks the idea that *Catastrophe* constitutes "Beckett's only direct political gesture." Morin stresses, however, that her book is not about "the grounds upon which Beckett may be considered a political writer."[24] I am interested in these grounds, which Morin's deep scholarship newly illuminates. Further, Morin's description of *Catastrophe* as a *gesture* opens up the question not of Beckett's politics, or of Beckett as a "political writer," but of the politics of his work, of his theater, of what it means to speak of a politics specific to the theater, of the politics of this short play. The idea of a political *gesture* tends to suggest that as a gesture such a form of expression falls short of genuine politics: mere gesture here; there, in the truly political realm, action. On the one hand, gesture, a movement that is legible as expression, which exhausts itself as expression; on the other hand, action, which—to count as political—must transcend the forms of expression that might lead to it. It is no accident that *Catastrophe* happens in a theater during a rehearsal: it is the catastrophe—the climactic culmination—of a career spent thinking through a politics particular to the theater. Morin demonstrates Beckett's complex and variegated engagement with politics, one that long predated this play from 1982. *Catastrophe* marks not the beginning but an end point to a long encounter with the terms of theatrical politics. The question of what constitutes a "direct political gesture" is complex, but as a writer for the stage, Beckett had long designed gestures that engage with the politics of mass culture precisely by working inside the theater.

24. Morin, *Beckett's Political Imagination*, 5, 2.

"*P raises his head, fixes the audience.*"[25] In his lectures from 1972–73, in which he concentrates on supervision and punishment, Foucault defines this pair as an "indispensable power relationship for fixing individuals to the production apparatus, for the formation of productive forces, and characterizes the society that can be called *disciplinary.*"[26] In response to this passage, Emily Apter zeroes in on the verb that finds its echo in *Catastrophe* and, through Foucault, ponders "the fixative or adhesive that binds individuals to production apparatuses." Foucault's micro-physics of power would chart the technologies of the body. "Micro-physics," observes Apter, "is no mere metaphor, then; it denotes a real physics of gesture and posture." Apter summarizes Foucault's attention to "all manner of orthopedic conformity to the architecture of schools, hospitals and prisons."[27] Such "orthopedic conformity" is one of Beckett's obsessions, one traceable from *Waiting for Godot* to his last plays. Again and again, Beckett stages the condition of the conforming or resistant body, and meditates on the ways these bodies do or do not find their reflection in the bodies of the audience.

The Protagonist, fixed by the Director to the apparatus of a theater of coerced consent, turns the tables on that apparatus and instead "fixes the audience." The Protagonist's fixing the audience contrasts with the couplet of surveillance and punishment: the fixing of the audience marks a micro-physical point of resistance to the disciplinary apparatus that controls the system of gestures and the drama of "orthopedic conformity":

D: Why hands in pockets?

A: To help have him all black.

D: They musn't.

A: I make a note. [*She takes out a pad, takes pencil, notes.*] Hands exposed.

[*She puts back pad and pencil.*]

D: How are they? [*A at a loss. Irritably.*] The hands, how are the hands?

A: You've seen them.

D: I forget.

A: Crippled. Fibrous degeneration.

D: Clawlike?

A: If you like.

D: Two claws?

25. Beckett, *Collected Shorter Plays*, 299.

26. Foucault, *The Punitive Society*, 196.

27. Apter, *Unexceptional Politics*, 39–40.

A: Unless he clench his fists.

D: He mustn't.

A: I make a note. [*She takes out a pad, takes pencil, notes.*] Hands limp.[28]

What is *Catastrophe* but a "real physics of gesture and posture"? To recall the discussion in my introduction: the theater as apparatus is a system of production that is not simply assimilable to what Foucault calls "production forces." The "storm of applause" enters the play as a synecdoche for the fixative or adhesive forms of mass culture: those applauding subjects are surely as shaped and molded as is the body of the Protagonist, whose look back kills the applause. Attention to the micro-physics of power, however, stresses the imbalance between the massive subject-forming powers of the apparatuses behind the canned applause and the staging of a rehearsal in a small theater where a gesture can point toward, but never enact, a disruption to that apparatus. Beckett's micropolitical investigations of theater never grant theater the privilege of political power and yet also never discount the value of micropolitical disruptions.

The putative division between gesture and "real" politics is part of a reading of Beckett—and of the aesthetic—that reproduces false antinomies. Benjamin's "The Author as Producer" once more helps to clarify what is at stake: "Rather than asking, 'What is the attitude of a work *to* the relations of production of its time?' I would like to ask, 'What is its position *in* them?' This question directly concerns the function the work has within the literary relations of production of its time. It is concerned, in other words, directly with the literary *technique* of works." Toward the end of the essay, Benjamin asks of the author: "Does he have proposals for the *Umfunktionierung* of the novel, the drama, the poem?"[29] The consensus is right: Beckett's plays do not contain clear attitudes toward the relations of production of his time, and they refuse direct political engagement. Beckett's techniques, however, mean that his plays take very particular positions *within* the theatrical "relations of production of its time." His dramatic works do offer a set of proposals for the *Umfunktionierung* of the drama. As the recorded applause in *Catastrophe* illustrates, these proposals and their attendant techniques often confront the media surround. That surround was inevitably part of those theatrical relations of production. What was not inevitable was the ensemble of techniques Beckett devised to position his plays within the theater.

28. Beckett, *Collected Shorter Plays*, 296.

29. Benjamin, "The Author as Producer," in *The Work of Art in the Age of Its Technological Reproducibility and Other Writings on Media*, 81, 93.

[TWENTY-THREE]

Endgame, Postwar Mass Culture, and Forms of Address

One technique of the *Umfunktionierung* of theater used in Beckett's plays was to reflect comically on a theatrical non-relation to the audience. In *Endgame*, Clov turns the telescope with which he views the wasted landscapes outside the windows of their room onto the audience:

HAMM: This is deadly.
> [*Enter Clov with telescope. He goes towards ladder.*]
CLOV: Things are livening up.
> [*He gets up on ladder, raises the telescope, lets it fall.*]
> I did it on purpose.
> [*He gets down, picks up the telescope, turns it on auditorium.*]
> I see . . . a multitude . . . in transports . . . of joy.
> [*Pause.*]
> That's what I call a magnifier.
> [*He lowers the telescope, turns towards Hamm.*]
> Well, don't we laugh?
HAMM [*after reflection*]: I don't.
CLOV [*after reflection*]: Nor I.
> [*He gets up on ladder, turns the telescope on the without.*]
> Let's see.
> [*He looks, moving the telescope.*]
> Zero. . . .
> [*he looks*]
> . . . zero . . .
> [*he looks*]
> . . . and zero.
HAMM: Nothing stirs. All is—
CLOV: Zer—
HAMM [*violently*]: Wait till you're spoken to!

ENDGAME, POSTWAR MASS CULTURE, AND FORMS OF ADDRESS > 191

> [*Normal voice.*]
> All is ... all is ... all is what?
> [*Violently.*]
> All is what?
> CLOV: What all is? in a word? Is that what you want to know? Just a
> moment.
> [*He turns the telescope on the without, looks, lowers the telescope,*
> *turns towards Hamm.*]
> Corpsed.
> [*Pause.*]
> Well? Content?[1]

The familiar word "deadly" and the more unusual "corpsed" frame this passage: these words are alike in appearing unambiguously to signify the deathly while having quite other connotations. "Deadly" in Hiberno-English can mean terrific, brilliant, lively, in short, "very cool," as in a "deadly" party.[2] Hamm's "deadly" might, then, describe the horror of their shared situation, or it might perfectly precede Clov's following line: things are "livening up" *because* they are "deadly" in the best way. "Corpsed," similarly, resembles some post-genocidal neologism but belongs to another discourse, intimately entangled with its appearance here. To corpse, as Christopher Ricks points out in relation to this passage, is theatrical slang and means "to blunder (whether unintentionally or not), and thus confuse other actors or spoil a scene; the blunderer is said to be 'corpsed.'"[3] Clov's emphatic "corpsed," that is, describes the deadened world of *Endgame*, and possibly the deadened world beyond *Endgame*; the unusual adjective also, however, carries along with it this theatrical meaning that bears a tricky relation to the term's seemingly primary and more obviously fatal or lethal connotation.

In their antithetical meanings, "deadly" and "corpsed" encapsulate the play's self-reflexive relationship to its audience. Hamm's "deadly" can easily appear to be descriptive not only of the situation he shares with Clov, but also of the situation he and the other pair onstage, Nagg and Nell, share

---

1. Beckett, *Endgame*, 36–37.

2. I am grateful to Conor Creaney for pointing this out in a seminar and for providing the example of the party.

3. "Corpse," in Partridge, *A New Dictionary of Slang and Unconventional English*. Partridge's entry also shows that the word is not absolutely a neologism, having had the meaning of "to kill" circa 1884. See Ricks, *Beckett's Dying Words*, 61. For a wider consideration of corpsing, see Nicholas Ridout's *Stage Fright, Animals, and Other Theatrical Problems* (130–46).

with the audience. "Deadly" and "corpsed" together, then, might best apply to the peculiarity of the relationship to the audience that typifies *Endgame*. "Corpsed" links breaking character to death. But it is unclear whether the fatality rests on the side of the unbreakable deadness of the theatrical character or on the destruction of that character. Corpsing produces the death of character by surprisingly pointing to a life that convention demands should be suppressed on behalf of that character's existence. "Things are livening up": liveliness in a contradictory way just as, one might say, a "deadly" party is, in certain precincts, the very party one most wants to attend.

These words complement the moment where Clov turns the telescope "on auditorium." Even the stage direction here participates in the gesture of annihilation: Clov turns the telescope not on an audience but on a space: the idiom suggests the aiming of a weapon. The lack of an article here—"auditorium," not *the* auditorium—on the one hand draws attention to the blankness of that space, which may as well be empty, and on the other hand marks a distinct contrast with the strange nominative that marks that space on the other three sides of the playing space in Beckett's English stage directions: "*the* without." The word embodies one of the play's many fierce binaries, emphasizing the divide between what's "in the shelter" and what is outside.[4] Those inside are already without so much—painkiller, bicycles, and so on—but the phrase insists on what is outside as the absolute location of lack: "the without." Meanwhile, the force of the joke directed to the auditorium—which is, after all, a broad joke—lies in its comic *mis*recognition of the probable situation of the audience: it is not a multitude, it is not in transports, and so on, and the telescope, in the small theaters in which *Endgame* usually plays, is not only unnecessary but will distort what it is trained on.

The peculiar and punctuated modernity of Beckett is legible in the form of his metatheatrical turns to the audience, but these turns mark an engagement with historical forms of spectatorship and in particular mass cultural forms of spectatorship. One way to clarify this claim is to focus on the particular instrument in question here: the telescope. A peculiarity of the English version is again constructive: in that version (and not analogously in French or German) Hamm and Clov consistently refer to the apparatus as a *glass* while the stage directions just as consistently insist on the apparatus as a *telescope*. Immediately before the "inspection of audience," for instance, the word "glass" insistently reappears:

CLOV: If I could kill him I'd die happy.
    [*Pause.*]

4. Beckett, *Endgame*, 9.

HAMM: What's the weather like?
CLOV: As usual.
HAMM: Look at the earth.
CLOV: I've looked.
HAMM: With the glass?
CLOV: No need of the glass.
HAMM: Look at it with the glass.
CLOV: I'll go and get the glass.
[*Exit Clov.*]
HAMM: No need of the glass!
[*Enter Clov with telescope.*]
CLOV: I'm back again, with the glass.[5]

Five consecutive lines end with "glass." If "glass" suggests that the telescope is merely a kind of pane between the viewer and the object under observation, "telescope" emphasizes the distance between the viewer and the object. The stage directions' "telescope" insists on the fundamentally technological nature of the form of looking that Clov engages in, but even "glass" cannot erase the problem of mediation: for reasons he does not feel the need to explain, Hamm insists that Clov look at the earth with the glass. Through repetition, Hamm repudiates Clov's insistence that there is "no need of the glass," and this insistence raises the question of what possible use the telescope might be. If the aim is to discover what the weather is like, then Clov's objection that there is "no need of the glass" seems sound: he has looked at the earth; the precision of the telescope is not needed to discover the general quality of the weather, just as, in a moment, it will not be needed to see the audience. And of course, once Clov obeys the order to "fetch the glass," Hamm echoes Clov and insists that there is no need for it. The mediation of sight by the telescope seems not only unnecessary but antithetical to the task at hand: "weather" is not a matter of a detail that the device might isolate.

Here Hamm's simple idiomatic question about the weather in the French text is worth stressing: "Quel temps fait-il?"[6] The divide between a question about time—"Quelle heure est-il?"—and one about weather separates weather as something *done* from time as something that simply *is*. The equally idiomatic English question, on the other hand, poses weather as a matter of likeness. Even though this is Hamm's question, it appears that likeness is what he does not want: his desire is to make weather knowable and measurable. During his

---

5. Beckett, *Endgame*, 35–36.

6. Beckett, *Fin de partie*, in *Dramatische Dichtungen in drei Sprachen*, 1:242.

story, he will similarly refer to increasingly arcane measurements: "zero by the thermometer," "fifty by the heliometer," "a hundred by the anemometer," and zero, again, "by the hygrometer."[7] This insistence on measurement recalls Martin Heidegger on the age of the world picture: "Man contends for the position in which he can be that particular being who gives the measure and draws up the guidelines for everything that is."[8] Heidegger's argument that to give the measure becomes normative—drawing up guidelines—suggests the assertion of an obscure authority behind Hamm's demand that Clov fetch the glass. To order Clov to report what the weather might be like changes nothing, but the order nevertheless reiterates a certain minimum of authority and of obedience that is one of the play's mysterious givens. Hamm's will to measurement equally recalls Heidegger's antagonists, Theodor Adorno and Max Horkheimer, who, discussing Edmund Husserl on "Galileo's mathematization of nature," write: "Mathematical procedure became a kind of ritual of thought. Despite its axiomatic self-limitation, it installed itself as necessary and objective: mathematics made thought into a thing—a tool, to use its own term."[9] The unreal regularity of Hamm's numbers—zero, fifty, one hundred, then down again to zero—suggests this ritual quality of mathematical procedure, just as the description of math as the tool that reifies thought recalls the reification of the weather through its being captured by the telescope: some distant place elsewhere has weather, and this can be known.

The weather first surfaces after Clov's declaration that if he "could kill him," he'd "die happy." Hamm's turn to asking about the weather is legible, then, as the everyday strategy of turning to the most banal topic after something awkward has been said. But this assumes that Hamm has heard those words, and that they are not as aside. Hamm will later excoriate Clov: "An aside, ape! Did you never hear an aside before?"[10] Nothing in the text except Hamm's failure to respond indicates that Clov's homicidal wish is itself such an utterance. Indeed, Beckett never uses "aside" as a stage direction in *Endgame*. Hamm's question sounds like a rhetorical one: of course, he implies, Clov has heard asides. Clov's announcement of his desire to kill Hamm could seem part of a secret between Clov and the audience: the audience then knows that his apparent consent conceals this homicidal desire. It may be, however, that Clov *has* never heard an aside, nor uttered one. The line in question begins by conceding the impossibility of the very rebellion Clov seems to desire: "If I could kill him . . ." It is after all unclear why Clov can't

---

7. Beckett, *Endgame*, 59–61.

8. Heidegger, "The Age of the World Picture," 134.

9. Adorno and Horkheimer, *Dialectic of Enlightenment*, 19.

10. Beckett, *Endgame*, 86.

kill Hamm: the question of this inability underlines mysteries of obedience and consent that mark the play.

The episode in question raises particular questions about Hamm's command and about Clov's obedience, or disobedience. First, Hamm never explicitly issues a command: he asks what the weather is like and demands that Clov fetch the telescope, but he leaves the link between question and demand implicit, never orders Clov to look out the window with the telescope in order to find out what the weather might be like. On the one hand, Hamm's indirection looks like a sleight of power: power means not having to be explicit, and obedience means knowing what one should do without having to be told. On the other hand, the lack of explicit command means that transgression or disobedience is never absolutely clear. Here, the inconspicuous detail of Clov's dropping the telescope resonates: the deliberateness with which he drops the telescope he has been ordered to fetch, and his declaration that he "did it on purpose," suggests a contrarian willfulness, not to mention a casual recklessness with a delicate device. If not genuine transgression, it is at least a slowdown. The stage direction does not specify, but when he drops the telescope, he is presumably looking through the right-hand window. The question, then, is how to understand Clov's turning the telescope "on auditorium." The "inspection" confirms nothing obvious about the weather. It may be part of the slowdown, a continuing refusal to do the work of finding out what the weather is like. If, however, there is a trace of disobedience in this telescopic examination of the audience, it is only a trace: there is no reason to think that Hamm has any idea where Clov has focused the telescope, and he might well imagine that Clov is joking about a multitude outside the window, not in the house. (It is when he has again turned the "telescope on the without," later, that Clov will claim to see the boy, who might as well count as a multitude.)[11]

"I see . . . a multitude . . . in transports . . . of joy." The audience is of course unlikely to be any of these things, although the sort of uneasy "stifled" laughter Wolfgang Iser described may well accompany—or have accompanied—this moment.[12] Here, comparison with the French and German texts is especially instructive:

Je vois . . . une foule en délire.

Ich sehe . . . eine begeistere Menge.[13]

11. Beckett, *Endgame*, 87.

12. See Iser, "The Art of Failure."

13. Beckett, *Fin de partie*, in *Dramatische Dichtungen in drei Sprachen*, 244, 245.

The audience is unlikely to be a "multitude," but, then again, what makes a "multitude"? The French *foule* and the German *Menge* alike point to the simpler word *crowd* as the most likely English translation. Beckett's "multitude" conjures the language of the King James Bible and locates this crowd squarely within the milieu of perverse New Testament echoes that Stanley Cavell may make too much of in his delirious essay on the play. But Cavell rightly sees that the play is, among other things, about the audience as a *problem*: "Practically, or conventionally, 'audience'—for theater in the period after Shakespeare through, say, the 19th century—means 'those present whom the actors ignore,' those beyond the fourth wall. Deny that wall—that is, recognize those in attendance—and the *audience* vanishes. It seems a reasonable hypothesis that if anything is sensibly grasped as 'modern theater' one of its descriptions would be the various ways in which modern dramatists have denied this wall."[14] Beckett, in Cavell's account, typifies the history of theatrical form in its modern incarnation in denying the fourth wall and in making a certain audience—a certain conception of the audience—vanish.

To repeat a sentence from Cavell: "Deny that wall—that is, recognize those in attendance—and the *audience* vanishes." This movement from the denial of the wall to the vanishing of the audience poses several questions. Put otherwise, the denial of the wall constitutes a form of address: denial of the barrier between audience and actors produces the recognition that makes the audience as audience vanish: it becomes something else. This recalls those experiments with overcoming the divide between performers and spectators that traversed the years of Beckett's work in the theater discussed above. A reader of Cavell will want to ask: what counts as recognition? Does the denial of the wall in itself constitute a form of recognition? To answer this question in relation to Cavell would necessitate thinking about the relationship between acknowledgment—a crucial term in his work—and recognition. For now, however, I want not so much to focus on the particular valences of this problem in Cavell's work but on the related problem that is central to understanding the form and the history of Beckett's metatheatricality.

To return to the scene that, later, Beckett would call the "inspection of the audience": it is remarkable that, at least immediately, Cavell's term, "recognition," would seem to be an exceptionally bad description of the telescope's being turned on the gathered audience. Training the

14. Cavell, "Ending the Waiting Game," 157. That nineteenth-century theater audiences were in many cases very voluble doesn't diminish the force of the comment for modern theater.

telescope on the audience draws attention to the audience but pointedly fails to see it: it quite literally distances the audience. This inspection of the audience is in certain ways continuous with a tradition of addressing the audience as old as theater, and Lionel Abel's coinage, *metatheater*, has seemed to describe that tradition. But the provenance of the word is significant: as mentioned above, it is only in the early 1960s, and partly in response to Beckett, that Abel invented the word *metatheater*. This invention signals the relative novelty of the situation in which Beckett's address to the audience occurs. As I have stressed, broadcast media had reshaped the public sphere in remarkable ways. The interpellation and shaping of mass audiences by radio and film had become, by the 1950s, a particular problem for those working in the theater: their audiences were not multitudes; their technologies were relatively crude (another reason for the naming of Hamm's arcane meteorological gadgets); mass cultural joys were, in the eyes of many, linked to manipulation. It was perfectly possible to respond to this situation by continuing to make theater more or less like the theater from decades before, and many did. But a large part of what defines the experimental theater of the postwar period lies in its grappling with the conditions of a remade world of spectatorship, of listening, and of subject formation. Recall the common complaint that the dialogue of point-to-point communications such as the telephone had been replaced by the monologue of media that could not be answered. The monological address of radio and film produces a range of fantasies that are not exactly mistakes: I am being addressed; I am being seen by the spectacle I see, by that luminous star on the screen. A set of responses that takes place on another scene is to a large extent always part of the situation of mass media. Beckett's theater typifies the force of postwar theater by staging this response to mass mediation: in that reversal of McLuhan's formulation, the content of an old medium is a new medium. By staging I do not mean at all to say that Beckett simply repeats or offers a mimetic version of the affective exchanges that the mass media at once provoke and frustrate. What Beckett stages is a whole set of desires and frustrations that attend the mass cultural reshaping of subjectivity. In a specifically Brechtian sense, Beckett makes the effects of an apparatus visible. Clov's telescope is the wrong instrument for the occasion if the point is to see an audience that, after all, needs no special equipment to see him. The apparatus guarantees that he will not and cannot see the audience, and that is part of the point of the joke about the multitude. This failure to see the audience is partly a joke about the fourth wall and about the convention that the actors "ignore" the audience, to use Cavell's word. But this malfunction of the apparatus also uneasily insists on the conditions of spectatorship that had become dominant: the spectacle that you can see cannot see you. But that spectacle pretends to look back at you.

Hugh Kenner was among the first critics to sense that Beckett worked in a theatrical environment that cinema had altered. Commenting on the inspection of the audience and similar passages, Kenner writes: "These, like comparable details in *Godot*, are sardonic authorizations for a disquiet that is certainly stirring in the auditorium. No one understands better than Beckett, nor exploits more boldly, the kind of fatalistic attention an audience trained on films is accustomed to place at the dramatist's disposal. The cinema has taught us to suppose that a dramatic representation moves inexorably as the reels unwind or the studio clock creeps, until it has consumed precisely its allotted time which nothing, no restlessness in the pit, no sirens, no mass exodus can hurry."[15] Kenner's fundamental assumption that Beckett addresses a theater audience "trained on films" seems to me fundamentally right. (And Kenner's sense of the training of audiences recalls Barthes.) Here, Kenner emphasizes the temporal aspect of that training. Beckett assumes and exploits the "clock-bound patience of a twentieth-century audience," a patience that is itself the product of a certain tautological understanding of cinema: the film will unvaryingly be as long as the film will be. Kenner's neglected suggestion seems to me correct but also, as will be clear, excessively delimited. If films trained audiences, that training extended well beyond questions of the temporal experience of film and theater. The implications of Kenner's "fatalistic attention" perhaps suggest as much. Filmic training instilled not simply certain assumptions about duration but also about "liveness," to evoke Philip Auslander's discussion once again. Film also taught audiences to expect that the audience could change nothing in the spectacles it witnessed. Bourgeois theater audiences had been trained to be decorous well before the advent of film, but if Kenner is right that decorum had changed in quality once film had trained Western audiences.

I stress that such an understanding of film was historically bound, and even in the postwar world in which it consolidated there were countercurrents as well. Nevertheless, this sense of film's pacification of its audience can illuminate the relatively narrow example with which I began this section. The simplest thing we can say about the telescope turned on the audience is that it makes the audience aware of itself as audience. In Kenner's terms, one might speculate that an audience watching *Endgame*

15. Kenner, *Samuel Beckett*, 161.

experiences the difference between its own "fatalistic attention" and the "transports of joy" Clov sardonically assigns to it. Beckett, more Brechtian than Brecht, alienating the audience without the reassurance of dialectical resolution: this trope is a familiar one. But what such a formulation continues to lack is a satisfactory account of how such an alienation might work or what, roughly, is alienated. One might plausibly venture to say that the moment supplied a means for the audience to attain a knowledge of itself. One might, however, equally plausibly claim that insofar as Clov's scrutiny of the audience makes it aware of the fatality of its own attention—Clov's senselessly mediated survey looks rather like its disciplined attention to the happenings onstage—that scrutiny reinforces the audience's absence of agency, its passive subjection to a spectacle that will not change for it. The telescope turned on the audience, that is, emphasizes the pointlessness of the device itself, while also producing a new sense of distance between performers and audience. The word chosen by Beckett's German translators, *Fernglas*, makes this point with peculiar clarity: the noun combines "distant" with "glass," but in the context of *Endgame* one must wonder if the glass *produces* distance. "That's what I call a magnifier": the telescope alters what it surveys.

Building on cuts that had already been introduced in his own English translation of *Fin de partie*, Beckett cut what he called the "inspection of the audience" from the production he directed at the Schiller Theater in 1967.[16] "He further cut all allusions to the audience, all comments that imply a public, keeping the work more insular, more hermetic."[17] The most available editions in English, then, are arguably not the most authoritative, where that word describes authorial intention, as they still include these passages. The cutting of "all allusions to the audience" and "comments that

16. Dirk Van Hulle and Shane Weller provide a full account of the genesis and published texts of *Fin de partie* and *Endgame* (and also *Endspiel*) in *The Making of Samuel Beckett's* Fin de partie/Endgame. For the phrase "the inspection of the audience," see Beckett, letter to Marek Kedzierski, November 15, 1981, quoted in Gontarski, introduction to Beckett, *The Theatrical Notebooks of Samuel Beckett: Endgame*, xviii; this passage also appears in Van Hulle and Weller, 107. Beckett writes of the cuts: "To another director they may not seem desirable." I thank Marcus Stern, who did not cut the inspection, for discussion of his production at the American Repertory Theater in 2009.

17. Gontarski, introduction to Beckett, *The Theatrical Notebooks of Samuel Beckett: Endgame*, xviii. Such revision, then, would be similar to the movement toward insularity and hermeticism that Gontarski, with evidence drawn from manuscripts, has reasonably argued typifies Beckett's labors of revision in general. For Beckett's revisions of *Fin de partie* and *Endgame*, for instance, see Gontarski, *The Intent of Undoing*, 25–54.

imply a public" could devastate my reading here. The available editions do, however, have the authority of stage practice behind them: many productions do stage the inspection of the audience. To cut any implication of a public in the theater is part of the Beckettian project of denying relation that Leo Bersani and Ulysse Dutoit have argued is central to Beckett's work: "The artist," they write, "may no longer feel compelled to deny the inherent unrelatedness of art to the world of objects." "If, as a consequence, Beckett's work is almost entirely devoid of social and political references and resonances, it is still unthinkable apart from the historical moment in which it was written."[18] Is it possible for Beckett's work to be devoid of social resonances? Bersani and Dutoit grant that Beckett's earlier works, including *Endgame*, "are expressive in ways that the later texts are not," and such expressiveness would seem to include the kinds of references and resonances that they claim his later work lacks.[19] One could see the paring away of those "allusions to the audience" in *Endgame* as bringing an earlier work in line with the more rigorous project of unrelatedness in the later work.

There are also more social and political references, and resonances, across Beckett's work that Bersani and Dutoit may be willing to grant. The canned laughter in *Catastrophe* is one of many examples of Beckett's pointed acknowledgment of the media surround that was a terrain, however alienated and however intimate—however intimately alienated—of social life. The desire for unrelatedness for which they make so compelling a case is the negation of an apparatus that seeks relation without end.

18. Bersani and Dutoit, *Arts of Impoverishment*, 26.

19. Bersani and Dutoit, *Arts of Impoverishment*, 27.

[TWENTY-FOUR]

Beckett, the Proscenium, Media

In Broadway theatres I sometimes imagine that the proscenium is filled in with glass, that the stage is really a huge television screen, that the actors are not really there.

Michael Smith, introduction to *Eight Plays from Off-Off Broadway*

A contradiction structures discourses on perspective and, therefore, discussions of the proscenium. On the one hand, perspective and the proscenium verify the position of the viewer in the field of vision, and hence the sovereignty of the subject. The spectator's sight of events on stage, distanced, framed, and controlled, confirms the subject's mastery of the spectacle. On the other hand, the perspectival image captures the subject, makes it subject. The technology of perspective, and the apparatus of the proscenium stage developed in its wake, anticipate the panoptic machine it resembles, placing the spectator in its sights: "Visibility is a trap."[1] (It is possible to see this contrast as no contradiction at all, but for a moment I want to pause inside it, to occupy it as a contradiction.) That court theaters of early modern Europe oriented the machine of the proscenium and the design of the theater such that the privileged spectatorial position belonged to the monarch is exemplary of the first approach: the sovereign occupied the best seat in the house, the seat designed for the best view of the perspectival grid of the stage framed by the proscenium.[2] The sovereign subject inherits something

1. Michel Foucault, *Discipline and Punish*, 200.

2. Stephen Orgel's *The Illusion of Power* remains a classic discussion. Until 1605, the "royal seat, that is, was placed directly on the stage. [. . .] After 1605, when perspective settings were introduced—and they were used *only* at court or when royalty was present—the monarch became the center of the theatrical experience in another way, and the aristocratic hierarchy grew even more apparent. In a theater employing perspective, there is only one focal point, one perfect place in the hall from which the illusion achieves its fullest effect. At court performances this is where the king sat" (10). The stage history here is more complicated than my account here can fully acknowledge: Pannill Camp's *The First Frame* challenges the idea that since the Renaissance proscenium theaters have consistently relied on the perspectival model.

like this privilege of sovereignty: the proscenium frames a picture that reinforces the subject's sense of itself as sovereign, in possession of the view before it. The second strand of this discourse stresses subjection to and through images as one of the primary engines of the ideological production of persons. Sights we do not and can never possess produce us in their image: not sovereignty, but alienation; not possession, but dispossession. This contradiction can be resolved by asserting that the privilege of sovereignty is precisely the result of our having been alienated through the power of images. Our sense of ourselves as sovereign is one of the most powerful effects of the perspectival system that assures us that we occupy a privileged position in relation to our field of vision. Our sovereignty is precisely a form of the captation we thought we had overcome by becoming subjects.

This problem of the powers and function of perspective and of the proscenium, with all its complex history, forms the background of the well-known fact that Beckett imagined his plays as designed for the proscenium stage. However experimental, his plays were conceived inside and not against that long-standing feature of theatrical architecture, the proscenium arch. This is true of *Endgame* as it is of *Not I*. Indeed, Beckett's engagement with the proscenium and the structures of subjectivation and sovereignty that surround it is important to what it means to call his work experimental. Further, this theatrical experiment within the ideological apparatus of the proscenium with its complicated modalities of address to the spectator must be understood in relation to histories of media. Beckett's work inside and against the media surround in which his plays were first staged offers an example of a technique typical of his theatrical work: the proscenium, the frame of the old medium, becomes the object of a Brechtian *Umfunktionierung*. Apparently unchanged, same as it ever was, the proscenium, in Beckett's theater, undergoes a refunctioning, precisely as a result of Beckett's encounter with media. To summarize many accounts: the proscenium made a picture of the stage, and this picture confirmed or produced—confirmed by reproducing—the subjectivity of the well-placed spectator. Beckett used the technology of the proscenium, but his technique militates against this traditional account of the proscenium as machine of subject formation. His use of it opposes such fantasies of subject formation with experiences of subject deformation.[3]

Beckett's plays have largely belonged to the proscenium stage, and he wanted it this way. A fairly early example resonates: in 1956, in a letter now,

---

3. An exchange with David Levine during an exploratory seminar at the Radcliffe Institute for Advanced Study I co-organized with Nicholas Ridout in August 2018 sharpened my sense of Beckett's refunctioning of the proscenium.

it seems, lost, Alan Schneider apparently proposed to Beckett that *Waiting for Godot* should be performed in the round. Beckett responded: "I don't in my ignorance agree with the round and feel Godot needs a very closed box. But I'd give it to you with joy if I were free to do so. So all you want— all!—is the OK from MM and Rosset."[4] Both the modest profession of ignorance and the quite confident assertion that the "closed box" is necessary for *Godot* are typical of Beckett's early communications on the theater and the place of his plays within it. Despite Beckett's conviction about the need for this more traditional staging, he does allow that with the permission of the producer Michael Myerberg and Beckett's US publisher, Barney Rosset, Schneider might go forward with his plan to stage the play in the round. Despite Beckett's apparent willingness to allow Schneider to proceed with his experiment (if only he were free) this passage has been taken as evidence of Beckett's insistence that his plays belong within the frame of the proscenium arch, and for good reason.[5] His own practice as director confirmed this belonging. Equally resonant is an anecdote from about decade later. When Beckett came to direct *Endgame* at the Schiller Theater in Berlin in 1967, he not only worked within a theater with a proscenium arch but insisted on the conventions of that apparatus. Michael Haerdter's diary of Beckett's work in the theater includes this explanation of his decision to cut certain metatheatrical moments: "All replies which refer to the public have been removed ('a multitude in transports of joy!' etc): the action is to be entirely concentrated on the dwellers of the lair [*Unterschlupf*]. There is surprise when Beckett explains this by means of a principle of naturalistic theater—'the play is to be acted as though there were a fourth wall where the footlights are.'"[6] As Haerdter's anecdote suggests, Beckett's insistence

4. Beckett, letter to Alan Schneider, in Beckett, *Letters*, 2:659.

5. The editors of Beckett's letters provide a germane passage in a letter from Alan Schneider to Thornton Wilder: "When I see the Brecht company or the Piccolo Teatro of Milan [. . .] they ignore the proscenium tho they don't destroy it. They 'open' it up in another way, physically and psychologically; and a special kind of theatricality [. . .] comes flying out to the audience" (Beckett, *Letters*, 2:660n2).

6. Haerdter, "A Rehearsal Diary," 204; "Samuel Beckett Inszeniert das 'Endspiel,'" in Sigal, *Materialen zu Becketts 'Endspiel,'* 38. This translation is partial, and skips over, for instance, a sentence that appears immediately after the quoted passage: "Um Becketts spöttische, puritanisch schmale Lippen spielt ein Lächeln der Verlegenheit" ("An embarrassed smile played over Beckett's mockingly, puritanically judgmental lips" [my trans.]). A further volume in which Haerdter's essay was reprinted as a supplement to a revised text, *Samuel Beckett Inszeniert das "Endspiel,"* is itself a remarkable document: with three sides that fold out on the top (a photograph of lighting instruments) and the sides (photographs of curtains), the horizontally oriented volume deliberately frames

that his plays were written for the proscenium theater seems to contrast with the challenge his work posed to dramatic convention: for Haerdter, the insistence on the fourth wall is a startling concession to the naturalist tradition. And yet the proscenium stage as an apparatus continued to be essential to Beckett's conception of his theatrical work. This insistence on the proscenium as theatrical frame is not, as Haerdter may be read to suggest, a concession to an outmoded theatrical naturalism but, instead, exemplary of Beckett's recognition of the altered situation of postwar theater in a transformed media surround. The proscenium was not, after 1945, what it had been. Beckett's deliberate uses of the apparatus of the theater respond to the proscenium-like frame of the cinema, a resemblance stressed (for instance) by the curtains that open two otherwise very different films about theater and performance, Marcel Carné's *Children of Paradise* (1945) and George Cukor's *A Star Is Born* (1954). The theater's proscenium had become something different in relation to what was perceived as the unprecedented subjectifying power of mass culture and of its perspectival productions. It was as though the cinema had succeeded in producing the illusions, and the subjects in thrall to them, of which the postwar theater was able only to dream. In the face of the power of the silver screen as fourth wall—the cinema's much-remarked power to include its spectators in scenarios from which they were structurally and materially excluded—Beckett rethought the proscenium and the relation between stage and audience. To repeat M's question in *Play*: "Am I as much as . . . being seen?"[7] You are, yes—but being seen does not confirm your sovereign subjecthood.

At stake is Beckett's relation to the so-called fourth wall, a concept often linked to the theories of Denis Diderot, though Diderot never uses precisely that phrase. Diderot thinks about the problem from the point of view of the stage and of the actors: "In a dramatic representation, the beholder is no more to be taken into account than if he did not exist. Is there something addressed to him? The author has departed from his subject, the actor has been led away from his part. They both step down from the stage. I see them in the orchestra, and as long as the speech lasts, the action is suspended for me, and the stage remains empty."[8] Diderot emphasizes a significant term: *action*. For Diderot, the barrier between stage and audience makes the continuation of action possible. When they acknowledge the audience, author

---

the text *Endspiel*, with accompanying photographs of the 1967 production, as a portable proscenium stage.

7. Beckett, *Collected Shorter Plays*, 160.

8. Diderot, *Discourse on The Natural Son*, quoted in Fried, *Absorption and Theatricality*, 94.

and actor together "step down from the stage," descending, as it were, into the audience. Part of the impropriety of this moment may be that the author becomes visible at all, but Diderot's main complaint is that *to address* the audience suspends the action. Diderot's emphasis here falls not on the desired invisibility of the author, but on the fiction of the beholder's nonexistence. It is that fiction that allows the action its continuity.

The proscenium, then, might seem to be an architectural materialization of theater as apparatus in the sense that Bertolt Brecht understood it: part of the material and institutional machinery that reproduces theater's "social function—that of providing an evening's entertainment." Roswitha Mueller succinctly describes the capaciousness of Brecht's understanding of "apparatus": it includes "every aspect of the means of cultural production, from the actual technological equipment to promotion agencies, as well as the class that is in possession of the mean of production."[9] Brecht writes of "musicians, writers, and critics": "As they hold the opinion that they own an apparatus that actually owns them, they defend an apparatus over which they no longer have any control—which is no longer, as they believe, a means for the producers, but has turned into a means directed against the producers, in other words against their own production."[10] The question of the proscenium, in this context, is subsidiary to the larger question of control of the apparatus. If the apparatus is directed "against the producers"—implicitly, here, against a group of producers who hope to produce a left-wing theater—then the innovations of those producers within the theater are relatively trivial: a change to the physical arrangement or structure of the theater, or a text that seems to challenge the class that controls the means of production, makes no difference to the apparatus as a whole. That apparatus will ensure that anything, no matter how apparently rebarbative, becomes a commodity to be delivered. This aspect of Brecht's media theory, then, is in conflict with the frequent attention, in Brecht's writing on the theater and in scholarly accounts of that theater, to Brecht's challenges to the arrangements of the traditional stage. Estrangement includes estrangement from the technologies of the production of illusion that produced the bourgeois theater.

Walter Benjamin stressed that Brecht's critique of the actually existing theaters of his day involved a concentrated challenge to the divide between audience and performer. That is, Brecht's understanding of the power of the apparatus to absorb innovation did not exclude thinking about the

---

9. Mueller, *Bertolt Brecht and the Theory of Media*, 15.

10. Brecht, "The Modern Theatre is the Epic Theatre," in *Brecht on Theatre*, 71.

possibilities of organizing theatrical space otherwise. Benjamin focused on the orchestra pit rather than the proscenium, but it is significant that he opens his discussion of epic theater with a hyperbolic description of the theater's traditional divide: "This abyss, which separates the players from the audience as though separating the dead from the living; this abyss, whose silence in a play heightens the sublimity, whose resonance in an opera heightens the intoxication; this abyss, which of all the theater's elements is the one that bears the most indelible traces of its origins in ritual, has steadily decreased in significance."[11] The point is not that one or another architectural feature produces this separation, that the orchestra pit or the proscenium produces this "abyss" through the inevitable force of the architectural arrangement. These aspects of the theater space are part of the same divide. As Benjamin's comparison of this separation to one between the dead and the living suggests, the separation is as much an effect of culture as of architecture. A desire to separate actors from audience, or the dead from the living, produces an apparatus that does this effectively. The stage is a sort of cemetery separated from the audience by the orchestra pit. Theodor Adorno imagined a residue of the magical in all art despite its reliance on rationalized technique or technology and despite "progressive disenchantment"; as if to form a corollary, here Benjamin attaches the "sacral" precisely to the divisions of the traditional Western theater.[12]

In 1970, Dan Isaac published a survey of experimental New York theater in 1969 under the guise of an obituary, "The Death of the Proscenium Stage." Isaac's thesis was that the proscenium belonged to a vanishing world, and that, while it might survive in New York inside Broadway theaters functioning more or less as museums, its era was passing. Isaac's argument synthesizes several critiques of the proscenium: "The proscenium stage, with its curtain that can be quickly pulled aside to reveal *everything*, feeds our secret voyeuristic longings. But at the same time, the proscenium stage represents one of the dearest values of the Renaissance man: the private life, the sanctified separateness that makes of a man an *individual*."[13] Isaac, embracing the environmental theater of Richard Schechner, Jerzy Grotowski, the Texas Combine, LeRoi Jones/Amiri Baraka and other theater artists, summarizes a critique of the traditional theater's production of perspectival space: it perversely encourages voyeurism while also working to maintain—presumably on both sides of the curtain—the value of privacy

11. Benjamin, "What Is the Epic Theater? (II)," trans. Harry Zohn, in *Selected Writings*, 4:307.

12. Adorno, *Aesthetic Theory*, 58.

13. Isaac, "The Death of the Proscenium Stage," 238.

and individuality. And yet the pleasures of voyeurism rest on an imbalance: the spectator "feeds" on the revelation of everything on the other side of the curtain, while revealing nothing. Privacy rests on the revelation of the other, but the fiction—or contract?—of the fourth wall assures everyone that there has been no exposure.

One can see why, then, experiments in postwar drama so often included challenges to the proscenium arch: theatrical critiques of the "sanctified separateness" the sovereignty of the subject needed to adopt other arrangements of theatrical space, arrangements that did not tend always already to confirm that sanctity and that sovereignty. Schneider was right to see a connection between Beckett's work and the project of undoing the subjectivity effects in Western theater by breaking down the fourth wall, with all its institutional support for the confirmation of the comfortable bourgeois *subject* in its safe entrances and exits.[14] Beckett's work gave that subject little solace, and less comfort. Precisely *because* that work for the stage is so exquisitely attentive to the long history of the theater's role in the maintenance of those subjectivity effects, Beckett's theater never abandoned the proscenium arch. The swerve to the theater in the round, and to the exploded or empty spaces of other experiments, recognized the power of the proscenium arch but left the apparatus intact. Beckett took up the apparatus of the proscenium, that old medium of subjectivity effects, at the moment when the new medium of film had perfected that architecture and apparatus of subjection, leaving the theater in the shade—or as a place to experiment with the aftermaths of its former power.

This quick survey of the proscenium has deliberately skipped from Brecht to experimental theater of the late 1960s. One response to the Brechtian critique of theater as apparatus was to imagine other spaces for the theater. Schneider's suggestion to Beckett that *Godot* might be staged in the round is a chapter in a larger history of imagining liberation from the ideological apparatus of the bourgeois theater through the demolition of the proscenium. Beckett, instead, works within the conventional technology of the proscenium, as if to stress that a new architecture of the theater alone is not sufficient to produce liberation. His dedication to the "closed box," with its suggestion of the stage as coffin for actors, echoes Benjamin's necropolitical understanding of the theatrical divide between stage and audience. "Now we'll make it all dead," Beckett once said in a rehearsal.[15] One might link the increasing deadness of Beckett's performers to the preservation of

14. This sentence alludes to Joel Fineman's *The Subjectivity Effect in Western Literary Tradition* and Nicholas Ridout's *Scenes from Bourgeois Life*.

15. Illig, "Acting Beckett's Women," 26.

the stage as a site of uninterrupted action in conventional accounts of the proscenium, and then place this in the context of Richard Halpern's discussion of the "eclipse of action" in Beckett's dramaturgy.[16]

The perseverance of the proscenium in Beckett's dramaturgy needs to be linked to the larger media surround. The particular negation of the proscenium, precisely through its use, is exemplary of Beckett's reworking of the theater and of the media surround. In the form of film and television, the perspectival box was, if anything, an increasingly dominant technology in the postwar period. Never had so many been subject to interpellation through the frame and its subjectivation through perspective. One might argue that there was simply a continuity between the theater proscenium and the similar frames of film and television: one technology across platforms. Beckett's dedication to the frame of the proscenium belongs, however, in the context of negation: he adopts the proscenium because of its hegemonic force outside the theater and because it cannot, inside the theater, take on that power. By working complexly with the forms of address the proscenium has promoted, Beckett performs a "refunctioning," to use Brecht's word again, of the now historical force of that theatrical frame. A caution is in order here: in this context, Beckett's notorious embrace of failure and of aesthetic poverty describes a real imbalance. His theater is an important site for the recognition, and defamiliarization, of the force of cinema's interpellation of its spectators. The counterpoint to this recognition is a refusal to exaggerate theater's power to counter this force. And yet a rigorous encounter with the proscenium is everywhere in Beckett's work for the stage.

The 1967 Berlin production of *Endgame* included an element that, directing a later production, in 1980, Beckett would cut: "*Hanging near door, its face to wall, a picture.*"[17] This faceless picture and the "closed box" of the proscenium both provoke questions about a familiar phrase: the stage picture. Beckett uses the proscenium to produce the illusion of the fourth wall; inside that "closed box" is an invisible picture, "its face to the wall." Photographs of the Berlin production suggest that that picture had a primitive frame and that a rag hung from it: as the play begins this object would then also recall the face of Hamm, covered with a handkerchief. This echo would have been redoubled at the play's end. Another stage direction preceding the "action" of *Endgame* ties these elements together: "*Brief tableau.*"[18] The movement in English from plainspoken "picture" to "tableau," a French

16. For a compelling treatment of Beckett and the postwar predicament of action, see Halpern's chapter, "Beckett's Tragic Pantry," in *Eclipse of Action*, 226–54.

17. Beckett, *Endgame*, 7.

18. Beckett, *Endgame*, 7.

loan word that, in English, indicates a picture belonging to or created on the stage, contrasts this reversed picture with the tableau produced by the proscenium. Is this picture in fact a *tableau*? What is gained in translation? It is striking that the French text of *Fin de partie* includes "*un tableau retourné*"—the picture hanging with "its face to the wall"—but there is no "brief tableau." This iteration of the French word, that is, belongs only to Beckett's English translation. (No equivalent to the "brief tableau" appears in the German translation with its "*umgedrehtes Gemälde*" on the wall, either). In every language, the texts insist on Clov's immobility; only *Endgame* links this immobility to the moments of charged, frozen signification in the melodramatic tableau.[19] This pattern repeats itself at the play's end, where the text of *Endgame* concludes with another "*Brief tableau*" with no equivalent in *Fin de partie* or *Endspiel*.

The promise of the proscenium is that it will give the spectator a picture, a stage picture, a slice of life; the reversed picture on the wall undercuts such a promise. The melodramatic tableau, writes Carolyn Williams, "establishes a moment of hieratic silence and stillness within the ongoing action of the play, a moment in which the representation is turned inside out."[20] The reversed painting on the wall in *Endgame* blankly literalizes this turning inside out of representation; it also emblematizes the inaction framed by those brief opening and closing tableaux. The picture on the wall, that is, might model the function of the larger frame of the proscenium here: it frames an image to which the audience does not have the access it expects. This frame does not enclose a picture. It is not—to open a can of worms—a picture of a world. The picture on the wall, the only decoration of *Endgame*'s set, unless one counts the alarm clock that for a time hangs on the wall, is never the subject of any discussion in the play. One of Hamm's narratives does, however, include a painter. The episode deserves careful consideration:

> I once knew a madman who thought the end of the world had come. He was a painter—and engraver. I had a great fondness for him. I used to go and see him, in the asylum. I'd take him by the hand and drag him to the window. Look! There! All that rising corn! And there! Look! The sails of the herring fleet! All that loveliness!
>
> [*Pause.*]
>
> He'd snatch his hand away and go back into his corner. Appalled. All he had seen was ashes.

19. For the French and German texts, see *Dichtungen*, 1:208 and 209.

20. Williams, "Moving Pictures: George Eliot and Melodrama," 109–10.

[Pause.]

He alone had been spared.

[Pause.]

Forgotten.

[Pause.]

It appears that the case is . . . was not so . . . so unusual.[21]

Hamm's hesitation around the question of grammatical tense points to the many strands at work in this passage. He corrects himself because there are no longer enough people for the situation to be usual or unusual: in the absence of others, no statistical norm. He corrects himself because he wants to distance himself from the resemblance between his own situation, seemingly one of the few "spared" or "forgotten" after some unnamed disaster, and that of the madman: having once compelled a madman to go to the window in order to cheer him up, he now orders Clov go to the two windows. Adorno observed, "The madman's perception coincides with that of Clov, who peers out the window on command."[22] The views Clov reports far more closely resemble the madman's descriptions of ashes than any scene of rural and maritime loveliness, and no one is cheered by the prospects. Hamm's correction of the tense of his observation also underlines the problem of the convergence, or the distance, between the present occupied by those on stage and the present of the spectators. His movement from present to past points to the postwar situation of *Endgame* and to the question of the temporality of the end of the world. What madman didn't think the end of a world had come? The evident parallel between the madman and Clov, however, could raise the question of whether Clov, too, misrecognizes, or even simply invents, what he sees. (This possibility becomes especially vivid around the episode with the boy.)[23] Hamm's narrative is not only a metatheatrical reflection on his own situation, but also contains a sort of rebus of the concerns of this section. In brief, the passage conjures a scene of looking framed by a window as a scene of education: you think the world has ended, but if you look at this view, you will see that the world perseveres, that there is still "All that loveliness." The one who looks sees something very different, a landscape of ashes. This scene of an enforced looking through a frame also stresses the continuum between the window—a figure for the

---

21. Beckett, *Endgame*, 52.

22. Adorno, "Trying to Understand *Endgame*," in *Notes to Literature*, 1:254.

23. On the boy, see Gontarski's note in Beckett, *The Theatrical Notebooks of Samuel Beckett*, 68.

frame of the perspectival painting at least since Alberti's *On Painting*—and the proscenium arch.

The premise of the story would seem to be, simply, that Hamm is correct, the madman wrong. Part of what is unsettling about this narrative, then, is that in it Hamm appears as an agent of what Herbert Marcuse called affirmative culture, insisting on dragging the painter and engraver, who has been deluded by pictures of desolation, to the window to see a landscape of remarkable loveliness. The metatheatricality of this moment is multiple: not only does the scene's reflection on the stage as picture underscore the frame of the stage, but the scenario of Hamm's encounter with the madman offers an anticipatory echo of the response of at least a part of the play's audience. The parallel with the many spectators who would respond to *Endgame* by insisting that things are after all not really so bad as all that links this episode, for instance, to the episode of Mr. Shower or Cooker in *Happy Days*: the resisting audience drags Beckett to yet another window, and Beckett returns to his corner. Here another detail unique to Beckett's English version resonates: only in *Endgame*, and not in *Fin de partie* or *Endspiel*, does Hamm repeat that the madman was "a painter—and engraver." The repeated dash suggests a self-correction and in its punctuated emphasis calls attention to the medial difference between painting and engraving, and also repeats the usual order of production, in which the engraving—black and white, and reproducible—follows the unique painting. At this moment located, as Thomas Dilworth and Christopher Langlois have pointed out, at the center of texts that have just stressed the importance of being in the center, *Endgame* introduces a distinction important to many reflections on media: the engraving as the original copy of copies, where the original begins to dissolve into generations of repetitions.[24]

Here direct comparison of *Fin de partie* and *Endgame* is illuminating. (*Endspiel* again follows the French text.) Who was the madman?:

J'ai connu un fou qui croyait que la fin du monde était arrivée. Il faisait de la peinture.

I once knew a madman who thought the end of the world had come. He was a painter—and engraver.[25]

---

24. Dilworth and Langlois, "The Nietzschean Madman Walter Benjamin," 167–68. To cite an especially germane and obvious instance, Benjamin discusses the engraving in the second section in "The Work of Art in the Age of Its Technological Reproducibility" (20).

25. Beckett, *Fin de partie*, in *Dichtungen*, 1:262; *Endgame*, 52.

The French text suggests that there is a connection between the madman's belief and the paintings he would make: the implication, I think, is that the paintings he used to make were responses to, and perhaps illustrations of, the end that he thought had already arrived. The unseen painting would then be an image of the end of the world, an image that cannot be seen. Like the "picture" of *Endgame* or the "tableau" of *Fin de partie* on the wall at the start of the play, the madman's paintings are not images and also something much less than ekphrasis: a tantalizing idea of a possible image rather than description. Further, *Fin de partie* stresses the making of paintings, not, as in *Endgame*, a profession. *Endgame*'s madman is both painter and engraver, combining two professions that were, in practice, very often separated.

The story of the madman encapsulates the problem of representing the end of the world. It also underlines the question of the medium of such representation: the madman works across media, as Beckett would increasingly do. Indeed, the striking repetition—"painter—and engraver"—recalls one of Beckett's descriptions of his own development as an artist: "I realised that Joyce had gone as far as one could in the direction of knowing more, in control of one's material. He was always adding to it; you only have to look at his proofs to see that. I realised that my own way was in impoverishment, in lack of knowledge and in taking away, in subtracting rather than in adding."[26] The pairing of painting and engraving echoes Beckett's sense of Joyce's work as endlessly additive, and of his own as an art of taking away and subtraction. The view through the window that Hamm wants to supply, with its surprising exclamations in praise of the lovely landscape, supplies the negative not only of something like Joyce's knowledge and control but also works also against Hamm's story of the window within the proscenium.[27] The proscenium figures those apparatuses that supplied the affirmative world pictures against which Beckett's theater reacted by working inside the perspectival system. In *Beckett's Thing: Painting and Theatre*, David Lloyd has described just this dynamic: "It is the gradual breakdown of that 'world picture' that can be descried across Beckett's theatre in a painstaking trajectory that is steadily informed by his engagement with painting. In part, the progress of his dramatic work involved the rupture with the dramatic image in which is preserved that dimension of the 'spectacle' that inherited, as Beckett's contemporary Guy Debord put is, 'all the *weaknesses* of the Western philosophical project which undertook to

26. Knowlson, *Damned to Fame*, 319.

27. My sense of the force of negativity in Beckett's work owes much to Julia Jarcho's chapter on Beckett in *Writing and the Modern Stage* (68–106).

comprehend activity in terms of the categories of seeing.'"[28] *Beckett's Thing* provides a rigorous and searching account of Beckett's engagement with vision and its technologies. And yet even as Lloyd's argument gestures to the mass-mediated affirmations to which Beckett's plays responded with their grave negatives, Lloyd tends to suggest that that theater responds to the predicament of vision as such. The understanding of "activity in terms of the categories of seeing" may have been a weakness of the "western philosophical project," but this understanding contributed to the massive power of spectacular apparatuses. The moment of Beckett's theater saw—is seeing, one might even say—the massive consolidation of the world picture in Heidegger's sense. *Endgame* is part of Beckett's ongoing critique of the solidity of that picture.[29] Its breakdown in the plays is the negative image of its power outside them.

28. Lloyd, *Beckett's Thing*, 17. The internal quotation is from Debord, *Society of the Spectacle*, thesis 19.

29. For related speculations, also with reference to Beckett, see my "The End of a Trope for the World."

[TWENTY-FIVE]

Product Placement

If Beckett's aim was to eliminate references to and even resonances of the social world, why didn't he succeed? Yes, Beckett eliminated the "inspection of the audience" in his own productions of *Endgame*, and this decision exemplifies his later work. That work became increasingly hermetic and the range of reference—and possibly also of resonance—narrows. But aren't advertisements part of the social world? Jennifer Wicke's argument about advertising and the novel, already cited above, also illuminates the theater: "Modern literature, and particularly the novel, has its reading parameters defined by the linguistic horizon of advertising—a language that emanates from everywhere and nowhere."[1] Similarly, modern theater has its parameters of spectatorship in part determined by that horizon, a horizon that is not only linguistic but also visual and aural. It's unsurprising when, in *A Streetcar Named Desire*, Steve specifies that Mitch should bring not just any old swill but "Jax beer" to their poker game.[2] Williams's plays are permeable to the stuff of advertising and of mass culture. Beckett's plays also, however, contain surprising moments when particular products are named.

One of the early exchanges in *Endgame* between Hamm and Clov involves food:

> HAMM I'll give you nothing more to eat.
> CLOV Then we'll die.
> HAMM I'll give you just enough to keep you from dying. You'll be hungry all the time.
> CLOV Then we won't die.
> [*Pause.*]
> I'll go and get the sheet.

1. Wicke, *Advertising Fictions*, 53.

2. Williams, *A Streetcar Named Desire*, 24. Elaine Freedgood's *The Ideas in Things* changed my thinking about objects on stage and props.

[*He goes towards the door.*]

HAMM No!

[*Clov halts.*]

I'll give you one biscuit a day.

[*Pause.*]

One and a half.[3]

A biscuit and a half would be the proper measure to keep Clov from dying while also assuring that he will be "hungry all the time." What is this biscuit, and where does it come from, and what is it made of? A few moments later, the biscuit—or *a* biscuit, in any case—makes another appearance. Nagg calls for his pap. "There's no more pap," Clov announces. Hamm once again invents a solution: "Give him a biscuit." Clov quickly fetches one:

[*He gives biscuit to Nagg who fingers it, sniffs it.*]

NAGG [*plaintively*] What is it?

CLOV Spratt's medium.

NAGG [*as before*] It's hard! I can't!

HAMM Bottle him![4]

Soon enough, this inedible biscuit becomes a treat Nagg offers to share with his partner, Nell: "I've kept you half," he says, and then revises it to "Three quarters," which would be, by Hamm's earlier calculation, half of the daily ration required in order for Clov not to die.[5]

"Dogs of the Empire Eat and Enjoy Spratt's," one of many advertisements for the biscuits in the London *Times* announced.[6] Why the entry of this familiar brand name into the seemingly sealed world of *Endgame*? Spratt's was for a century or more the best-known manufacturer of animal food in Britain. The company's success illustrates the familiar complaint about advertising: that it produces a need where none previously existed. Spratt's, and the other manufacturers of pet food that followed in the company's wake, had to convince their publics that the old ways of feeding pets with scraps from the table or with greaves—"fibrous matter or skin found in animal fat, which forms a sediment on melting and is pressed into cakes

---

3. Beckett, *Endgame*, 12–13.

4. Beckett, *Endgame*, 17.

5. Beckett, *Endgame*, 25.

6. London *Times*, Wednesday, May 24, 1911.

to serve as meat for dogs or hogs, fish-bait, etc."[7]—needed to give way to (to use the language of the *Times* ad once more) the "dietetically perfect" biscuit: this is what dogs of the empire eat. Dogs had always eaten, and humans had very often fed dogs deliberately, but the production of a food made especially for dogs dates to roughly 1860, when an American named James Spratt began to manufacture dog biscuits under his own name in England. Spratt, or so the origin narrative goes, spotted dogs eating hardtack discarded by sailors after sea voyages on London docks.[8] Rations for sailors become trash; this trash becomes food for dogs. A relationship between waste and dog food is a constant of its history. Katherine C. Grier writes: "'Feed tankage' (the slurry of odds and ends of commercial slaughter that was mixed with crackling and blood, dried, and pressed into 'cheeses'), sold by packers for use in feed mixes for hogs and chickens, could just as easily be cooked up into food for dogs."[9] "Spratt's Patent Meat Fibrine Dog Cakes," to give one proper name for the biscuits in question, were, it seems, similarly produced from the byproducts of other processed meats and fish.[10] In naming Spratt's, Beckett invokes a company that would have been familiar to the British audience for whom he first translated his *Fin de partie*. (In *Fin de partie*, the treat appears simply as "*biscuit classique*," with no suggestions of animal consumption; the German translation similarly has "*klassische Zwieback*.")[11] That Beckett wanted the reference to be recognized is clear in a letter to Alan Schneider: "If in US there is no particularly well known brand of dog biscuit you could fall back on 'classic biscuit' or 'standard biscuit' or [as if remembering the fable of Spratt's origins] 'hard tack.'"[12]

Beckett's corpus includes one especially compact and succinct comment about advertising. In *Molloy*, the narrator describes a period during which his sleeping and waking were scarcely distinguishable: "But it is useless to dwell on this period of my life. If I go on long enough calling that my life I'll end up by believing it. It's the principle of advertising."[13] Roughly, the

---

7. *Oxford English Dictionary*, s.v. "Greaves."

8. See Katherine C. Grier, *Pets in America*, 281.

9. Grier, *Pets in America*, 281; 283.

10. Because Scott and Shackleton's team fed Spratt's biscuits to its dogs and left biscuits behind, scientists were recently able to examine the biscuits: see Fraser-Miller et al., "Feeding the Team: Analysis of a Spratt's Dog Cake from Antarctica."

11. Beckett, *Fin de partie*, in *Dramatische Dichtungen in drei Sprachen*, 220; 221.

12. Harmon, *No Author Better Served*, 22. To my knowledge, no American production has substituted "Milkbone" for "Spratt's medium," but Beckett's authority for such a change, if wanted, seems to me solid.

13. Beckett, *Molloy*, in *Three Novels*, 53.

"principle of advertising" here seems to be that repetition produces belief. The passage becomes more resistant as one reads it more closely, however. The divorce of the "principle of advertising" here from any object to be sold—from any object or commodity with a use-value that can be given a meaning unrelated to that use-value—suggests that "life," far from being a zone of exclusion advertising cannot touch, is the location of advertising's far-reaching effects, or even the site of the origin of those effects. It is "the principle of advertising"—repeatedly calling any life mine?—that produces belief in one's possession of a singular life. The passage refuses the logic of a "life" vulnerable to reification but instead implies that the sense of such a life owes something to a "principle of advertising" prior to "my life," prior also, perhaps, to an industry of advertising in the narrower sense. Advertising produces the belief in a life that advertising can then violate.

Beckett, that is, leaves undecidable whether "the principle of advertising," as a mode of psychic repetition that produces the phenomenon of a life someone could possess, existed before the industry of advertising, or if advertising as a distinct and historically delimited cultural force has produced a new form of belief in what Molloy designates "my life." We can ask not only why the name "Spratt's" appears in Beckett's very English translation of his play but what the temporality and historical conditions of this appearance are. At the close of her *Advertising Fictions*, Jennifer Wicke compares advertising's cultural work to that of literature. Advertising, she argues, is "unlike literature in that it gains this power only across the range of its artifacts, only in its constellation as a floating cultural corpus—the individual instances of advertisement are too embedded in the discursive matrix of advertising for them to be anything but slight when taken in isolation. Literature's power is discrete and accretive; advertising's power is aggregate, cumulative—almost, one might say, immanent."[14] To return to *Endgame*: one of the leitmotifs of the play has to do with what is running out: "There is no more painkiller," there are no more bicycles, there is no more pap, and so on. When Hamm threatens to put Clov on a near-starvation diet, this seems simply sadistic, but the threat also underlines the scarcity that haunts many exchanges in the play. That Nagg's treat is a dog biscuit is a reflection on a scene of scarcity where food for a dog can become a human luxury; this mildly grotesque scenario certainly recalls the harsher deprivations that were part of wartime and the postwar years. (Indeed, Spratt's became scarce due to "World Food Conditions.")[15] Beckett's scenes

14. Wicke, *Advertising Fictions*, 175.

15. See, for instance, the announcements in *The Times* (London) on Saturday, June 22, 1946, and Tuesday, September 30, 1947.

of an emptied-out object world become legible—let us say, in Paris and in London, in 1957, when the play was first staged—as extreme examples of a familiar scarcity. But the situation of *Endgame* is also something more than scarcity: the commodity form and its great medium, advertising, are also dying out. In Wicke's terms, it is as though the advertisement is returning to the condition of literature. The "aggregate, cumulative" power of advertising dissolves in the singularity of a name, instantly familiar, that belongs to a world of multitudinous commodities that no longer exists. "Spratt's," "taken in isolation," evokes a discourse and set of material practices that, in *Endgame*, seem extinct. The play, however, pictures that extinction in a social world where advertising thrives—where, indeed, *Endgame* could and did become the stuff of advertising.

"Spratt's medium": as far as I have found, Beckett took liberties with that second term. There were many varieties of Spratt's animal feed, and for many kinds of creatures, but I have not yet found "Spratt's medium" advertised or mentioned anywhere outside Beckett. The French and German texts, the "*biscuit classique*" and "*klassische Zwieback*" mix everyday food with exalted aesthetic aspirations, so, in the English, "Spratt's medium" suggests the emphasis on the materiality of art that was part of the discourse of art in Beckett's milieu. If an insistence on the actual materiality of the artwork became a way to distance art from the mass fetishism of commodities that surrounded art—a way to rescue a modernist "thing culture" from commodity culture, so to speak—such a strategy met a strange and paradoxical challenge on stage. "Spratt's medium" introduces the discourse of advertising in the context of its death: there are no masses to address, and what Wicke calls "advertising's uncanny you personally/you-all mode of address" becomes strangely nonfunctional in the situation of an imagined evacuation of human culture.[16]

"Spratt's medium" appears in the English *Endgame*, as "Milkbone" should appear in the American, to invoke the familiarity of a discourse that does not need to be named. In a setting where the commodity dies out, advertising dies with it. But that uncanny mode of address—to "you personally/you-all"—has belonged not only to advertising but also to drama (and not only drama: each form is, perhaps, vulnerable in its own way). Spratt's, that is, stands as the crumbled fragment of an allegory of the medium in which Beckett works—that is, the stage, or, that is, the Milkbone medium.

Take another example, from *Play*:

16. Wicke, *Advertising Fictions*, 160.

M: Perhaps they meet, and sit, over a cup of that green tea that they
both so loved, without milk or sugar, not even a squeeze of lemon—
[*Spot from M to W2.*]

W2: Are you listening to me? Is anyone listening to me? Is anyone
looking at me? Is anyone bothering about me at all?
[*Spot from W2 to M.*]

M: Not even a squeeze of—
[*Spot from M to W1.*]

W1: Is it something I should do with my face, other than utter? Weep?
[*Spot from W1 to W2.*]

W2: Am I taboo, I wonder. Not necessarily, now that all danger is
averted. That poor creature—I can hear her—that poor creature—
[*Spot from W2 to W1.*]

W1: Bite off my tongue and swallow it? Spit it out? Would that placate
you? How the mind works still to be sure!
[*Spot from W1 to M.*]

M: Meet, and sit, now in the one dear place, now in the other, and
sorrow together, and *compare*—[*hiccup*]—pardon—happy memories.
[*Spot from M to W1.*]

W1: If only I could think, There is no sense in this . . . either, none
whatsoever. I can't.
[*Spot from W1 to W2.*]

W2: That poor creature who tried to seduce you, what will ever became
of her, do you suppose?—I can hear her. Poor thing.
[*Spot from W2 to M.*]

M: Personally I always preferred Lipton's.[17]

M differentiates himself from W1 and W2 by preferring a brand most remarkable for its ubiquity: that "personal" preference for the brand everyone prefers, the obverse of the aspiration to produce distinction through drinking green tea, is surely the point. Just as the scenario of *Play* recalls that most clichéd of the plots of the bourgeois stage, the adulterous triangle, so M's effort to distinguish himself from the others stresses the very sameness that effort would deny. This preference for Lipton's also illuminates the plaintive litanies about being heard and being seen that recur throughout *Play.* "Are you listening to me? Is anyone listening to me? Is anyone looking at me? Is anyone bothering about me at all?" W2's questions are at once specific to the excruciating dramaturgy of *Play*, with its spitfire manipulations

17. Beckett, *Play*, in *Collected Shorter Plays*, 156–57. In *Comédie*, M used to prefer another familiar brand, "l'Eléphant" (2:420); Lipton's also prevails in *Spiel* (2:261).

of the inquisitorial spotlight, and a motif in Beckett's work. The movement from the relative intimacy of the second-person pronoun to the anonymity of "anyone" describes something analogous to the modes of mass cultural address: "You deserve a break today." That second person might refer at once to some particular listener, and perhaps even to M; to any particular embodied listener; and to the mass of listeners, who understand that they are addressed corporately. Comparison with the German and French translations of *Play* is instructive here:

Are you listening to me? Is anyone listening to me?

Est-ce que tu m'écoutes? Est-ce que quelqu'un m'écoute?

Hörst du mir zu? Hört irgend jemand mir zu?[18]

The transition from the familiar second-person forms *du* and *tu* to the anonymity of "*irgend jemand*" or "*quelqu'un*," even more than that from "you" to "anyone," stresses the gap between the ideal of an intimate interlocutor and addressee and the indefinite referent of "anyone." The referential uncertainty that accompanies the English "you," an awkward and permanent fact of English grammar, now also bears the traces of mass cultural address: you, there in the theater, are listening, but you are and are not described by the "you." To answer the question—"Are you listening to me?"—would evince a misunderstanding of convention just as deep as Septimus Smith's when he imagines that the skywriting plane writes messages directed exclusively to him in *Mrs. Dalloway*. That is to say, Septimus is not wrong to imagine that he is addressed by the plane's message, but he mistakes its address to an urban collective as a cryptic message meant for his eyes only.

Such a "mistake," however, is precisely the mode of interiorization that advertising demands: the product offered to all becomes the thing that one desires oneself: "Personally I always preferred Lipton's." With the precision of that redundant "Personally," *Play* marks this claim to "personal" difference just where the banality of the preference would seem to erase that personality itself. However satirical this treatment of M's desire, *Play* cannot, however, simply expel such desire or the structures that produce it. This is already clear in the uncertainty that surrounds the pronoun "you." It is clearer still in the play's convention: "*Their speech is provoked by a spotlight projected on faces alone.*" In a note that follows the text Beckett calls the

18. Beckett, *Comédie* and *Spiel* in *Dramatische Dichtungen in drei Sprachen*, 2:419; 2:259.

spotlight a "unique inquisitor": the convention evokes a tool of torture.[19] The spotlight is also the tool of, and a principal metaphor for, mass cultural visibility: these three ghastly figures in the spotlight are at the same time ready for their close-ups and afraid of them. The only thing more frightening than the glare of exposure is its utter absence. "Bite off my tongue and swallow it? Spit it out? Would that placate you?" Here W1 may address the spotlight itself as "you": the personification of a set of inscrutable demands, the light seems to demand self-mutilation and silence, even while its effect is to provoke speech.[20] M's preference for Lipton's is also a register of the extent to which he cannot hear what the women next to him on their urns are saying. With all the care Beckett takes to specify the size of the urns and the movements of the inquisitorial light, there is evidently no need to specify what is clear to any spectator: these figures cannot hear each other.

The passage oscillates between M's imagining untormented reunions of his wife and lover and the affectless and yet intense anguish that characterizes the lines of W1 and W2. In his fantasy of friendship based in shared sorrow, W1 and W2 nevertheless compare "happy memories." Meanwhile, W1 and W2, equally unaware of each other or of M, are nonetheless alike in addressing that "you," who may or may not be watching and may or may not be "bothering about" them. W2's lines are especially resonant: "Are you listening to me? Is anyone listening to me? Is anyone looking at me? Is anyone bothering about me at all?" This passage exemplifies the place of the second-person pronoun in *Play*, and also of the condition of theater after film. On the one hand, the pathetic survivor, left behind by its audience, asks for attention. On the other, this is an example of Huyssen's remediation in reverse: the old, renewed medium dislocates the place of the spectator and complicates the direction and misdirection of performed address that constitutes a public. The dramaturgical situation implies that that second person addresses the just barely personified spotlight: insofar as that light seems to address the figures in the urns, however violently, it can in turn be addressed. The logic of *Play* encapsulates, then, an aspect of the phenomenology of mass cultural address: the audience member experiences itself

---

19. Beckett, *Play*, in *Collected Shorter Plays*, 149, 161. Hugh Kenner calls this a variation on Beckett's "Gestapo theme" (*A Reader's Guide to Samuel Beckett*, 109 and, with direct reference to *Play*, 153). See also Anna McMullan, *Theatre on Trial*, 24, and Tyrus Miller, "Beckett's Political Technology."

20. Ruby Cohn writes: "Separately, the Man and the rival Women address the light as 'you,' questioning its purpose. At times the spotlight seems a manic deity, but rationally we in the audience know that a theatre spotlight is manipulated by a technician" ("Ghosting through Beckett," 9).

as addressee. To be addressed is to imagine the solicitation of a reply and to reply may be to a greater or lesser degree psychotic. But who has not experienced this psychosis? Something like it is the enabling condition of cinematic spectatorship. *Play* puts its captive and unmoving audience in something like the position of those in the urns: "Are you listening to me?" Are you anyone? *Play* perfectly allows the audience to renounce the second person: that "you" addresses an apparatus of which I am not a part. And yet W2's translation of *you* to *anyone* implicitly opens a divide in the second person who may be listening: you *or* anyone. The audience may not be "you" but cannot disavow being that anonymous or anonymized someone who is, at the very least, listening and looking. "Is anyone bothering about me at all?" This question caps the sequence: to bother about someone implies some concern—a form of care so minimal as to add up to bother—that exceeds the basic spectatorial activities of watching and listening. Late in *Play*, M takes on this scrutiny of spectatorship, asking repeatedly the question that has also repeated through these pages, "Am I as much as . . . being seen?"[21] For M, to be seen would maybe be bother enough. This emphasis, however, may only emphasize the machinic nature of the apparatus that seems to see. Beckett's insistence that the spotlight belongs to the "ideal space" of the performers accentuates the inhuman aspect of the illusion of such address: the projection doesn't bother about you at all. The automatic response of the figures in the urns and the silence of the audience in the theater are related. After film, the theatrical convention that the audience should not respond resembles the anonymity of the apparatus that produces second persons it does not address.

---

21. Beckett, *Play*, in *Collected Shorter Plays*, 160.

∴

ADRIENNE KENNEDY

∵

[TWENTY-SIX]

Theater after Hollywood

It may be true that every visit to the cinema left Theodor Adorno, "against all [his] vigilance, stupider and worse."[1] It may, conversely, be true that every visit to the cinema left Adrienne Kennedy smarter, better, more vigilant to the contradictions of American culture. Kennedy, who increasingly appears to be among the most captivating and thought-provoking American playwrights of the latter half of the twentieth century and the first decades of the twenty-first, took on the problem of making theater after film in a way few other playwrights of the period can match. Film, in her case, was largely the Hollywood of what film historians have called the classical era; her theater, by contrast, belongs to those venues open to experimentation, to the world of downtown, Off-Broadway, and regional theater and its equivalents abroad. In his critical account of Black abstraction, Phillip Brian Harper includes her among the practitioners of what he calls "abstractionist aesthetics," and his description of Kennedy's *The Owl Answers* might apply to many of her plays: "The work's disavowal of naturalistic dramatic norms [. . .] actually facilitates its disclosure of the social-historical relations that constitute black racial identity, which in turn potentially engenders 'epistemological critique' on the part of the audience."[2] The relation of her plays to Hollywood is a particular site of this disclosure and potential critique. As in the cases of Williams and Beckett, her theater comes after a particular conjuncture of cinema and a particular life of moviegoing.

Throughout, I have argued that the works on which I focus are at once excellent and telling—to my mind, central—examples of the theatrical response to the postwar order of film and mass media. I don't, however, think of these examples as typical of postwar theater. They are not typical because, on the one hand, the typical drama in the period that interests

1. Adorno, *Minima Moralia: Reflections*, 25.

2. Harper, *Abstractionist Aesthetics*, 175. Harper draws on the important critical account of Kennedy in Kimberly Benston's *Performing Blackness* (71–82, 228–44).

me—if by typical one means dominant or, more simply, the theater seen by most spectators—continued along formal, generic, and presentational lines as though nothing at all had happened to perturb the theater's peace. Box office magic, as often as not, colored by numbers: for every disruptive encounter with *Marat/Sade*, so many more happy evenings were caught in *The Mousetrap*. That *The Mousetrap* was by a significant order of magnitude more popular arguably makes it more significant, but that blockbuster doesn't belong to the kind of theater that interests me here. Even were one to narrow one's focus and to seek the work typical of that narrower category of dramatic experiment on which I focus, to make a claim for any single work's exemplarity would be to risk making a formula of a disparate and discontinuous collection of theatrical responses to the postwar order of mass culture. To picture that order as monolithic is in itself to ignore its internal contradictions and variations. Contradictions are legible inside even the most familiar of the productions of the culture industry; and yet a picture of that industry as an ideological factory held sway with many observers. As I have stressed throughout this book, the construction of mass cultural hegemony as an objective structure of solicitation enabled, even made necessary, theatrical works that challenged the codes and apparatuses of such solicitation. The lasting strangeness of these works is, not least, evidence of their quite exceptional and quite singular forms of resistance to the force of mass cultural forms. Further, that picture had concrete historical effects. Among those effects are the dramatic strategies of refunctioning or detournement or remediation in reverse that this book considers.

Just as there can be no absolutely exemplary singular work along the way, this book could also have had many endings.[3] And yet, just as *Endgame* in its resolute refusal to resemble anything else, in all its singularity, stands out as exemplary of a theatrical movement that refuses exemplarity, so Adrienne Kennedy's *A Movie Star Has to Star in Black and White*, her idiosyncratic and singular play of 1976, stands out as the example with which to conclude. In crudely dialectical terms, Kennedy's play performs a kind of synthesis of Williams and Beckett. If Williams's thesis is that drama

---

3. Sam Shepard's *Tooth of Crime*, first performed in London in 1972, might have offered a conclusion to a book concentrating on the relationship between rock music and theater. Recent plays, among them Young Jean Lee's *The Shipment* (2009), Julia Jarcho's *Dreamless Land* (2011), Anne Washburn's *Mr. Burns, A Post-Electric Play* (2012), and Annie Baker's *The Flick* (2013), are related to my concerns but involve, I think, a different conjunction of theater and mass media, and different responses to that conjunction.

can be made through the distillation of an openness to the myths of mass culture, and Beckett's antithesis that drama can continue only through attempts at mass culture's negation, Kennedy's synthesis adopts the affective logic of Williams's embrace of the mass cultural surround and yet combines it with Beckett's insistence on negation and a remade dramatic form. Her work shares with Williams a saturation in the world of mass culture and of stardom; it shares with Beckett a disfiguration or paring down of theatrical genres. Not for nothing was the first collection of her work titled *In One Act*. Immersed though she is in the pleasures of the narrative structures of Hollywood, her own short plays resist the machinery of identification in which she herself so evidently revels. In *A Movie Star*, she experiments with what happens to some of the effects of the Hollywood apparatus—particularly to stardom, more particularly to stardom in relation to Black spectators—when one empties out the narrative forms and the logic of character that provide its most basic architecture.

In a 1996 interview with Kennedy, Suzan-Lori Parks illuminates the intimacy and intensity of Kennedy's identifications with stars with a provocative observation:

> SLP You have your immediate family, and then you have what I call your extended family, in Hollywood—the Hollywood stars. Their ghosts are still out there. A lot of them are on hiatus but . . .
> AK They haven't been in a movie in a while . . .

These ghosts "on hiatus" continue to haunt: there is no telling when they may return from their long breaks, even if these breaks bear a close resemblance to death. In Parks's formulation, kinship with stars makes them, at least for Kennedy, "extended family." To equate the stars who populate Kennedy's work with a family not nuclear but nevertheless intimately related captures something of the intensity of Kennedy's engagement with luminaries of the star system. On the one hand, Kennedy's devotion to her "extended family" of stars is not exceptional: Kennedy responds to Hollywood's claim to address everyone, to a system of movies and fan magazines, the whole machinery of modern stardom. On the other hand, her representations of the importance of stars to psychic life transcends more familiar forms of this devotion. In the interview, Parks recalls a visit she and Kennedy made to Universal Studios:

> That was so much fun for me, to watch *you* interact with these . . .
> AK These ghosts.
> SLP Yes. These ghosts of Hollywood.

AK I have no idea why I fell so in love with the movies. I guess it was so common. All of my childhood friends were in love with them, we'd see the double feature on Saturdays. I could spend days being a character. And then my mother was crazy about them. She took drama lessons when she was at Atlanta University and she always talked about that so fondly. She was so enamored with all those people: Joan Crawford, Bette Davis, Ginger Rogers. If I'd had my druthers, I would have loved to have been a movie star, a '40s movie star!

SLP They had the best clothes.

AK Their outfits! Thulani Davis and I were talking and she said, "They got to wear cocktail dresses in the daytime."

SLP And those shoes, their hair! But at the same time, there weren't any black movie stars . . . I mean, to fall in love with being a '40s movie star is to fall in love with something that didn't include who you are.

AK As a child, I was blinded to that.

SLP I think it's puberty or adolescence when you realize, my hair!

AK I was blinded to that, too. But I'm still totally crazy about that particular period.[4]

Those Hollywood ghosts are the ghosts of previous, but also of ongoing, attachments. While claiming not to know why she loved the movies, Kennedy points toward structures of triangular desire with great explanatory power: all of her "childhood friends," and especially her mother, loved the movies. And to love the movies, in the period she is talking about, was the love of stars: to love those stars was also, as the psychoanalytic discourse on identification would insist, to want to be them, spending "days being a character."[5] And that desire persists: Kennedy inherits her mother's love of women who were stars, and especially of Bette Davis. She gently but firmly resists Parks's critique: "To fall in love with being a '40s movie star is to fall in love with something that didn't include who you are." Parks relegates this love to the past: Kennedy, still "blinded," insists that she remains "totally

4. Suzan-Lori Parks, interview with Adrienne Kennedy. See also the importance of Bette Davis to Elin Diamond's account of a public interview with Kennedy (*Unmaking Mimesis*, 125–26). Black playwrights working in her wake have inspired some of Kennedy's best interviews. See also "Unraveling the Landscape: An Interview with Adrienne Kennedy by Branden Jacobs-Jenkins," in Kennedy, *He Brought Her Heart Back in a Box*, 29–35.

5. On identification and the desire to be as the desire to have another, see Diana Fuss, *Identification Papers*, 11–12.

crazy about that particular period." As her mother was, so she remains, "so enamored with all those people," "crazy about them."

For Parks, there is something damaging in Kennedy's identifications; in speaking of herself as "blinded," Kennedy seems to agree. And yet Kennedy also resists this rhetoric of mass cultural inclusion and exclusion. In her fundamental *Unmaking Mimesis*, Elin Diamond demonstrates the centrality of identification to Kennedy's work. Because Diamond takes seriously the psychoanalytic proposition that our selves are made of our histories of identification, her reading of Kennedy is acutely alert to Kennedy's staging of identifications, including mass cultural ones. Noting the "passivity and masochism of the female viewing position" described by film theorists, Diamond writes: "What Kennedy contributes is the pleasurable possibility of (to paraphrase Cixous) becoming, inhabiting, entering, as well as the particular historicity of that process. Kennedy's identifications *are* her history, the 'character of [her] ego is [not only] a precipitate of her abandoned object-cathexes' but *'the history of those object choices.'*"[6] These object choices, that is, are never fully abandoned: those precipitates never fully dissolve. Here, the question of exemplarity splits. On the one hand, Kennedy's work is exemplary in that it unapologetically chronicles and stages the ways that identification makes the ego—her ego, every ego. This is everybody's autobiography. On the other hand, however familiar her constellation of stars might have been—"I guess it was so common"— that history remains singular, as virtually any page of *People Who Led to My Plays* demonstrates. Her history of identifications, like any such history, is exemplary in its singularity.

That Hollywood stars had to star in her unconscious is also not a matter of chance. Few writers are so aware of the cast of characters who have made them or, more generally, of the force of mass culture in the shaping of the psyche. This book traces different forms of the acknowledgment of this force in drama. Throughout, I have tried to emphasize the historical character of this entwinement of drama and mass culture. Diamond emphasizes the history of the identifications that made Kennedy. In these sections on Kennedy, I will emphasize the historical character of the mass cultural formations that made this drama, paying special attention to the first, workshop production of *A Movie Star* in 1976. People may still lead to plays, but they won't be the same people, and they won't lead to the same plays.

The exchange between Parks and Kennedy invokes a debate about race, cinema, theater, and performance that is structured by an antinomy. This

---

6. Diamond, *Unmaking Mimesis*, 126 (Diamond's italics). The interior quotation is from Freud's "The Ego and the Id."

debate concerns not so much the historical question whether the Holly-wood cinema of the 1940s excluded the Black spectator as whether cinema continues to exclude—cannot not exclude—Black life and whether, given this exclusion, theater and performance provide an alternative medium for inclusion. Can theater and performance, after and within this ongoing history of film, address Black spectators in a different, potentially more inclusive mode? Can theater and performance make the apparatus of mass cultural address, of exclusion and the potential for inclusion, more visible?

Twentieth-century playwrights went to the movies, but what moviegoing meant varied. In an immensely generative essay first published in *Screen* in 1988, Manthia Diawara, responding to what had become a set of premises about cinematic spectatorship (also largely first established in the pages of *Screen*), pointed out that these theories overlooked the particular situation of the Black spectator. The Black spectator, Diawara argued, is interchangeable with the "resisting spectator."[7] Diawara elaborates his argument: "Resisting spectators are transforming the problem of passive identification into active criticism which both informs and interrelates with contemporary oppositional film-making."[8] Maybe Kennedy as spectator, immersed in her identifications, resists this paradigm of resistance. But the evidence of the stage is that she transforms "the problem of passive identification" *into* the form of "active criticism" that is her own theater after film. Diawara's theory assumes that there is either passively receptive or actively resistant spectatorship. Kennedy's example suggests a sequence from identification to resistance to or alienation from that identification, to staging that alienation as a mode of theater.

But identification with what? As the interview with Parks suggests, Kennedy consistently returns, across interviews and in her writing, to her attachments to the classical Hollywood cinema.[9] As Kennedy reveals again and again, these are contradictory attachments. Cedric Robinson made an especially rich historical argument that Hollywood cinema was designed to "inferiorize" Blacks: this inferiorization, he argues, served capital by splitting the working class by giving white workers the symbolic assurance of white supremacy: "White patrimony deceived some of the majority of Americans, patriotism and nationalism others, but the more fugitive reality was the theft

7. Diawara, "Black Spectatorship," 66. This essay has since been republished frequently, including in Diawara's influential collection of 1993, *Black American Cinema*.

8. Diawara, "Black Spectatorship," 75–76.

9. Kennedy also notes the importance of European cinema to her formation. See, for instance, Paul Bryant-Jackson and Lois More Overbeck, "Adrienne Kennedy: An Interview," in their *Intersecting Boundaries*, 10. This excellent collection opened up many important conversations in the scholarship on Kennedy.

they themselves endured and the voracious expropriation of others they facilitated. The scrap which was their reward was the installation of black inferiority into their shared national culture. It was a paltry dividend, but it still serves."[10] Film, central to the production of "national culture" in the twentieth century, was, Robinson argues, crucial to this installation. This argument sharpens the question of Kennedy's identification: what part, if any, of this "shared national culture" could she in fact share? One answer might be that of Jacques Rancière, who rejects the idea that the "collective power shared by spectators" stems "from the fact that they are members of a collective body": "It is the power each of them has to translate what she perceives in her own way, to link it to the unique intellectual adventure that makes her similar to all the rest in as much as this adventure is not like any other."[11] Alike in unlikeness, spectators translate their perceptions; no power can dictate the language of these translations. Even, or especially, a Black spectator may translate a cinematic language that buttresses Black inferiorization into her own "intellectual adventure." The fiercest response to this translation of Rancière to the terrain of the racialization of Black spectatorship might, in turn, be that of Frank Wilderson. For Wilderson, the possibility of such a translation would assume an impossible subjectivity: "Afro-pessimism explores the meaning of Blackness not—in the first instance—as a variously and unconsciously interpellated identity or as a conscious social actor, but as a structural position of noncommunicability in the face of all other positions."[12] From this perspective, the picture of the Black spectator's free translations of cinematic discourse via Rancière fails to recognize that spectator's "structural position," that "noncommunicability," which forecloses unconscious interpellation and conscious social action alike.[13]

The line between the poles of the antimony structuring debates about Black cinematic spectatorship, then, stretches from the possibility of vigilantly resistant spectatorship to the impossibility of any agency at all. Adrienne Kennedy responds to, even contains, this antinomy. Her work for the

---

10. Robinson, *Forgeries of Memory and Meaning*, 126.

11. Rancière, "The Emancipated Spectator," 16–17. Jenny Spencer has pursued Rancière's rethinking of spectatorship in relation to Kennedy in "Emancipated Spectatorship in Adrienne Kennedy's Plays."

12. Wilderson, *Red, White & Black*, 58.

13. Wilderson is suspicious of arguments that suggest that "specific cultural practices (e.g., countercinema or performance art)" can redress the dispossession that is the structural "rebar" of cinema studies (*Red, White & Black*, 67). Wilderson discusses theater directly in "Grammar & Ghosts" and in Jaye Austin Williams's discussion, "Staging (within) Violence."

stage celebrates, and yet resists, immersion in the identificatory pleasures of cinematic spectatorship. That spectatorship proves at once a privileged site of subject formation and yet is also marked, as Parks suggests, by structural exclusion. Michele Wallace describes a dynamic that recalls Kennedy's socialization into the pleasures of cinematic spectatorship, remembering how her grandmother and mother taught her "to know and love Lana Turner, Rita Hayworth, Gloria Swanson, Joan Crawford, Ingrid Bergman, Gloria Grahame, Barbara Bel Geddes, and Barbara Stanwyck, not because they were 'white' but because they were 'stars.'" Wallace's argument about "a way in which these films were possessed by Black female viewers" is suggestive for reading Kennedy's work as it cuts through the antinomies of theories of spectatorship: "The process may have been about problematizing and expanding one's racial identity instead of abandoning it. It seems crucial here to view spectatorship not only as potentially bisexual but also multiracial and multiethnic. Even as the 'Law of the Father' may impose its premature closure on the filmic 'gaze' in the coordination of suture and classic narrative, disparate factions in the audience, not all equally well indoctrinated in the dominant discourse, may have their way, now and then, with interpretation."[14] The central technique of the play central to these sections on Kennedy—white movie stars speak for Clara, the "protagonist" of *A Movie Star*—encapsulates Kennedy's having her way with interpretation. Wallace points to the possibilities of renegade Black forms of spectatorship even inside a discourse that remains dominant. Stuart Hall, in another classic essay, stresses that popular culture "is a theater of popular desires, a theater of popular fantasies. It is where we discover and play with the identifications of ourselves, where we are imagined, where we are represented, not only to the audiences out there who do not get the message, but to ourselves for the first time."[15] Kennedy's project is to make theater out of this "theater of popular fantasies." This second order of representation—a theater made of the stuff of these representations, a theater made of Black *re*presentations of popular cultural presentations—is not a repetition of Hall's "theater of popular desires." If, as for many of us, popular culture was the place Kennedy represented herself to herself "for the first time," the theater became, so to speak, the space for the second time, the space for taking distance from these representations.

14. Wallace, "Race, Gender, and Psychoanalysis in Forties Films: *Lost Boundaries, Home of the Brave*, and *The Quiet One*," in Diawara, *Black American Cinema*, 264. A comparative study of the art of Wallace's mother, Faith Ringgold, and the writing of Kennedy might illuminate both bodies of work.

15. Hall, "What Is This 'Black' in Black Popular Culture?," 32. This essay was first published as part of a project organized by Michele Wallace.

[TWENTY-SEVEN]

A Movie Star in 1976

Glamour is fact. When I or you or Adrienne Kennedy adore stars, we respond to a structure of solicitation engineered to produce that adoration.[1] The production of movie stars and of fans are two aspects of the same, very effective apparatus. To say this is not, however, to imagine that what becomes of stardom is wholly determined or to claim that any apparatus can thoroughly capture, much less control, what viewers make of the stars they adore, as Wallace suggests. Kennedy's multivalent title, *A Movie Star Has to Star in Black and White*, implies at once that the only real stars were those who reigned before color technologies came to dominate the silver screen and that stardom means soliciting spectators across the color line. The title also suggests that "to star" happens not on screen at all, but in writing—stardom as something put down, so to speak, "in black and white." An imperative also lurks: however much a star of a newer age might think otherwise, or however strenuously an unwritten Jim Crow law might decree against the practice, a movie star, any movie star, has no choice but to star in black and white. There is a utopian suggestion that whatever the genius of the system might have collectively planned when it produced stars, those stars *must* violate those boundaries legislating whatever segregated spaces of fantasy and identification that system might have imagined it could maintain and control.

In *Place for Us*, D. A. Miller has written incisively about what he calls at once mass culture and—the term is especially germane here—"first culture":

> The stuff of mass culture (as our first culture) conducts psychic flows with an efficiency that the superior material of no second, later culture ever comes close to rivaling. It is by way of *Shane*, not Sophocles or Freud,

---

1. Participants in a 2024 American Comparative Literature Association seminar, especially Shonni Enelow and Julia Jarcho, provoked my thinking about glamour.

that Oedipus stalks our dreams, just as the Beach Boys have a power of refreshing our memories unknown to Brahms. We do not begin to understand how fundamentally this stuff outfits our imagination of social space, and of our own (desired, represented, real) place in it, by refusing to acknowledge the stains that such flows may have deposited in a given sample. On the contrary, our cathexes correspond to an objective structure of soliciting, shaping, and storing them that contributes far more to the significance of a work of mass culture than the hackneyed aesthetic design, or the see-through ideological proposition, that is all that remains when they are overlooked.[2]

A remarkable willingness to acknowledge those "flows" marks Kennedy's work; indeed, her work is unusual because of its resolute avoidance of the shaming rhetoric of "stains" and the like. Few texts so powerfully acknowledge, as Kennedy's *People Who Led to My Plays* and *A Movie Star* do, how mass culture as first culture "outfits our imagination of social space, and of our own (desired, represented, real) place in it." These texts also chart gaps between those categories—the fissures between the desired and the represented and the real—but the first move is the refusal of divisions between high and low and an equally fierce determination not to accept any racial division among representations. The "see-through ideological proposition" may propose or assume or even seek to determine forms of correct reception and belonging along racial lines, but the "objective structure of soliciting, shaping, and storing" cathexes—precisely to the extent that it is objective and the effect of an apparatus—broadcasts without discrimination.

This is not to say that the context for these broadcasts is not a thoroughly racist cultural and national landscape. Throughout Kennedy's work, her insistence on receptivity to mass cultural apparatuses of solicitation contrasts with—or complements?—her equally adamant insistence on the way that racism structures US culture. *A Movie Star* conjures a star system belonging to what David Bordwell, Janet Staiger, and Kristin Thompson decisively dubbed the classical Hollywood cinema. At the time of the first performances of *A Movie Star* in 1976, that system had long since collapsed, but Kennedy could count on memories of and investments in its leading players and its power to shape psychic life. Bordwell, Staiger, and Thompson date the end of Hollywood's classical period to 1960: Kennedy's career begins in the immediate aftermath of this ending. *People Who Led to My Plays*, her experimental biography, ends roughly at the beginning of her career; her plays variously experiment with the history of identifications which that

2. D. A. Miller, *Place for Us*, 68–69.

biography so disarmingly chronicles. Kennedy's work belongs as the conclusion to this book because of, among other things, how the occasion of *A Movie Star* marks a particular formation in the history of theater through its response to a specific formation in the history of film.

A Movie Star is a particularly charged work in a career made, in part, of making experimental theater and texts in other genres out of fragments of the classical Hollywood cinema and other aspects of mass culture. Consider the first stage direction from *A Movie Star*: "*The movie music throughout is romantic.*"[3] Kennedy can assume that the audience and those producing her plays have a sense, from lifetimes of moviegoing, of the mode of that romanticism, of those strings and swelling motifs. And she is not alone in using "movie music" as a shorthand. When early in *The Classical Hollywood Cinema* Bordwell lists the familiar "devices" of that cinema, he includes "three-point lighting, continuity editing, 'movie music,' centered framings, dissolves, etc."[4] The scare quotes signal Bordwell's acknowledgment that this term is insufficiently technical, but also his trust, in a book published about a decade after *A Movie Star* was first performed, that the reader will know, more or less, what "movie music" sounds like, just as Kennedy trusts that her readers and interpreters will. We know it when we hear it. (Or knew it when we heard it? More on this later.) To score *A Movie Star* with "movie music" is to draw on one device of the classical Hollywood cinema in order to harness its power to solicit its audience. Stage directions in *A Movie Star* mention "movie music" mostly between scenes and at the end of the play, as though that music might suture the play's disjunctive scenes or, instead, as though the familiar "romantic" soundtrack were there in the background to emphasize the contrast between classical Hollywood's drives to narrative continuities and comforts and Kennedy's refusal of those lures. "Stravinsky's comparison of film music to wallpaper is apt," writes Bordwell, "not only because it is so strongly decorative but because it fills in cracks and smoothes down rough textures."[5] In *A Movie Star*, those reparative and decorative qualities might be precisely what alienates: the "movie music" emphasizes, rather than smoothing down, the discordances that structure the play. If the color line structures the casting of the play, does it also inform its soundtrack? What is the race of movie music? Bordwell's brief overview stresses the Wagnerian roots of movie music, and this would seem to be the idiom that Kennedy has in mind.

3. Kennedy, *A Movie Star*, in *The Adrienne Kennedy Reader*, 62.

4. Bordwell et al., *Classical Hollywood Cinema*, 6.

5. Bordwell et al., *Classical Hollywood Cinema*, 33.

A Movie Star Has to Star in Black and White begins, absolutely conventionally, with a note about the first production: "*A Movie Star Has to Star in Black and White* was done as a work in progress at the New York Shakespeare Festival in New York on November 5, 1976, with the following cast . . ." In 1976, the play and production could assume a mediascape that has now largely vanished: "Eddie and I went to the Thalia on 95th and Broadway. There's a film festival this summer. We saw *Double Indemnity*, *The Red Shoes* and *A Place in the Sun*. Next week *Viva Zapata* is coming. Afterwards we went to Rienzis on Macdougal Street and had Viennese coffee. We forced an enthusiasm we didn't feel."[6] This dialogue belongs to and describes 1963, but in 1976 a New Yorker might still plausibly have made an evening of a similar, ambitious itinerary. (Many might have thought of heading to the Village for a coffee after a double feature at the Thalia, but how many would have gotten themselves on the train?) The Thalia continued to serve as a beloved revival house until 1987. The general coordinates—an Upper West Side revival house and a café in Greenwich Village—would have been on the maps of Manhattan cinephiles. But, while the streets remain, those landmarks are long gone. The constellations that orient fantasy change. Think of Michele Wallace's list: the stars who had to star in black and white are no longer the stuff of fantasy for many as they were. The generation for whom those stars might have provided the stuff of what Miller calls "first culture" has passed, or is passing, and is probably not to come. This might also mean that the stardom these stars represented, as the title suggests, has also passed. If a star had to star in black and white, a medium now reserved for certain prestige pictures, then stardom—in the sense that it informs *A Movie Star*—has also passed. That historical formation of stardom is one of the features of the media surround that contributed to the equally historical formation of theater after film. *A Movie Star* belongs at the end of this book in part because the very specificity of the world of mass culture that the play limns also marks, in a general if not a punctual way, the end of the historical formation that produced the drama this book has been tracing.

Objective structures of solicitation captured many. What they made of these structures, or how they resisted them: this is another story. The waning of the age of the classical Hollywood cinema contributed to a period of theatrical experiment. The 1976 production of *A Movie Star* is at once one culmination and an end to that period. To insist on one production as a punctual ending would be to pretend to a clarity that would distort any aesthetic movement and exaggerate the claims of any single event. With

---

6. Kennedy, *A Movie Star*, in *The Adrienne Kennedy Reader*, 62, 67.

that caveat, I nevertheless end in 1976 with *A Movie Star*. Threads I have been following come together in that play and that production. *People Who Led to My Plays* is the best document of the overdetermined histories that inform Kennedy's work: the book also ends, as its title implies, with the beginnings of her career as a playwright and theater maker. Kennedy's catalog also points, with its daunting heterogeneity and openness to all manner of influence, to the impossibility of any absolutely thorough genealogy of *A Movie Star*. Given the perspective of this book, especially important threads include the world of downtown and Off-Broadway theater in New York; currents in experimental writing, especially Black experimental writing; and histories and theories of stardom and of spectatorship. The deep roots of *A Movie Star* in two performance cultures—that of New York in the 1960s and 1970s on the one hand and of that scene's supposed antithesis, Hollywood, on the other—produce an experiment that remains startling in its bringing together of sources that adamantly refuse synthesis. It is no accident that each of these cultures is notorious for its failures to include—in the many senses of this word—Black writers, performers, or audiences. In 1976, with *A Movie Star*, Kennedy and her collaborators staged an encounter with a mass cultural formation that only ambivalently included her on a stage that had, in her words, "forgotten" her.[7] Kennedy uses that word when recounting her vivid memories of Joseph Chaikin's direction of *A Movie Star*: "Joe . . . is very important because when people had totally forgotten about me, in the mid-seventies, Joe was one of the people saying quite extravagant things about me, and working on my plays at his workshops. What he did with *Movie Star* [1976] was a total moving image; it just never stopped moving. It was a masterpiece the way he did it."[8] As a stay against the oblivion into which Kennedy felt herself to be falling, the production was a mixed success. Kennedy's testimony and archival remains suggest that it was an impressive staging of her text. As a "totally moving image," this *Movie Star* may almost have reached the cinematic condition to which the text aspires. And yet, unlike the movies the play evokes and recalls, *A Movie Star*'s first production was—even given familiar laments about theatrical archives—more than usually evanescent. Few saw this masterpiece.

7. Amiri Baraka wrote a sympathetic letter to Kennedy about the difficulties of getting a play produced in New York, remarking that Joe Papp had "nixed" a play of his (Amiri Baraka, undated letter to Kennedy, Adrienne Kennedy Papers, Harry Ransom Center, container 9.1).

8. Paul Bryant-Jackson and Lois More Overbeck, "Adrienne Kennedy: An Interview," in their *Intersecting Boundaries*, 3. This interview strikingly begins here, in the middle of things, with discussion about Chaikin's importance to Kennedy.

There appear to have been only six performances, including the opening: a schedule annotated by Kennedy lists these as "open rehearsals." These open rehearsals were not publicly advertised. Despite an "embargo," the *Village Voice* ran a "mixed review."[9]

While it is unclear when Kennedy began the text, the production came together with some speed. Chaikin and Mira Rafalowicz wrote to Kennedy (on Performing Artservices Inc. stationery) in April 1976 soliciting scripts for a collective project around storytelling and work with "inherited material as well as new material." Chaikin mentions Walter Benjamin's essay on the storyteller from *Illuminations* as "a source and a challenge" for thinking about how to narrate experience.[10] This letter reveals something about what Chaikin hoped for in approaching Kennedy in the spring of 1976, but not necessarily anything about how Kennedy came to write the play. Nevertheless, the letter's stress on the narration of experience, especially coupled with the reference to Benjamin, emphasizes a problem at the heart of Kennedy's play. Both Chaikin and Kennedy exemplify Benjamin's central claim in that essay that modernity had made experience less communicable. And this is true because and not despite of Kennedy's often-cited claim, in an interview published in 1977, that "autobiographical work is the only thing that interests me."[11] No oeuvre better exemplifies the expressive challenge of autobiographical writing than Kennedy's. When Chaikin and Rafalowicz describe "inherited material," they may have had classic theatrical or poetic texts in mind—at any rate, work already published. *A Movie Star* includes varieties of "inherited material." Verbatim passages from Kennedy's *The Owl Answers*, first staged in 1965, posit her own previous work as one kind

9. For various copies of this schedule, see the Adrienne Kennedy Papers, Harry Ransom Center, container 9.20. In her chronology of the career of the career of Joseph Chaikin, Eileen Blumenthal writes of 1976: "On October 11, Chaikin starts rehearsals at the Public Theater for Adrienne Kennedy's *A Movie Star Has to Star in Black and White*, the only new script he has ever directed that was not connected to one of his laboratories. The show is performed the weekend of November 9–12 in the Public's workshop series; there is no advertising and the press is not invited" (Blumenthal, *Joseph Chaikin*, 221–22). For the embargo and review, see Marc Robinson's chronology in the Library of America *Collected Plays and Other Writings* (980).

10. Joseph Chaikin and Mira Rafalowicz to Adrienne Kennedy, April 30, 1976. Adrienne Kennedy Papers, Harry Ransom Center, container 9.1. On Performing Artservices, see Fischer, *Mabou Mines: Making Avant-garde Theater in the 1970s*, 54. See also Richard Foreman's comment in an interview with Sara Farrington: "In those days, Artservices managed sort of everybody, from Phil Glass to you name it. But managing an artist didn't mean very much. They just did tasks for you occasionally" (Farrington, *The Lost Conversation*, 21).

11. Kennedy and Lehman, "A Growth of Images," 42.

of inheritance. It is unlikely that Chaikin and Rafalowicz had the legacy of Hollywood stars in mind when they thought about inheritance, but *A Movie Star* posits that, too, as inheritance of a kind. The emphasis in their letter falls on finding words, whether inherited or new, that allow for the telling of experience. Kennedy changes the emphasis, imagining the bodies and voices of movie stars as the surprising ventriloquists for her words.

The question of her re-use of her own earlier writing for the stage concerned Edward Albee, to whom Kennedy, in a letter of August 1976, had sent a draft of *A Movie Star*. Albee, who had co-produced the Kennedy's *Funnyhouse of a Negro*,[12] admired the play but wondered about how audiences would respond to its debts to her earlier work, "how it will seem to someone who doesn't know your other work—who doesn't have the references, for this new play fits so tightly with the other plays."[13] What appears to concern Albee here is that the incorporation of pieces of Kennedy's own work and the possibility that such self-reflexivity will alienate audiences. Albee, born in 1928, three years before Kennedy, shared a similar constellation of stars and movies: the play's cinematic inheritance does not appear to trouble him.[14] At any rate, Kennedy did not excise the passages from *The Owl Answers* from the working script for the Public Theater production or from any subsequent version.

Drafts of *A Movie Star Has to Star in Black and White* are sometimes collages: where Kennedy quotes *The Owl Answers*, for instance, she has simply taped cut sections of pages from the play's publication in *Cities in Bezique* onto her typewriter paper. Kennedy also taped pieces of other typed versions onto the pages: some leaves of the manuscript are remarkable

12. Kennedy's participation in Albee's workshop at Circle in the Square in 1962 was consequential (Kennedy, *Deadly Triplets*, 100–101). On Albee's importance to Kennedy, see also her description of herself as "a product of the time when *Zoo Story* and *American Dream* were the models of success"; in this interview she also recalls that she "studied with Albee at one point" (Kennedy and Lehman, "A Growth of Images," 47). "Visited by a Phantom," the final, brief prose text in the Library of America edition of Kennedy's work, drastically revises earlier pictures of Albee's place in her life, picturing him as a supernatural, almost vampiric force, "catastrophic." "It was," she writes, "as if Clark Gable (my childhood Gable of *It Happened One Night*) walked down from the screen and we had a grand wedding. And then disappeared" (*Collected Plays and Other Writings*, 966).

13. Edward Albee to Adrienne Kennedy, August 3, 1976. Adrienne Kennedy Papers, Harry Ransom Center, container 9.1.

14. At the start of *Who's Afraid of Virginia Woolf?*, Martha, imitating Bette Davis, famously declares, "What a dump"; this quotation leads to discussion about what movie this line belongs to (Albee, *Who's Afraid of Virginia Woolf?*, 3). Yet this discussion already concerns the problem of remembering Hollywood movies.

palimpsests of pieces of her own typescript, handwritten additions, and cut-out sections of print. One of these pages records a set of remarkable revisions.[15] In the published text, Clara, speaking for once, despite having a "bit role," describes her torment:

July.

    I can't sleep. My head always full of thoughts night and day. I feel so nervous. Sometimes I hardly hear what people are saying. I'm writing a lot of my play, I don't want to show it to anyone though. Suppose it's no good. (*Reads her play.*)[16]

The draft records some wavering around the status of the text that Clara reads: "I'm writing alot on my novel," Kennedy had initially typed, later crossing out "novel," replacing that word with "play" in handwriting. (Kennedy's archive includes a long draft for an unpublished novel set in the same period and milieu as the New York sections of *A Movie Star*.) More remarkably, this page includes the handwritten stage direction "(Reads her play)," with "my" written directly above "her." Neither word is crossed out; this draft hovers between the two possessive pronouns. Her play or my play: whose play is this? The published text of *A Movie Star* settles on "her play": when Clara reads, "her" text belongs to a play published by Kennedy. Kennedy claims ownership of these words only through a persona, a persona who reads dialogue that belongs, on the relevant page of *The Owl Answers*, to the speech prefix "SHE," to a persona who embodies a whole dramatis personae within herself, "SHE who is CLARA PASSMORE who is the VIRGIN MARY who is the BASTARD who is the OWL."[17] This unsettling device—the deliberateness with which Kennedy invites her audience to read the multiple Claras of *The Owl Answers* and the Clara of *A Movie Star* as surrogates for herself—might lead to overly simple readings of the plays as auto-fictions. The effect of this staging of the authorship of plays published under the name of Adrienne Kennedy is, instead, to emphasize one among the several implications of the title of her later *People Who Led to My Plays*: that their authorship belongs not solely to a single figure or to a single name, but both to that individual who owns copyright and to some cast of authors as multiple and heterogeneous as the figures who collectively make up the "SHE" of *The Owl Answers*.

15. Manuscript page of *A Movie Star Has to Star in Black and White*, in Adrienne Kennedy Papers, Harry Ransom Center, container 4.11, p. 10.

16. Kennedy, *A Movie Star*, in *The Adrienne Kennedy Reader*, 68.

17. Kennedy, *The Owl Answers*, in *The Adrienne Kennedy Reader*, 40–41, 29.

The lines from *A Movie Star* that introduce the passage from *The Owl Answers* describe thoughts so intense that Clara hardly hears "what people are saying": thoughts about the words of others shut out the words of others. The nervousness and thoughts that mean that she scarcely hears others complements the play's distribution of words that "should" belong to Clara and to the movie stars who speak for her, to Bette Davis, Jean Peters, and Shelley Winters. If writing a play, here, is linked to the shutting out of speech, that writing also produces speech. That those movie stars speak in a first person that seems properly to be Clara's is central to the play's complex negotiation of mass-mediated identifications. Here, another page from Kennedy's archive resonates. A photocopy of a skewed image of the logo for Columbia Pictures is interleaved among the pages of one of Kennedy's drafts.[18] The icon of only a relatively minor studio in the era Kennedy adored, the Columbia logo nevertheless becomes for Kennedy (and maybe for others) something like the icon of Hollywood as such.[19] The only logo of a well-known studio to feature a human figure, the Columbia logo invites personification in a way that even the growling lion of MGM may not. Filed among the pages of a draft, this sheet is the sole image Kennedy interleaved with those pages. At once mnemonic device and, precisely as a photocopy, an icon for Kennedy's own project, the page reproduces the mystic writing pad on which Hollywood leaves its traces.

The first icon in *A Movie Star* who speaks for Clara is precisely the "Columbia Pictures Lady," a figure whose usual role is, at least in the most literal sense, a nonspeaking one. To make this logo speak recalls semiotic projects like Barthes's articulation of national visual icons in *Mythologies*, bringing the unspoken but organized logic of silent, powerful images into discourse: "even objects will become speech, if they mean something."[20] But if Barthes aimed to explicate the active but implicit historical significations of mythical mass cultural material, Kennedy at once acknowledges her own psychic engagements with such material and uses these icons to ventriloquize speeches that make no claim to the general. A Barthesian analysis of the Columbia Pictures logo might examine its debts to the iconography of feminized national belonging in such figures as Marianne in France, the Statue of Liberty, and so on. Even the photocopy between the sheets of Kennedy's draft resonates with these connotations: with a torch in her right

18. Adrienne Kennedy Papers, Harry Ransom Center, container 4.11.

19. Columbia was not among the major "five integrated major motion picture companies" during the "so-called classical era of Hollywood" listed by Jerome Christensen (*America's Corporate Art*, 3).

20. Barthes, "Myth Today," in *Mythologies*, 219.

hand and a sword in her left, this embodiment of an enlightened readiness to head to the barricades. Rather than bringing the unspoken but hegemonic discourse of this image to speech, however, Kennedy defamiliarizes this image—and the power of its discourse—by making it speak for Clara. First, the Columbia Pictures Lady functions something like a program, neutrally describing the settings, the actors, the scenes, the date. But then she switches to the first person:

> My producer is Joel Steinberg. He looks different from what I once thought, not at all like that picture in *Vogue*. He was in *Vogue* with a group of people who were going to do a musical about Socrates. In the photograph Joel's hair looked dark and his skin smooth. In real life his skin is blotched. Everyone says he drinks a lot.
>
> Lately I think often of killing myself. Eddie Jr. plays outside in the playground. I'm very lonely. . . . Met Lee Strasberg: the members of the playwrights unit were invited to watch his scene. Geraldine Page, Rip Torn and Norman Mailer were there. . . . [21]

To name a producer follows the logic of this hybrid opening sequence: the producer's name is an opening credit to add to the setting and the other details with which the Columbia Pictures Lady begins. And yet even this word, "producer," raises questions: does this maintain the cinematic fiction and refer to the lists of producers that roll across the screen at the start of Hollywood films? Or does this suggest that this theatrical event itself has a producer, and that the Columbia Pictures Lady is, on Clara's behalf, biting the hand that feeds her? The question of whether Joel Steinberg looks like his photo picks up on a question of likeness to celebrities that is very clear in the text—Bette Davis, Paul Henreid, Jean Peters, Marlon Brando, Montgomery Clift, and Shelley Winters are played by actors who look "*exactly like*" them.[22] In performance, this question of likeness would be clear enough once we hear from the Columbia Pictures Lady that the "leading roles" are played by those stars: however powerful we may imagine Joel Steinberg to be, we know that he has not in fact gathered this star-studded cast—back from the dead, in one case—for a workshop production at the Public Theater in New York in 1976. The disparaging description of Steinberg installs an anxiety about being like a photographic image at the start. If even Joel Steinberg, with his blotchy skin, can't live up to his glamorous

---

21. Kennedy, *A Movie Star*, in *The Adrienne Kennedy Reader*, 63–64.

22. Kennedy, *A Movie Star*, in *The Adrienne Kennedy Reader*, 63.

photo in *Vogue*—can't "in real life," that is, look "exactly like" himself—what hope is there for the actors who play Bette Davis and company?

"Joel Steinberg" contrasts with all of the other names in this opening speech: where the other names all belong to figures along the spectrum of real-world celebrity from Bette Davis to (later in the monologue) Ted Joans, Steinberg appears to be fictional. But *A Movie Star* did have a producer. As if to stress this, in its publication in *Adrienne Kennedy in One Act*, this phrase appears in a box below other information about the first staging: "Original production by Joseph Papp, at the New York Shakespeare Festival, 1976, directed by Joseph Chaikin."[23] What is the relationship between this note and the Columbia Pictures' Lady's lapidary declaration, "My producer is Joel Steinberg"? At the simplest phonemic level, *Joel* Steinberg echoes the names of the two *Josephs* who were important to this first production. (That sound, "Jo," echoes through the speech: "Joel's," "Jones," "Joans.") That the name is evidently a Jewish one also resonates with Papp and Chaikin and points toward a long and complex history of Black art promoted by Jewish men. This history puts special emphasis on the pronoun here: "*My* producer." This possessive dispossesses: the claim to ownership disappears in the ascription of production to someone else. The question of who is speaking here also matters: this moment when the anonymous voice of the production—a personified program given speech and an iconic costume and voice ("The leading roles are played by")—begins to ventriloquize Clara's experience begins with that disorienting first-person pronoun, "My." What corporate person claims this first person? "My," that is, precisely marks the transition from the staccato description of details of the production to a first-person narration that quickly becomes so intimate that it can belong only to someone who speaks of her own experience and not as the embodiment of corporate personhood. For the Columbia Pictures Lady to describe herself as having a producer conflicts with her identity as the icon of the studio that produces. Or, put otherwise, this seeming contradiction emphasizes a question essential to *A Movie Star*: How does production make speech possible? (Such a question may also be implicit in another title, *People Who Led to My Plays*.)

A Movie Star, "a tiny-budget Public Theatre workshop," in fact required little of Joseph Papp's prodigious energy as a producer in 1976.[24] This play

---

23. Kennedy, *In One Act*, 79. This box and this language appear neither in the initial 1984 publication of the play in the collection *Word Plays 3* nor in the 2001 *The Adrienne Kennedy Reader*; *Collected Plays and Other Writings* does include a version of this information in a note (1017).

24. Blumenthal, *Joseph Chaikin*, 30.

about production, in its widest senses, did not receive a full production in that narrower sense. That this quintessential play about mass-mediated subjectivity initially had a minute private audience is an ironic culmination of the situation of theater after film. This almost invisible premiere happened in a period when, as Hillary Miller has shown, New York was the site of a lively debate in theatrical circles precisely about production. Miller's discussion of playwrights' efforts to establish their own theaters and to "dilute the divinity of agents and producers," in the words of Tom Eyen, illuminates the particular strangeness of the Columbia Pictures Lady's portrait of Joel Steinberg: divine in the pages of *Vogue*, "in real life" he has the blotchy skin of a perennial drinker.[25] That the Columbia Pictures Lady claims to speak for "real life" is not the least of this play's ironies. In *A Movie Star*, the mass-mediated conditions that enable expression also distort it. Kennedy accepts the situation of theater after film and that the apparatuses of mass culture conditions have established the conditions for expression—and explodes these conditions.

The most striking of the discordant techniques that structure *A Movie Star* is no doubt that white actors who look "*exactly like*" Hollywood stars speak for the Black actors who have been relegated to "supporting roles."[26] It's an impossible list of dramatic personae:

CLARA
"Leading roles" are played by actors who look exactly like:
BETTE DAVIS
PAUL HENREID
JEAN PETERS
MARLON BRANDO
MONTGOMERY CLIFT
SHELLEY WINTERS
(They all look exactly like their movie roles.)
Supporting roles by
THE MOTHER

25. Miller, *Drop Dead*, 40–41. Miller discusses Kennedy's involvement with groups of theater makers who hoped to find alternative venues and funding for theater production in New York City (38–41).

26. Kennedy, *A Movie Star*, in *The Adrienne Kennedy Reader*, 63. Early in James Baldwin's long essay on the movies, *The Devil Finds Work* (also notably a text from 1976), he writes about being aware as a child "that Joan Crawford was a white lady. Yet, I remember being sent to the store sometime later, and a colored woman, who, to me, looked exactly like Joan Crawford, was buying something" (4). The work of that "yet" is astonishing.

THE FATHER
HER HUSBAND
*(They all look like photographs CLARA keeps of them except when they're
in the hospital.)*[27]

The first parenthetical note is not quite redundant: it is not just that these
actors must "look exactly like" these stars, but that they must "look exactly
like" the stars as they appear in their "movie roles" in the three films central
to the play, *Now Voyager, Viva Zapata,* and *A Place in the Sun.* The public
availability of the models for the leading roles contrasts with the privacy of
those photos that Clara keeps. These photos, too, are subject to idealization,
and the stage direction blurs several lines at once. If one follows the various
clues equating Clara with Kennedy—the author, after all, of the older works
that are thinly disguised, in *A Movie Star,* as Clara's work—then one might
refer to the various photos of her father and mother in *People Who Led to
My Plays.* A portrait that appears to be that of Kennedy's mother appears
toward the end of the section titled "Junior High," illustrating these entries:

My mother, Lena Horne and myself as a grown-up:

My mother looked to me to be a combination of Lena Horne and Ingrid Bergman. I thought she was the prettiest person I'd ever seen. But
I couldn't look forward to growing up and looking like her . . . everyone
said we looked nothing alike. I was often unhappy about this fact that
when I grew up (no matter what else happened to me) I would never look
like this beautiful woman with brown curly hair, pale luminous skin and
keen elegant features.

My mother and my face:

My face as an adult will always seem to be lacking because it is not my
mother's face.[28]

27. Kennedy, *A Movie Star,* in *The Adrienne Kennedy Reader,* 63. In *The Ride across
Lake Constance,* a play first performed in 1971, Peter Handke names characters after
famous figures in silent German film, including Emil Jannings, Henny Porten, and Erich
von Stroheim. Handke's use of this device is quite different, however, and the names
are resonant placeholders rather than objects to produce likenesses: "When the play is
staged, the characters should bear the names of the actors playing the roles: the actors
are and play themselves at one and the same time" (*Ride across Lake Constance,* 69).

28. Kennedy, *People Who Led to My Plays,* 50–51.

On one hand, these are utterly familiar desires: to look like a star, to look like one's mother. On the other hand, everything seems a barrier in the way of these intense desires for intimate resemblance. One barrier is the generalized belief in the essential singularity of each person, the common sense conviction that no one, really—if only we look closely, if we consider each person in their essential humanity, etc.—looks like anyone else. Whether declared as fact or clung to as a remnant, however thoroughly secularized, of Christian belief, this article of faith is everywhere. Another barrier is the particular difficulty, in this world of differences, of finding actors who "look exactly" like any of these movie stars. A production might convey the desire for likeness—might, through makeup and costumes, convey this desire. A peculiarity of stardom lies in the ubiquity of the star's face matched by another article of faith: that the star looks like no one else. The star's ubiquity is, strangely enough, a function of their quintessential difference from everyone else.

Given the various kinds of impossibility in play here, it is worth asking where this desire for exact likeness comes from. How is the desire to cast an actor who looks "exactly like" Bette Davis different from the desire to cast Bette Davis? Davis, who died in 1989, would in theory (and ignoring, for the moment, every other kind of spectacular unlikelihood) have been available for the role in 1976. This theoretical possibility stresses the point made by Kennedy's insistence on the need for the actors to look "*exactly like their movie roles*": Bette Davis, in 1976, was not the Bette Davis who had starred in *Now Voyager* in 1942. Folded into the desire for likeness is the knowledge that there will be no one like that Bette Davis, that Bette Davis, indeed, is no longer like herself. The peculiar poignancy of Kennedy's acknowledgment of the situation of theater after film lies in the registration of a historical chasm at the heart of the desire for likeness. *A Movie Star*, even or especially at the moment that it aspires to recreate a star turn from a black-and-white film, marks the necessary failure of that re-creation.

[TWENTY-EIGHT]

The Author as Produced

Hollywood/Jim Crow

A Movie Star coordinates a particular formation of mass culture, the glamour of classical Hollywood cinema, with a particular formation of US racial politics, the Jim Crow era.[1] That coordination is singular, yet it also makes visible something of the shared historicity of what Adrienne Kennedy combines. Adolph Reed writes: "My age cohort is basically the last, black or white, for which the Jim Crow regime is a living memory—for good and ill."[2] A similar age cohort is also the last for which there is a living memory of the moviegoing practices associated with classical Hollywood cinema. Cinema-going as a regular practice (every Saturday, for instance); the print culture surrounding stardom (fan magazines like *Modern Screen*); the whole habitus of that era of Hollywood as first culture (the very different cinemas of Cleveland, Ohio, and Montezuma, Georgia): in 1976, Kennedy could assume the "living memory" of that world.[3] Jim Crow and Hollywood

---

1. Cedric Robinson stresses the coincidence of Jim Crow and Hollywood's ascendancy: "The appearance of moving pictures coincides with Jim Crow and the development of American national identity in the midst of dramatic demographic and economic change" (*Forgeries of Memory and Meaning*, xv). Robinson's argument is that this is more than coincidence, that Hollywood was crucial to "the formulation of the new racial regime" in the early twentieth century (181).

2. Reed, *The South*, 4–5.

3. *People Who Led to My Plays*, among many other things, catalogs some of these practices: see, for instance, Kennedy's story of hiding *Modern Screen* under her mattress along with her diary (17); her scrapbooks "from my favorite pictures" and a scrapbook devoted to Ingrid Bergman (41); the lists of studios, beginning with MGM, to which she sends "penny postcards to the movie stars to get their autographed photos" (43); and the "penny postcard" Kennedy sends to Orson Welles for an "autographed photo" (44). An online Library of America interview with Marc Robinson, editor of Kennedy's *Collected Plays and Other Writings*, includes an image of a page from one of Kennedy's "homemade movie star scrapbooks" as well as remarkable photos of the 1976 *A Movie Star* ("Experimental in the Fullest Sense").

combine in the Mother's speech about the Georgia town in which she grew up:

> When a Negro bought something in a store he couldn't try it on. A Negro couldn't sit down at the soda fountain in the drugstore but had to take his drink out. In the movies at Montefore you had to go in the side and up the stairs and sit in the last four rows.[4]

Reed's analytical memoir resonates here:

> The relatively superficial mechanisms that were elements of enforcement—the petty apartheid of Jim Crow take-out windows at restaurants, separate water fountains, toilets, and so on—were never trivial to those who endured them on a daily basis and were never less than massively inconvenient and humiliating. And everyone understood that they were extrusions inseparably linked—as the tip is to the submerged 90 percent of an iceberg—to that larger system that included denial of due process and equal protection under the law and the extremes of economic exploitation made possible by elimination of citizenship rights.[5]

The movie theater in Montefore is at once an example of these "relatively trivial mechanisms" of Jim Crow segregation and a particular reminder that movie stars starred in movies screened not in utopian black and white but in separate and unequal spaces divided by race. *A Movie Star* stages but does not reconcile the contradiction between the lived experience of movie audiences segregated by race and the sense of cinema as a medium that stars for everyone and addresses every spectator. The mise-en-scène of *A Movie Star* on one level looks like the imaginary solution to a real problem: white stars, at last, speak about the Black life excluded by the films in which they had starred. In *People Who Led to My Plays*, Kennedy herself describes being haunted by Shelley Winters, Montgomery Clift, Marlon Brando, and Jean Peters: "These people would become characters in a play called *A Movie Star Has to Star in Black and White*, a play in which the movie fantasies of the heroine overshadow her life."[6] This powerful formation of

---

4. Kennedy, *A Movie Star*, in *The Adrienne Kennedy Reader*, 65.

5. Reed, *The South*, 8.

6. Kennedy, *People Who Led to My Plays*, 97.

fantasy, however, does nothing to alter the damaged lives about which the white actors impersonating movie stars speak:

> JEAN PETERS: This reminds me of when Eddie was in Korea and I had the miscarriage. For days there was blood on the sheets. Eddie's letters from Korea were about a green hill. He sent me photographs of himself. The Red Cross, the letter said, says I cannot call you and I cannot come.
> For a soldier to come home there has to be a death in the family.
> MOTHER: (*In the hallway she breaks down further.*) I have never wanted to go back to the south to live. I hate it. I suffered nothing but humiliation and why should I have gone back there?[7]

Pregnant and confined to her bed, Jean Peters, speaking for Clara, remembers the aftermath of a miscarriage and a loss that does not, to the Red Cross, count as a death. The scene pairs this couple's enforced separation with the divorce of Clara's parents—a conflict that Jean Peters has said, earlier, Clara's mother associated with Clara's loss of her baby.[8] The scene multiplies the levels of mediation: Jean Peters, speaking for Clara, describes the letters and photos Eddie sends in place of phone calls or coming home. Those letters, maybe because of censorship, remain silent about Eddie's experience and instead are "about a green hill." Nothing spells out the reason for the juxtaposition of this conflict and loss with her mother's refusal to return to the humiliations of the South.

The problem of medium in the large sense implied by Benjamin's work of art essay—the "way in which human perception is organized—the medium in which it occurs"—is persistent in Kennedy's work.[9] Cinema is preeminent but not alone among the forms of mass culture that organize perception. To be separated from the ability to speak takes several forms here: the military protocols that forbid Eddie even to call Clara oddly recall the play's convention according to which Shelley Peters speaks for Clara. But the order of media under Jim Crow also remains a persistent formation in *A Movie Star*.

The script for the 1976 Public Theater production of *A Movie Star* largely resembles familiar published versions, with one striking exception. In the first, *Now Voyager* scene, the Mother's bitter speech about her small

---

7. Kennedy, *A Movie Star*, in *The Adrienne Kennedy Reader*, 73.

8. Kennedy, *A Movie Star*, in *The Adrienne Kennedy Reader*, 70.

9. Benjamin, "Work of Art," 23.

hometown in Georgia includes five paragraphs that have never appeared in print:

> When I was five I was sent to a boarding school where I stayed until I was eighteen. Summers I lived with my grandmother in a little house behind the colored cemetery.
>
> In Montefore there was a cemetery for white people and a cemetery for Negroes and the white people's cememtery had a gate around it and grass and huge headstones and the Negroes had a little field with weeds and no markings.
>
> You just had to remember where the dead person was.
>
> In boarding school I spent the holidays with the headmaster because my mother was dead. Even though my father paid for my schooling I only saw him a few times a year when he sent for me. I always hoped noone at the school knew I was illegitimate and had a white father.
>
> I loved it when my grandmother took me to church with her. We'd come home and have fried chicken and lemonade on her red and white calico table. I wish I could drink water from the dipper in her kitchen again.[10]

The location of her grandmother's house leads to a description of the cemetery, with its moving picture of the Jim Crow's regime extension beyond the architecture of everyday segregation to the precincts of the dead. The know-how needed to navigate this cemetery—a memory of "where the dead person was"—resonates in a play that refuses to provide the standard markers. The gated community of the white dead with its "huge headstones" is a continuation of the town described in the published text: "In our Georgia town the white people lived on one side. It had pavement on the streets and sidewalks and mail was delivered. The Negroes lived on the other side and the roads were dirt and had no sidewalk and you had to go to the post office to pick up your mail."[11] If *A Movie Star* is a kind of memorial to the vanishing regime of the classical Hollywood cinema, it also remembers the Jim Crow regime that, if by no means vanished in 1976, had also seen its legal foundations substantially dissolved. The play does not suggest a structural or historical symmetry between these two very different historical formations; it does experiment with understanding them alongside

10. *A Movie Star Has to Star in Black and White*, New York Shakespeare Festival Draft, in Adrienne Kennedy Papers, Harry Ransom Center, container 4.13, p. 6 (as typed). Courtesy of Adrienne Kennedy.

11. Kennedy, *A Movie Star*, in *The Adrienne Kennedy Reader*, 65.

each other. That white stars speak for Black lives jarringly emphasizes the racial divisions that structured actually existing Hollywood cinema during the classical era. Recalling lived experiences of the Jim Crow South in straightforward terms underlines social facts that cinema's realism could never acknowledge. *A Movie Star* repairs what Hollywood refused or was unable to do, or imagines what repair might look like: movie stars never did have to star in black and white in the strong sense that the play imagines, but what if they had had to?

This deleted passage, perhaps especially because it is unfamiliar, underlines qualities of the dialogue in *A Movie Star*. There is nothing difficult in the language of this passage—nothing, that is, which challenges usual protocols of syntax or habits of making sense. Consistent with the published texts of this speech, it describes a small Georgia town in the Jim Crow South. Different from these texts, in the deleted passage the Mother speaks in the first person: she describes intimate details those texts lack, most especially about her father. The existing texts also lack anything like the last nostalgic turn here, with the memory of Sunday dinners, "red and white calico table," and the vivid evocation of the dipper. All of this is to say that difficulty at the level of language in *A Movie Star* belongs almost entirely to the four surreal, interpolated passages from *The Owl Answers*.[12] The difficulty of taking in the play's monologues mostly stems not from the semantic or syntactic complexity of the content, but in understanding who is speaking. If the acousmatic voice achieves its uncanny effects by separating voice from body, as in Antonin Artaud's radio broadcast, Kennedy produces a different but related effect by assigning speeches to bodies to whom they evidently do not belong. The voice belongs to that body—to the body, say, of the actors who "look exactly like" Bette Davis or Jean Peters—but the words clearly do not. And it's striking that Kennedy does not say anything at all about what the voices of the actors who look like movie stars sound like. She never specifies in a stage direction or otherwise whether the actors also sound like the stars they resemble, and no stage direction specifies anything about the delivery of any line spoken by them. (An exception that says nothing about the question of sonic resemblance: Bette Davis delivers a line to Eddie, and her delivery is described as "*very remote.*") Kennedy does specify that the movie stars should never be "*camp or farcical,*" and this might suggest that too complete an impersonation—a Bette Davis, say,

---

12. Elinor Fuchs's argument for a break between Kennedy's work of the 1960s and that of the 1970s is relevant here: see "Kennedy and the First Avant-Garde," in Bryant-Jackson and Overbeck, *Intersecting Boundaries*, 76–84.

who not only looks but also sounds "exactly like" the unmistakable voice of the star—would militate against the desired atmosphere of seriousness.[13]

A somewhat belated stage direction describes Clara:

> *She has a passive beauty and is totally preoccupied. She pays no attention to anyone, only writing in a notebook. Her movie stars speak for her.* CLARA *lets her movie stars star in her life.*[14]

What does it mean that the stars "speak for her"? On the one hand, the movie stars seem to have colonized Clara, unjustly claiming the right to speak on her behalf. Letting them "speak for her" is an aspect of a learned passivity that buttresses a culture that refuses her subjectivity. And it is worth emphasizing that they speak *only* for Clara: the Father, Mother, and Eddie speak in their own persons. On the other hand, Clara has ceded this speech to "her movie stars": they have relieved her of a burden, and she gets to keep writing. In the final scene of *A Movie Star*, Clara ascribes exactly this criticism to Eddie:

> Eddie says I've become shy and secretive and I can't accept the passage of time, and that my diaries consume me and that my diaries make me a spectator watching my life like watching a black and white movie.
>
> He think sometimes . . . to me my life is one of those black and white movies that I love so . . . with me playing a bit part.

Closely echoing the Columbia Pictures Lady's opening speech—"A bit role is played by Clara"—it is easy to mistake this criticism for the last word on Clara's consuming spectatorship.[15] The diagnosis here, however, is not principally about spectatorship but, instead, about writing—or, that is, Eddie sees the danger of writing in the way that Clara does as turning her into a spectator. The problem for Eddie is not that Clara has become lost in the cinema that structurally excludes her but that her private writing in her diaries has turned her into a spectator of her own life. Or, maybe more accurately, Eddie speaks to the fear that a certain kind of private writing turns

---

13. Kennedy, *A Movie Star*, in *The Adrienne Kennedy Reader*, 68, 62.

14. Kennedy, *A Movie Star*, in *The Adrienne Kennedy Reader*, 68.

15. Kennedy, *A Movie Star*, in *The Adrienne Kennedy Reader*, 75, 63. For a compelling argument that stresses the play as the representation of an encounter with an apparatus that excludes Clara, see Deborah R. Geis, "'A Spectator Watching My Life': Adrienne Kennedy's *A Movie Star Has to Star in Black and White*," in Bryant-Jackson and Overbeck, *Intersecting Boundaries*, 170–78.

THE AUTHOR AS PRODUCED: HOLLYWOOD/JIM CROW › 253

against the very interiority it would seem to preserve and becomes alienation: the diary, site of the most private thoughts, becomes a mechanism of exclusion through writing. (And one can imagine Clara's speech as itself a transcription of—and a mode of making public—a passage from a diary.) The complex dramaturgical arrangement of the third scene is important:

> (MONTGOMERY CLIFT *silently rows dark boat across.* CLARA *has on a nightgown and looks as if she has been very sick, and heartbroken by her brother's accident.* MONTGOMERY CLIFT, *as were* HENREID *and* BRANDO, *is mute. If they did speak, they would speak lines from their actual movies. As the boat comes across* BRANDO *and* PETERS *are still. Movie music.* EDDIE *comes in room with* JEAN PETERS *and* BRANDO. *He still has his textbook and briefcase.* SHELLEY WINTERS *sits opposite* MONTGOMERY CLIFT *as in* A Place in the Sun. CLARA *is writing in her notebook.*)
> EDDIE: (*To* JEAN PETERS; *simultaneously* CLARA *is writing in her diary.*) Are you sure you want to go on with this?
> JEAN PETERS: This?
> EDDIE: You know what I mean, this obsession of yours?
> JEAN PETERS: Obsession?
> EDDIE: Yes, this obsession to be a writer?
> JEAN PETERS: Of course I'm sure.

The palimpsest of scenes here stages Jean Peters in what an earlier stage direction calls the *"Zapata teach-me-to-read scene"* alongside the emergence of the boat from the pivotal scene in *A Place in the Sun* in which George Eastman (Montgomery Clift) arranges for an "accident" and, at the very least, does nothing to prevent Alice Tripp (Shelley Winters) from drowning.[16] *Viva Zapata* stages learning to read as erotic encounter; *A Movie Star* appropriates this scene but also produces its obverse: Eddie wants Clara—or Clara in the person of Jean Peters, who is starring as, or in the place of, Clara—not to write, to get over, not to "go on with" her obsession. Jean Peters objects to the word "obsession": she insists, with a clarity Clara cannot muster in her own person, on her certainty about her need to continue to write. Ventriloquism of the stars, or the stars' ventriloquism of Clara, is the condition of possibility that makes this writing, and this theater, possible.

16. Kennedy, *A Movie Star*, in *The Adrienne Kennedy Reader*, 74–75, 71.

[TWENTY-NINE]

Diary of Lights

Kennedy's *Diary of Lights*, a dance theater piece written in 1973, first staged in Chicago in 1978, and published only in 2012, anticipates the milieu and the material of *A Movie Star*.[1] The piece begins, for instance, at the Thalia Theater and includes a scene at Rienzi's. *Diary of Lights* reads as an earlier draft, in a happier, more bohemian mode, in the writing and revision of a difficult past. Passages from the earlier play appear, lightly revised, in *A Movie Star*. The conflicted relationship of the central character (here called Billie) with a husband called Eddie and her struggle to write are at the heart of both plays. And yet where *A Movie Star* focuses on the repetition of family traumas, *Diary of Lights* foregrounds friendships and elective affinities. Choral passages spoken by all include: "Let's go to Rienzi's. It's the greatest coffee house in the Village. Let's all go to Rienzi's."[2] A scene of dancing on MacDougal Street, laconically described in a stage direction, follows. When Clara narrates an outing to "Rienzis" in *A Movie Star*, she laments, "We forced an enthusiasm we didn't feel."[3] In relation to *A Movie Star*, *Diary of Lights* may feel like an exercise in forced enthusiasm.[4] The mode of *A Movie Star* contrasts markedly with that of *Diary of Lights*, an amalgam of dance and drama featuring tortured eggheads who argue about whether Arthur Miller or Tennessee Williams is "the greatest playwright in

1. For a thorough account of the play's composition and production history, see Johanna Frank, "Reintroducing Adrienne Kennedy's *Diary of Lights*." I believe an additional source of the text may be two drafts of a novel contained in the Kennedy archive at the Ransom Center: see the loosely interleaved typed drafts of a novel "about New York" (Adrienne Kennedy Papers, Harry Ransom Center, containers 8.7 and 8.8). Frank's article introduces a cluster of articles about the play.

2. Kennedy, *Diary of Lights*, 113.

3. Kennedy, *A Movie Star*, in *The Adrienne Kennedy Reader*, 67.

4. It is notable that until the 2023 Library of America edition, Kennedy had not included *Diary of Lights* in any of the collections of her work.

America" and listen to Lead Belly and wonder whether Jung is greater than Freud.[5] One could derive a checklist of passions and interests, the names of writers, painters, musicians, and other figures, from the play's forty pages.[6] And when the friends are done talking, they dance. If *Diary of Lights* has a cinematic frame, it is the movie musical, not the Hollywood melodrama. Exuberant dance replaces cinematic ventriloquism.

Given this striking difference in modes, it is remarkable that Kennedy integrates passages from *Diary of Lights* verbatim into the text of *A Movie Star*. Where *A Movie Star* introduces passages from her published play, *The Owl Answers*, the text makes it clear that Clara is reading from her own literary work. *A Movie Star* subsumes passages from *Diary of Lights* without such acknowledgment. The most extensive of these debts to *Diary of Lights* is the section from *A Movie Star* on the segregation of a town in rural Georgia discussed above, only very lightly revised: "In Georgia the white people lived on one side of the town . . ."[7] This self-quotation emphasizes that this play about an idealized Gotham of lights and dancing has also been a play about racialized exclusion: Eddie protests the racism he encounters as a PhD student in psychology, and Roy, his brother, also protests the racism he encounters on the faculty at Brooklyn College. In *A Movie Star*, the lines belong to Clara's mother, who speaks bitterly. In *Diary of Lights*, Billie reads the passage from her diary, near the end of the play, "*partly to herself and partly to EDDIE.*" The narrative of apartheid counters the play's ebullient staging of interracial and international camaraderie. If the dramaturgical mode suggests a utopian version of downtown bohemia, Adrienne Kennedy as staged by the MGM musical unit or Jacques Demy, this passage undercuts that euphoric strand.

The play is full of names; it also forms a fascinating node in the complex web of Kennedy's practice of naming. "In perhaps its simplest formulation," writes Diana Fuss, "identification is the detour through the other that defines a self."[8] How many detours through other selves can one self endure? The profusion of names across Kennedy's work points to her ongoing concern with identifying and mapping these paths and divagations through a complex set of others. Very early in *People Who Led to My Plays*, Kennedy recalls the circumstances of her own naming:

5. Kennedy, *Diary of Lights*, 109, 112.

6. In their overview of the cultural and historical moment of *Diary of Lights*, Harvey Young and Megan Geigner count "the names of nearly sixty artists and novelists" ("A Racial Concern," 42).

7. Kennedy, *Diary of Lights*, 121.

8. Fuss, *Identification Papers*, 2.

Adrienne Ames (my mother and my name)

My mother often told the story of how when she was pregnant she went to a movie and saw Adrienne Ames and decided to name me for her. How could I see then that my name was responsible for inspiring in me a curiosity about celebrity and glamour?[9]

Compare *Diary of Lights*: "My mother named me after Billie Holiday."[10] A slight idiomatic difference here reveals much about the dynamics of naming in Kennedy's work: what is the difference between being named *for* and being named *after*? The prepositions emphasize different ways of thinking about a predecessor and the child who is named: naming *for* emphasizes the honorific function of the name, the name as given not only to the as yet nameless child but also to the person for whom the child has been named. To be named *after* conjures the larger world that that name carries with it and the changes that name made to the world, the world, in this case, of Billie Holiday. The passage from *People Who Led to My Plays* stresses the performative effects of naming: being named after Adrienne Ames, a story repeatedly told, inspired in Adrienne Kennedy "a curiosity about celebrity and glamour." In this childhood story as in *Diary of Lights*, the mother alone names. Implicit in the entry is that this act of maternal naming inaugurates the complexities of identification with white actors: Adrienne Ames had appeared in only a few movies when, in 1931, Etta Hawkins decided on her daughter's name. Billie Holiday, too, named herself after a white actress, taking her first name from Billie Dove.[11] The name of the movie star has to star in black and white.

Diary of Lights reads, then, as an experiment in imagining what Kennedy might have become had she been named "after Billie Holiday": what if her theater had come after jazz? "Their whole youthful summer is a dance / and the dances all reflect this," reads an author's note that prefaces the play. In the first scene, all of the performers together speak these words: "On a night like this New York is full of possibilities the possibilities of being a part of a history of people who've achieved and set the world on fire."[12] The play's manic, sometimes comic, concatenation of names is not only intellectual history in shorthand but also an assemblage that points toward this

9. Kennedy, *People Who Led to My Plays*, 10.

10. Kennedy, *Diary of Lights*, 111.

11. Farrah Jasmine Griffin, *In Search of Billie Holiday*, 23.

12. Kennedy, *Diary of Lights*, 102; 104.

potentiality: the names are synecdochal of a utopian and glamorous whole, a world of lights, a history in which one might take part, of which one might become part. Like *People Who Led to My Plays*, *Diary of Lights* ends with the beginning of writing—in this alternative history, her determination to be a poet. Being named after Billie Holiday makes her a poet ready to set the world on fire. Being named after Adrienne Ames makes her a playwright forever struggling with the plight of writing plays after film.

Such determination through the force of the name rests on some residual magic that suggests that maybe the signifier is after all not so arbitrary. The fantasy of a life as Billie in *Diary of Lights* counters the lives as Clara in *The Owl Answers* and *A Movie Star*: Kennedy's plays often draw on autobiography but are always variations on the life actually lived, the staging of identifications and disidentifications that, however vital, are nevertheless not exactly the story of Kennedy's life—unless one allows that life is the story of one's identifications. Kennedy's concern with identification as selfhood and her practice of staging identifications as one form of autobiographical writing, however, do not mean that her plays imply one can remake oneself through renaming. Passages such as the repeated account of the violently segregated town in Georgia suggest that the new name changes nothing.

Diary of Lights stands on its own but is also a chapter in the prehistory of *A Movie Star*. Recalling Tennessee Williams's idea of "material" that could take different generic forms, *Diary of Lights* reads as an earlier attempt to graft the stuff of *A Movie Star* onto the form of the musical. The contrast suggests the labor of working through the power of mass culture's interpellation on stage. *Diary of Lights* presents the immersion in mass culture as the potential compensatory reward for a life of solitary writing. As the play closes, having been told by "an editor at *Dial*" that she has talent, Billie speaks about wanting to be a rebel and an author of poems that will "tell the utter truth about life as it really is. I have so many thoughts I want to express." She "*walks further into the blazing lights*."[13] The scene represents the desire to express and the thrill of walking into those lights—those "*larger than life lights that are the replica of the real life lights of New York Places*" (that is, the lights of the Thalia, Rienzi's, and so on)—which, a choral line early in the play stresses, are "like stars."[14] *A Movie Star* breaks down this fantasy supernova, this devouring black hole of stardom, by imagining the desires those lights cannot satisfy and the suffering they cannot alleviate, by reworking the material of film for the theater.

13. Kennedy, *Diary of Lights*, 125.
14. Kennedy, *Diary of Lights*, 102, 104.

[THIRTY]

Afterword/After Theater

In 2006, the Classical Theater of Harlem staged *Waiting for Godot* with a Black cast on a partly flooded stage designed to evoke the wreckage of New Orleans after Hurricane Katrina. The production, directed by Christopher McElroen, is now best known as the basis for the later collaboration with Paul Chan that moved the performance location from Harlem to New Orleans.[1] This *Godot* had a particular force in Harlem before its adaptation to the specific site of the Lower Ninth Ward. Vladimir's speech in the second act, as Lucky and Pozzo lay neglected and calling for help in a forlorn pile, had a new, terrible plangency in Wendell Pierce's performance:

> Let us not waste our time in idle discourse! [*Pause. Vehemently.*] Let us do something, while we have the chance! It is not every day that we are needed. Not indeed that we personally are needed. Others would meet the case equally well, if not better. To all mankind they were addressed, those cried for help still ringing in our ears! But at this place, at this moment of time, all mankind is us, whether we like it or not. Let us make the most of it, before it is too late! Let us represent worthily for once the foul brood to which a cruel fate consigned us! What do you say?[2]

Vladimir channels a humanist discourse all too familiar in the postwar world years in which the play emerged. Pozzo has cried for help, and already Vladimir allegorizes this direct appeal—to whom else but to Didi and Gogo?—as an address to "all mankind," the perfect alibi for those actually present who might do something. In the Classical Theater of Harlem production, this scene of an abstraction from a direct address to particular persons for

---

1. For documentation, see Chan, *Waiting for Godot in New Orleans*. Alys Moody's "*Waiting for Godot* in New Orleans" and Shane's Vogel's "*Waiting for Godot* and the Racial Theater of the Absurd" offer ways into thinking about this public art piece.

2. Beckett, *En attendant Godot / Waiting for Godot*, 289.

help, here and now, resonated with the horrible contrast between unambiguous appeals for help from those in danger of drowning—the signs in block letters written on rooftops, which the production echoed—and the mass-mediated spectacle of the catastrophic flooding of the city. All mankind was us, and we talked, and—think of the photos of George W. Bush viewing the devastation through the window of Air Force One—we watched.

Godot, that is, reflects on the theater's relation—"at this place, at this moment in time"—to mass cultural forms of address that more plausibly address that abstraction called "all mankind." Vladimir's speech, then and there in New York City, retained those echoes of the mass appeal to "all mankind," but these echoes were sutured not to some vague allegory of a disconnection between hearing an appeal and remaining in one's seat (as, of course, the audience did) but directly to the unavoidable disjunction between the mass dissemination of appeals for help and the criminally inadequate response. *Waiting for Godot*, too, addresses its audience, and that address happens—and happened from the start—in relation to a mass cultural surround addressed to everyone and no one. *Godot* cannot replicate that appeal, but sometimes, even now, it can estrange it.

Acknowledgments

The preface begins with one story of where the book began. Another story might go farther back, to another performance, staged by Julian Schlusberg, a teacher and director to whom I owe much of my love for theater. Some time around 1980, before I had met Mr. Schlusberg or performed under his direction, I saw his production of *Wait Until Dark* at the Michael J. Whalen Junior High School in my hometown of Hamden, Connecticut. That production began, as I recall, with a short black-and-white film: in it, Mimi Schmir, the actress playing Suzy Hendrix, descended the stairs of a brownstone. (I believe that the late Bill Burns, who told me years afterward that he had been a childhood friend of P. Adams Sitney, filmed the sequence.) This short, prefatory film made me wonder about the seam between theater and film, and in some form or other I have been wondering about it ever since. Thinking back to this episode also lets me meditate on the difference Julian made to my life in those years in junior high and high school in the Hamden public schools, and what that difference has continued to mean in the years since.

Other teachers also changed my thinking. This is my chance to thank other superb teachers in the Hamden schools: Frances Bennett, Lucien Boisvert, Mrs. Fox, Haywoodene Hines, and Raymond Rapuano. When I was an undergraduate at Columbia University, David Damrosch challenged me to think comparatively in ways I may yet learn to do, and Andreas Huyssen's exemplary, theoretically complex readings of texts set a high pedagogical and scholarly standard. In graduate school at Yale University, I owe special debts to Michael Levine, David Marshall, and Jennifer Wicke. Jonathan Freedman brilliantly practiced the art of being at once teacher, mentor, and friend.

I have worked out ideas in this book across many talks. I am especially grateful to audiences at Brown University, the English Institute, Harvard University, New York University, the Graduate College on Forms of Life and Forms of Knowledge at the University of Potsdam, Queen Mary University of London, Princeton University, Rutgers University, the University of Pittsburgh, and various seminars and panels at the American Comparative Literature Association, the American Society for Theater Research, and the Modernist Studies Association.

Since the late 1990s, I have taught courses related to this book at Princeton University, New York University, and the University of California, Irvine. Over those years, I have learned from more students than I can name. I must single out Elizabeth Bonapfel, Jennifer Buckley, Jen Cayer, Emily Cone-Miller, Conor Creaney, Garrett Eisler, Jane Han, Francesca Heng, and Mirabelle Ordinaire. At Irvine, an ongoing writing group with Sharece Boghozian, Mo Brouwer, Vincent Hiscock, Bridget O'Reilly, Olivia Rall, and Madeleine Read has helped to sustain my work.

A Frederick Burckhardt Residential Fellowship from the American Council of Learned Societies gave me an invaluable year at the Radcliffe Institute for Advanced Study (2009). Rather than finishing this book that year, as I had planned to do, I learned how much I had yet to think about. Learning that among such an excellent assembly of scholars and artists—especially in conversation with Gwyneth Lewis, Sarah Messer, Chiori Miyagawa, and Björn Weiler—was inspiring.

A seminar I taught at the inaugural Mellon School of Theater and Performance in the summer of 2011 continues to prove immensely important to me. I thank Martin Puchner for the gift of the invitation. That scintillating group—Heidi Bean, Katherine Biers, Julie Buckler, Matt Cornish, Shonni Enelow, Craig Iturbe, Julia Jarcho, Nicole Jerr, Uri McMillan, Christine Mok, John Muse, Magda Romanska, Ameer Sohrawardy, Lawrence Switzky, and Ariel Watson—offered one of the most memorable experiences of my career of thinking together. Not only was the seminar in itself enriching, but the Mellon School also initiated collaborations and friendships that have been crucial to me in the years since: Julia and Shonni have been among my most glamorous, thought-provoking, and sympathetic interlocutors. Nick Ridout visited the school as a lecturer, and we have been talking, corresponding, and collaborating ever since.

With her astonishing good humor and insights—practical, utopian, and otherwise—Una Chaudhuri supported this project from the start. Friends sustain me, and I could (and should, and will) write a paragraph for every name that follows: Laurien Alexandre, Michael Altman, Eyal Amiran, Emily Apter, Ian Balfour, Sean Belman, Norma Bowles, Margaret Bruzelius, Ted Byfield, Suzan Bymel, Radiclani Clytus, Pat Crain, Daniela Hernández Chong Cuy, Elin Diamond, Ed Dimendberg, Lisa Gitelman, Stathis Gourgouris, Anselm Haverkamp, Michelle Latiolais, Rodrigo Lazo, Elias Leight, Peter Leight, Heather Lukes, Meredith Martin, Saloni Mathur,

ACKNOWLEDGMENTS > 263

Molly McGarry, Meredith McGill, Sarah Mesle, Aamir Mufti, Alan Page, Neni Panourgía, Andrew Parker, Joanna Picciotto, Adela Pinch, Yopie Prins, Henrik Rehbinder, Urmila Seshagiri, Alisha Sett, Caleb Smith, Rei Terada, Michael Warner, Orlagh Woods, and Rishona Zimring. Tony Vidler remains a vital presence. Reading together remotely through the pandemic with Jennie, Craig Dworkin, Stefanie Sobelle, and the late and much-missed Marjorie Perloff made that unbearable time less so.

An anonymous reader offered generous and searching comments, and Marc Robinson went above and beyond in making this a better book. At the University of Chicago Press, Alan Thomas and Randy Petilos have all my thanks for their enthusiasm for and their patient stewardship of this book. Charles Dibble's painstaking copyediting has proved invaluable. I am also grateful to Elizabeth Ellingboe for her careful eye on production and to Meredith Nini for thinking about how to find readers. Ted Byfield, in a shocking act of friendship for which I am beyond grateful, devised the index.

My mother died in September 2021, and a small, but also not negligible, part of that loss is that I cannot share this book with her. I miss her every day. Her absence also makes me grateful for the precious company of a vibrantly alive family. Karsten Harries and Elizabeth Langhorne exemplify some rare and mysterious ability to share their dedication to the life of the mind and their indefatigable love of life. Lisa Harries Schumann is lovingly attentive to and thoughtful about everything. Lisa and Roman Schumann and Peter and Ute Harries and their families keep things tasty, interesting, and delightful. Jenn Whiting reminds me to lift my head out of that book. Walker Teiser keeps me alert to the present. Sadye, Kyle, and Jackson Teiser-Simmons remind me that there's a future. And every day Jennie shares the ongoing pleasures of our life together—then, now, and always.

∴

Fragments of two articles appear in this book: "Theater and Media Before 'New' Media: Beckett's *Film* and *Play*" was published in *Theater* 42 (2012): 7–25; and "Theater after Film, or Dismediation" appeared as part of a cluster of essays edited by Bill Brown and Bradin Cormack in *Medium: Essays from the English Institute*, in *ELH* 83, no. 2 (Summer 2016): 345–61, Copyright © 2016 Johns Hopkins University Press. An earlier version of section 24 appears in *Beckett and Media*, edited by Mark Nixon, Balazs Rapcsak, and Philipp Schweighauser (Manchester: Manchester University Press, 2022).

Bibliography

Abel, Lionel. *Metatheatre: A New View of Dramatic Form*. New York: Hill and Wang, 1963.

Ackerman, Alan. "Samuel Beckett's *Spectres du Noir*: The Being of Painting and the Flatness of *Film*." In Ackerman, *Seeing Things: From Shakespeare to Pixar*, 65–96 Toronto: University of Toronto Press, 2011.

Ackerman, Alan, and Martin Puchner, ed. *Against Theatre: Creative Destructions of the Modernist Stage*. Basingstoke: Palgrave Macmillan, 2006.

Adler, Thomas P. "The Glass Menagerie." In *Tennessee Williams: A Guide to Research and Performance*, ed. Philip C. Kolin, 34–50. Westport, CT: Greenwood Press, 1998.

Adorno, Theodor W. *Aesthetic Theory*. Ed. and trans. Robert Hullot-Kentor. Theory and History of Literature 88. Minneapolis: University of Minnesota Press, 1997.

Adorno, Theodor W. *Minima Moralia: Reflections from Damaged Life*. Trans. E. F. N. Jephcott. London: Verso, 1978.

Adorno, Theodor W. *Minima Moralia: Reflexionen aus dem Beschädigten Leben*. 1951. Frankfurt: Suhrkamp, 1970.

Adorno, Theodor W. *Negative Dialectics*. Trans. E. B. Ashton. New York: Seabury Press, 1973.

Adorno, Theodor W. *Noten zur Literatur*. Ed. Rolf Teidemann. Frankfurt am Main: Suhrkamp, 1981.

Adorno, Theodor W. "Notes on Beckett." Trans. Dirk Van Hulle and Shane Weller. *Journal of Beckett Studies* 19, no. 2 (2010): 157–78.

Adorno, Theodor W. *Notes to Literature*. 2 volumes. Ed. Rolf Tiedemann. Trans. Shierry Weber Nicholsen. New York: Columbia University Press, 1992.

Albee, Edward. *Who's Afraid of Virginia Woolf?* New York: Atheneum, 1962.

Albright, Daniel. *Beckett and Aesthetics*. Cambridge: Cambridge University Press, 2003.

Althusser, Louis. "Ideology and Ideological State Apparatuses (Notes towards an Investigation)." Trans. Ben Brewster. In *Lenin and Philosophy and Other Essays*. New York: Monthly Review Press, 1971.

Amiran, Eyal. *Modernism and the Materiality of Texts*. Cambridge: Cambridge University Press, 2016.

Apter, Emily S. *Unexceptional Politics: On Obstruction, Impasse, and the Impolitic*. Brooklyn, NY: Verso, 2018.

Arjomand, Minou. *Staged: Show Trials, Political Theater, and the Aesthetics of Judgment*. New York: Columbia University Press, 2018.

266 ‹ BIBLIOGRAPHY

Armitage, F. S., Camera. American Mutoscope and Biograph Company, and Paper Print Collection. *Star Theatre*. United States: American Mutoscope and Biograph Company, 1902. Accessed August 2, 2024. Video. https://www.loc.gov/item/00694388/.

Aronson, Arnold. *Looking into the Abyss: Essays on Scenography*. Ann Arbor: University of Michigan Press, 2005.

Arsić, Branka. *The Passive Eye: Gaze and Subjectivity in Berkeley (via Beckett)*. Stanford, CA: Stanford University Press, 2003.Artaud, Antonin. *Selected Writings*. Ed. and intro. Susan Sontag. Trans. Helen Weaver. Notes by Sontag and Don Eric Levine. Berkeley: University of California Press, 1988.

Artaud, Antonin. *Œuvres complètes*. 26 vols. Paris: Gallimard, 1956.

Artaud, Antonin. *Pour en finir avec le jugement de dieu*. 1947. Sub Rosa: Aural Documents, SR92, 1995. CD-ROM.

Artaud, Antonin. *Watchfiends and Rack Screams: Works from the Final Period*. Trans. and ed. Clayton Eshleman with Bernard Bador. Boston: Exact Change, 1995.

Auslander, Philip. *Liveness: Performance in a Mediatized Culture*. London: Routledge, 1999.

Bair, Deirdre. *Samuel Beckett: A Biography*. New York: Touchstone, 1978.

Bak, John S. "'May I Have a Drag . . . ?': Mae West, Tennessee Williams, and the Politics of a Gay Identity." *Journal of American Drama and Theatre* 18, no. 3 (2006): 5–32.

Baker, Annie. *The Flick*. New York: Theatre Communications Group, 2014.

Baldwin, James. *The Devil Finds Work*. 1976. New York: Vintage, 2011.

Balme, Christopher B. *The Theatrical Public Sphere*. Cambridge: Cambridge University Press, 2014.

Barthes, Roland. "Diderot, Brecht, Eisenstein." *Screen* 15, no. 2 (Summer 1974): 33–39.

Barthes, Roland. "*Godot* adulte." In *Écrits sur le théâtre*. Paris: Éditions du Seuil, 2002.

Barthes, Roland. *Mythologies*. Trans. Richard Howard and Annette Lavers. New York: Hill and Wang, 2012.

Bataille, Georges. *The Accursed Share: An Essay on General Economy*. Trans. Robert Hurley. New York: Zone Books, 1988.

Bay-Cheng, Sarah. *Mama Dada: Gertrude Stein's Avant-Garde Theatre*. London: Routledge, 2004.

Bay-Cheng, Sarah. "Theatre Squared: Theatre History in the Age of Media." *Theatre Topics* 17, no. 1 (2007): 37–50.

Bay-Cheng, Sarah, Jennifer Parker-Starbuck, and David Z. Saltz. *Performance and Media: Taxonomies for A Changing Field*. Ann Arbor: University of Michigan Press, 2015.

Beckett, Samuel. *The Collected Shorter Plays*. New York: Grove, 1984.

Beckett, Samuel. *Disjecta: Miscellaneous Writings and a Dramatic Fragment*. Ed. Ruby Cohn. New York: Grove, 1984.

Beckett, Samuel. *Dramatic Works*. The Grove Centenary Edition. Vol. 3, ed. Paul Auster. New York: Grove, 2006.

Beckett, Samuel. *Dramatische Dichtungen in drei Sprachen*. 2 vols. in one. Frankfurt: Suhrkamp, 1981.

Beckett, Samuel. *En attendant Godot / Waiting for Godot: Tragicomedy in 2 Acts*. Bilingual ed. New York: Grove Press, 2006.

Beckett, Samuel. *Endgame* and *Act without Words*. New York: Grove, 1957.

BIBLIOGRAPHY > 267

Beckett, Samuel. *The Letters of Samuel Beckett.* 4 vols. Ed. Martha Dow Fehsenfeld and Lois More Overbeck; George Craig and Daniel Gunn, associate eds. Cambridge: Cambridge University Press, 2009–2016.

Beckett, Samuel. *Samuel Beckett Inszeniert das "Endspiel."* Frankfurt am Main: Suhrkamp, 1969.

Beckett, Samuel. *The Theatrical Notebooks of Samuel Beckett: Endgame.* Ed. S. E. Gontarski. New York: Grove, 1992.

Beckett, Samuel. *Three Novels: Molloy, Malone Dies, The Unnamable.* New York: Grove, 1965.

Benjamin, Walter. *The Arcades Project.* Trans. Howard Eiland and Kevin McLaughlin. Ed. Rolf Tiedemann. Cambridge, MA: Belknap Press, 1999.

Benjamin, Walter. *Gesammelte Schriften,* 7 vols. in 14. Ed. Rolf Tiedemann and Hermann Schweppenhäuser. Frankfurt am Main: Suhrkamp Verlag, 1972–89.

Benjamin, Walter. *One-Way Street.* Trans. Edmund Jephcott. Introduction by Michael W. Jennings. Cambridge, MA: Harvard University Press, 2016.

Benjamin, Walter. "The Work of Art in the Age of Its Technological Reproducibility: Second Version." Trans. Edmund Jephcott and Harry Zohn. In Benjamin, *The Work of Art in the Age of Its Technological Reproducibility and Other Writings on Media,* ed. Michael W. Jennings, Brigid Doherty, and Thomas Y. Levin, 19–55. Cambridge, MA: Harvard University Press, 2008.

Benjamin, Walter. *The Work of Art in the Age of Its Technological Reproducibility and Other Writings on Media,* ed. Michael W. Jennings, Brigid Doherty, and Thomas Y. Levin. Cambridge, MA: Harvard University Press, 2008.

Benston, Kimberly W. *Performing Blackness: Enactments of African-American Modernism.* London: Routledge, 2000.

Ben-Zvi, Linda. "Samuel Beckett's Media Plays." *Modern Drama* 28, no. 1 (March 1985): 22–37.

Ben-Zvi, Linda, and Angela Moorjani, eds. *Beckett at 100: Revolving It All.* New York: Oxford University Press, 2008.

Berlant, Lauren. *The Female Complaint: The Unfinished Business of Sentimentality in American Culture.* Durham, NC: Duke University Press, 2008.

Bernhardt, Sarah. "Phèdre: La déclaration." Edison Amberol: 35008. UCSB Audio Cylinder Archive.

Bernstein, Jay. "Philosophy's Refuge: Adorno in Beckett." In *Philosophers' Poets,* ed. David Wood, 177–91. New York: Routledge, 1990.

Bersani, Leo. *The Freudian Body: Psychoanalysis and Art.* New York: Columbia University Press, 1986.

Bersani, Leo. "Is the Rectum a Grave?" *October* 43 (1987): 197–222.

Bersani, Leo, and Ulysse Dutoit. *Arts of Impoverishment: Beckett, Rothko, Resnais.* Cambridge, MA: Harvard University Press, 1993.

Bersani, Leo, and Ulysse Dutoit. *Forms of Being: Cinema, Aesthetics, Subjectivity.* London: British Film Institute, 2004.

Biers, Katherine. *Virtual Modernism: Writing and Technology in the Progressive Era.* Minneapolis: University of Minnesota Press, 2013.

Bignell, Jonathan. *Beckett on Screen: The Television Plays.* Manchester: Manchester University Press, 2009.

Binder, Wolfgang, and Adrienne Kennedy. "A MELUS Interview: Adrienne Kennedy." *MELUS* 12, no. 3 (Autumn 1985): 99–108.

Biner, Pierre. *The Living Theatre*. New York: Horizon Press, 1972.

Blau, Herbert. *The Impossible Theater: A Manifesto*. New York: Macmillan, 1964.

Bloch, Ernst. *The Utopian Function of Art and Literature: Selected Essays*. Trans. Jack Zipes and Frank Mecklenburg. Cambridge, MA: MIT Press, 1988.

Blumenthal, Eileen. *Joseph Chaikin: Exploring at the Boundaries of Theater*. Cambridge: Cambridge University Press, 1984.

Bodek, Richard. "Red Song: Social Democratic Music and Radicalism at the End of the Weimar Republic." *Central European History* 28, no. 2 (Summer 1995): 209–27.

Bohn, Willard. "Lorca, Buster Keaton, and the Surrealist Muse." *Revista Hispánica Moderna* 53, no. 2 (2000): 413–24.

Bolter, Jay David, and Richard Grusin. *Remediation: Understanding New Media*. Cambridge, MA: MIT Press, 2000.

Bordwell, David, Janet Staiger, and Kristin Thompson. *The Classical Hollywood Cinema: Film Style and Mode of Production to 1960*. New York: Columbia University Press, 1985.

Bottoms, Stephen J. "The Efficacy/Effeminacy Braid: Unpacking the Performance Studies / Theatre Studies Dichotomy." *Theatre Topics* 13, no. 2 (September 2003): 173–87.

Boyle, Michael Shane. "Brecht's Gale." *Performance Research* 21, no. 3 (2016): 16–26.

Boyle, Michael Shane, Matt Cornish, and Brandon Woolf, eds. *Postdramatic Theatre and Form*. London: Methuen Drama, 2019.

Brandt, George W., ed. *Modern Theories of Drama: A Selection of Writings on Drama and Theatre, 1840–1990*. Oxford: Oxford University Press, 1998.

Brantlinger, Patrick. *Bread and Circuses: Theories of Mass Culture as Social Decay*. Ithaca, NY: Cornell University Press, 1983.

Brecht, Bertolt. *Arbeitsjournal*. Ed. Werner Hecht. 2 vols. Frankfurt: Suhrkamp, 1973.

Brecht, Bertolt. *Brecht on Film and Radio*. Trans. Marc Silberman. London: Methuen, 2000.

Brecht, Bertolt. *Die Maßnahme: Kritische Ausgabe mit einer Spielanleituung von Reiner Steinweg*. Frankfurt: Suhrkamp, 1972.

Brecht, Bertolt. *Journals: 1934–1955*. Trans. Hugh Rorrison. Ed. John Willett. New York: Routledge, 1993.

Brecht, Bertolt. *The Measures Taken and Other Lehrstücke*. Trans. Carl R. Mueller, Ralph Mannheim, and Wolfgang Sauerlander. London: Methuen, 1977.

Bresson, Robert. *Notes on the Cinematographer*. Trans. Jonathan Griffin. Copenhagen: Green Integer, 1997.

Brewster, Ben. "The Fundamental Reproach: Bertolt Brecht and the Cinema." In *Explorations in Film Theory: Selected Essays from Ciné-Tracts*. Ed. Ron Burnett. Bloomington: Indiana University Press, 1991.

Brewster, Ben, and Lea Jacobs. *Theatre to Cinema: Stage Pictorialism and the Early Feature Film*. Oxford: Oxford University Press, 1997.

Brooks, Daphne A. *Bodies in Dissent: Spectacular Performances of Race and Freedom, 1850–1910*. Durham, NC: Duke University Press, 2006.

Bryant-Jackson, Paul K., and Lois More Overbeck, ed. *Intersecting Boundaries: The Theatre of Adrienne Kennedy*. Minneapolis: University of Minnesota Press, 1992.

Buckley, Jennifer. *Beyond Text: Theater and Performance in Print after 1900*. Ann Arbor: University of Michigan Press, 2019.

BIBLIOGRAPHY > 269

Buck-Morss, Susan. "Aesthetics and Anaesthetics: Walter Benjamin's Artwork Essay Reconsidered." *October* 62 (1992): 3–41.

Bulson, Eric. "Literature and Close Reading: An Interview with Andreas Huyssen." *Los Angeles Review of Books*, February 19, 2016.

Bürger, Peter. *Theory of the Avant-Garde.* Trans. Michael Shaw. Minneapolis: University of Minnesota Press, 1984.

Burges, Joel. "Adorno's Mimeograph: The Uses of Obsolescence in *Minima Moralia.*" *New German Critique* 118, special issue on Adorno (Winter 2013): 65–92.

Burgin, Victor. "Diderot, Barthes, *Vertigo.*" In *Formations of Fantasy*, ed. Victor Burgin, James Donald, and Cora Kaplan, 159–81. New York: Methuen, 1986.

Calendo, John. "Tennessee Talks to John Calendo." *Interview*, April 1973. https://www .interviewmagazine.com/culture/new-again-tennessee-williams#.

Camp, Pannill. *The First Frame: Theatre Space in Enlightenment France.* Cambridge: Cambridge University Press, 2014.

Cantwell, Robert. *When We Were Good: The Folk Revival.* Cambridge, MA: Harvard University Press, 1996.

Carlson, Marvin. *The Haunted Stage: The Theatre as Memory Machine.* Ann Arbor: University of Michigan Press, 2001.

Cavell, Stanley. "Ending the Waiting Game: A Reading of *Endgame.*" In *Must We Mean What We Say?* Cambridge: Cambridge University Press, 1976, 115–62.

Cavell, Stanley. *The World Viewed: Reflections on the Ontology of Film.* Enlarged ed. Cambridge, MA: Harvard University Press, 1979.

Certeau, Michel de. *The Practice of Everyday Life.* Trans. Steven Rendall. Berkeley: University of California Press, 1984.

Chabas, Paul. *September Morn* (ca. 1912). Accessed July 17, 2024. https://www .metmuseum.org/art/collection/search/488977.

Chan, Paul, ed. *Waiting for Godot in New Orleans: A Field Guide.* New York: Creative Time, 2010.

Chapple, Freda, and Chiel Kattenbelt, eds. *Intermediality in Theatre and Performance.* Amsterdam: Rodopi, 2006.

Children of Paradise. Dir. Michel Carné. With Arletty, Jean-Louis Barrault, and María Casares. 1945.

Christensen, Jerome. *America's Corporate Art: The Studio Authorship of Hollywood Motion Pictures.* Stanford, CA: Stanford University Press, 2012.

Clark, T. J. Introduction. In *Farewell to an Idea: Episodes from a History of Modernism*, 1–13. New Haven, CT: Yale University Press, 1999.

Clum, John M. "The Sacrificial Stud and the Fugitive Female in *Suddenly Last Summer, Orpheus Descending*, and *Sweet Bird of Youth.*" In *The Cambridge Companion to Tennessee Williams*, ed. Matthew C. Roudané, 128–46. Cambridge: Cambridge University Press, 2006.

Cohen, Debra Rae, and Michael Coyle, eds. *Broadcasting Modernism.* Gainesville: University of Press of Florida, 2009.

Cohn, Ruby. *A Beckett Canon.* Ann Arbor: University of Michigan Press, 2001.

Cohn, Ruby. "Ghosting through Beckett." *Samuel Beckett Today/Aujourd'hui* 2 (1993): 1–12.

Connor, Steven. *Beckett, Modernism and the Material Imagination.* Cambridge: Cambridge University Press, 2014.

Connor, Steven. *Samuel Beckett: Repetition, Theory and Text*. Oxford: Basil Blackwell, 1988.

Cosgrove, Ben. "Brando Takes Broadway: *LIFE* on the Set of 'A Streetcar Named Desire' in 1947." https://www.life.com/arts-entertainment/brando-takes-broadway-life-on-the-set-of-a-streetcar-named-desire-in-1947/.

Critchley, Simon. "To be or not to be is not the question: Samuel Beckett's *Film*." *Film-Philosophy* 11, no. 2 (August 2007): 108–21.

Cronin, Anthony. *Samuel Beckett: The Last Modernist*. New York: HarperCollins, 1997.

Crow, Thomas. "Modernism and Mass Culture in the Visual Arts." In Crow, *Modern Art and the Common Culture*, 3–37. New Haven, CT: Yale University Press, 1996.

Cunningham, David. "Trying (Not) to Understand: Adorno and the Work of Beckett." In *Beckett and Philosophy*, ed. Richard J. Lane, 125–39. Houndmills, Basingstoke, Hampshire: Palgrave, 2002.

Dardis, Tom. *Keaton, The Man Who Wouldn't Lie Down*. New York: Scribner, 1979.

Days of Being Wild. Dir. Wong Kar-Wai. With Leslie Cheung, Andy Lau, Maggie Cheung, Carina Lau, Jacky Cheung, and Tony Leun. 1990.

Debord, Guy. *The Society of the Spectacle*. 1967. Trans. Donald Nicholson-Smith. New York: Zone, 1995.

Defraeye, Piet. "You! Hypocrite Spectateur. A Short History of the Production and Reception of Peter Handke's *Publikumsbeschimpfung*." *Seminar* 42, no. 4 (November 2006): 412–38.

DeFrantz, Thomas, and Anita Gonzalez, eds. *Black Performance Theory*. Durham, NC: Duke University Press, 2014.

Deleuze, Gilles. *Cinema I: The Movement Image*. Trans. Hugh Tomlinson and Barbara Habberjam. Minneapolis: University of Minnesota Press, 1986.

Deleuze, Gilles. "The Greatest Irish Film (Beckett's Film)." In *Essays Critical and Clinical*, trans. Daniel W. Smith and Michael A. Greco, 23–26. Minneapolis: University of Minnesota Press, 1997.

DeWitt, M. E. *Dramaticules for Choric Recitation with Group Movement: Light, Youth and the Haunted Old, Maelstrom, The Unknown, the Living and Their Ghosts, Endow the Oral Arts, Sound and Movement*. Boston: Expression Company, 1936.

Diamond, Elin. "Re: Blau, Butler, Beckett, and the Politics of Seeming." *TDR* 44, no. 4 (2000): 31–43.

Diamond, Elin. *Unmaking Mimesis: Essays on Feminism and Theater*. New York: Routledge, 1997.

Diawara, Manthia, ed. *Black American Cinema*. New York: Routledge, 1993.

Diawara, Manthia. "Black Spectatorship: Problems of Identification and Resistance." *Screen* 29, no. 4 (Autumn 1988): 66–76.

Dilworth, Thomas, and Christopher Langlois. "The Nietzschean Madman in Beckett's *Endgame*." *The Explicator* 65, no. 3 (2007): 167–71.

Dinerstein, Joel. *The Origins of Cool in Postwar America*. Chicago: University of Chicago Press, 2020.

Dolar, Mladen. *A Voice and Nothing More*. Cambridge, MA: MIT Press, 2006.

Dowd, Garin. *Abstract Machines: Samuel Beckett and Philosophy after Deleuze and Guattari*. Amsterdam: Rodopi, 2007.

Eck, Hélène. "Radio, culture et démocratie en France: Une ambition mort-née (1944–1949)." *Vingtième siècle, Revue d'histoire* 30 (April–June 1991): 55–67.

Editorial. *Theatre Arts Magazine* 4, no. 2 (April 1920).

BIBLIOGRAPHY > 271

Eisenstein, Sergei. "Through Theater to Cinema" [1934]. In *Film Form: Essays in Film Theory*. Ed. and trans. Jay Leyda., 3–17. San Diego, CA: Harcourt, 1977.

Eisler, Hanns, and Bertolt Brecht. *Die Maßnahme*. DR Leipzig Radio Choir & MDR Leipzig Kammerphilharmonie. MDR1207.

Elsaesser, Thomas. "Early Film History and Multi-Media: An Archaeology of Possible Futures?" In *New Media / Old Media: A History and Theory Reader*, ed. Wendy Hui Kyong Chun, Anna Watkins Fisher, and Thomas Keenan, 13–25. New York: Routledge: 2006.

The Encyclopedia of Philosophy. Ed. Paul Edwards. 8 vols. New York: Macmillan, 1967.

Enelow, Shonni. *Method Acting and Its Discontents: On American Psycho-Drama*. Evanston, IL: Northwestern University Press, 2015.

Enelow, Shonni. "Sweating Tennessee Williams: Working Actors in *A Streetcar Named Desire* and *Portrait of a Madonna*." *Modern Drama* 62, no. 2 (2019): 129–48.

Enzensberger, Hans Magnus. *The Consciousness Industry: On Literature, Politics, and the Media*. Ed. Michael Roloff. New York: Seabury, 1974.

Esslin, Martin. *Mediations: Essays on Brecht, Beckett, and the Media*. Baton Rouge: Louisiana State University Press, 1980.

Esslin, Martin. *The Theatre of the Absurd*. Rev. ed. Garden City, NJ: Anchor, 1969.

"'Experimental in the Fullest Sense': Marc Robinson on the Convention-Shattering Works of Adrienne Kennedy." Library of America, accessed August 2, 2024. https:// www.loa.org/news-and-views/2174-experimental-in-the-fullest-sense-marc -robinson-on-the-convention-shattering-works-of-adrienne-kennedy/.

Farrington, Sara. *The Lost Conversation: Interviews with an Enduring Avant-Garde*. Brooklyn, NY: 53rd State Press, 2022.

Feshbach, Sidney. "Unswamping a Backwater: On Samuel Beckett's *Film*." In *Samuel Beckett and The Arts: Music, Visual Arts, and Non-Print Media*, ed. Lois Oppenheim, 333–63. New York: Garland, 1999.

Filene, Benjamin. *Romancing the Folk: Public Memory and American Roots Music*. Chapel Hill: University of North Carolina Press, 2000.

Fineman, Joel. *The Subjectivity Effect in Western Literary Tradition: Essays toward the Release of Shakespeare's Will*. Cambridge, MA: MIT Press, 1991.

Fischer, Ernst. "Samuel Beckett: *Play* and *Film*." Trans. Anna Bostock. *Mosaic* 2, no. 2 (Winter 1969): 96–116.

Fischer, Iris Smith. *Mabou Mines: Making Avant-garde Theater in the 1970s*. Ann Arbor: University of Michigan Press, 2011.

Fischer-Lichte, Erika. *The Show and the Gaze of Theatre: A European Perspective*. Trans. Jo Riley. Iowa City: University of Iowa Press, 1997.

Foucault, Michel. *Discipline and Punish: The Birth of the Prison*. Trans. Alan Sheridan. New York: Vintage, 1979.

Foucault, Michel. *The Punitive Society: Lectures at the Collège de France, 1972–1973*. Ed. Bernard E. Harcourt and trans. Graham Burchell. Houndmills, Basingstoke, Hampshire: Palgrave Macmillan, 2015.

Frank, Johanna. "Reintroducing Adrienne Kennedy's *Diary of Lights*." *Modern Drama* 55, no. 1 (2012): 1–18.

Fraser-Miller, S. J., J. S. Rooney, K. Gordon, C. R. Bunt, and J. M. Haley, "Feeding the Team: Analysis of a Spratt's Dog Cake from Antarctica." *Polar Record* 57 (2021): e19.

Freedgood, Elaine. *The Ideas in Things: Fugitive Meaning in the Victorian Novel*. Chicago: University of Chicago Press, 2006.

Freedman, Jonathan. "Autocanonization: Tropes of Self-Legitimation in 'Popular Culture.'" *Yale Journal of Criticism* 1, no. 1 (1987): 203–17.

Fried, Michael. *Absorption and Theatricality: Painting and Beholder in the Age of Diderot.* Chicago: University of Chicago Press, 1988.

Fried, Michael. *Art and Objecthood: Essays and Reviews.* Chicago: University of Chicago Press, 1998.

Friedel, Robert. *A Culture of Improvement: Technology and the Western Millennium.* Cambridge, MA: MIT Press, 2007.

The Fugitive Kind. Dir. Sidney Lumet. With Marlon Brando, Joanne Woodward, and Anna Magnani. 1960.

Fuss, Diana. *Identification Papers.* New York: Routledge, 1995.

Gallagher-Ross, Jacob. "Mediating the Method." *Theatre Survey* 56, no. 3 (2015): 291–313.

Garner, Stanton B., Jr. *Bodied Spaces: Phenomenology and Performance in Contemporary Drama.* Ithaca, NY: Cornell University Press, 1994.

Gillett, John, and James Blue. "Keaton at Venice." *Sight and Sound* 35 (1965): 26–30.

Gilroy, Paul. *The Black Atlantic: Modernity and Double Consciousness.* Cambridge, MA: Harvard University Press, 1993.

Gitelman, Lisa. *Always Already New: Media, History and the Data of Culture.* Cambridge, MA: MIT Press, 2006.

Gitelman, Lisa, and Geoffrey B. Pingree, eds. *New Media, 1740–1915.* Cambridge, MA: MIT Press, 2003.

Goldsby, Jacqueline. *A Spectacular Secret: Lynching in American Life and Literature.* Chicago: University of Chicago Press, 2006.

Goldthwaite, Charles A., Jr. "All Shook Up: Elvis, Bo, and the White Negro in Tennessee Williams's *Orpheus Descending.*" *Tennessee Williams Annual Review* 8 (2006): 95–107.

Gontarski, S. E. *The Intent of Undoing in Samuel Beckett's Dramatic Texts.* Bloomington: Indiana University Press, 1985.

Goodman, Paul. *Growing Up Absurd.* New York: Vintage, 1960.

Goodman, Paul. "Notes on the Underworld." *The Nation* 192, no. 10 (March 11, 1961): 215–17.

Gordon, Lois. *The World of Samuel Beckett, 1906–1946.* New Haven, CT: Yale University Press, 1996.

Gourgouris, Stathis. "The Lyric in Exile (Meditations on the *Hollywooder Liederbuch*)." *Qui Parle* 14, no. 2 (2004): 145–75.

Graver, Lawrence, and Raymond Federman, eds. *Samuel Beckett: The Critical Heritage.* London: Routledge & Kegan Paul, 1979.

Greenberg, Clement. "Modernist Painting" [1960]. In *The Collected Essays and Criticism*, vol. 4, *Modernism with a Vengeance, 1957–1969*, ed. John O'Brian, 85–93. Chicago: University of Chicago Press, 1993.

Greenberg, Clement. "Towards a Newer Laocoon" [1940]. In *The Collected Essays and Criticism*, vol. 1, *Perceptions and Judgments, 1939–1944*, ed. John O'Brian, 23–38. Chicago: University of Chicago Press, 1986.

Grier, Katherine C. *Pets in America: A History.* Chapel Hill: University of North Carolina Press, 2006.

Griffin, Farrah Jasmine. *In Search of Billie Holiday: If You Can't Be Free, Be a Mystery.* New York: Ballantine, 2001.

Grobe, Christopher. "Why It's 'Easier to Act with a Telephone than a Man'." *Theatre Survey* 57, no. 2 (2016): 175–99.

Grotowski, Jerzy. *Towards a Poor Theatre*. New York: Touchstone, 1968.

Guillory, John. "Genesis of the Media Concept." *Critical Inquiry* 36, no. 2 (2010): 321–62.

Gunn, Drewey Wayne. "The Various Texts of Tennessee Williams's Plays." *Educational Theatre Journal* 30, no. 3 (1978): 368–75.

Gunning, Tom. "An Aesthetic of Astonishment: Early Film and the (In)Credulous Spectator." In *Viewing Positions: Ways of Seeing Film*, ed. Linda Williams, 114–33. New Brunswick, NJ: Rutgers University Press, 1995.

Gunning, Tom. "Buster Keaton or the Work of Comedy in the Age of Mechanical Reproduction." *Cineaste* 21, no. 3 (1995): 14–16.

Guralnick, Peter. *Last Train to Memphis: The Rise of Elvis Presley*. Boston: Little, Brown, 1994.

Habermas, Jürgen. *The Structural Transformation of the Public Sphere: An Inquiry into a Category of Bourgeois Society*. Trans. Thomas Burger with the assistance of Frederick Lawrence. Cambridge, MA: MIT Press, 1991.

Hadot, Pierre. *Philosophy as a Way of Life: Spiritual Exercises from Socrates to Foucault*. Ed. Arnold Davidson. Trans. Michael Chase. Malden, MA: Blackwell, 1995.

Haerdter, Michael. "A Rehearsal Diary." Trans. Britta von Diezelski. In *Beckett in the Theatre: The Author as Practical Playwright and Director*, ed. Dougald McMillan and Martha Fehsenfeld, 204–38. London: J. Calder, 1988.

Hall, Stuart. "What Is This 'Black' in Black Popular Culture?" In *Black Popular Culture: A Project by Michele Wallace*, ed. Gina Dent. Seattle, WA: Bay Press, 1992.

Halliwell, Stephen, and Daniel Mendelsohn. Letters to the Editor, *New York Review of Books*, June 23, 2013.

Halpern, Richard. *Tragedy and Political Economy*. Chicago: University of Chicago Press, 2017.

Hamilton, James. "Unearthing Broadcasting in the Anglophone World." In *Residual Media*, ed. Charles R. Acland, 383–400. Minneapolis: University of Minnesota Press, 2007.

Handke, Peter. *Ich bin ein Bewohner des Elfenbeinturms*. Frankfurt: Suhrkamp, 1972.

Handke, Peter. *A Journey to the Rivers: Justice for Serbia*. Trans. Scott Abbott. New York: Viking, 1997.

Handke, Peter. *Kaspar and Other Plays*. Trans. Michael Roloff. New York: Hill and Wang, 1969.

Handke, Peter. *Once Again for Thucydides*. Trans. Tess Lewis. New York: New Directions, 1998.

Handke, Peter. *Prosa Gedichte Theaterstücke Hörspiel Aufsätze*. Frankfurt: Suhrkamp, 1970.

Handke, Peter. *The Ride across Lake Constance and Other Plays*. Trans. Michael Roloff with Karl Weber. New York: Farrar, Straus and Giroux, 1976.

Handke, Peter. *Stücke 1*. Frankfurt: Suhrkamp, 1972.

Handke, Peter. "Theater and Film: The Misery of Comparison." In *Theater and Film: A Comparative Anthology*, ed. Robert Knopf, 184–92. New Haven, CT: Yale University Press, 2005.

274 ‹ BIBLIOGRAPHY

Hansen, Miriam Bratu. *Babel and Babylon: Spectatorship in American Silent Film.* Cambridge, MA: Harvard University Press, 1991.

Hansen, Miriam Bratu. "Benjamin's Aura." *Critical Inquiry* 34, no. 2 (2008): 336–75.

Hansen, Miriam Bratu. *Cinema and Experience: Siegfried Kracauer, Walter Benjamin, and Theodor W. Adorno.* Berkeley: University of California Press, 2012.

Hansen, Miriam Bratu. "The Mass Production of the Senses: Classical Cinema as Vernacular Modernism." *Modernism/Modernity* 6, no. 2 (1999): 59–77.

Harmon, Maurice, ed. *No Author Better Served: The Correspondence of Samuel Beckett and Alan Schneider.* Cambridge, MA: Harvard University Press, 1998.

Harper, Phillip Brian. *Abstractionist Aesthetic: Artistic Form and Social Critique in African American Culture.* New York: New York University Press, 2015.

Harries, Martin. "Beckett's Ghost Light." In *Popular Ghosts: The Haunted Spaces of Everyday Culture,* ed. María del Pilar Blanco and Esther Peeren, 19–34. New York: Continuum, 2010.

Harries, Martin. "The End of a Trope for the World." In *"If Then the World a Theatre Present . . .": Revisions of the Theatrum Mundi Metaphor in Early Modern England,* ed. Björn Quiring, 221–39. Berlin / New York: De Gruyter, 2014.

Harries, Martin. "Theater after Film, or Dismediation." In *Medium: Essays from the English Institute,* ed. Bill Brown and Bradin Cormack. Special issue of *ELH* 83, no. 2 (Summer 2016): 345–61.

Harries, Martin. "Theater and Media before 'New' Media: Beckett's *Film* and *Play.*" *Theater* 42, no. 2 (2012): 6–25.

Heidegger, Martin. "The Age of the World Picture" [1938]. In *The Question concerning Technology and Other Essays,* ed. and trans. William Lovitt, 115–54. New York: Harper, 1977.

Hoberman, J. *Film after Film: Or, What Became of 21st Century Cinema?* New York: Verso, 2012.

Horkheimer, Max, and Theodor W. Adorno. *Dialectic of Enlightenment: Philosophical Fragments.* Ed. Gunzelin Schmid Noerr, trans. Edmund Jephcott. Stanford, CA: Stanford University Press, 2002.

Hurt, James, ed. *Focus on Film and Theatre.* Englewood Cliffs, NJ: Prentice-Hall, 1974.

Huyssen, Andreas. *After the Great Divide: Modernism, Mass Culture, Postmodernism.* Bloomington: Indiana University Press, 1986.

Huyssen, Andreas. *Miniature Metropolis: Literature in an Age of Photography and Film.* Cambridge, MA: Harvard University Press, 2015.

Illig, Nancy. "Acting Beckett's Women." In *Women in Beckett: Performance and Critical Perspectives,* ed. Linda Ben-Zvi, 24–26. Urbana: University of Illinois Press, 1990.

Isaac, Dan. "The Death of the Proscenium Stage." *Antioch Review* 31, no. 2 (Summer 1971): 235–53.

Iser, Wolfgang. "The Art of Failure: The Stifled Laugh in Beckett's Theater." In Iser, *Prospecting: From Reader Response to Literary Anthropology,* 152–93. Baltimore, MD: Johns Hopkins University Press, 1989.

Israel, Nico. *Outlandish: Writing between Exile and Diaspora.* Stanford, CA: Stanford University Press, 2000.

Jackson, Shannon. *Professing Performance: Theatre in the Academy from Philology to Performativity.* Cambridge: Cambridge University Press, 2004.

BIBLIOGRAPHY > 275

Jakovljević, Branislav. "Fording the Stream of Conscience: Peter Handke's River Journeys." In *Theatre in the Context of the Yugoslav Wars*, ed. Jana Dolečki, Stefan Hulfeld, and Senad Halilbašić, 243–70. Cham: Palgrave Macmillan, 2018.

James, Henry. *Autobiography*. Ed. and intro. Frederick W. Dupee. Princeton, NJ: Princeton University Press, 1983.

Jameson, Fredric. *Brecht and Method*. London: Verso, 1998.

Jannarone, Kimberley. *Artaud and His Doubles*. Ann Arbor: University of Michigan Press, 2010.

Jarcho, Julia. *Dreamless Land*. In *Minor Theater: Three Plays*. Brooklyn, NY: 53rd State Press, 2017.

Jarcho, Julia. *Writing and the Modern Stage: Theater beyond Drama*. Cambridge: Cambridge University Press, 2017.

Jarcho, Julia, and Martin Harries. "Dividing the Audience." In *The Very Thought of Herbert Blau*, ed. Joseph R. Roach and Clark D. Lunberry, 61–77. Ann Arbor: University of Michigan Press, 2018.

Jay, Martin. *Downcast Eyes: The Denigration of Vision in Twentieth-Century French Thought*. Berkeley: University of California Press, 1993.

Jenemann, David. *Adorno in America*. Minneapolis: University of Minnesota Press, 2007.

Jenkins, Henry. *Convergence Culture: Where Old and New Media Collide*. New York: New York University Press, 2006.

Jenkins, Henry. "'This Fellow Keaton Seems to Be the Whole Show': Buster Keaton, Interrupted Performance, and the Vaudeville Aesthetic." In *Buster Keaton's* Sherlock Jr., ed. Andrew Horton, 29–66. Cambridge: Cambridge University Press, 1997.

Jones, LeRoi [Amiri Baraka]. *Home: Social Essays*. New York: William Morrow, 1966.

Joselit, David. *Feedback: Television against Democracy*. Cambridge, MA: MIT Press, 2007.

Kahn, Douglas, and Gregory Whitehead, eds. *Wireless Imagination: Sound, Radio, and the Avant-Garde*. Cambridge, MA: MIT Press. 1992.

Keaton, Buster, with Charles Samuels. *My Wonderful World of Slapstick*. London: George Allen & Unwin, 1967.

Keil, Charlie. "'All the Frame's a Stage': (Anti-Theatricality) and Cinematic Modernism." In *Against Theatre: Creative Destructions on the Modernist Stage*, ed. Alan Ackerman and Martin Puchner, 76–91. New York: Palgrave Macmillan, 2006.

Kennedy, Adrienne. *The Adrienne Kennedy Reader*. Minneapolis: University of Minnesota Press, 2001.

Kennedy, Adrienne. *Collected Plays and Other Writings*. Ed. Marc Robinson. New York: Library of America, 2023.

Kennedy, Adrienne. *Deadly Triplets: A Theatre Mystery and Journal*. Minneapolis: University of Minnesota Press, 1990.

Kennedy, Adrienne. *Diary of Lights*. With lyrics by Sandy Chapin. *Modern Drama* 55, no. 1 (Spring 2012): 100–145.

Kennedy, Adrienne. He Brought Her Heart Back in a Box *and Other Plays*. New York: Theatre Communications Group, 2020.

Kennedy, Adrienne. *In One Act*. Minneapolis: University of Minnesota Press, 1990.

Kennedy, Adrienne. *A Movie Star Has to Star in Black and White*. In *Wordplays 3: An Anthology of New American Drama*. New York: Performing Arts Journal, 1984.

Kennedy, Adrienne. *People Who Led to My Plays*. New York: Theatre Communications Group, 1987.

Kennedy, Adrienne, and Lisa Lehman. "A Growth of Images." *Drama Review* 21, no. 4 (1977): 41–48.

Kenner, Hugh. *The Mechanic Muse*. New York: Oxford University Press, 1987.

Kenner, Hugh. *A Reader's Guide to Samuel Beckett*. New York: Farrar, Straus and Giroux, 1973.

Kenner, Hugh. *Samuel Beckett: A Critical Study*. New ed. Berkeley: University of California Press, 1967.

King, W. D. "Blau-Blooded Thought: Recent Writings of Herbert Blau." *Theater* 16, no. 1 (1984): 80–85.

Klaver, Elizabeth. *Performing Television: Contemporary Drama and the Media Culture*. Bowling Green, KY: Bowling Green State University Popular Press, 2000.

Klaver, Elizabeth. "Spectatorial Theory in the Age of Media Culture." *New Theatre Quarterly* 11, no. 44 (1995): 309–21.

Kline, Jim. *The Complete Films of Buster Keaton*. New York: Citadel Press, 1993.

Knabb, Ken, ed. and trans. *Situationist International Anthology*. Berkeley, CA: Bureau of Public Secrets, 1981.

Knopf, Robert. *Theater and Film: A Comparative Anthology*. New Haven, CT: Yale University Press, 2005.

Knowlson, James. *Damned to Fame: The Life of Samuel Beckett*. New York: Simon and Schuster, 1996.

Koepnick, Lutz P. "Negotiating Popular Culture: Wenders, Handke, and the Topographies of Cultural Studies." *German Quarterly* 69, no. 4 (1996): 381–400.

Krauss, Rosalind. *"A Voyage on the North Sea": Art in the Age of the Post-Medium Condition*. London: Thames and Hudson, 1999.

Lahr, John. *Tennessee Williams: Mad Pilgrimage of the Flesh*. New York: Norton, 2014.

Laplanche, Jean. "To Situate Sublimation." Trans. Richard Miller. *October* 28, Discipleship: A Special Issue on Psychoanalysis (Spring 1984): 7–26.

Lee, Young Jean. *The Shipment; Lear*. New York: Theatre Communications Group, 2010.

Lehmann, Hans-Thies. *Postdramatic Theatre*. Trans. Karen Jürs-Munby. London: Routledge, 2006.

Levin, Thomas Y. "Iconology at the Movies: Panofsky's Film Theory." *Yale Journal of Criticism* 9, no. 1 (1996): 27–55.

Leyda, Jay. *Kino: A History of Russian and Soviet Film*. New York: Macmillan, 1960.

Lloyd, David. *Anomalous States: Irish Writing and the Post-Colonial Moment*. Dublin: Lilliput Press, 1993.

Lloyd, David. *Beckett's Thing: Painting and Theatre*. Edinburgh: Edinburgh University Press, 2016.

Loiperdinger, Martin, and Bernd Elzer. "Lumière's 'Arrival of the Train': Cinema's Founding Myth." *Moving Image* 4, no. 1 (2004): 89–118.

Loomis, Jeffrey B. "'Cassandra, Meet Leadbelly': Tennessee Williams Battles to Become Orpheus." *Text and Presentation*, 2013: 123–39.

Lorca, Federico García. *The Unknown Lorca: Dialogues, Dramatic Projects, Unfinished Plays and a Filmscript*. Ed. and trans. John London. London: Atlas, 1996.

BIBLIOGRAPHY > 277

Lott, Eric. *Love and Theft: Blackface Minstrelsy and the American Working Class.* Oxford: Oxford University Press, 1993.

Magid, Marion. "The Innocence of Tennessee Williams." *Commentary* 35, no. 1 (January 1963): 34–43.

Malamud, Marc D. Email to author. April 27, 2020.

Malina, Judith. *The Diaries of Judith Malina, 1947–1957.* New York: Grove Press, 1984.

Malina, Judith, and Julian Beck. Letter to the Drama Mailbag, *New York Times*, April 7, 1957.

Malina, Judith, and Julian Beck. *Paradise Now: Collective Creation of the Living Theatre.* New York: Random House, 1971.

Marvin, Wanda. "CBS." Review of television. *Billboard*, September 2, 1944, 12.

Maslan, Susan. *Revolutionary Acts: Theater, Democracy, and the French Revolution.* Baltimore, MD: Johns Hopkins University Press, 2005.

Mast, Gerald, Marshall Cohen, and Leo Braudy, eds. *Film Theory and Criticism: Introductory Readings.* 4th ed. New York: Oxford University Press, 1992.

Materialen zu Becketts 'Endspiel.' Frankfurt am Main: Suhrkamp, 1968.

McCarthy, Mary. *Mary McCarthy's Theatre Chronicles, 1937–1962.* New York: Noonday, 1963.

McDonough, Tom, ed. *Guy Debord and the Situationist International: Texts and Documents.* Cambridge, MA: MIT Press, 2004.

McGill, Meredith L. "What is a Ballad? Reading for Genre, Format, and Medium." *Nineteenth-Century Literature* 71, no. 2 (2016): 156–75.

McGinley, Paige A. "Reconsidering 'the American Style': Black Performers and Black Music in *Streetcar* and *Cat.*" *Theatre Journal* 68, no. 1 (March 2016): 1–15.

McGuigan, Jim. *Raymond Williams: Cultural Analyst.* Bristol: Intellect, 2019.

McLaughlin, Robert. *Broadway and Hollywood: A History of Economic Interaction.* New York: Arno Press, 1974.

McLuhan, Marshall. 1954. "Sight, Sound, and the Fury." In *Mass Culture: The Popular Arts in America*, ed. Bernard Rosenberg and David Manning White, 489–95. Glencoe, IL: Free Press, 1957.

McLuhan, Marshall. *Understanding Media: The Extensions of Man* [1964]. Ed. W. Terrence Gordon. Corte Madera, CA: Gingko Press, 2003.

McMillan, Dougald, and Martha Fehsenfeld. *Beckett in The Theatre: The Author as Practical Playwright and Director.* Vol. 1. London: John Calder, 1988.

McMullan, Anna. *Theatre on Trial: Samuel Beckett's Later Drama.* New York: Routledge, 1993.

Melville, Stephen W. "Gaze." In *Encyclopedia of Aesthetics*, ed. Michael Kelly. 4 vols. New York: Oxford University Press, 1998.

Melville, Stephen W. *Philosophy Beside Itself: On Deconstruction and Modernism.* Theory and History of Literature 27. Minneapolis; University of Minnesota Press, 1986.

Menke, Christoph. *The Sovereignty of Art: Aesthetic Negativity in Adorno and Derrida.* Trans. Neil Solomon. Cambridge, MA: MIT Press, 1999.

Metz, Christian. *The Imaginary Signifier: Psychoanalysis and the Cinema.* Trans. Celia Britton, Annwyl Williams, Ben Brewster, and Alfred Guzzetti. Bloomington: Indiana University Press, 1981.

Miller, D. A. *Place for Us: Essay on the Broadway Musical.* Cambridge, MA: Harvard University Press, 1998.

Miller, Edward. *Emergency Broadcasting and 1930s American Radio*. Philadelphia: Temple University Press, 2002.

Miller, Hillary. *Drop Dead: Performance in Crisis, 1970s New York*. Evanston, IL: Northwestern University Press, 2016.

Miller, Tyrus. "Beckett's Political Technology: Expression, Confession, and Torture in the Later Drama." *Samuel Beckett Today/Aujourd'hui*, 2000: 255–78.

Mitchell, Tom. "Tennessee Williams Wrestles with Race in Three Unpublished Works: 'Goat Song,' 'Heavenly Grass,' and 'Why Did Desdemona Love the Moor?'" *Tennessee Williams Annual Review* 18 (2019): 57–76.

Moody, Alys. "Waiting for Godot in New Orleans: Modernist Autonomy and Transnational Performance in Paul Chan's Beckett." *Theatre Journal*, 65, no. 4 (2013): 537–57.

Moretti, Franco. *Signs Taken for Wonders: Essays in the Sociology of Literary Forms*. London: Verso, 1983.

Morin, Emilie. *Beckett's Political Imagination*. Cambridge: Cambridge University Press, 2017.

Morin, Emilie. "Political Theatre and the Beckett Problem." In *Beckett and Politics*, ed. William Davies and Helen Bailey, 177–93. Basingstoke: Palgrave Macmillan, 2020.

Moschovakis, Nick. "Tennessee Williams's American Blues: From the Early Manuscripts through *Menagerie*." *Tennessee Williams Annual Review* 7 (2005): 15–36.

Moten, Fred. "The Case of Blackness." *Criticism* 50, no. 2 (2008): 177–218.

Mowitt, John. *Radio: Essays in Bad Reception*. Berkeley: University of California Press, 2011.

Mueller, Roswitha. *Bertolt Brecht and the Theory of Media*. Lincoln: University of Nebraska Press, 1989.

Mueller, Roswitha. "Learning for a New Society: The *Lehrstück*." In *The Cambridge Companion to Brecht*, ed. P. Thomson and G. Sacks, 101–17. Cambridge: Cambridge University Press, 2006.

Mulvey, Laura. "Visual Pleasure and Narrative Cinema." In *Feminism and Film Theory*, ed. Constance Penley, 57–68. New York: Routledge, 1988.

Musser, Charles. "Towards a History of Theatrical Culture: Imagining an Integrated History of Stage and Screen." In *Screen Culture: History and Textuality*, Stockholm Studies in Cinema 3, ed. John Fullerton, 3–20. Eastleigh: John Libbey, 2004.

Nägele, Rainer. "Peter Handke: Aspekte eines experimentellen Theaters." *Colloquia Germanica* 14, no. 3 (1981): 220–28.

Nägele, Rainer. "Peter Handke: The Staging of Language." *Modern Drama* 23, no. 4 (Winter 1980): 327–38.

Negt, Oskar, and Alexander Kluge. *Public Sphere and Experience: Toward an Analysis of the Bourgeois and Proletarian Public Sphere*. Trans. Peter Labanyi, Jamie Owen Daniel, and Assenka Oksiloff. London: Verso, 2016.

Nirvana. *MTV Unplugged in New York*. Geffen: DGCD-24727, 1994.

Niver, Kemp R. *Early Motion Pictures: The Paper Print Collection in the Library of Congress*. Ed. Bebe Bergsten. Washington, DC: Library of Congress, 1985.

Noland, Carrie. *Poetry at Stake: Lyric Aesthetics and the Challenge of Technology*. Princeton, NJ: Princeton University Press, 1999.

North, Michael. *Machine-Age Comedy*. Oxford: Oxford University Press, 2009.

Notfilm: A Kino Essay. Dir. and written by Ross Lipman. With Kevin Brownlow, Walter Karen, James Knowlson, Jeannette Seaver, and Billie Whitelaw. Milestone, 2016. DVD.

Offizielle deutsche Charts. Accessed July 11, 2024, https://www.offiziellecharts.de.

Olf, Julian M. "The Play as a Moving Picture: Toward a Phenomenology of Theatre." PhD diss., New York University, 1971.

Oliver, Edith. "The Theatre: Off Broadway." *New Yorker*, June 27, 1983, 75.

Oliver, Kelly. "The Look of Love." *Hypatia* 16, no. 3 (Summer 2001): 56–78.

Orgel, Stephen. *The Illusion of Power: Political Theater in the English Renaissance.* Berkeley: University of California Press, 1975.

Ovid. *Metamorphoses.* Trans. Charles Martin. New York: Norton, 2004.

Owens, Craig N. "Applause and Hiss: Implicating the Audience in Samuel Beckett's *Rockaby* and *Catastrophe*." *Journal of the Midwest Modern Language Association* 36, no. 1 (2003): 74–81.

"Palace Theater: Edward Albee's Showplace on Playhouse Square." Accessed July 17, 2024. https://clevelandhistorical.org/items/show/246.

Panofsky, Erwin. *Three Essays on Style.* Ed. Irving Lavin. Cambridge, MA: MIT Press, 1995.

Parker, Andrew, and Eve Kosofsky Sedgwick, ed. and intro. *Performativity and Performance.* Essays from the English Institute. London: Routledge, 1995.

Parks, Suzan-Lori. Interview with Adrienne Kennedy. *Bomb*, January 1, 1996. https://bombmagazine.org/articles/1996/01/01/adrienne-kennedy/.

Pasquier, Sylvain du. "Buster Keaton's Gags." Ed. and trans. Norman Silverstein. *Journal of Modern Literature* 3, no. 2 (April 1973): 269–91.

Pedullà, Gabriele. *In Broad Daylight: Movies and Spectators after the Cinema.* Trans. Patricia Gaborik. London: Verso, 2012.

Peymann, Claus. "Directing Handke." Trans. Claus Brucher-Herpel. *Drama Review* 16, no. 2 (1972): 48–54.

Phelan, Peggy. "Performance, Live Culture, and Things of the Heart: Peggy Phelan in Conversation with Marquard Smith," *Journal of Visual Culture* 2, no. 3 (2003): 291–302.

Phelan, Peggy. *Unmarked: The Politics of Performance.* New York: Routledge, 1993.

Pompe, Anja. *Peter Handke: Pop als poetisches Prinzip.* Cologne: Böhlau, 2009.

Post, Tina. *Deadpan: The Aesthetics of Black Inexpression.* New York: New York University Press, 2022.

Powdermaker, Hortense. *Hollywood, the Dream Factory: An Anthropologist Looks at the Movie-Makers.* Boston: Little, Brown, 1950.

Puchner, Martin. *Stage Fright: Modernism, Anti-Theatricality, and Drama.* Baltimore, MD: Johns Hopkins University Press, 2002.

Rancière, Jacques. "The Emancipated Spectator." In *The Emancipated Spectator*, trans. Gregory Elliott, 1–23. London: Verso, 2009.

Rancière, Jacques. *The Ignorant Schoolmaster.* Trans. Kristin Ross. Stanford, CA: Stanford University Press, 1991.

Rapcsak, Balazs, Mark Nixon, and Philipp Schweighauser, eds. *Beckett and Media.* Manchester: Manchester University Press, 2022.

Reed, Adolph. *The South: Jim Crow and Its Afterlives.* London: Verso, 2022.

Retman, Sonnet. *Real Folks: Race and Genre in the Great Depression.* Durham, NC: Duke University Press, 2011.

Ricks, Christopher. *Beckett's Dying Words*. Oxford: Clarendon Press, 1993.

Ridout, Nicholas. *Passionate Amateurs: Theatre, Communism and Love*. Ann Arbor: University of Michigan Press, 2013.

Ridout, Nicholas. *Scenes from Bourgeois Life*. Ann Arbor: University of Michigan Press, 2020.

Ridout, Nicholas. *Stage Fright, Animals, and Other Theatrical Problems*. Cambridge: Cambridge University Press, 2006.

Ridout, Nicholas. *Theatre & Ethics*. Houndmills: Palgrave Macmillan, 2009.

Robinson, Cedric J. *Forgeries of Memory and Meaning: Blacks and the Regimes of Race in American Theater and Film before World War II*. Chapel Hill: University of North Carolina Press, 2007.

Rodenbeck, Judith F. *Radical Prototypes: Allan Kaprow and the Invention of Happenings*. Cambridge, MA: MIT Press, 2011.

Ros, Xon de. "Cinema." In *A Companion to Federico García Lorca*. Ed. Federico Bonaddio. Woodbridge: Tamesis, 2007.

Rosen, Philip, ed. *Narrative, Apparatus, Ideology*. New York: Columbia University Press, 1986.

Rosenberg, Bernard, and David Manning White, ed. *Mass Culture: The Popular Arts in America*. Glencoe, IL: The Free Press & The Falcon's Wing Press, 1957.

Ross, Andrew. *No Respect: Intellectuals and Popular Culture*. New York: Routledge, 1989.

Ross, Kristin. *Fast Cars, Clean Bodies: Decolonization and the Reordering of French Culture*. Cambridge, MA: MIT Press, 1996.

Sartre, Jean-Paul. *Being and Nothingness*. 1943. Trans. Hazel E. Barnes. New York: Washington Square Press, 1992.

Savran, David. *Communists, Cowboys, and Queers: The Politics of Masculinity in the Work of Arthur Miller and Tennessee Williams*. Minneapolis: University of Minnesota Press, 1992.

Savran, David. *Highbrow/Lowdown: Theater, Jazz, and the Making of the New Middle Class*. Ann Arbor: University of Michigan Press, 2009.

Schallert, Edwin. "Sex Problems Tormented in 'Orpheus Descending.'" *Los Angeles Times*, November 6, 1957.

Schechner, Richard. "The New Look." *Tulane Drama Review* 11, no. 1 (1966): 22–23.

Schechner, Richard. "Who's Afraid of Edward Albee?" *Tulane Drama Review* 7, no. 3 (1963): 7–10.

Schlueter, June. *The Plays and Novels of Peter Handke*. Pittsburgh, PA: University of Pittsburgh Press, 1981.

Schlusberg, Julian S. *Letters from the Prophets: A Theater Teacher's Memoir*. New York: Author's Choice Press, 2001.

Schnapp, Jeffrey T. "Border Crossings: Italian/German Peregrinations of the *Theater of Totality*." *Critical Inquiry* 21, no. 1 (Autumn 1994): 80–123.

Schnapp, Jeffrey T. *Staging Fascism: 18 BL and the Theater of Masses for Masses*. Stanford, CA: Stanford University Press, 1996.

Schneider, Alan. "On Directing *Film*," In Samuel Beckett, *Film*, 63–94. New York: Grove, 1969.

Schneider, Rebecca. *Performing Remains: Art and War in Times of Theatrical Reenactment*. London: Routledge, 2011.

BIBLIOGRAPHY > 281

Schwab, Gabriele. *Moments for Nothing: Samuel Beckett and the End Times.* New York: Columbia University Press, 2023.

Seibert, Peter, ed. *Samuel Beckett und die Medien: Neue Perspektiven auf einen Medienkünstler des 20. Jahrhunderts.* Bielefeld: Transcript, 2008.

Seldes, George. *The Great Audience.* New York, Viking Press, 1950.

Sellar, Tom. "Theater Director with a Filmmaker's Eye." *New York Times,* November 28, 2008.

Sennett, Richard. *The Fall of Public Man.* London: Faber, 1986.

Shaw, George Bernard. *Heartbreak House* [1919.]. London: Penguin, 2000.

Singer, Ben. *Melodrama and Modernity: Early Sensational Cinema and Its Contexts.* New York: Columbia University Press, 2001.

Smith, Michael. Introduction. In *Eight Plays from Off-Off Broadway.* Ed. Nick Orzel and Smith. Indianapolis, IN: Bobbs-Merrill, 1966.

Smith, Russell, ed. *Beckett and Ethics.* London: Continuum, 2008.

Sontag, Susan. "Film and Theatre." *Tulane Drama Review* 11, no. 1 (Autumn 1966): 24–37.

Spencer, Jenny. "Emancipated Spectatorship in Adrienne Kennedy's Plays." *Modern Drama* 55, no. 1 (2012): 19–39.

Stalin, Joseph. Speech of February 9, 1946. In *The Strategy and Tactics of World Communism.* Washington, DC: Government Printing Office, 1948.

Stam, Robert. *Reflexivity in Film and Literature: From Don Quixote to Jean-Luc Godard.* New York: Columbia University Press, 1992.

Stans, Lea. "In Memory of Buster and Eleanor's House." *Silent-ology,* December 6, 2020. https://silentology.wordpress.com/2020/12/06/in-memory-of-buster-and -eleanors-house/.

A Star Is Born. Dir. George Cukor. With Judy Garland and James Mason. 1954.

Starobinski, Jean. *Jean-Jacques Rousseau: Transparency and Obstruction.* Trans. Arthur Goldhammer. Chicago: University of Chicago Press, 1988.

States, Bert O. "*Catastrophe*: Beckett's Laboratory/Theatre." *Modern Drama* 30, no. 1 (1987): 14–22.

States, Bert O. *Great Reckonings in Little Rooms: On the Phenomenology of Theater.* Berkeley: University of California Press, 1985.

Stewart, Jacqueline Najuma. *Migrating to the Movies: Cinema and Black Urban Modernity.* Berkeley: University of California Press, 2005.

Stewart, Jacqueline Najuma. "Negroes Laughing at Themselves?: Black Spectatorship and the Performance of Urban Modernity." *Critical Inquiry* 29, no. 4 (2003): 650–77.

Stoehr, Taylor. "Paul Goodman, the Living Theater, and the Great Despair." *Theater* 21, nos. 1 and 2 (1990): 17–22.

Strauss, Neil. *Radiotext(e).* New York: Semiotext(e), 1993.

"'A Streetcar Named Desire': Tennessee Williams Has Written the Broadway Season's Best New Play." *Life.* December 15, 1947, 101–4.

Szanto, George H. *Theater and Propaganda.* Austin: University of Texas Press, 1978.

Terada, Rei. *Looking Away: Phenomenality and Dissatisfaction, Kant to Adorno.* Cambridge, MA: Harvard University Press, 2009.

Turner, Fred. *The Democratic Surround: Multimedia and American Liberalism from World War II to the Psychedelic Sixties.* Chicago: University of Chicago Press, 2013.

"Two Bands Please Local Bugs; Cootie and Satchmo Grade A." *Cleveland Call and Post,* September 16, 1944: 11.

Tyler, Parker. Review of *The Fugitive Kind*. *Film Quarterly* 13, no. 4 (Summer 1960): 47–49.

Van Hulle, Dirk, and Mark Nixon. *Samuel Beckett's Library*. Cambridge: Cambridge University Press, 2013.

Van Hulle, Dirk, and Shane Weller. *The Making of Samuel Beckett's* Fin de partie/Endgame. Beckett Digital Manuscript Project 7. London: Bloomsbury, 2018.

Vardac, A. Nicholas. *Stage to Screen: Theatrical Method from Garrick to Griffith*. Cambridge, MA: Harvard University Press, 1949.

Vidal, Gore. *Palimpsest: A Memoir*. New York: Random House, 1995.

Vogel, Shane. "Waiting for Godot and the Racial Theater of the Absurd." *PMLA* 137, no. 1, (2022): 19–35.

Voigts-Virchow, Eckart. *Mediated Drama/Dramatized Media*. Contemporary Drama in English, vol. 7. Trier: WVT Wissenschaftlicher Verlag Trier, 2000.

von Herrman, Hans-Christian. "Stimmbilding: Zum Verhältnis von Theater- und Mediengeschichte." *MLN* 120 (2005): 620–32.

Vos, Erik. "*Prometheus* as Total Theatre: Production Notes." *Educational Theatre Journal* (1970): 19–34.

Walsh, Martin. *The Brechtian Aspect of Radical Cinema*. London: British Film Institute Publishing, 1981.

Warner, Michael. *Publics and Counterpublics*. New York: Zone Books, 2005.

Washburn, Anne. *Mr. Burns and Other Plays*. New York: Theatre Communications Group, 2017.

Wasser, Audrey. "A Relentless Spinozism: Deleuze's Encounter with Beckett." *SubStance* 41, no. 1 (2012): 124–36.

Weber, Samuel. *Mass Mediauras: Form, Technics, Media*. Ed. Alan Cholodenko. Stanford, CA: Stanford University Press, 1996.

Weber, Samuel. *Theatricality as Medium*. New York: Fordham University Press, 2004.

Weiss, Allen S. *Phantasmic Radio*. Durham, NC: Duke University Press, 1995.

Wicke, Jennifer. *Advertising Fictions: Literature, Advertisement, and Social Reading*. New York: Columbia University Press, 1988.

Wild at Heart. Directed by David Lynch. With Nicholas Cage and Laura Dern. 1990.

Wilderson, Frank B., III. "Grammar & Ghosts: The Performative Limits of African Freedom." *Theatre Survey* 50, no. 1 (2009): 119–25.

Wilderson, Frank B., III. *Red, White & Black: Cinema and the Structure of US Antagonisms*. Durham, NC: Duke University Press, 2010.

Wilke, Tobias. "Tacti(ca)lity Reclaimed: Benjamin's Medium, the Avant-Garde, and the Politics of the Senses." *Grey Room* 39, Walter Benjamin's Media Tactics: Optics, Perception, and the Work of Art (Spring 2010): 39–56.

Willett, John. *The Theatre of Erwin Piscator: Half a Century of Politics in the Theatre*. New York: Holmes and Meier, 1979.

Williams, Carolyn. "Moving Pictures: George Eliot and Melodrama." In *Compassion: The Culture and Politics of an Emotion*, ed. Lauren Berlant, 105–44. London: Routledge, 2004.

Williams, Jaye Austin. "Staging (within) Violence: A Conversation with Frank Wilderson and Jaye Austin Williams." *Rhizomes: Cultural Studies in Emerging Knowledge* 29 (2016).

Williams, Raymond. "Drama in a Dramatized Society." In Williams, *Writing in Society*, ed. Jim McGuigan, 161–71. London: Verso, 1991.

BIBLIOGRAPHY > 283

Williams, Raymond. *Politics and Letters: Interviews with the New Left Review*. London: Verso, 1979.

Williams, Raymond, and Michael Orrom. *Preface to Film*. London: Film Drama, 1954.

Williams, Tennessee. *Collected Poems*. Ed. David Roessel and Nicholas Moschovakis. New York: New Directions, 2002.

Williams, Tennessee. *Fugitive Kind*. Ed. Allean Hale. New York: New Directions, 2001.

Williams, Tennessee. *Memoirs*. New York: New Directions, 1975.

Williams, Tennessee. *Orpheus Descending*. New York: Dramatists Play Service, 1959.

Williams, Tennessee. *Plays 1937–1955*. New York: Library of America, 2000.

Williams, Tennessee. *Plays 1957–1980*. New York: Library of America, 2000.

Williams, Tennessee. *A Streetcar Named Desire*. Intro. Arthur Miller. New York: New Directions, 2004.

Wittgenstein, Ludwig. *Philosophical Investigations*. 3rd ed. Trans. G. E. Anscombe. New York: Macmillan, 1958.

Wizisla, Erdmut. *Walter Benjamin and Bertolt Brecht: The Story of a Friendship*. Trans. Christine Shuttleworth. London: Verso, 2016.

Wolfe, Charles K., and Kip Lornell. *The Life and Legend of Leadbelly*. New York: HarperCollins, 1992.

Wollen, Peter, "On Gaze Theory." *New Left Review* 91 (March–April 2007): 91–106.

Young, Harvey, and Megan Geigner. "A Racial Concern: Adrienne Kennedy's *Diary of Lights*." *Modern Drama* 55, no. 1 (2012): 40–54.

Youngblood, Gene. *Expanded Cinema*. Intro. R. Buckminster Fuller. New York: Dutton, 1970.

Zilliacus, Clas. *Beckett and Broadcasting: A Study of the Works of Samuel Beckett for and in Radio and Television*. Acta Academiae Aboensis, ser. A, vol. 51, no. 2. Abo: Abo Akademi, 1976.

Zischler, Hanns. *Kafka Goes to the Movies*. Trans. Susan H. Gillespie. Chicago: University of Chicago Press, 2003.

Žižek, Slavoj. *The Sublime Object of Ideology*. London: Verso, 1989.

Zolotow, Sam. "'Village' to Get an Unusual Show; 'Flickadisc' to Happen Nights at Circle in the Square." *New York Times*, May 25, 1966.

Index

Abel, Lionel, 26, 197

abstraction, 8, 15, 19, 30, 94, 258–59; Black, 225; and commodities, 105; in painting, 75; technologies of, 96, 160

absurdism, 76; and Beckett, 155, 258n1; *The Theatre of the Absurd* (Esslin), 74–76

Ackerman, Alan, 161n22

actors: "actor/audience" system, 60; Artaud on, 93; in Beckett, 1, 191, 196–98, 207–8; Benjamin on, 34–37, 206; Brecht on, 39–40, 56–60; Diderot on, 204–5; Esslin on, 74–75; Handke on, 97–108, 155; in Kennedy, 242–46, 249; Malina on, 66; in Shakespeare, 196; Michael Smith on, 201; stage vs. screen, 34–37; Wilderson on, 231. *See also* Blackness

Adorno, Theodor, 44, 206; *Aesthetic Theory*, 45–46, 47, 48, 206; on Beckett, 76n36, 179n2, 210; and Benjamin, 31, 56; and Bloch, 48; and Brecht, 56–57, 179n2; on cinema, 22, 42, 225; *Dialectic of Enlightenment*, 130n3, 194; and Esslin, 76n36; and Hegel, 47–48; and Heidegger, 194; and the Holocaust, 50; and Horkheimer, 22, 130n3, 194; Huyssen on, 45; *In Search of Wagner*, 45; *Lectures*, 47–48; on mass media, 45, 50; *Minima Moralia*, 2, 42, 43–44, 45–47, 49–50, 225; on negation, 22, 43, 47–48, 95; and theater, 43–44, 95; and "timeliness," 44; Fred Turner on, 50

advertising, 24n14, 144, 171, 220; language of, 118, 152, 215; and literature, 80–81, 214–22

aesthetics, 17, 31n1, 185n20; abstractionist, 225; of attention, 105; Baraka's, 83; Beckett's, 46, 158n13; Buck-Morss on, 31n1; Wittgenstein's, 83. *See also* Adorno, Theodor

Afro-pessimism, 231

Albee, Edward, 239, 239n12; grandfather of, 24n14; *Who's Afraid of Virginia Woolf?*, 71n26, 239n14

alienation, 73, 81–82, 83, 199, 202, 230

allegory, 8n1, 153, 217, 258–59; Barthes on, 153–54; and Plato, 22; for radio, 89; in *Sunset Blvd.*, 163

Althusser, Louis, 26

Anderson, Benedict, 95

anonymity: of audience, 29, 142–43; in Beckett, 220–22; Rancière on, 61

apparatus, 26–27; and Adorno, 45; and Beckett, 177, 182, 192, 197, 203–4, 222; and Benjamin, 38–40; and Brecht, 39, 55–58, 62, 205; cinematic, 21–22, 24, 29, 36, 166; critique of, 47; and Debord, 62–64; and Foucault, 188; Hollywood, 27, 227; ideological, 26–27, 70, 202; and Keaton, 165, 169, 175; and Kennedy, 27, 234, 252n15; and Krauss, 165; mass cultural, 106, 130, 177, 230, 244; negation and, 200; "one-way," 63; proscenium as, 201–2, 204–6; public sphere as, 94–96; and radio, 56; of scholarly book, 1–2; spectacular, 213; theatrical, 64, 95, 186, 189, 206 applause, 180–82

Apter, Emily, 188

architecture: and Beckett, 202, 207; and Benjamin, 206; and Foucault, 188; racial dimensions of, 227, 250; theatrical, 202, 205–7. *See also* proscenium

archives, theater as, 143, 237

Arsić, Branka, 160

Artaud, Antonin, 85–93, 251; and Brecht, 61–62, 77; *The Conquest of Mexico*, 83; Eck on, 86; and Malina, 73; and Miller, 88; Rancière on, 61–62; theater of cruelty, 82; *The Theatre and Its Double*, 86; *To have done with the judgment of god*, 85–86, 87–88, 90–93. *See also* audience(s); radio

attendance, 196; as ritual, 107n26

attention: "fatalistic," in Beckett, 198–99; in Handke, 98, 101, 103, 105

audience(s), 61–84, 160; and Artaud, 86, 90–92; Auslander on, 198; Baraka on, 83; Barthes on, 153–54; and Beckett, 29, 153–78, 179–89, 190–200, 201–13, 214, 221–22; and Benjamin, 35–36, 205–6; and Brecht, 57–59, 205–6; British, 216; camera as, 34; Cavell on, 196; cinema and, 24–25, 35–36, 52, 118, 153–78, 248; Debord on, 63–64; Esslin on, 75–76; Grotowski on, 74; and Handke, 97–108; and happenings, 64; history of, 60, 61–62, 64; "inspection of," in Beckett, 192, 195–97; Kennedy and, 225, 232, 235, 240; Kenner on, 198; Living Theatre and, 64, 72–73, 77n39 (*see also* Malina, Judith); moviegoing and, 24–25; Panofsky on, 48; and profit, 39; proscenium and, 201–13; and race, 140–41, 225, 235; Rancière on, 63–64; Schechner on, 78, 80; Fred Turner on, 50; understanding of, 7n2; and Williams, 115, 139, 144, 145–46. *See also* Blackness; spectacle

aura: Adorno on, 44; Benjamin on, 32–38; and cinema, 35–37, 41; Hansen on, 31n1, 34–35; and theater, 37–38

Auslander, Philip, 9, 11–12, 14, 198

authenticity: American, 140; *Echtheit*, 31; and Greenberg, 158–59; jargon of, 143; and kitsch, 130–31; and truth, 117

author: and Beckett, 199, 204–5; Benjamin on, 38–39, 55, 189; effects of adaptation on, 111; Handke on, 99; in Kennedy, 240, 245, 247–53

autobiography. *See* Kennedy, Adrienne

autographs, 136, 139–40, 247n3

avant-gardes: and Broadway, 65, 83; and kitsch, 159n15; in the 1960s, 64, 83, 251n12; in the 1970s, 238n10, 251n12; and theater, 12, 22–23, 74, 81, 153

Baldwin, James, 244n26

ballad, 142–43

Baraka, Amiri (LeRoi Jones): on art, 83; Isaac on, 206; and Kennedy, 237

Barrault, Jean-Louis, 72, 73

Barthes, Roland: on Beckett, 153–54; on Brecht, 22n8; and cameras, 174; and Kennedy, 241; and Kenner, 198; *Mythologies*, 130n3, 241

Baudrillard, Jean, 80, 186

Baudry, Jean-Louis, 22

Bay-Cheng, Sarah, 4n1, 19n14

Beatles, 101

Beck, Julian, 146n48; and Broadway, 66

Beckett, Samuel: *Catastrophe*, 1, 179–89; *Endgame*, 46n13, 76n36, 172, 179n2, 190–200, 202–3, 208–13, 214–22; *Endgame*, French text (*Fin de partie*), 193n6, 195n13, 199, 209, 211–12, 216; *Endgame*, German text (*Endspiel*), 199n16, 203n6, 209, 211; *Film*, 28, 151–52, 153–78; *Happy Days*, 151, 211; *Krapp's Last Tape*, 174; *Molloy*, 216–17; *Nacht und Träume*, 179; *Not I*, 202; *Ohio Impromptu*, 1; *Play*, 160–61, 218–22; *Play*, French (*Comédie*) and German (*Spiel*) texts, 219–20; *Quad*, 179; *Waiting for Godot*, 152, 153–54, 157, 178, 188, 198, 203, 207, 258–59; *Waiting for Godot*, French text (*En attendant Godot*), 178; *What Where*, 1

Bel Geddes, Barbara, 232

Benjamin, Walter, 184, 206; "The Author as Producer," 38–39, 55, 189; *One-Way*

Street, 2; "The Work of Art," 31–40, 41–51, 56–57, 163, 189, 211n24, 249
Bergman, Ingrid, 232, 247n3
Berkeley, George, 160, 175, 177–78. *See also* perceptions
Bersani, Leo, 105n15, 123n19, 179n2, 200
Blackness, 157n11, 147; and abstraction, 225; Afro-pessimism, 231; appropriation or representation of, 137, 142n37, 147, 225n2, 232, 243, 248, 251; audiences, 24, 227, 230–32; Black studies, 147; Hall on, 232; inferiorization of, 230; and Jim Crow, 233, 247; and Keaton, 157n11; and law, 147; marginalized characters, 131–32, 244, 248; mass culture of, 146; and music, 130–32, 140–41, 146, 148; Parks on, 227–28; performers, 136, 139, 148, 237, 244; and racial authenticity, 131; and racist violence, 134, 145; Reed on, 247; of writers and playwrights, 228n4, 237. *See also* Kennedy, Adrienne
Blake, William, 116
Blau, Herbert: "atmosphere" and "counter-atmosphere," 67–68, 72, 74, 83; on illusion, 69–70; *The Impossible Theater*, 67–68, 71; and Malina, 72–73; on mass culture, 67–68, 71; on mystification, 67–68, 70, 76; and Niebuhr, 69; and power, 71, 73; and theatrical history, 68–69; and Peter Weiss, 76
Blin, Roger, 157
Bloom, Claire, 126–27
blues, 132, 139n29, 140, 142–43
Bolter, Jay David, 16–17, 103
Bordwell, David, 234–35
Bottoms, Stephen, 71–72
bourgeois: apparatus of production and publication, 55; art, 45; audiences, 185n20, 198; era, 44; subject, 207; theater, 57, 107, 185, 198, 205, 207, 219
Bowles, Paul, 142
Brando, Marlon: as actor, 114, 116–17, 129; in *The Fugitive Kind* (Lumet), 147; Kennedy and, 242, 248, 253; Williams and, 143

Brecht, Bertolt: and Benjamin, 39–40, 55–56; *Die Maßnahme*, 59n21; *Galileo*, 57, 70, 194; *The Measures Taken*, 57–60; "The Radio as a Communications Apparatus," 55–56
Bresson, Robert, 104–5
Brewster, Ben, 5n2, 15–16, 56
bricolage, 138
broadcast: Artaud and, 85–93, 251; audiences, 92, 197; Beckett and, 156n6; Brecht and, 56, 156n6; as distribution vs. communication, 56, 67, 99; and embodiment, 86; *Emergency Broadcasting* (Miller), 88; and gramophones, 54; indiscriminate, 56, 234; as media, 56, 137, 180; and race, 234; radio and television, 28, 85–93; telephones (Budapest), 14
Broadway, 6–7, 13, 21n5, 236; Baraka on, 83; and Hollywood, 65–66; Isaac on, 206; Malina on, 65–66; Michael Smith on, 201; Williams and, 49, 118, 139n29, 146. *See also* Off-Broadway
Buck-Morss, Susan, 31n1

camera: as actor, 35, 161, 165; as audience, 34; and Beckett, 161, 164, 171–75; "Camera Men" (North), 165, 171; in *The Fugitive Kind* (Lumet), 147; and Keaton, 170, 174–75; as mediation, 38; redemptive (Kracauer), 104; and time-lapse techniques, 6
Camus, Albert, 76
canons, 28, 105n15, 138–40
capital: anticapitalism, 10; and art, 31; and audiences, 91; in Beckett, 153; capitalism, 153; and Hollywood, 21; and mass media (Brecht), 55; and painting, 17; and photographic reproduction, 11; and race, 230
Carné, Marcel, 204
casting. *See* Blackness
categories: "border," 185n20; mass vs. first culture, 151, 234; as reification, 141–42; of seeing, 213
Cavell, Stanley, 11n9, 20, 179n2, 196–97
Certeau, Michel de, 106
Chaikin, Joseph, 237–39, 243

288 < INDEX

Chan, Paul, 258
Chaplin, Charlie, 81, 157
characters: in Beckett, 151, 171, 192; and
  cinema, 151–52; and gender, 115–16;
  in Handke, 107, 245n27; and Keaton,
  167–68; in Kennedy, 227–29, 248, 254;
  and race, 131–32, 139, 145; in Williams,
  112, 115–16, 123, 124n22, 131, 139. *See
  also* Blackness
children: in Artaud, 87; and naming, 256;
  vulnerability of, 123n19
Children of Paradise (Carné), 204
choreography, 134, 175
cinematography, 104, 105n15; and
  Beckett, 163n30; of Kaufman, 164
Cixous, Hélène, 229
class: in Brecht, 55, 205; "high," 43, 45, 49;
  "low" (in Beckett), 178n58; middle, 140;
  and race, 230; working, 60, 92, 230
Classical Theater of Harlem, 258
Clift, Montgomery, 242, 244, 248, 253
clowns, 155
Cobain, Kurt, 147n52
Cobb, Lee J., 102
Cold War, 21n7, 68–71, 89
collaborations, 77n39, 87, 157, 258
Columbia Pictures, 241–44, 252
comedy: and gender, 168; and Keaton,
  174n52; *Machine-Age Comedy* (North),
  157
consciousness: in art (Adorno), 45;
  in Beckett, 49, 176; of cinema,
  52; "consciousness industry"
  (Enzensberger), 160; in Kluge, 94; in
  Lefebvre, 82; public, 75; saturation
  by film, 42, 154; self-consciousness
  (Enelow), 116; in Williams, 49
continuities: in Diderot, 205;
  discontinuities of books, 2; in editing
  (Bordwell), 235; intellectual, 10n4; in
  theater and media, 97, 185, 208
contradictions: and alienation, 202; of
  American culture, 225; in Beckett,
  164, 184; in Brecht, 57, 81–82; in
  drama, 226; in Kennedy, 243, 248; in
  Lehrstück, 60; in mass culture, 130;
  and the proscenium, 201; in Williams,
  113, 127, 133

conventions: and absurdism, 76;
  audiences as, 196–97; Bazin on, 104;
  in Beckett, 161, 186, 192, 203, 220–22;
  bourgeois, 57; comparative, 29; in
  Handke, 98, 107–8; in Kennedy, 249;
  new, 79; in realism, 187; theatrical, 57,
  101, 108, 203–4
copyright, 6, 240
counterpublics: *Publics and
  Counterpublics* (Warner), 91–92, 95;
  and Williams, 130–48
crafts, 66n14
Crawford, Joan, 228, 232, 244n26
crises: in Benjamin, 32–33, 36–37, 39;
  in Blau, 68–69; in Brecht, 70–71; in
  Greenberg, 158
Critchley, Simon, 160, 163n29
criticism: of Albee, 71; and Adorno, 42,
  47, 50; and Barthes, 154; of Beckett,
  153–54, 158–61, 176–77, 198; and
  Brecht, 57, 205; and Bürger, 64; of
  film as "hypnotic" or "hegemonic,"
  21; of film vs. theater, 57; and the
  Frankfurt School, 31; and Godard, 105;
  and intermediation, 4; and Kenner,
  198; and "metatheater" (Abel), 26;
  as resistance to spectatorship, 230;
  and status of theater, 9; of theater as a
  medium, 20
Cukor, George, 204

Dadaism, 65
dance, 78, 254
Davis, Bette, 228, 239n14, 241–43, 246,
  251–52
death: in Beckett, 218; in Benjamin,
  35–36; "The Death of the Proscenium
  Stage" (Isaac), 206; in Kennedy,
  227, 249; language of, 191–92; and
  resurrection, 133; of theater, 37, 74; in
  Williams, 136
Debord, Guy, 62–64, 212–13
decades: early twentieth century, 24, 75;
  early twenty-first century, 225; 1920s,
  14, 54, 175; 1930s, 24, 33, 41, 43, 54, 57–
  58, 59n21, 88, 139n27, 143; 1940s, 24,
  33, 46, 143, 230; 1950s, 23, 27, 73, 77,
  138, 144, 160, 197; 1960s, 20, 23; 1970s,

4, 10, 13, 21, 23, 27, 237, 238n10; 1990s, 9, 143n41; postwar, 5, 12, 30, 43
defamiliarization, 208, 242
Deleuze, Gilles, 160
Demy, Jacques, 255
detournement, 106, 226
dialectics: Adorno and, 43–44, 194; and Beckett, 158, 186; Benjamin and, 33, 40, 184; Brecht and, 57, 82, 186, 199; Bürger and, 64; film vs. theater, 158; and folk revival, 139; and the Frankfurt School, 31; Handke and, 98, 103; and Kennedy, 226; Lefebvre and, 82; of love and theft (Lott), 141; Rodenbeck on, 64; and sound, 184; and theater, 28; *Verfremdungseffekt*, 82; Peter Weiss and, 76; Williams and, 82, 130, 143
Diamond, Elin, 69n22, 228–29
Diawara, Manthia, 230, 232n14
Diderot, Denis, 204, 205
diegesis, 168, 184
dismediation. *See* remediation
dissemination: mass, 62, 75, 89, 135, 160, 259; and radio, 56, 89; vs. representation, 186; and the spectacle, 62; and theater, 75
documentary theater, 76–78
drafts: of Kennedy's plays, 239, 241, 254n1; of Williams's plays, 130n1, 142
dramaturgy: of Beckett, 28, 208, 219; Brechtian, 40, 70, 81, 82; of the Living Theatre, 77; of Williams, 123
dreams: and Artaud, 86; cinematic, 65, 204; as compensation, 169; Elsaesser on, 177; as escape, 82; "Hollywood dream factory," 26; and Keaton, 166–69; mass culture as dream or nightmare (Adorno), 45, 234
Dutoit, Ulysse, 105n15, 179, 200

effects: in Beckett, 197; Brechtian, 197; of detournement/mediation in reverse, 226; filmic, 7, 16, 19; of Hollywood, 227; of naming, 256; of newer media, 111; psychic, of film, 21; sound, 83; in theater, 39, 65, 82, 207; uncanny, 251
Eisenstein, Sergei, 163n30, 170
Eliot, T. S., 135

Elsaesser, Thomas, 16n4, 177
Enelow, Shonni, 116, 117–18, 122, 233n1
environmental theater, 206
Enzensberger, Hans Magnus, 160
Epic Theater: in Benjamin, 39–40, 206; in Brecht, 205n10
eroticism, 61, 71, 84, 115, 124, 253
esotericism, 34, 75
Esslin, Martin, 74–76, 156n6
estrangement: in Beckett, 259; and bourgeois theater, 205; in Pirandello, 35; of time, 59
exclusion, 217, 229–30, 253, 255
existentialism, 76n36, 175–76. *See also* Sartre, Jean-Paul
expressionism, 65
eye: in Beckett, 161, 178, 185; of camera, 161, 165, 173; evil, 177n56; Keaton's, 169–70; Wittgensteinian, 106. *See also* gaze

faith: in God, 177; in others' humanity, 246; in perception, 177; in progress, 33n6
fandom, 106
fascism: Adorno on, 45, 50; anti-, 139n29; Benjamin on, 36, 38; and film, 42; and Guthrie, 138; and "one-to-many" media, 51; and publics, 21; Schnapp on, 52
Faust, Gretchen, 10n5
feminisms, 10, 175. *See also* Cixous, Hélène; Mulvey, Laura
festivals: film, 28; Shakespeare Festival (NYC), 236, 243, 250n10
Filene, Benjamin, 138n23, 140–41
Fischer, Ernst, 160n17
folk: counterpublic, 140; folkways, 106; and mass culture, 143; music, 139, 142–43; opera, 142; verse, 142–43
Foucault, Michel, 176–77, 188–89, 201n1
Frank, Johanna, 254n1
Frankfurt School, 31. *See also* Adorno, Theodor; Horkheimer, Max
Freedgood, Elaine, 214n2
Freedman, Jonathan, 142
Fried, Michael, 20–21, 78–79, 159n15, 204n8

Fuchs, Elinor, 251n12
Fugitive Kind, The (Lumet), 130n2, 147;
and Elvis, 132n9; as a phrase, 131, 145–
46; reception, 143. *See also* Williams,
Tennessee: (*The*) *Fugitive Kind*
Fuss, Diana, 228n5, 255

Gable, Clark, 239n12
gags, 166–69, 169n40
Gauguin, Paul, 13
gaze: in Beckett, 160, 162, 170–71; filmic,
232; Keaton's, 170; male, 115; Melville
on, 175–76; of the Other, 176; Sartre's,
175–76; Wollen on, 176n55. *See also*
eye
Geis, Deborah R., 252n15
gendering: ambiguous, 88; of audiences,
24, 169; and Blau, 71; Hansen on, 24;
and Keaton, 168; Mulvey on, 102; and
race, 24, 232n14; and Sartre, 175; and
Schaulust, 102; Stewart on, 24; in
Williams, 115, 128
Genet, Jean, 71n26
genocide, 50, 102, 191
genre: and authenticity, 143; in Beckett,
160, 227, 235; Grotowski on, 74; in
Kennedy, 227, 235; Sontag on, 79; in
Williams, 112–13, 227
gestures: Adorno on, 45–46, 48; Apter
on, 188–89; in Beckett, 46, 181, 186–
89; in Handke, 102; in Keaton, 165,
173; literary, 1–2; in Shaw, 53; in silent
films, 53; utopian, 146
ghosts, in Kennedy, 227–28
Gilroy, Paul, 131
Gitelman, Lisa, 14–15
glossolalia, 90
Godard, Jean-Luc, 27, 105
Gontarski, S. E., 172n47, 199, 210n23
Goodbye, Dragon Inn (Tsai), 8n1
Goodman, Paul, 66n14, 72, 77
Gourgouris, Stathis, 57n16
Grahame, Gloria, 232
gramophones, 53–54
Grant, Cary, 117
Greenberg, Clement, 158–59
Grotowski, Jerzy, 23, 44, 74, 206
Grusin, Richard, 16–17, 103

guilds, 66
Guilly, René, 86n4, 91–92
Guralnick, Peter, 132, 133n10
Guthrie, Woody, 138

Habermas, Jürgen, 94
Hadot, Pierre, 102
Hall, Stuart, 232
hallucination, 181, 184; in Beckett, 181;
and Blau, 67; in Williams, 184
Halpern, Richard, 208
Handke, Peter, 23, 155, 245; *A Journey
to the Rivers*, 97, 106; *Offending the
Audience*, 97–108; *The Ride across
Lake Constance*, 245n27
Hansen, Miriam Bratu, 24–25, 31n1, 33n6,
34–35, 169n41
Havel, Václav, 182–83, 185
Hawkins, Etta, 256
Hayworth, Rita, 232
hegemony: and Artaud, 88; and Beckett,
208; and capitalism, 21, 42; of cinema,
5, 7, 12; and Hollywood, 21, 42; in
Kennedy, 242; of media and mass
culture, 12, 28, 30, 49, 73–74, 226; of
the proscenium, 208; of radio, 88; of
sound, 163; of the spectacle, 83; and
theater, 43, 49, 83, 208
Henreid, Paul, 242, 244, 253
hipsters, 143–44
historians: Blau and, 67n18; and film and
theater, 8, 16, 79n45; on Hollywood,
7n3, 225; and media, 79n45, 86
historicity: and Beckett, 157, 173–75, 178;
and Benjaminian aura, 34; of cinema,
178; Gitelman on, 15; in Kennedy, 229,
247; of theater, 9, 26; and theories of
spectatorship, 156
historiography, 46–47
Holbein, Hans, 17
Holiday, Billie, 256–57
Holocaust, 49–50
homophobia, 71n26
homosexuality, 71n26
Horkheimer, Max, 22, 130n3, 194
Horne, Lena, 24n14; Kennedy on, 245
human: ahistorical, 155; Artaud on, 92;
and Beckett, 162, 171, 222; Benjamin

on, 32, 34, 36–38, 41, 249; bodies, 23; condition, 30; and God, 177, 246; identity, 80–81; in movie studio logos, 241; nature (Blau), 69; and objectification, 175; perception (Benjamin), 41; response to cameras, 171–72; in the theater, 37, 70; and Williams, 80, 130, 134
humanitarianism, 55
Hunter, Kim, 114, 119
Hurwitz, Leo, 138n25
Huyssen, Andreas, 18, 45, 221

icon: of the body, 91; Keaton as, 163; in Kennedy, 241, 243; of kitsch, 144; and *Orpheus Descending*, 142; and Panofsky, 42n3; *Streetcar* as, 114; Mae West as, 128
identification: and Beckett, 29–30, 180; Blackness and, 230–31, 256–57; and Brecht, 30, 81–82; and cinema, 23, 29–30, 232; of Handke, 101; Keaton and, 166–67; in Kennedy, 227–32, 233–34, 241, 255–57; Lefebvre on, 81–82; and naming, 255; in Parks, 229; theatrical, 29–30; and Williams, 29–30, 114–15, 125, 142n38
ideologies: and Artaud, 87, 91; avant-garde on, 81; Baudry on, 22n10; Blau on, 69; and "canned laughter," 184; of capital, 11; and captioning, 118, 140n30; culture industry as, 226; "first culture," 233; images in, 202; and modernism, 52n2; patriarchal, 115; of state radio, 87; and theater, 27; of the unified subject, 24–25; Žižek on, 184. *See also* apparatus
illusion, 185; and anti-illusion, 69–70; in Beckett, 222; cinematic, 104, 115, 204; in Documentary Theatre, 77; of the fourth wall, 208; and Handke, 107–8; *The Illusion of Power* (Orgel), 201n2; of immediacy, 17; and reality, 65
images: and alienation, 202; Bazin on, 104; in Beckett, 209, 212; filmic images, 78, 165, 166; and Keaton, 166, 168; in Kennedy, 237, 238n11, 239n12, 241–42; Lefebvre on, 82;

"literarization" of (Brecht), 118; mass dissemination of, 62; mediated desire, 130; perspectival, 201; pleasures of, 100; "sound images," 184, 186; and speech, 242; and Williams, 80, 124–25, 144; of women, 115, 128. *See also* scopophilia
improvisation: Adorno on, 44; in Cassavetes, 19n13; Peter Weiss on, 77; Williams and, 126
incorporation: in Keaton, 167; in Kennedy, 239; of media, 4, 17–18; and negation (Adorno), 22, 48; in Williams, 116
intermedial condition, 4, 8, 76, 78, 105n15
Ionesco, Eugène, 154

Jacobs, Lea, 5n2, 15–16, 228n4
Jakovljević, Branislav, 97n1
James, Henry, 70
Jarcho, Julia, 13n17, 22n9, 47–48, 146, 155n5, 212n27, 226n3, 233n1
Jefferson, Blind Lemon, 137–39
Jenkins, Henry, 78, 103, 158n12, 228n4
Jones, LeRoi. *See* Baraka, Amiri (LeRoi Jones)
Joyce, James, 75, 212
Jung, Carl, 255

Kafka, Franz, 75; *The Trial*, 73
Kaprow, Allan, 64
Kaufman, Boris, 164
Kazan, Elia, 119, 133–24, 139n29
Keaton, Buster: *Go West*, 157; *Hearts and Pearls, or the Lounge Lizard's Lost Love*, 166–67; *My Wonderful World of Slapstick*, 164n32; *Sherlock Jr.*, 165–69
Kennedy, Adrienne: *Diary of Lights*, 254–57; *Funnyhouse of a Negro*, 239; *A Movie Star Has to Star in Black and White*, 24, 27, 226–27, 232, 233–46, 247–53, 254–55, 257; *The Owl Answers*, 225, 238–41, 251, 255, 257; *People Who Led to My Plays*, 24, 229, 234, 240, 245, 247–48, 255–57
"kino-essay," 157
kitsch, 128, 130–31, 144
Kluge, Alexander, 94

292 ‹ INDEX

Knowlson, James, 157n7, 162n24, 212n26
Krauss, Rosalind, 159, 165, 175

Lahr, John, 115n3, 129, 142n38
laughter: canned, 184, 200; stifled, 195
Lead Belly, 137–42, 147, 147n52, 255
Lefebvre, Henri, 81–82
Lehmann, Hans-Thies, 12, 65n12
Leigh, Vivien, 114
Levine, David, 202n3
Life (magazine), 118–23, 127, 140
Lipman, Ross, 157, 171–72, 174
Living Theatre: and Broadway,
  66–67; early visions of, 64, 72;
  experimentation of, 23; influences on,
  73n30, 77; and mass culture, 76; and
  Williams, 146n48
Lloyd, David, 212–13
London, 81, 218, 226n3; *Times*, 215–16,
  217n15
Lorca, Federico García: *Blood Wedding*,
  54; *Buster Keaton's Outing*, 53–54;
  Yerma, 54
Los Angeles: Brecht in, 56, 57n16; and
  film industry, 7; Schneider on, 164;
  Times, 132n9
Lott, Eric, 141
Lumet, Sidney, 147
lynchings, 134–35

magazines: Adorno on, 43; and Artaud,
  92; *Modern Screen*, 247; *The Nation*,
  139n29; *New Yorker*, 182; *Screen*, 22n8,
  230; *Theatre Arts Magazine*, 52; and
  visuality, 175; *Vogue*, 242. See also *Life*
  (magazine)
Mailer, Norman, 141, 242
Malina, Judith: and Beck, 146; and
  Broadway, 65–66; experimentation of,
  67, 73–74; and Gide, 64–65, 74; and
  Piscator, 66; and spectatorship, 77
manifestoes: Blau's, 73; Surrealist, 43
Marat/Sade (P. Weiss), 226
Marcuse, Herbert, 211
Marx Brothers, 155
masochism, 123n19, 177n56, 229
McElroen, Christopher, 258
McGhee, Brownie, 139n29

McGill, Meredith, 15, 142
McLuhan, Marshall, 14–17; and
  Beckett, 160–61, 197; on spectators, 23
melodrama: in Beckett, 209; Berlant on,
  169; and gender, 169; and Keaton,
  166, 168–69; and Kennedy, 255;
  across media, 15, 116; Rancière on, 62;
  and Williams, 114, 116, 123; Carolyn
  Williams on, 209
metaphysics, 9n2; Artaud on, 86
metatheater (Abel), 26, 197
MGM, 24n14, 111, 133, 241, 247n3, 255
Miller, Arthur, 254–55; on Brando and
  Streetcar, 116–17, 127
Miller, D. A., 233–34, 236
Miller, Edward, 88
Miller, Henry, 68n20
Miller, Hillary, 244
mimeographs, 44–45, 47
mimesis, 17, 228–29
minstrelsy, 141
modernism, 52–60; Adorno on, 45;
  and Beckett, 19n14, 151, 158, 173, 196;
  Benjamin on, 42; and Blau, 68–69;
  Brecht on, 205; and bricolage, 138;
  cityscape, 173; Crow on, 158–59;
  Debord and Situationists on, 63–64;
  and Eliot, 135–36; Esslin on, 75;
  Greenberg and, 158–59; Jarcho
  on, 47–48, 146, 155n5, 212n27; and
  Kennedy, 227; literature, 81, 214; mass
  commodity culture, 45, 151, 218; mass
  culture and (Huyssen), 18; and media,
  227–28, 247; "modernist miniature"
  (Huyssen), 18; and Moretti, 135–
  36; and negativity, 19n14; painting,
  158–59; Panofsky on, 42; primitivist
  impulse, 13; reductivist tendencies,
  26; and stardom, 227; and theater, 47–
  48, 69, 75, 196, 214; Peter Weiss on, 76
modernity: Beckett and, 192; Benjamin
  and, 34, 238; and experience, 13n16;
  Lorca and, 54; Singer on, 169n41
monarchism, 201
monologues, 89, 197, 243, 251
montage: as aesthetic, 2; Beckett and,
  151, 170; and cinema, 16, 40, 151; and
  Documentary Theatre, 77; Keaton

and, 168, 170; and theater, 40; Peter
Weiss and, 78
Moody, Alys, 258n1
Morin, Emilie, 182n11, 187
Morton, Jelly Roll, 138
Moten, Fred, 147
Mueller, Roswitha, 54–55, 60, 205
Mulvey, Laura, 102, 115
museums, 206
musicians: Brecht on, 205; Goodman on,
66n14; in Kennedy, 255; in Williams,
132, 136–39, 141–43. *See also individual
musicians*
mystifications: critical (Auslander), 11;
"epidemic of" (Blau), 68, 76

narrative: Althusser on, 26; and
apparatus, 26; in Beckett, 209–11,
227; Benjamin on, 33n6; and cinema,
5, 24–25, 27, 115, 158; and Handke,
102n12, 103; historical, 5; illusionistic,
115; in Kennedy, 232, 235, 255; Mulvey
on, 102; realist, 27; and soundtracks,
235; and theater, 5, 158–59; theater
vs. cinema, 5, 24–25, 103, 115, 158;
transhistorical suspicion of, 23; and
Williams, 129
naturalism, 163, 203–4, 225
negation: Adorno on, 22, 43–44, 46–48,
95; and Beckett, 49, 155, 161, 182, 200,
208, 227; Blau on, 68; and Handke, 98,
101; Jarcho on, 47–48; and Keaton,
165; in Kennedy, 227; Krauss on, 165;
and mass culture, 68, 155, 182, 227;
Menke on, 47; remediation in reverse,
27; and theater vs. cinema, 5, 26, 95,
151; and Williams, 49
newspapers, 67; Anderson on, 94–95;
and Artaud, 89, 91; in Beckett, 151–52;
Combat, 91; in Keaton, 173–74
New York: aesthetic debates in, 10, 244;
Barrault and, 72; happenings, 64;
Isaac on, 206; nineteenth-century,
6; Schechner on, 78; Shakespeare
Festival, 236, 243, 250n10; significant
stagings, 27, 118, 139n29, 181, 236, 242,
259; and theater, 1, 66, 206, 237, 244
(*see also* Broadway; Off-Broadway);

and Williams, 29, 112, 118, 146. *See also*
Classical Theater of Harlem
Niebuhr, Reinhold, 69
Nietzsche, Friedrich, 13n16, 130n1, 211n24
noise, 90, 108, 163
Noland, Carrie, 51, 153
norms: Adorno on, 49–50; and Beckett,
172, 210; Brecht on, 81–82; cinematic,
22, 30; and gags, 166; Handke on,
106; Heidegger on, 194; and Kennedy,
225; Lefebvre on, 81–82; radio and,
88; Rancière on, 61; of spectators, 29,
73, 172; unified subject as (Hansen),
24, 62
North, Michael, 157, 163, 165, 171
Notfilm (Lipman), 157, 171–72, 174
Now Voyager (film), 245–46, 249

Off-Broadway: applause in, 181;
influences on, 29; and Kennedy, 29,
225, 237; Off-Off-Broadway, 83, 201
Olf, Julian, 16n4
Oliver, Edith, 176n55, 181
Ono, Yoko, 44
ontology, 9–12, 160; and Beckett, 160,
178; Elsaesser on, 177; and Genet,
71n26; and media, 14
opera, 20, 142. See also *Threepenny
Opera, The*
Ovid, 140n31

Page, Geraldine, 242
painting: in Beckett, 144, 161, 209, 211–
12; Benjamin and, 32–33, 37; Dutch,
17–18; Gide on, 64–65; and literature,
75; and performance, 78–79; and the
proscenium, 211; reproduced, 18, 32,
37, 144; Schechner on, 78; Sontag on,
78–79; and theater, 33, 37, 64–65, 75,
79, 158, 159, 211–12; in Williams, 146.
See also remediation
Panofsky, Erwin, 41–42, 48
Papp, Joseph, 237n7, 243
Paradise Now (Living Theatre), 60, 64, 73
paratexts, 98, 101, 108, 143, 182
Paris: and Beckett, 23, 29, 176, 218;
Berliner Ensemble and, 81; and James,
70n24

Parks, Suzan-Lori, 227–29, 232
Pasquier, Sylvain du, 166, 169
perceptions: in Beckett, 162, 172, 210;
    Benjamin on, 35, 41–43, 249; Handke
    on, 107; mass cultural, 107, 175; and
    media, 177; postwar, 50; spectators', 231
periods. *See* decades
personification, 221, 241, 243
Peters, Jean, 241–42, 248–49, 251, 253
Phelan, Peggy, 9–12, 17
phenomenology, 10, 16n4;
    phenomenophilia, 106
philosophy: and Beckett, 155–56, 160,
    175–78, 179; and mediation, 13n16, 47;
    and negation, 47; postwar, 23; and
    theater, 12, 62, 76, 156; weakness of
    (Debord), 212–13. *See also individual
    philosophers*
photography: Bazin on, 104; and Beckett,
    162, 170, 174, 203n6, 208; Benjamin on,
    32; in Kennedy, 242, 247, 249; Phelan
    on, 10–11; and *Streetcar*, 118, 127
Pirandello, Luigi, 35, 37
Piscator, Erwin, 52n2, 66, 72–73
Plato's cave, 22, 67–68
pleasures: of being photographed, 174;
    of cinema, 23, 232; of comparison,
    105; and gender, 115; of identificatory
    structures, 114, 232; in Kennedy,
    227, 232; of narrative, 227;
    phenomenophilic, 106; of seeing,
    100–101, 106, 115, 171–72; visual, 102,
    172; of voyeurism, 207; in Williams,
    124. See also *Schaulust*; scopophilia
poems, 189, 257
Presley, Elvis, 132, 143
primitivism, 12–13, 116
prisons: Apter on, 188; and Havel, 182–83;
    and Lead Belly, 140; Oliver on, 181
pronouns, 220–21, 240, 243
proscenium: as apparatus, 201–7; and
    Beckett, 201–13; contradictions of,
    201; "Death of" (Isaac), 206; and
    painting, 211
psychoanalysis: and audiences, 232;
    influence on Phelan, 10; and Kennedy,
    228–29; and Sartre, 177n56; and
    Schaulust, 101; and Williams, 132n9

psychosis, 222
Public Theater (New York), 242. *See also*
    Papp, Joseph

queerness, 29, 115, 117n9, 129

radio: Artaud and, 85–93, 251; BBC, 86;
    and Beckett, 49, 156n6, 158, 161, 179;
    Benjamin on, 38–40, 55–56; Brecht on,
    38–40, 54–55; Handke on, 99; Kennedy
    and, 251; and mass culture, 28, 197; as a
    medium, 86–87; "phantasmic" power
    of, 88–89; Radio Luxembourg, 99;
    "radiophonic" body without organs,
    90; "radiovoice," 88; Schechner on, 78;
    state, 86–87, 91; Fred Turner on, 50;
    Voice of America, 86; Allen Weiss on,
    88; Williams and, 28, 124
Rafalowicz, Mira, 238–39
Rancière, Jacques, 61–63, 73, 77, 231
rape, 116–17, 119, 122, 123, 125–26, 145
reading, 1, 10n5, 24, 31, 56, 61, 67, 81, 82,
    88, 117, 118, 122, 127, 130n1, 140, 155n5,
    156, 176, 184, 185, 186, 187, 189, 200,
    214, 229, 232, 240, 255
redemption, 104, 140
Reed, Adolph, 247–48
reflexivity: in Beckett, 191; Blau on,
    70; and Brecht, 60; and film, 7; and
    Greenberg, 158–59; in Kennedy, 239;
    Stam on, 168; and theater, 26
rehearsals: Beckett and, 180, 183, 186, 189,
    207; Kennedy and, 238
remediation, 17–19, 22, 27, 156n6;
    alternatives to, 18; and Beckett, 163;
    Bolter and Grusin on, 16–17, 103;
    in Godard, 27; in Handke, 103; and
    Huyssen, 221; and Jenkins, 103; and
    Kennedy, 19; mass, 118; and McLuhan,
    16–17; in reverse, 22, 27, 156n6; and
    television, 156n6; theater as, 21n5; and
    Williams, 113
revolution: Baraka on, 83; and Beckett,
    181; Benjamin on, 55; Goodman on,
    72, 77n29; Malina on, 72, 77n29;
    technical, 44; and Williams, 113, 117n9
Ridout, Nicholas, 108n, 185n20, 207n14
Robinson, Cedric, 230–31, 247n1, 247n3

Theatre of the Absurd, The (Esslin), 74–76;
and race, 258n1
Thévenin, Paule, 87, 93n18
Threepenny Opera, The, 57
Torn, Rip, 242
Toscanini, Arturo, 44
totalitarianism, 50. *See also* fascism
tropes, 199, 213n29
Tsai Ming-Liang, 8n1
Turner, Fred, 50
Turner, Lana, 232
Tyler, Parker, 130n2, 132n9, 143

Umfunktionierung (refunctionalization),
55, 189–90

Vardac, A. Nicolas, 5n2, 15–16
ventriloquism, and Kennedy, 239, 253, 255
Verfremdungseffekt. See alienation
Vinson, Eddie,"Cleanhead," 24n14
violence: in Artaud, 82; in Beckett,
172–73, 176–77, 221; in Brecht, 58; in
Handke, 107; Keaton and, 172–73;
in Kennedy, 231, 257; Living Theatre
on, 77n39; and race, 134, 145, 231,
257; Sartre on, 176–77; state, 145;
theatrical, 82–83; in Williams, 114–29,
134–35, 145
Viva Zapata (film), 236, 245, 253
voice: and Artaud, 85–93; in Handke,
99, 106; in Kennedy, 239, 243, 251–52;
"radiovoice," 88; in silent films, 35; in
Williams, 136–37, 140, 145
von Hove, Ivo, 19, 19n13
von Stroheim, Erich, 245n27
voyeurism, 206–7

Wagner, Richard: Adorno on, 45;
Meistersinger, 55; and movie music,
235
Warhol, Andy: and Benjamin, 191n11;
Exploding Plastic Inevitable, 78n41;
visual style of, 101n11
Warner, Michael, 91, 95
Washburn, Anne, 226n3
Weimar Republic, 52n2, 60
Weiss, Allen, 85n1, 88
Weiss, Peter, 76–78
West: artworks in, 34; audiences in, 198;
and Baraka, 83; and Beckett, 207, 212–
13; media of (Esslin), 74; philosophy,
212–13; and theater, 206–7
West, Mae, 128–29, 131
Whitehead, Gregory, 88
Wicke, Jennifer, 80–81, 214, 217–18
Wilder, Thornton, 117, 203n5, 231
Williams, Raymond, 21n6, 42, 79–81, 83
Williams, Tennessee: *Cat on a Hot Tin
Roof*, 132; (*The*) *Fugitive Kind*, 132n9,
143, 146–47, 147n50, 147n52; "The
Gentleman Caller," 111–12; *The Glass
Menagerie*, 111; "Heavenly Grass," 141–
42, 146; *Orpheus Descending*, 112–13;
130–48; "Portrait of a Girl in Glass,"
111–12; *A Streetcar Named Desire*,
114–29
Winters, Shelley, 241–42, 244, 248, 253
Wong Kar-Wai, 132n6
Woolf, Virginia, *Mrs. Dalloway*, 220

Youngblood, Gene, 78

Žižek, Slavoj, 184

INDEX > 295

Robinson, Marc, 238n9
Rodenbeck, Judith, 51n21, 64
Rolling Stones, 98–99
Romanticism, 143; in Kennedy, 235
Ross, Andrew, 21n7
Rosset, Barney, 203
Rousseau, Jean-Jacques, 13n16, 60

Sartre, Jean-Paul, 76, 175–77, 177n56
Schaulust, 100–102, 105
Schauspiel, 100
Schechner, Richard, 71n26, 78, 206
Schneider, Alan, 157, 163–64, 171n46, 182n9, 203, 216
scopophilia, 100, 105, 115, 172–73. *See also* images
segregation, 248, 250, 255, 257
Shakespeare, William, 117, 196. *See also* New York: Shakespeare Festival
Shaw, George Bernard, 52–53
silence: audience, 185; and Barthes, 241; and Beckett, 157, 163, 173–74, 185, 209, 221–22; Benjamin on, 35, 206; in Brecht, 59; and film, 25, 53, 164; and Handke, 245; and Keaton, 157, 164; Pirandello on, 35
simulations: Baudrillard on, 80–81; Greenberg on, 158
Situationism, 62, 62n3, 64n9. *See also* Debord, Guy
slapstick, 155
Smith, Bessie, 136–38
Sontag, Susan, 20–21, 78–79, 104
sovereignty: and Beckett, 204, 207; Benjamin on, 37; Menke on, 47; and theater history, 201–2
spectacle, 6, 64, 77–78, 82; and audiences, 64, 198–99, 201; and Baraka, 83; Beckett and, 186, 197–99, 212–13; and Blau, 71, 83; and cinema, 198; Debord on, 62–64, 212–13; and gender, 71, 145; Handke on, 100–101; and happenings, 64; Lefebvre on, 82; lynching as, 135; mass, 62, 65–66, 186, 197–98, 259; and McLuhan, 197; and the proscenium, 201; Rancière on, 61–62; Reinhardt on, 65–66; society of, 62, 82; Peter Weiss on, 78; and Williams, 129, 145

Stam, Robert, 168
Stanwyck, Barbara, 23–24, 232
Star Is Born, A (Cukor), 204
Starobinski, Jean, 13n16, 177
States, Bert, 184
Stein, Gertrude, 19n14
Steinberg, Joel, 242–44
Steinweg, Reiner, 60
Stern, Marcus, 199n16
Stewart, Jacqueline, 24
Strasberg, Lee, 242
Stravinsky, Igor, 43–44, 47
Strindberg, August, 13
styles: acting, 19; in motion pictur (Panofsky), 41–42; Warner on, Williams, 117, 132n8, 139n29
suicide, 128–29
Sunset Blvd. (film), 163–64
surrealism: Adorno on, 43; and Ke 53–54, 166; in Kennedy, 251; an Lorca, 53–54; Malina on, 65; Surrealism, 75
Swanson, Gloria, 163–64, 232
symphonies, 43, 45, 47
Szanto, George, 19n14

Tandy, Jessica, 117, 119
teleology, 16, 18
telephones: and acting, 19n14; Gitel on, 14; as two-way medium, 56, 197
telescope, as prop, 190–99
television: Adorno on, 43–44, 49; a Beckett, 20, 49, 156, 158, 179, 208 Esslin on, 74–75; Grotowski on, and Guthrie, 138; impact, 4; Klav on, 19n14; and Lead Belly, 147n5; Malina, 66; on stage, 17; perspec and, 208; proscenium and, 208; a remediation, 21 (*see also* remedia Michael Smith on, 201; Fred Turr on, 50; Raymond Williams on, 79 Žižek on, 184
Terada, Rei, 106
terror: and Keaton, 174n52; and sexu 126–29; and theater (Blau), 71; an Williams, 116–17, 122, 126–29
Thalia (cinema), 236

Theatre of the Absurd, The (Esslin), 74–76; and race, 258n1
Thévenin, Paule, 87, 93n18
Threepenny Opera, The, 57
Torn, Rip, 242
Toscanini, Arturo, 44
totalitarianism, 50. *See also* fascism
tropes, 199, 213n29
Tsai Ming-Liang, 8n1
Turner, Fred, 50
Turner, Lana, 232
Tyler, Parker, 130n2, 132n9, 143

Umfunktionierung (refunctionalization), 55, 189–90

Vardac, A. Nicolas, 5n2, 15–16
ventriloquism, and Kennedy, 239, 253, 255
Verfremdungseffekt. See alienation
Vinson, Eddie, "Cleanhead," 24n14
violence: in Artaud, 82; in Beckett, 172–73, 176–77, 221; in Brecht, 58; in Handke, 107; Keaton and, 172–73; in Kennedy, 231, 257; Living Theatre on, 77n39; and race, 134, 145, 231, 257; Sartre on, 176–77; state, 145; theatrical, 82–83; in Williams, 114–29, 134–35, 145
Viva Zapata (film), 236, 245, 253
voice: and Artaud, 85–93; in Handke, 99, 106; in Kennedy, 239, 243, 251–52; "radiovoice," 88; in silent films, 35; in Williams, 136–37, 140, 145
von Hove, Ivo, 19, 19n13
von Stroheim, Erich, 245n27
voyeurism, 206–7

Wagner, Richard: Adorno on, 45; *Meistersinger*, 55; and movie music, 235
Warhol, Andy: and Benjamin, 191n11; Exploding Plastic Inevitable, 78n41; visual style of, 101n11
Warner, Michael, 91, 95
Washburn, Anne, 226n3
Weimar Republic, 52n2, 60
Weiss, Allen, 85n1, 88
Weiss, Peter, 76–78
West: artworks in, 34; audiences in, 198; and Baraka, 83; and Beckett, 207, 212–13; media of (Esslin), 74; philosophy, 212–13; and theater, 206–7
West, Mae, 128–29, 131
Whitehead, Gregory, 88
Wicke, Jennifer, 80–81, 214, 217–18
Wilder, Thornton, 117, 203n5, 231
Williams, Raymond, 21n6, 42, 79–81, 83
Williams, Tennessee: *Cat on a Hot Tin Roof*, 132; (*The*) *Fugitive Kind*, 132n9, 143, 146–47, 147n50, 147n52; "The Gentleman Caller," 111–12; *The Glass Menagerie*, 111; "Heavenly Grass," 141–42, 146; *Orpheus Descending*, 112–13, 130–48; "Portrait of a Girl in Glass," 111–12; *A Streetcar Named Desire*, 114–29
Winters, Shelley, 241–42, 244, 248, 253
Wong Kar-Wai, 132n6
Woolf, Virginia, *Mrs. Dalloway*, 220

Youngblood, Gene, 78

Žižek, Slavoj, 184

INDEX > 295

Robinson, Marc, 238n9
Rodenbeck, Judith, 5n21, 64
Rolling Stones, 98–99
Romanticism, 143; in Kennedy, 235
Ross, Andrew, 21n7
Rosset, Barney, 203
Rousseau, Jean-Jacques, 13n16, 60

Sartre, Jean-Paul, 76, 175–77, 177n56
Schaulust, 100–102, 105
Schauspiel, 100
Schechner, Richard, 7n26, 78, 206
Schneider, Alan, 157, 163–64, 171n46,
   182n9, 203, 216
scopophilia, 100, 105, 115, 172–73. *See also*
   images
segregation, 248, 250, 255, 257
Shakespeare, William, 117, 196. *See also*
   New York: Shakespeare Festival
Shaw, George Bernard, 52–53
silence: audience, 185; and Barthes, 241;
   and Beckett, 157, 163, 173–74, 185,
   209, 221–22; Benjamin on, 35, 206; in
   Brecht, 59; and film, 25, 53, 164; and
   Handke, 245; and Keaton, 157, 164;
   Pirandello on, 35
simulations: Baudrillard on, 80–81;
   Greenberg on, 158
Situationism, 62, 62n3, 64n9. *See also*
   Debord, Guy
slapstick, 155
Smith, Bessie, 136–38
Sontag, Susan, 20–21, 78–79, 104
sovereignty: and Beckett, 204, 207;
   Benjamin on, 37; Menke on, 47; and
   theater history, 201–2
spectacle, 6, 64, 77–78, 82; and audiences,
   64, 198–99, 201; and Baraka, 83;
   Beckett and, 186, 197–99, 212–13; and
   Blau, 71, 83; and cinema, 198; Debord
   on, 62–64, 212–13; and gender, 71, 145;
   Handke on, 100–101; and happenings,
   64; Lefebvre on, 82; lynching as, 135;
   mass, 62, 65–66, 186, 197–98, 259; and
   McLuhan, 197; and the proscenium,
   201; Rancière on, 61–62; Reinhardt
   on, 65–66; society of, 62, 82; Peter
   Weiss on, 78; and Williams, 129, 145

Stam, Robert, 168
Stanwyck, Barbara, 23–24, 232
Star Is Born, A (Cukor), 204
Starobinski, Jean, 13n16, 177
States, Bert, 184
Stein, Gertrude, 19n14
Steinberg, Joel, 242–44
Steinweg, Reiner, 60
Stern, Marcus, 199n16
Stewart, Jacqueline, 24
Strasberg, Lee, 242
Stravinsky, Igor, 43–44, 47
Strindberg, August, 13
styles: acting, 19; in motion pictures
   (Panofsky), 41–42; Warner on, 91; in
   Williams, 117, 132n8, 139n29
suicide, 128–29
Sunset Blvd. (film), 163–64
surrealism: Adorno on, 43; and Keaton,
   53–54, 166; in Kennedy, 251; and
   Lorca, 53–54; Malina on, 65;
   Surrealism, 75
Swanson, Gloria, 163–64, 232
symphonies, 43, 45, 47
Szanto, George, 19n14

Tandy, Jessica, 117, 119
teleology, 16, 18
telephones: and acting, 19n14; Gitelman
   on, 14; as two-way medium,
   56, 197
telescope, as prop, 190–99
television: Adorno on, 43–44, 49; and
   Beckett, 20, 49, 156, 158, 179, 208;
   Esslin on, 74–75; Grotowski on, 74;
   and Guthrie, 138; impact, 4; Klaver
   on, 19n14; and Lead Belly, 147n52; and
   Malina, 66; on stage, 17; perspective
   and, 208; proscenium and, 208; and
   remediation, 21 (*see also* remediation);
   Michael Smith on, 201; Fred Turner
   on, 50; Raymond Williams on, 79–81;
   Žižek on, 184
Terada, Rei, 106
terror: and Keaton, 174n52; and sexuality,
   126–29; and theater (Blau), 71; and
   Williams, 116–17, 122, 126–29
Thalia (cinema), 236